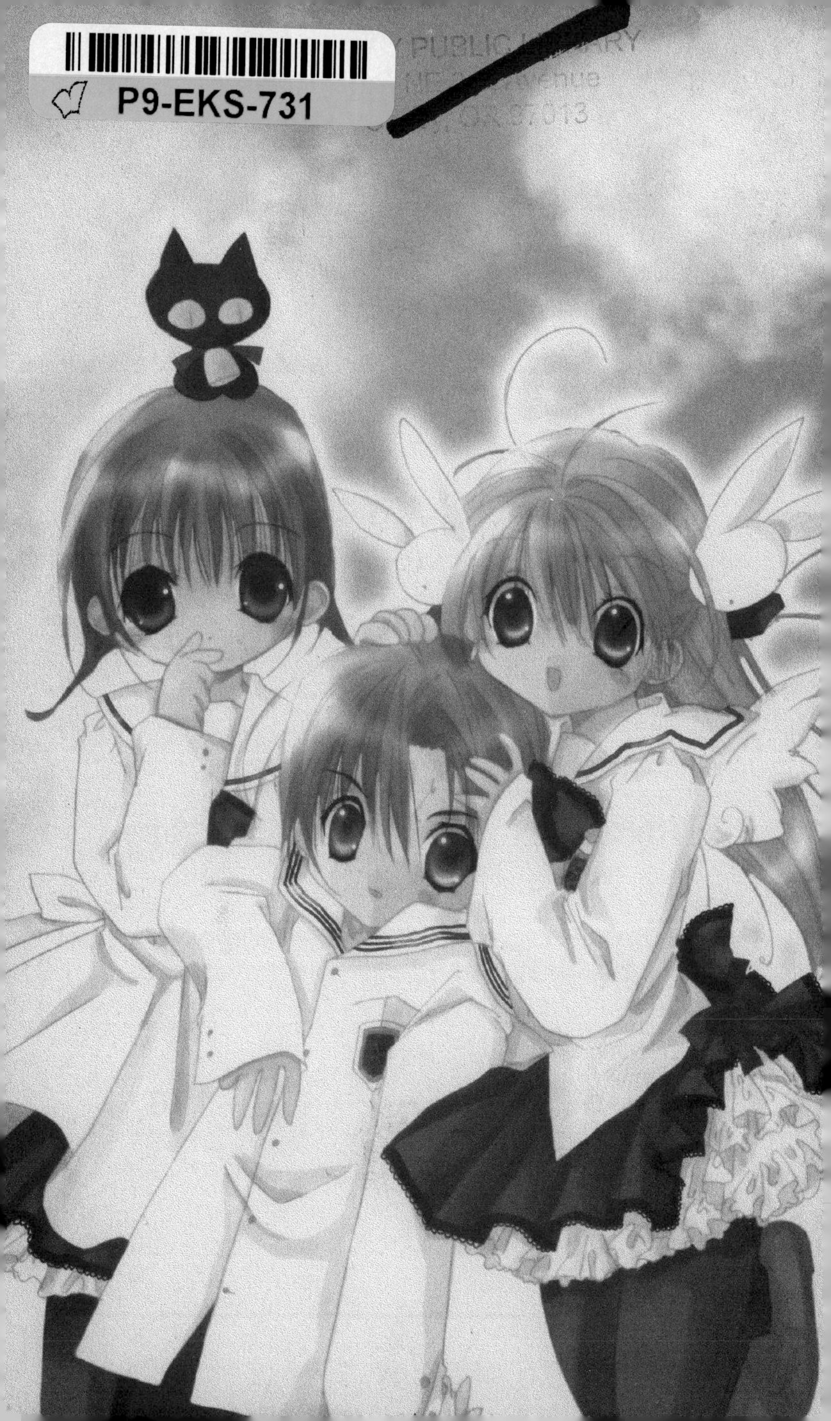

Volume 3

by
Koge-Donbo

Los Angeles • Tokyo • London

Translator - Nan Rymer
English Adaptation - Adam Arnold
Copy Editor - Tim Beedle
Retouch and Lettering - Abelardo Bigting
Cover Layout - Raymond Makowski
Graphic Designer - James Dashiell

Editor - Paul Morrissey
Digital Imaging Manager - Chris Buford
Pre-Press Manager - Antonio DePietro
Production Managers - Jennifer Miller and Mutsumi Miyazaki
Art Director - Matt Alford
Managing Editor - Jill Freshney
VP of Production - Ron Klamert
President & C.O.O. - John Parker
Publisher & C.E.O. - Stuart Levy

E-mail: info@TOKYOPOP.com
Come visit us online at www.TOKYOPOP.com

A  Manga

TOKYOPOP Inc.
5900 Wilshire Blvd. Suite 2000
Los Angeles, CA 90036

Pita-Ten Volume 3
© 2001 Koge-Donbo.
First published in Japan in 2001 by Media Works Inc., Tokyo, Japan.
English publication rights arranged through Media Works Inc.

English text copyright ©2004 TOKYOPOP Inc.

ISBN: 1-59182-629-2

First TOKYOPOP printing: May 2004

10 9 8 7 6 5 4 3 2 1

Printed in the USA

Contents

CHARACTERS

SHIA
A very polite and quiet girl who is great at cooking and cleaning. Little is known about her life before she became Misha's new roommate.

MISHA
This insanely perky girl is Kotarou's new next-door neighbor and her main passion in life is stalking and glomping Kotarou! Is she really an angel?

KOTAROU HIGUCHI
A calm and collected sixth grader who lives alone with his father. He's currently trying to study for his upcoming middle school entrance exams.

KAORU MITARAI
Hiroshi's pretty younger sister is a 5th grader who is a highly skilled culinary expert with a serious infatuation for Takashi.

HIROSHI MITARAI
Nicknamed both Dai-chan and Poops, Hiroshi is a prepubescent eccentric who is totally obsessed with trying to outdo Takashi no matter what.

KOBOSHI UEMATSU
This semi-sweet loudmouth has the hots for Kotarou and can't stand the fact that Misha is honing in on her territory.

TAKASHI AYANOKOJI
Nicknamed Ten-chan, Takashi is nothing short of a ladies' man. He's great at sports, is outgoing and he never has to study!

The Story Until Now:

Quiet elementary school student Kotarou Higuchi is worse off than most kids. His mother died in a traffic accident and his workaholic father is never at home. This leaves Kotarou struggling to make it to school on time, cook his own meals, go shopping and trying to keep up with his studies.

Yet, his so-called normal life has thrown him a curveball in the form of a mysterious girl named Misha who has not only moved in next door, but also started to attend the very same middle school as him! Sensing his loneliness and sorrow, Misha decides to make it her life's work to chase after, "abuse" and latch onto Kotarou. But somehow, Kotarou adapts and life settles back down...that is until another strange girl by the name of Shia appears and ends up as Misha's new roommate!

And so, Kotarou's life begins anew with two beautiful next-door neighbors. One day however, after falling asleep at Misha's place, Shia stumbles upon a sleeping Kotarou, bares fangs and bites him on the neck! Upon waking, Kotarou cannot help but sense some sort of change has occurred within his body. Then on his way home, he collapses... and Shia along with him.

Lesson 14

How to Wake Up

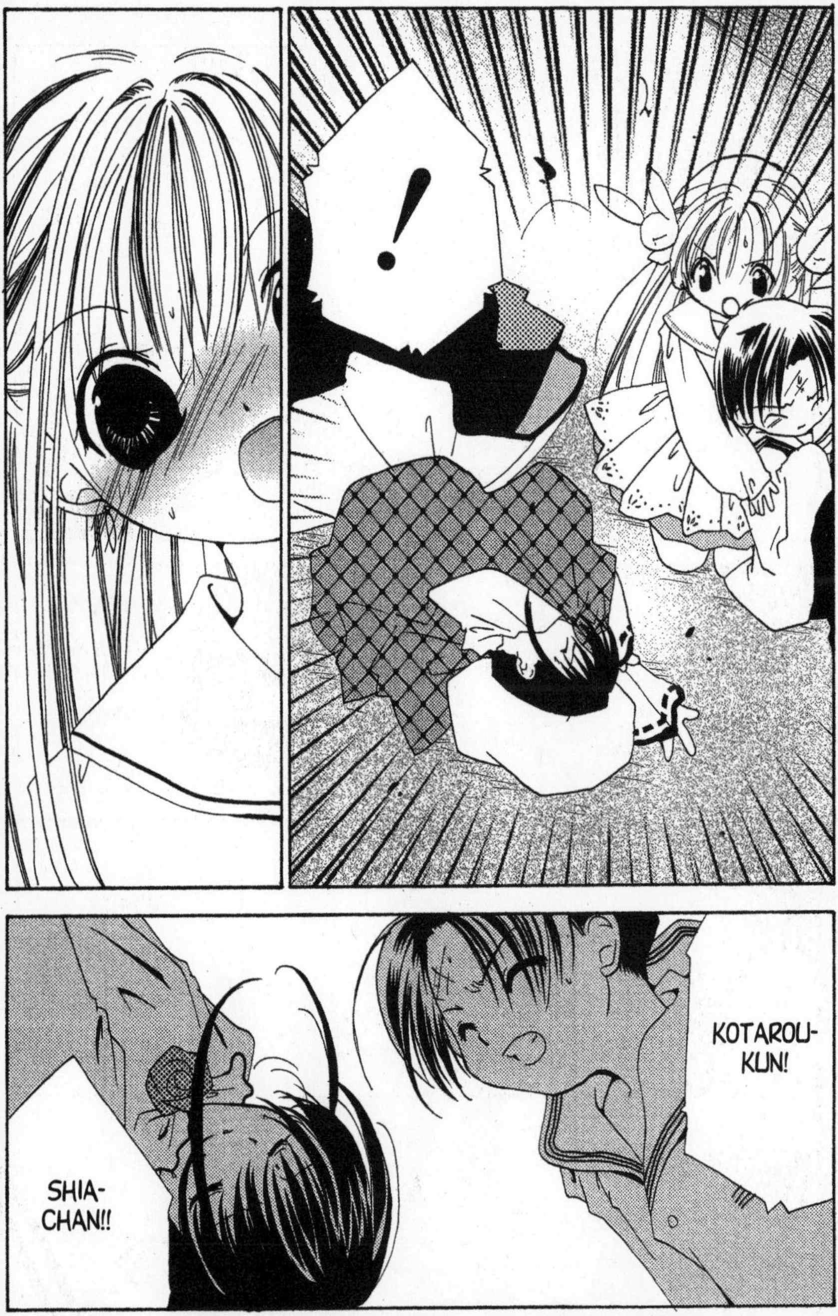
!
KOTAROU-KUN!
SHIA-CHAN!!

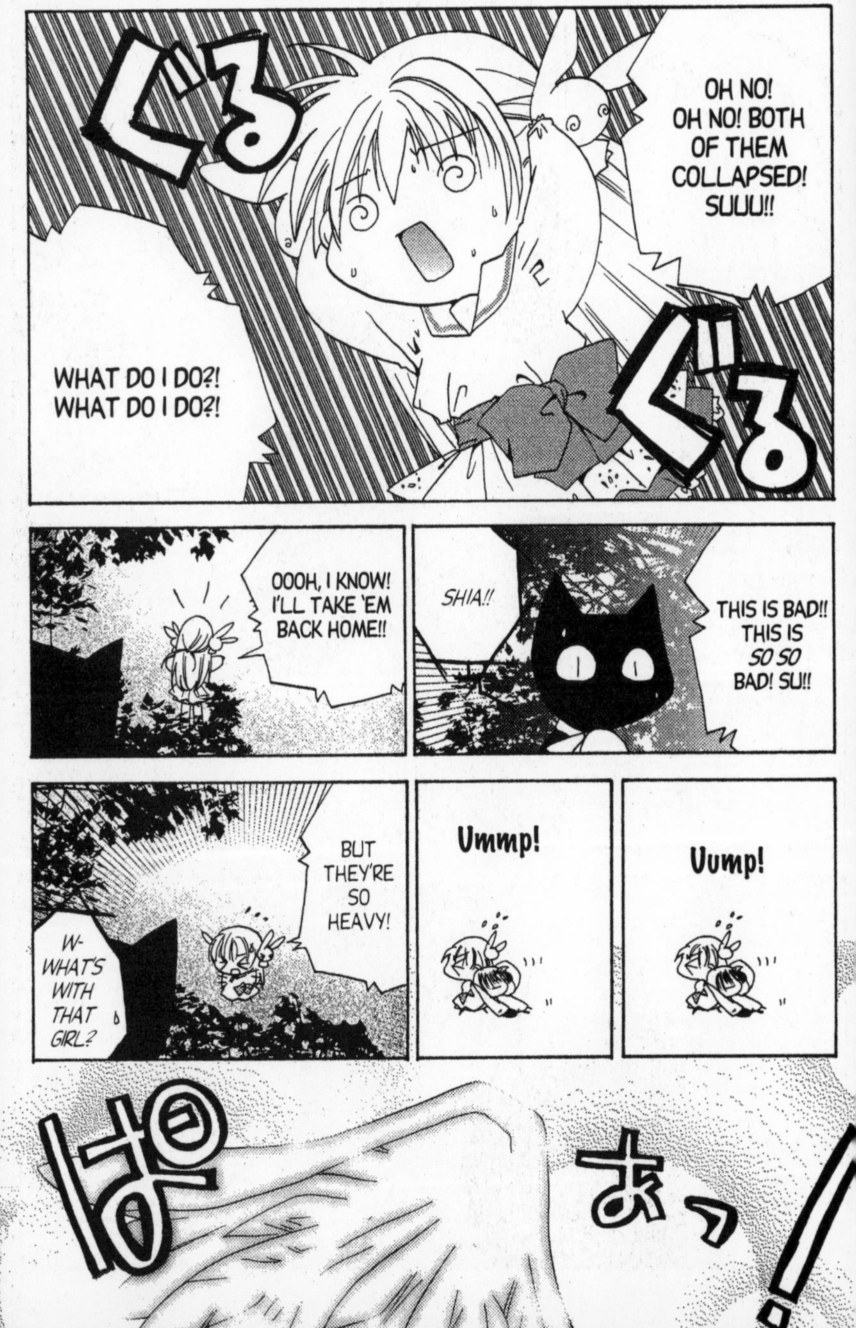
OH NO! OH NO! BOTH OF THEM COLLAPSED! SUUU!!
ぐる
WHAT DO I DO?! WHAT DO I DO?!
ぐる
THIS IS BAD!! THIS IS *SO SO* BAD! SU!!
SHIA!!
OOOH, I KNOW! I'LL TAKE 'EM BACK HOME!!
Vump!
Ummp!
BUT THEY'RE SO HEAVY!
W-WHAT'S WITH THAT GIRL?
ぱあっ!

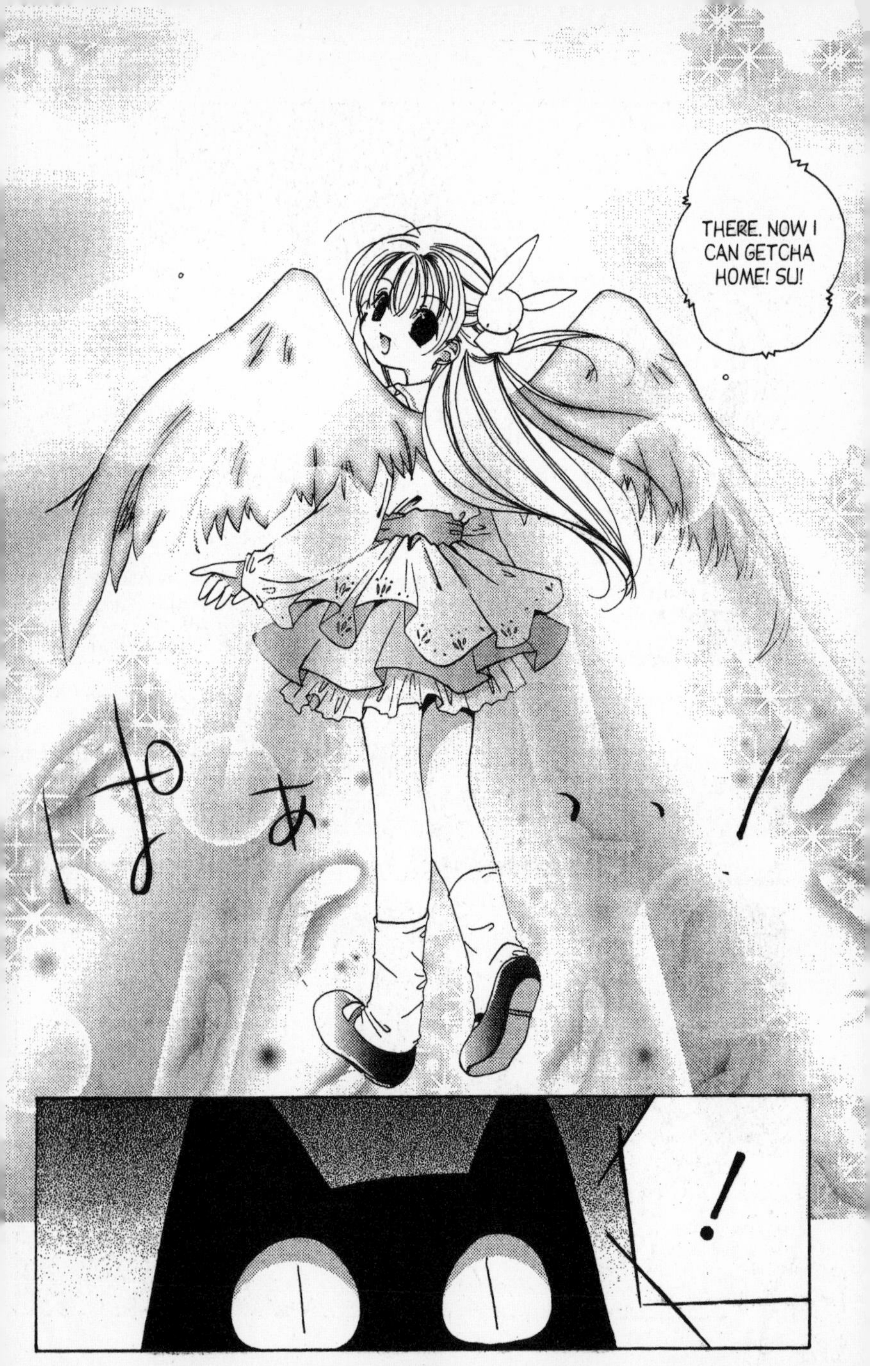
THERE. NOW I CAN GETCHA HOME! SU!
はぁっ！
!

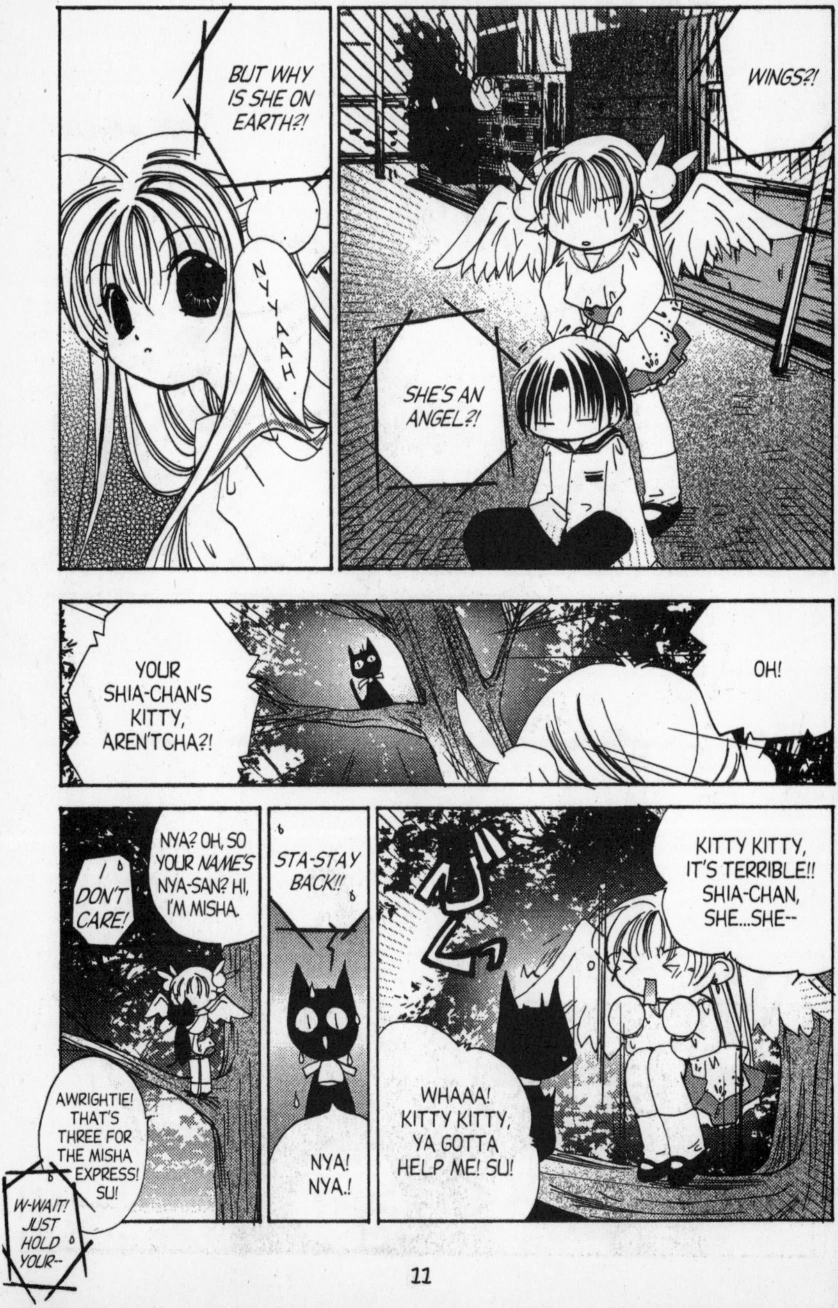
WINGS?!
SHE'S AN ANGEL?!
BUT WHY IS SHE ON EARTH?!
NYYAAAH.
OH!
YOUR SHIA-CHAN'S KITTY, AREN'TCHA?!
KITTY KITTY, IT'S TERRIBLE!! SHIA-CHAN, SHE...SHE--
WHAAA! KITTY KITTY, YA GOTTA HELP ME! SU!
STA-STAY BACK!!
NYA! NYA.!
NYA? OH, SO YOUR NAME'S NYA-SAN? HI, I'M MISHA.
I DON'T CARE!
AWRIGHTIE! THAT'S THREE FOR THE MISHA EXPRESS! SU!
W-WAIT! JUST HOLD YOUR--

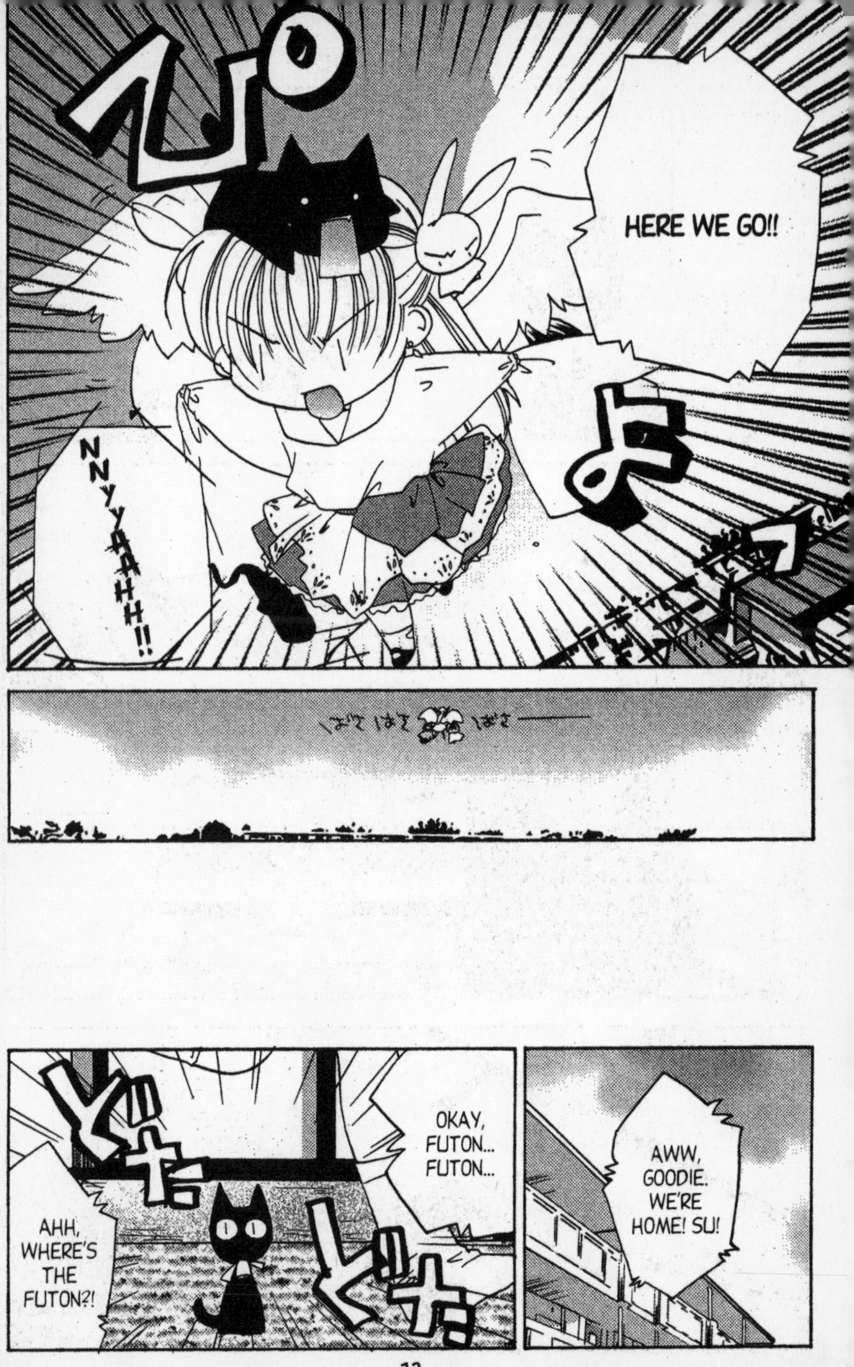
HERE WE GO!!
NNyyAAHH!!
AWW, GOODIE. WE'RE HOME! SU!
OKAY, FUTON... FUTON...
AHH, WHERE'S THE FUTON?!

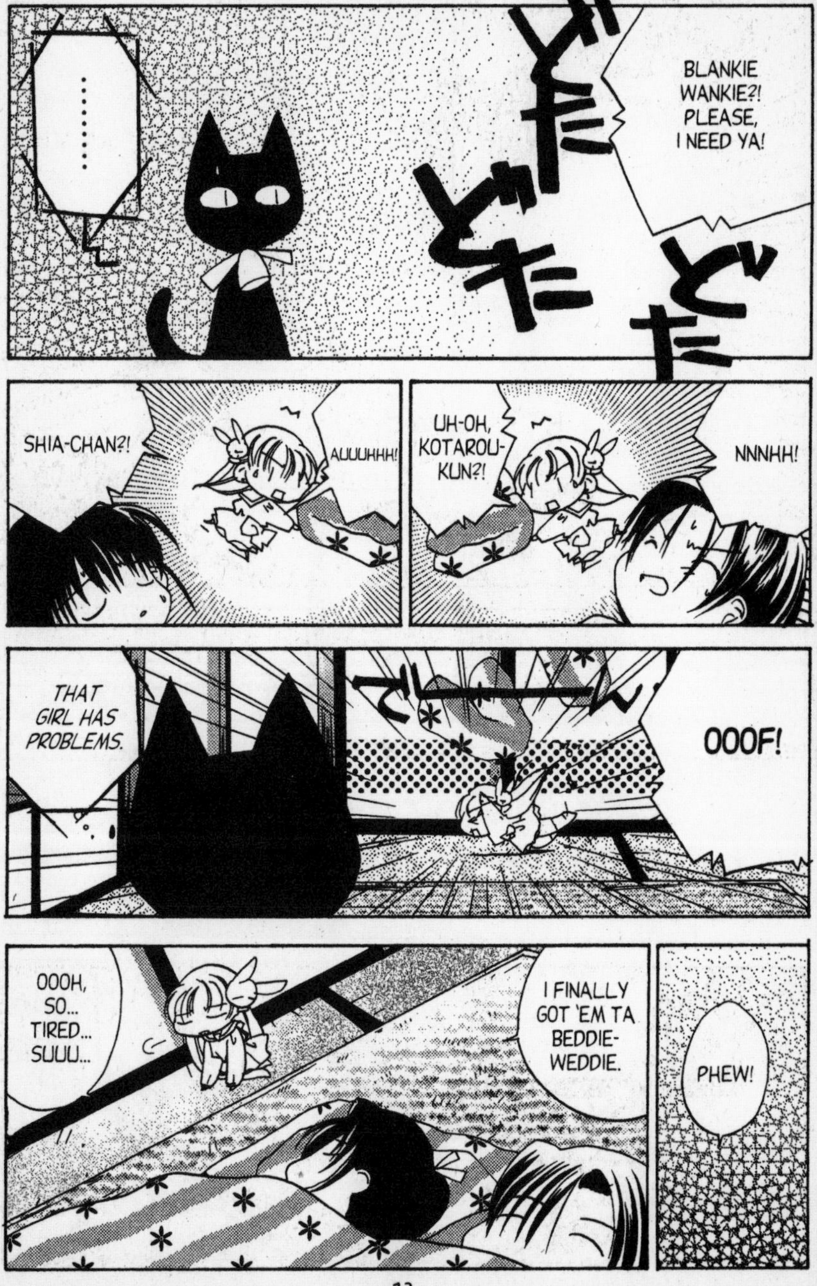
BLANKIE WANKIE?! PLEASE, I NEED YA!
......
NNNHH!
UH-OH, KOTAROU-KUN?!
AUUUHHH!
SHIA-CHAN?!
OOOF!
THAT GIRL HAS PROBLEMS.
PHEW!
I FINALLY GOT 'EM TA BEDDIE-WEDDIE.
OOOH, SO... TIRED... SUUU...

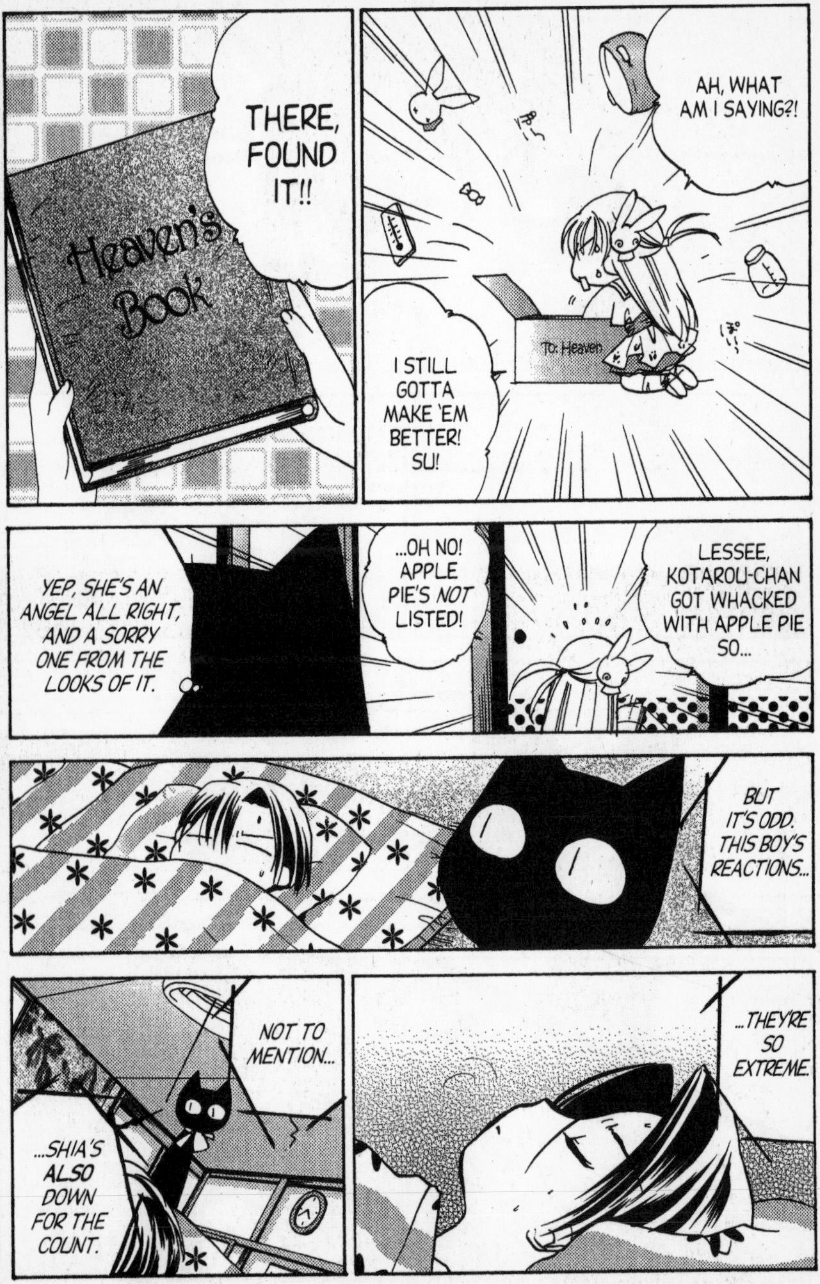
AH, WHAT AM I SAYING?!
I STILL GOTTA MAKE 'EM BETTER! SU!
To: Heaven
THERE, FOUND IT!!
Heaven's Book
LESSEE, KOTAROU-CHAN GOT WHACKED WITH APPLE PIE SO...
...OH NO! APPLE PIE'S *NOT* LISTED!
YEP, SHE'S AN ANGEL ALL RIGHT, AND A SORRY ONE FROM THE LOOKS OF IT.
BUT IT'S ODD. THIS BOY'S REACTIONS...
...THEY'RE SO EXTREME.
NOT TO MENTION...
...SHIA'S ALSO DOWN FOR THE COUNT.

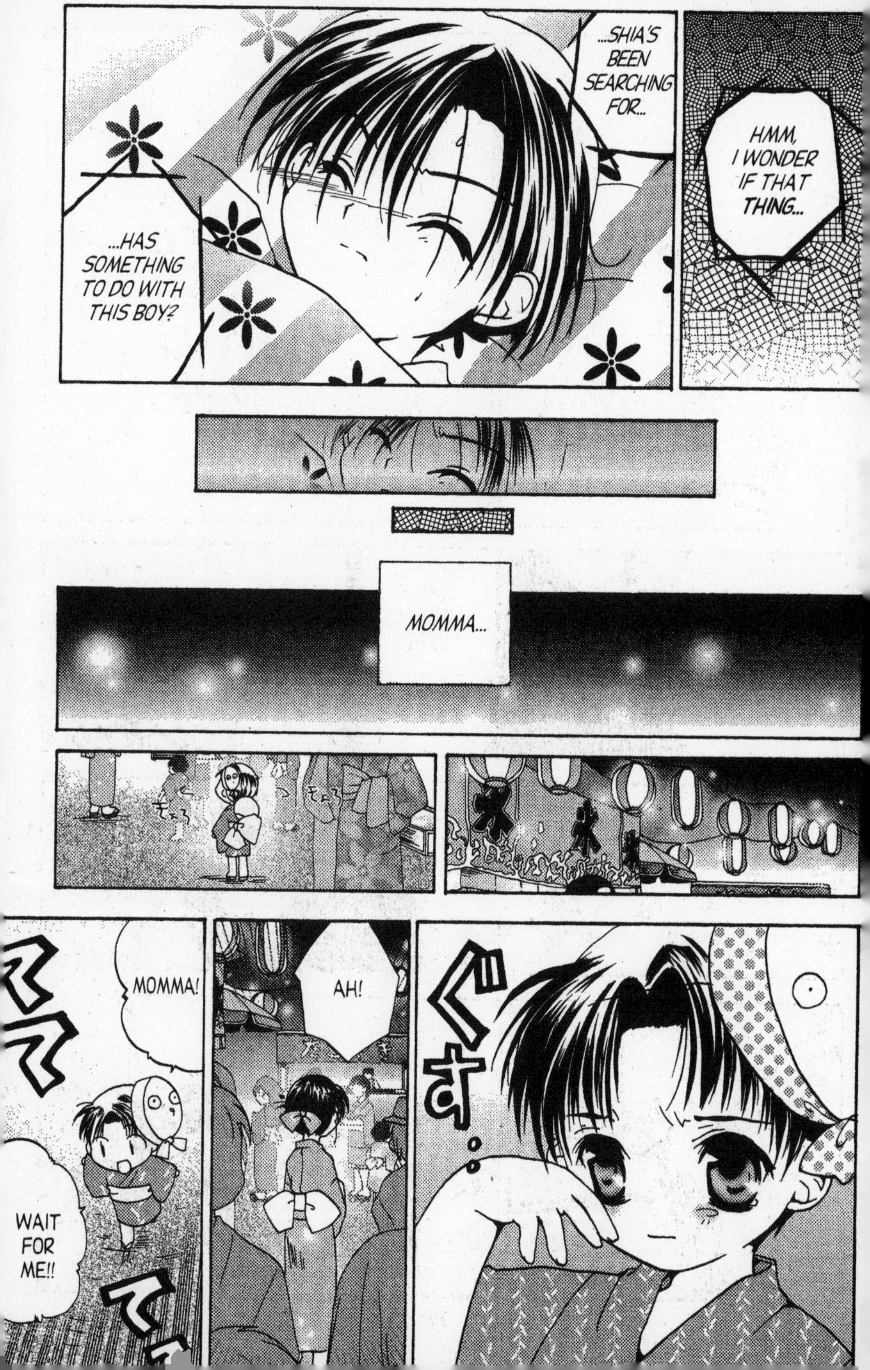
HMM, I WONDER IF THAT THING...
...SHIA'S BEEN SEARCHING FOR...
...HAS SOMETHING TO DO WITH THIS BOY?
MOMMA...
ぐす
AH!
MOMMA!
ママ
WAIT FOR ME!!

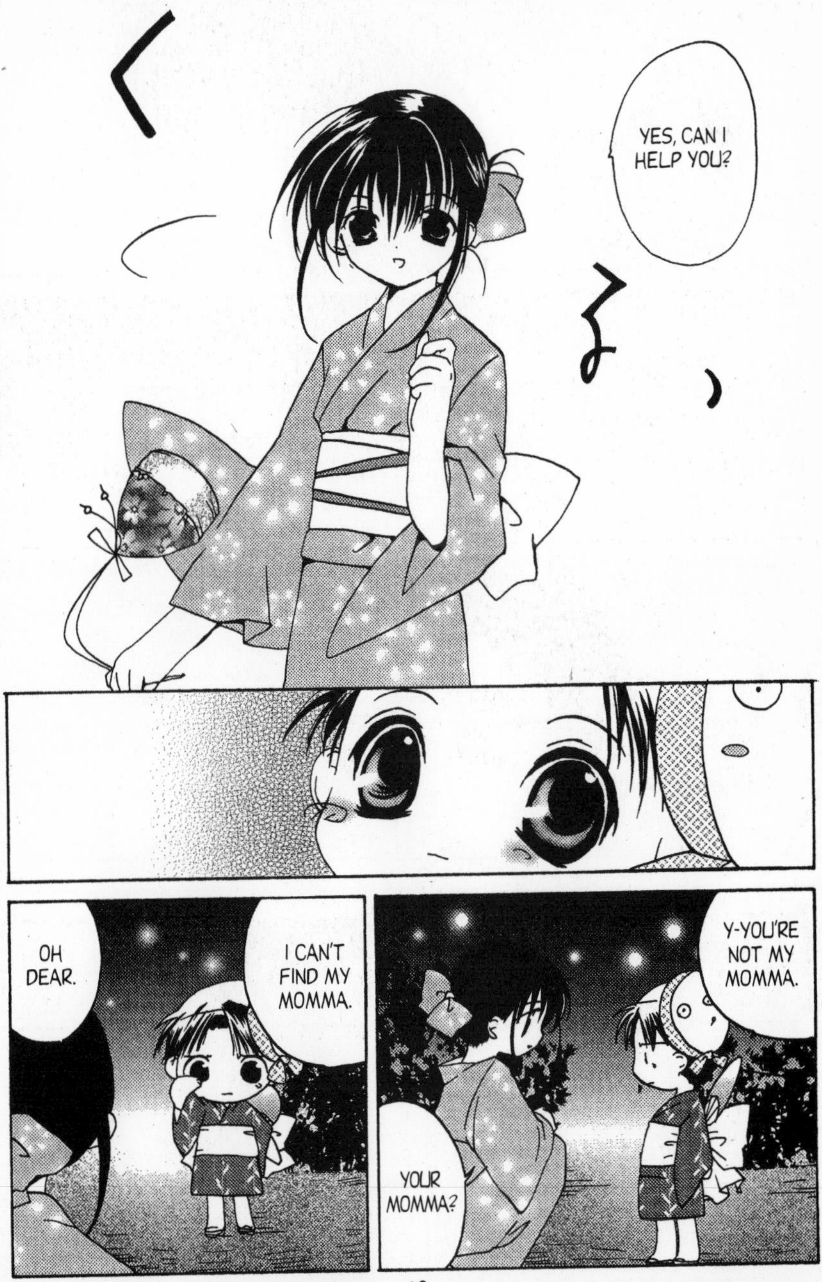
YES, CAN I HELP YOU?
Y-YOU'RE NOT MY MOMMA.
YOUR MOMMA?
I CAN'T FIND MY MOMMA.
OH DEAR.

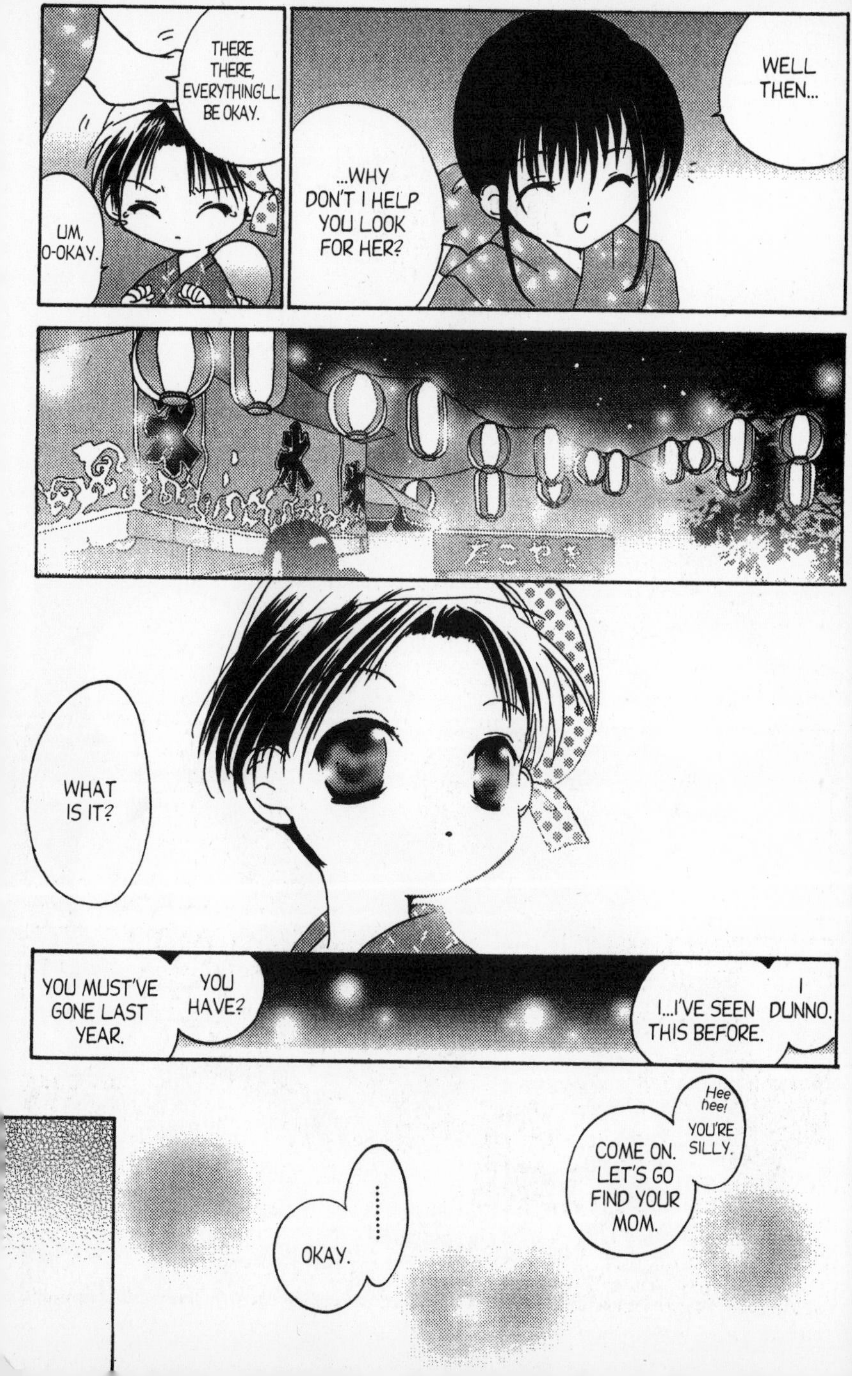
WELL THEN...
...WHY DON'T I HELP YOU LOOK FOR HER?
THERE THERE, EVERYTHING'LL BE OKAY.
UM, O-OKAY.
たこやき
WHAT IS IT?
I DUNNO.
I...I'VE SEEN THIS BEFORE.
YOU HAVE?
YOU MUST'VE GONE LAST YEAR.
Hee hee! YOU'RE SILLY.
COME ON. LET'S GO FIND YOUR MOM.
......
OKAY.

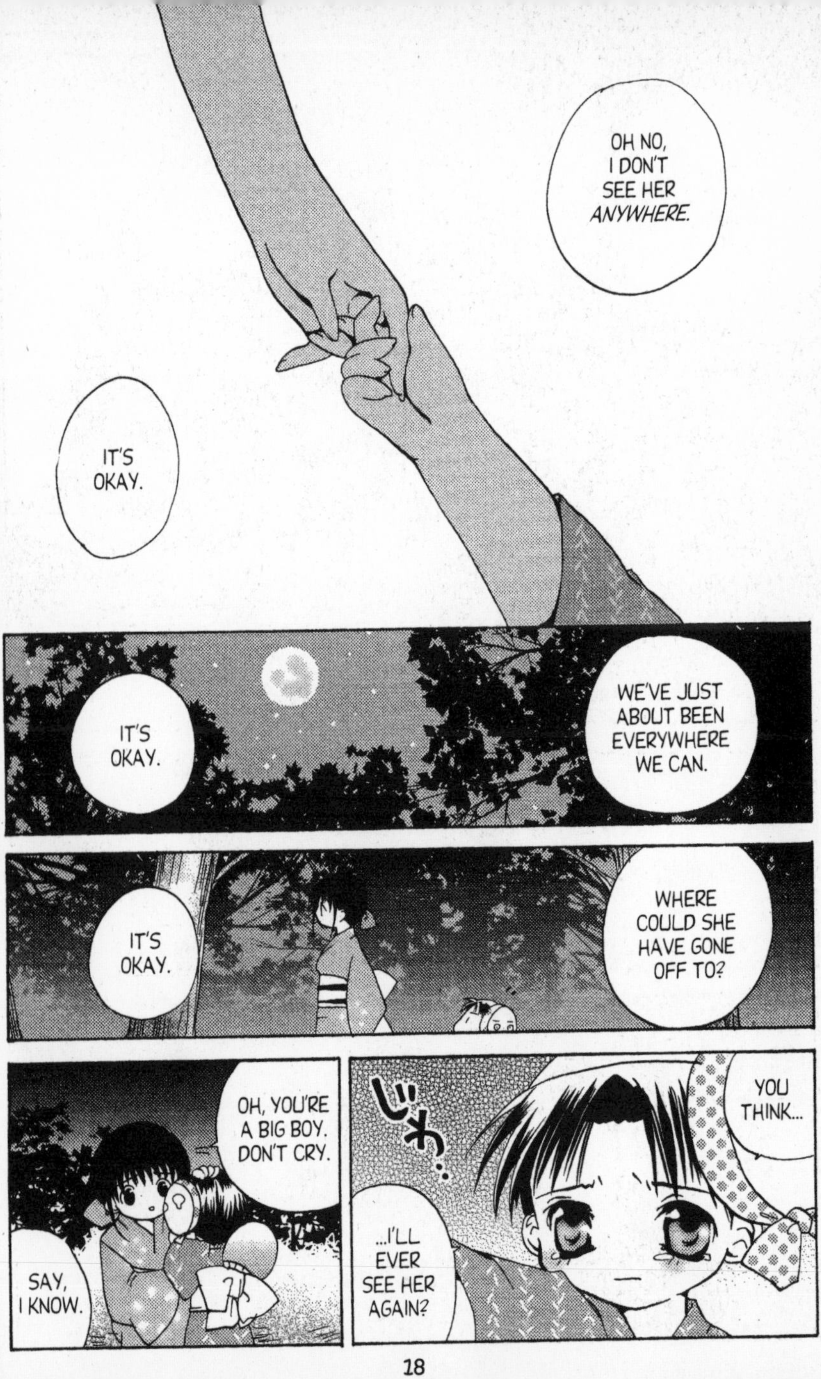
OH NO, I DON'T SEE HER *ANYWHERE.*
IT'S OKAY.
WE'VE JUST ABOUT BEEN EVERYWHERE WE CAN.
IT'S OKAY.
WHERE COULD SHE HAVE GONE OFF TO?
IT'S OKAY.
YOU THINK...
じわ..
...I'LL EVER SEE HER AGAIN?
OH, YOU'RE A BIG BOY. DON'T CRY.
SAY, I KNOW.

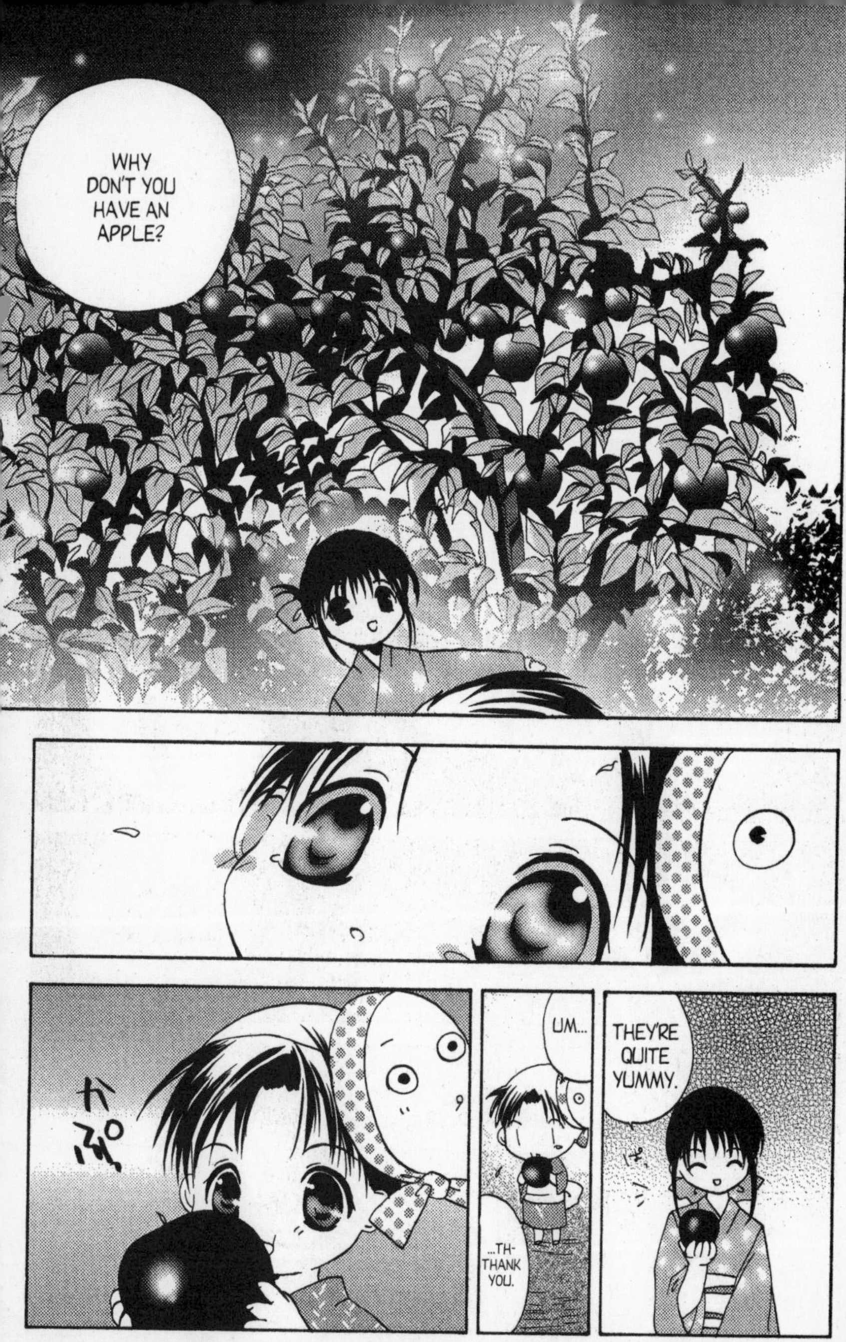
WHY DON'T YOU HAVE AN APPLE?
THEY'RE QUITE YUMMY.
UM...
...TH- THANK YOU.

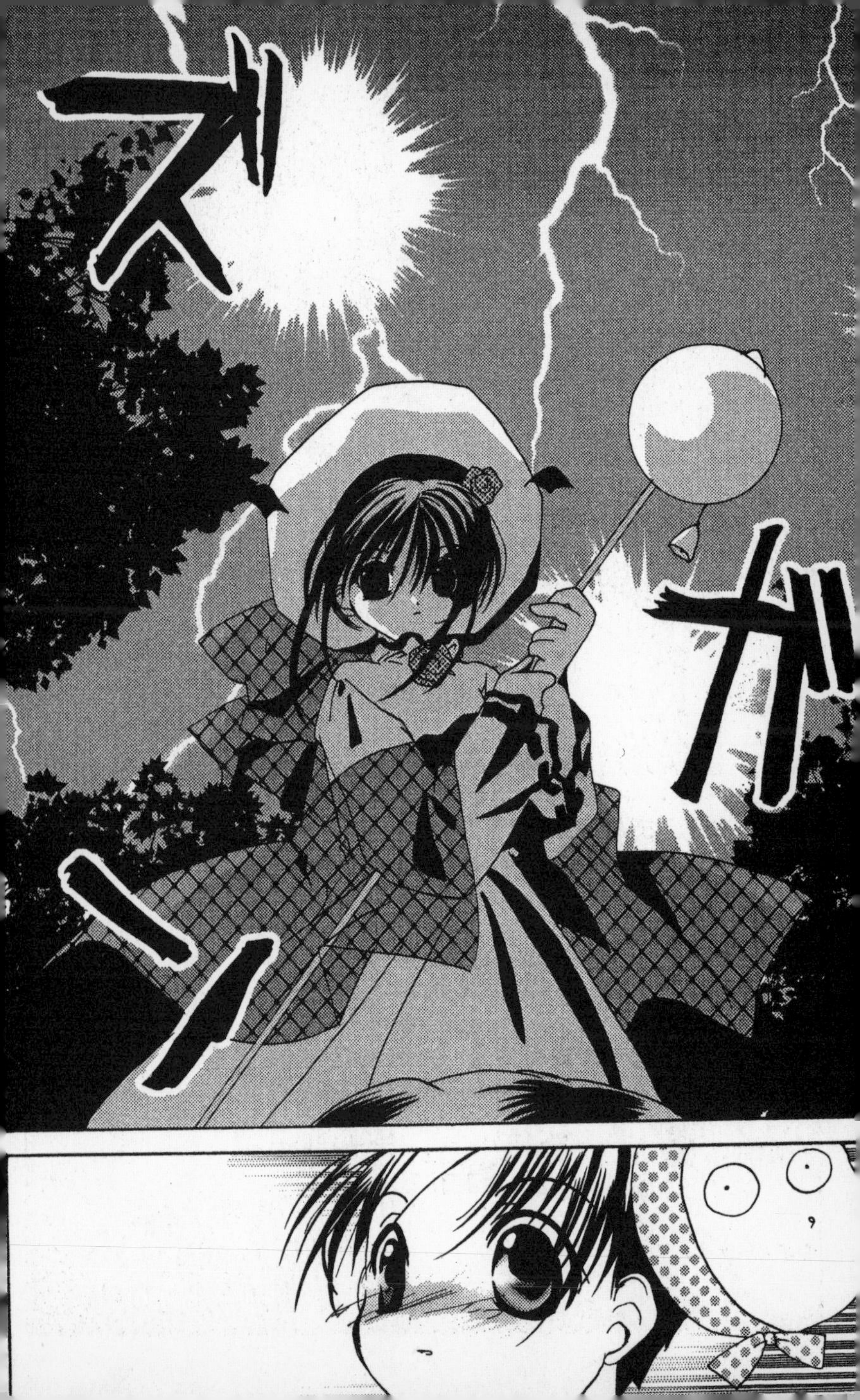
ズン
ガ

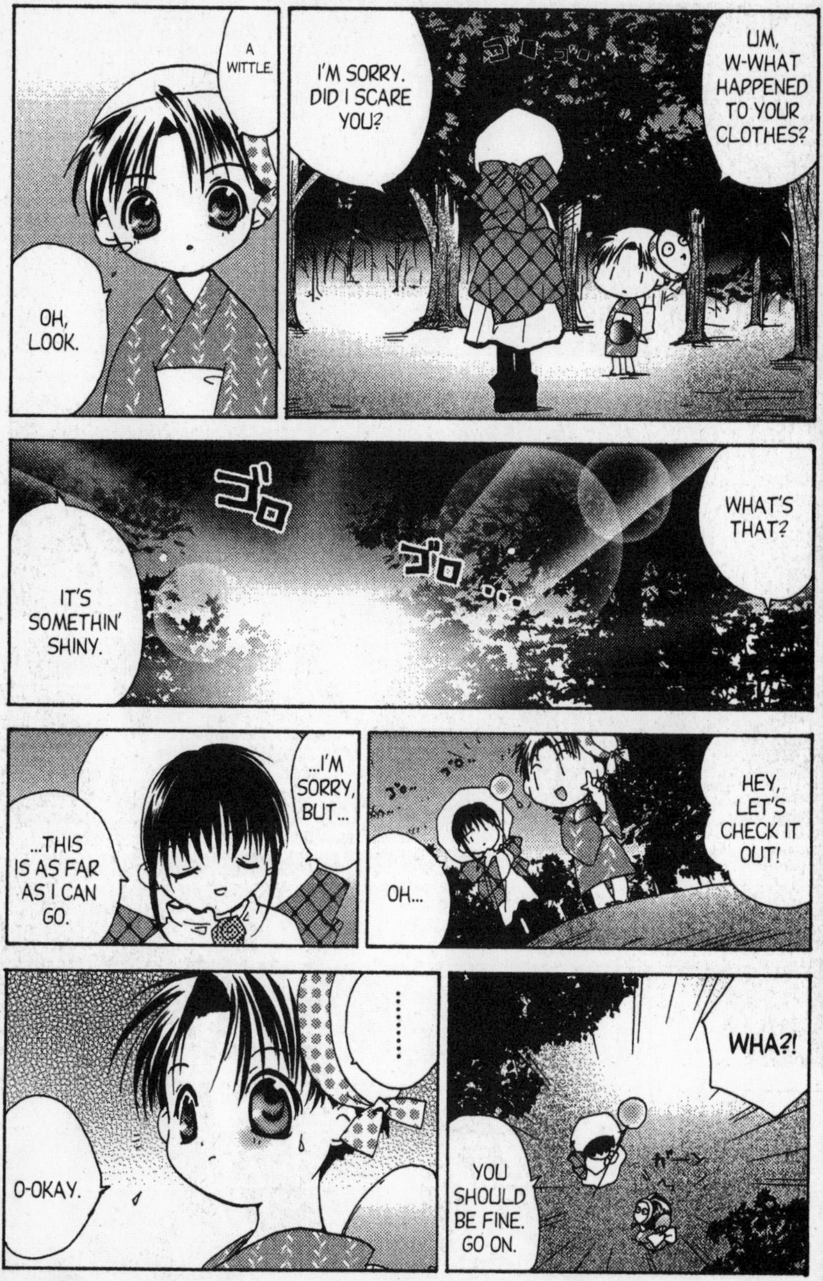
UM, W-WHAT HAPPENED TO YOUR CLOTHES?
I'M SORRY. DID I SCARE YOU?
A WITTLE.
OH, LOOK.
WHAT'S THAT?
ゴロ
ゴロ
IT'S SOMETHIN' SHINY.
HEY, LET'S CHECK IT OUT!
OH...
...I'M SORRY, BUT...
...THIS IS AS FAR AS I CAN GO.
WHA?!
YOU SHOULD BE FINE. GO ON.
......
O-OKAY.

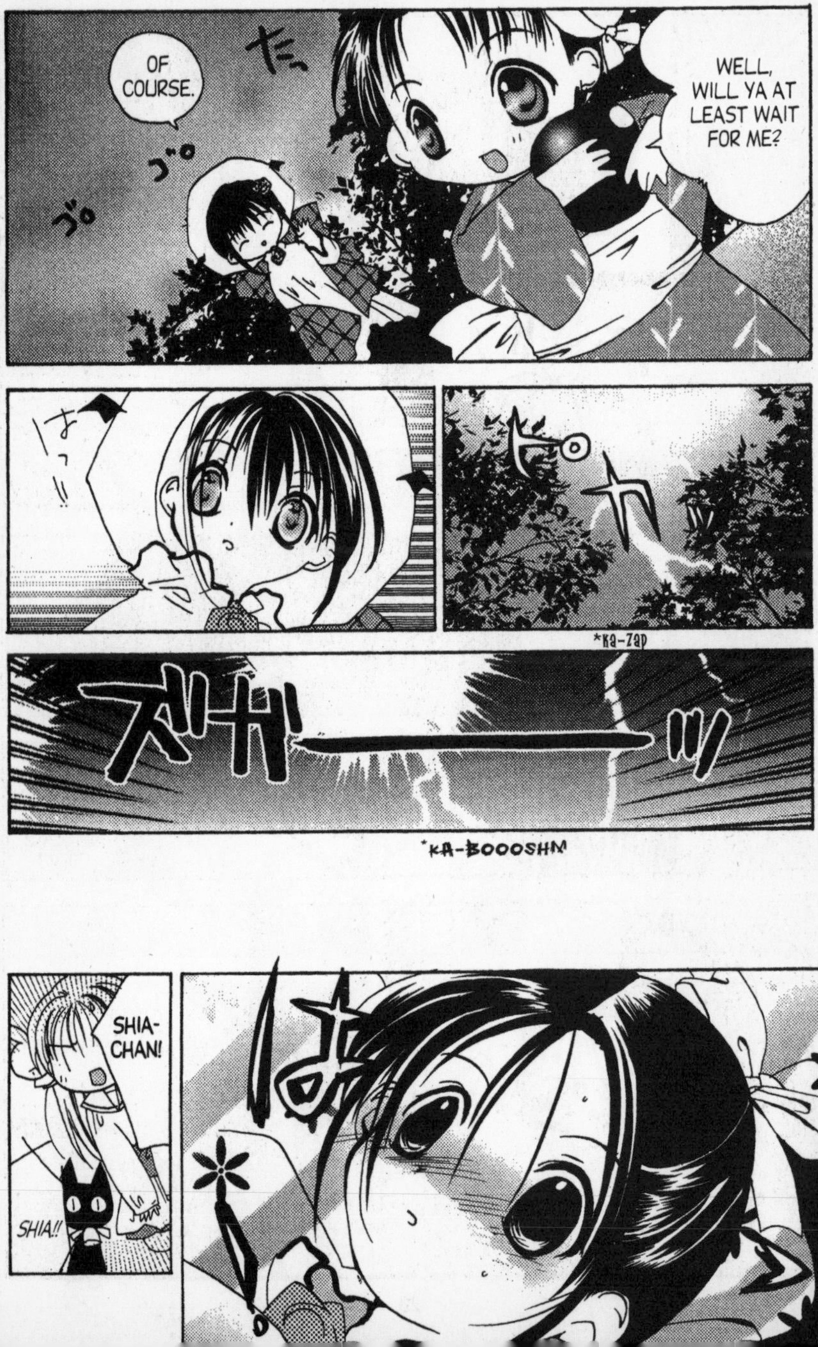
WELL, WILL YA AT LEAST WAIT FOR ME?
OF COURSE.
*ka-zap
*KA-BOOOSHM
SHIA-CHAN!
SHIA!!

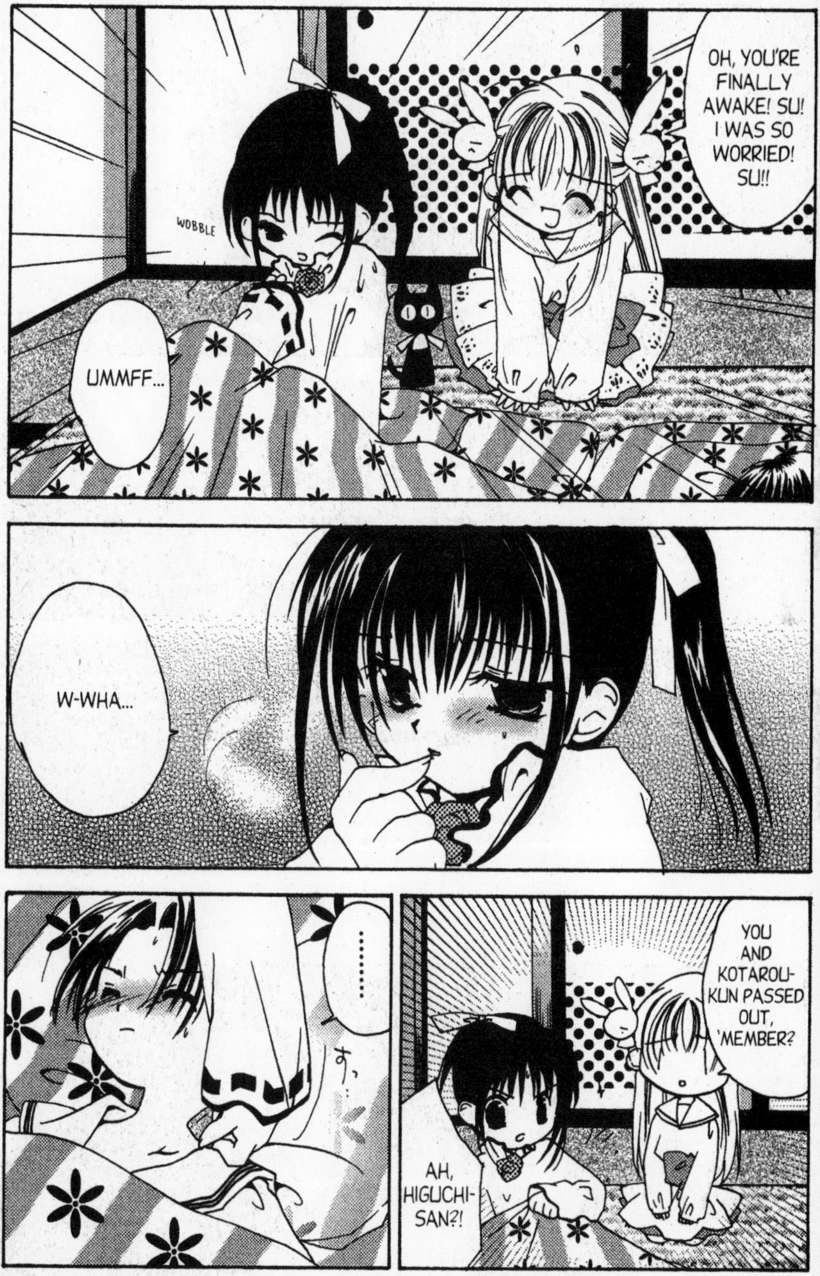
OH, YOU'RE FINALLY AWAKE! SU! I WAS SO WORRIED! SU!!
WOBBLE
UMMFF...
W-WHA...
YOU AND KOTAROU-KUN PASSED OUT, 'MEMBER?
AH, HIGUCHI-SAN?!
......
すっ

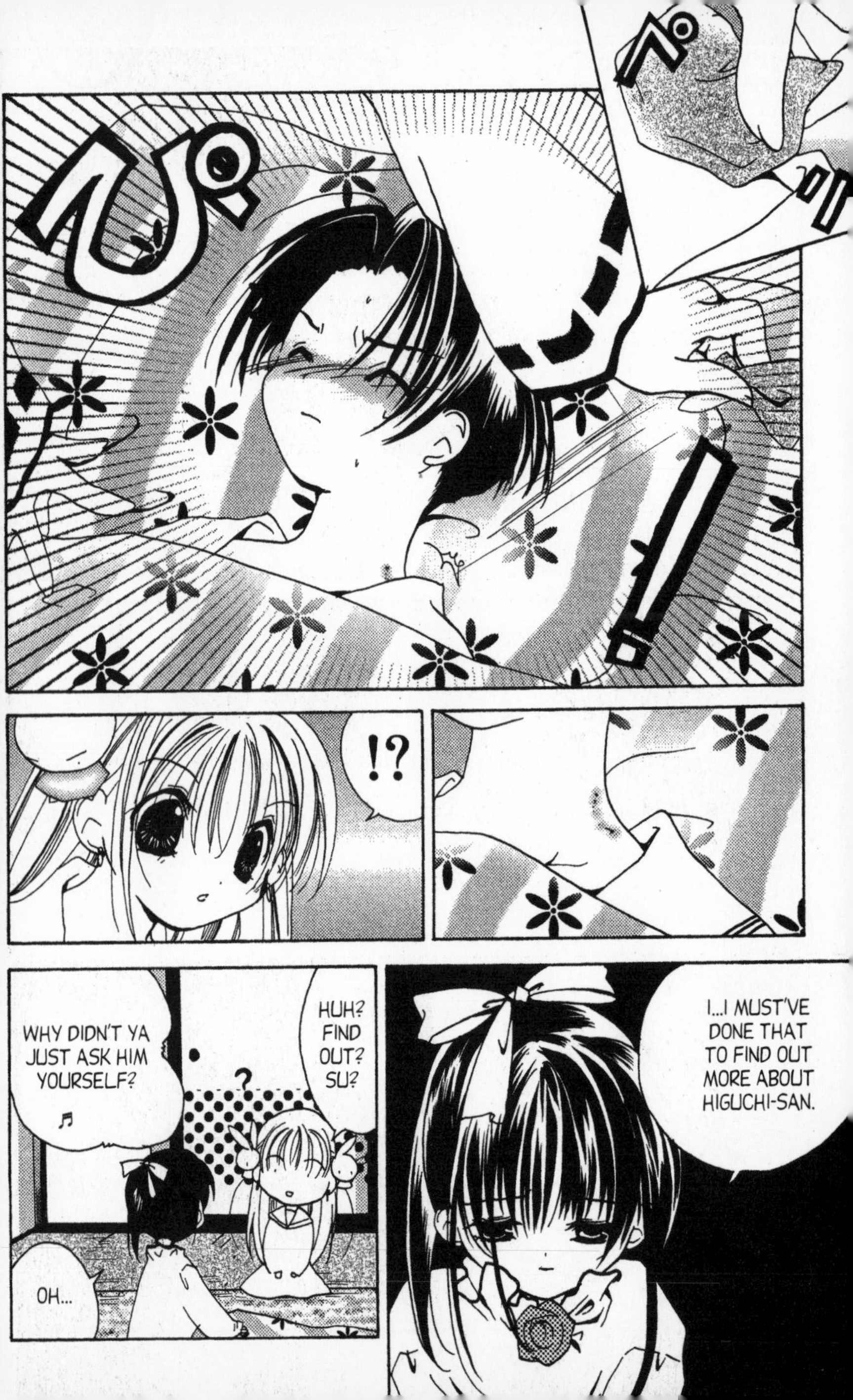

!?
I...I MUST'VE DONE THAT TO FIND OUT MORE ABOUT HIGUCHI-SAN.
HUH? FIND OUT? SU?
WHY DIDN'T YA JUST ASK HIM YOURSELF? ♪
OH...

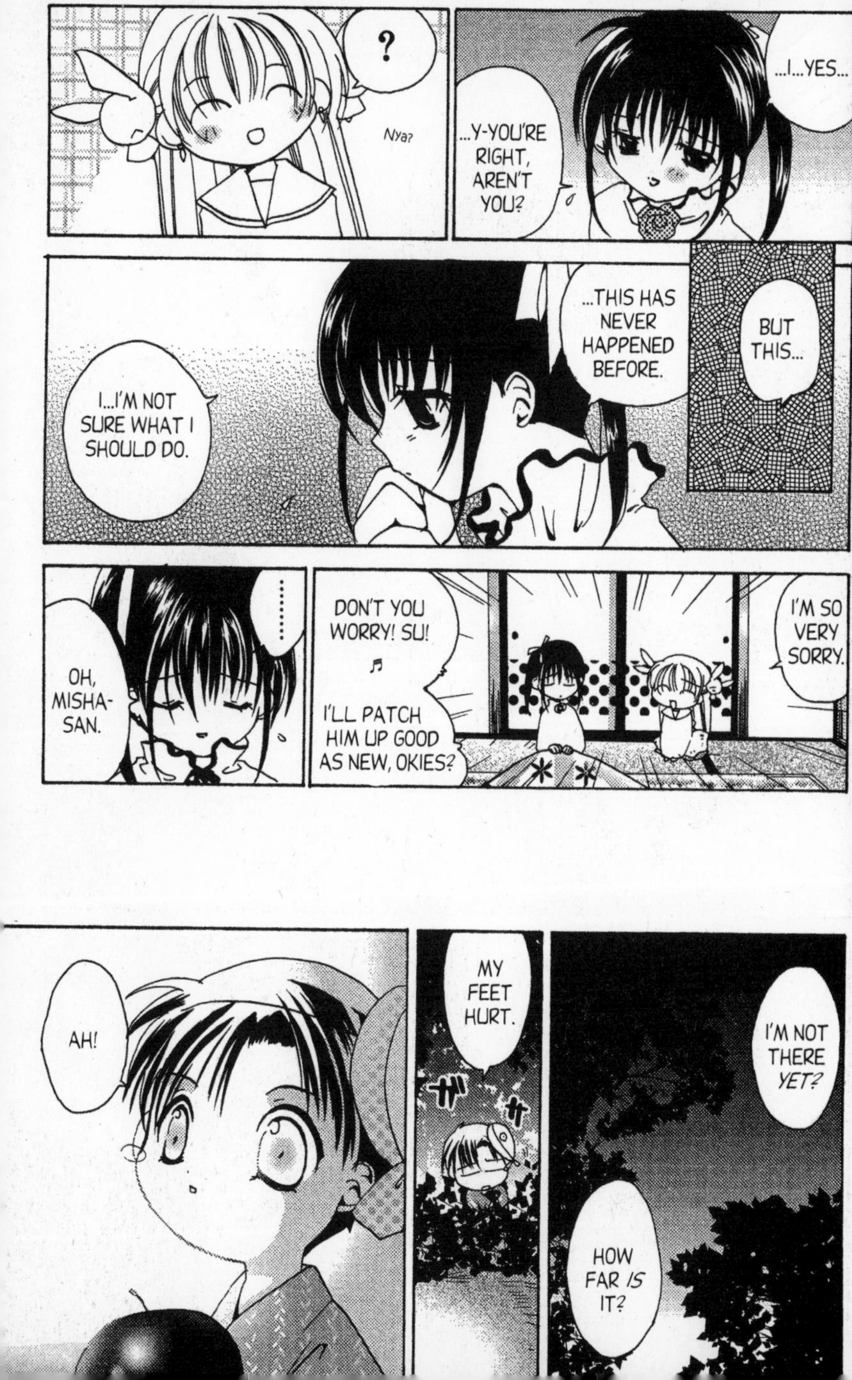
...I...YES...
...Y-YOU'RE RIGHT, AREN'T YOU?
?
Nya?
BUT THIS...
...THIS HAS NEVER HAPPENED BEFORE.
I...I'M NOT SURE WHAT I SHOULD DO.
I'M SO VERY SORRY.
DON'T YOU WORRY! SU! ♪
I'LL PATCH HIM UP GOOD AS NEW, OKIES?
......
OH, MISHA-SAN.
I'M NOT THERE *YET?*
HOW FAR *IS* IT?
MY FEET HURT.
AH!

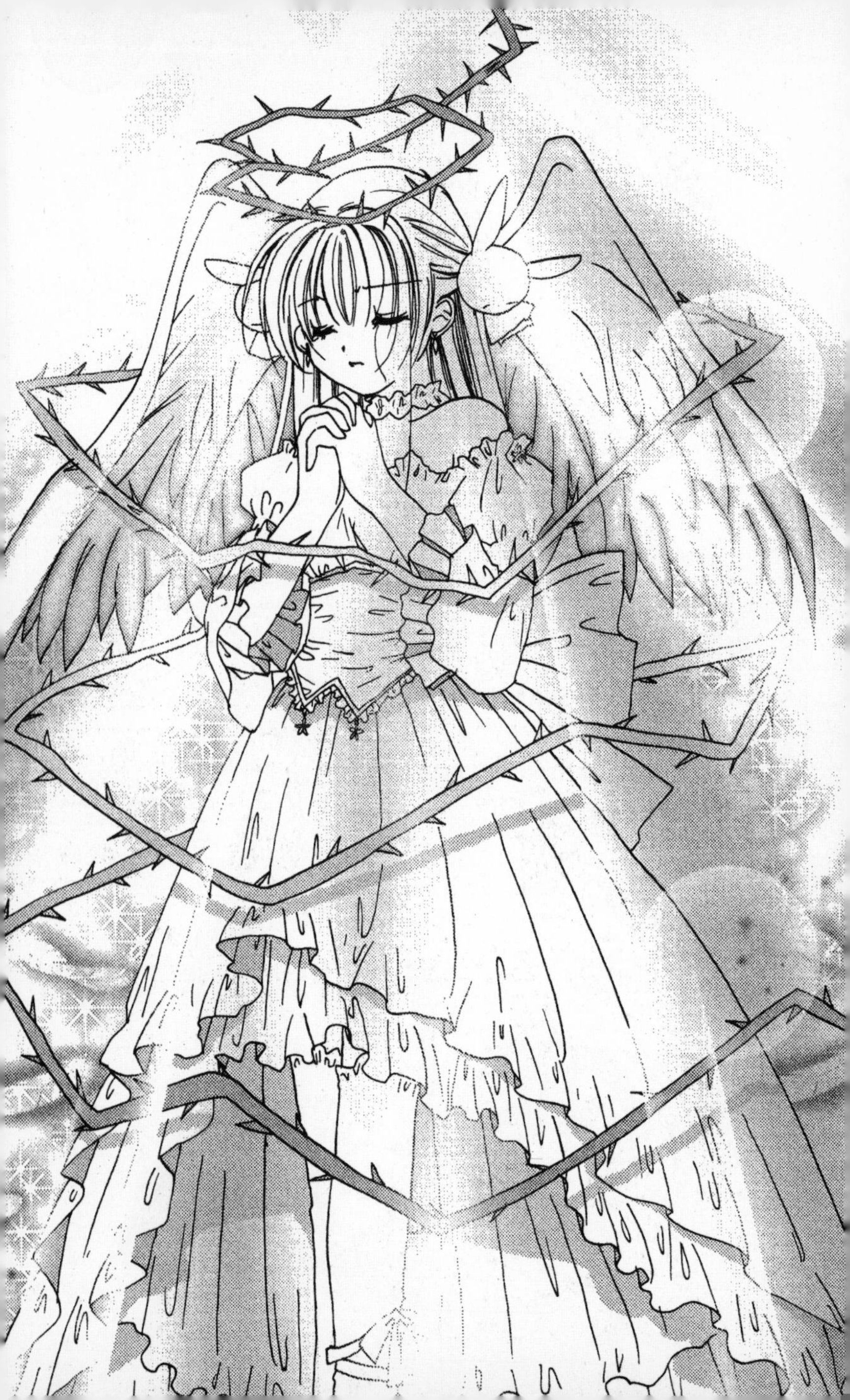

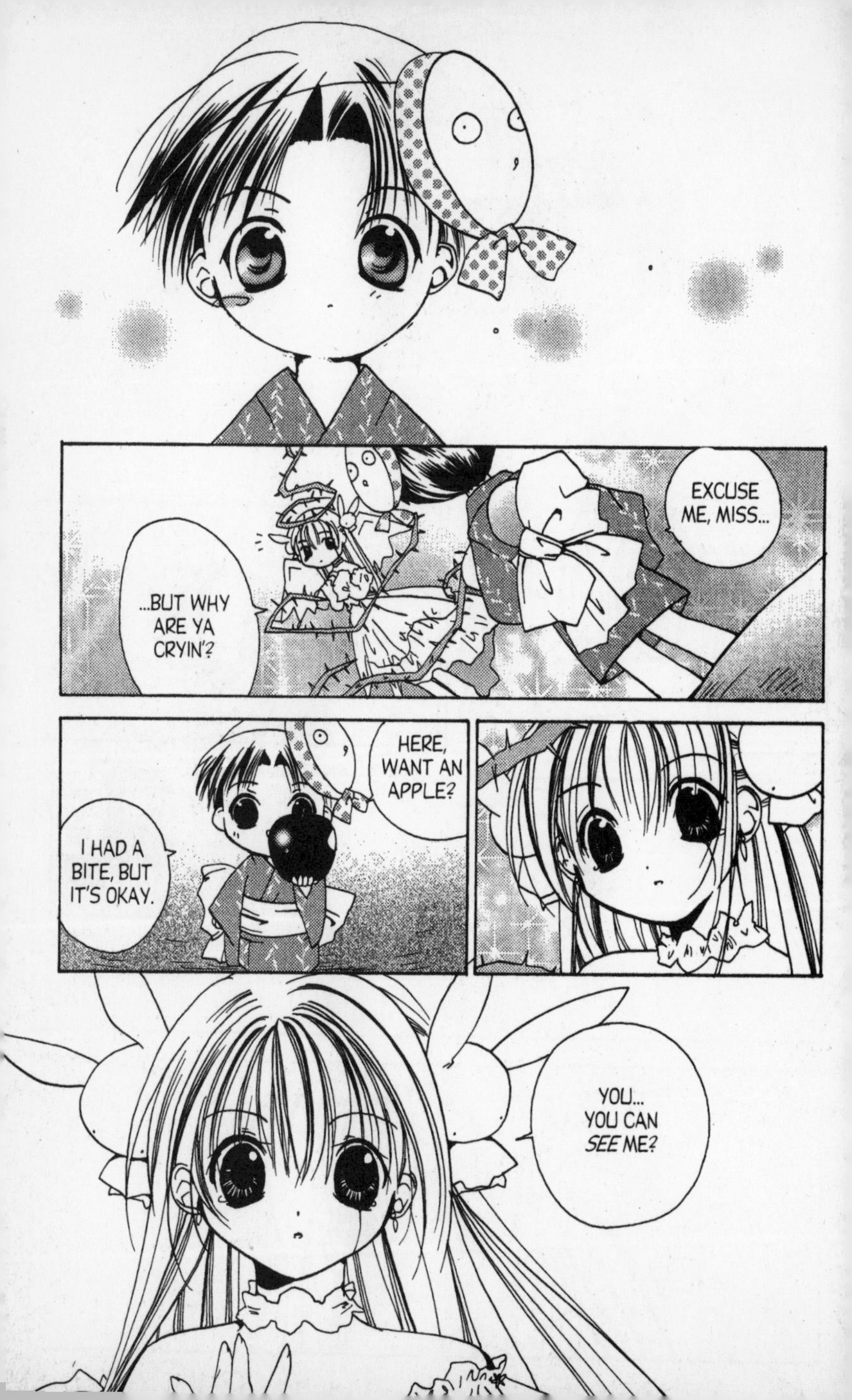
EXCUSE ME, MISS...
...BUT WHY ARE YA CRYIN'?
HERE, WANT AN APPLE?
I HAD A BITE, BUT IT'S OKAY.
YOU... YOU CAN *SEE* ME?

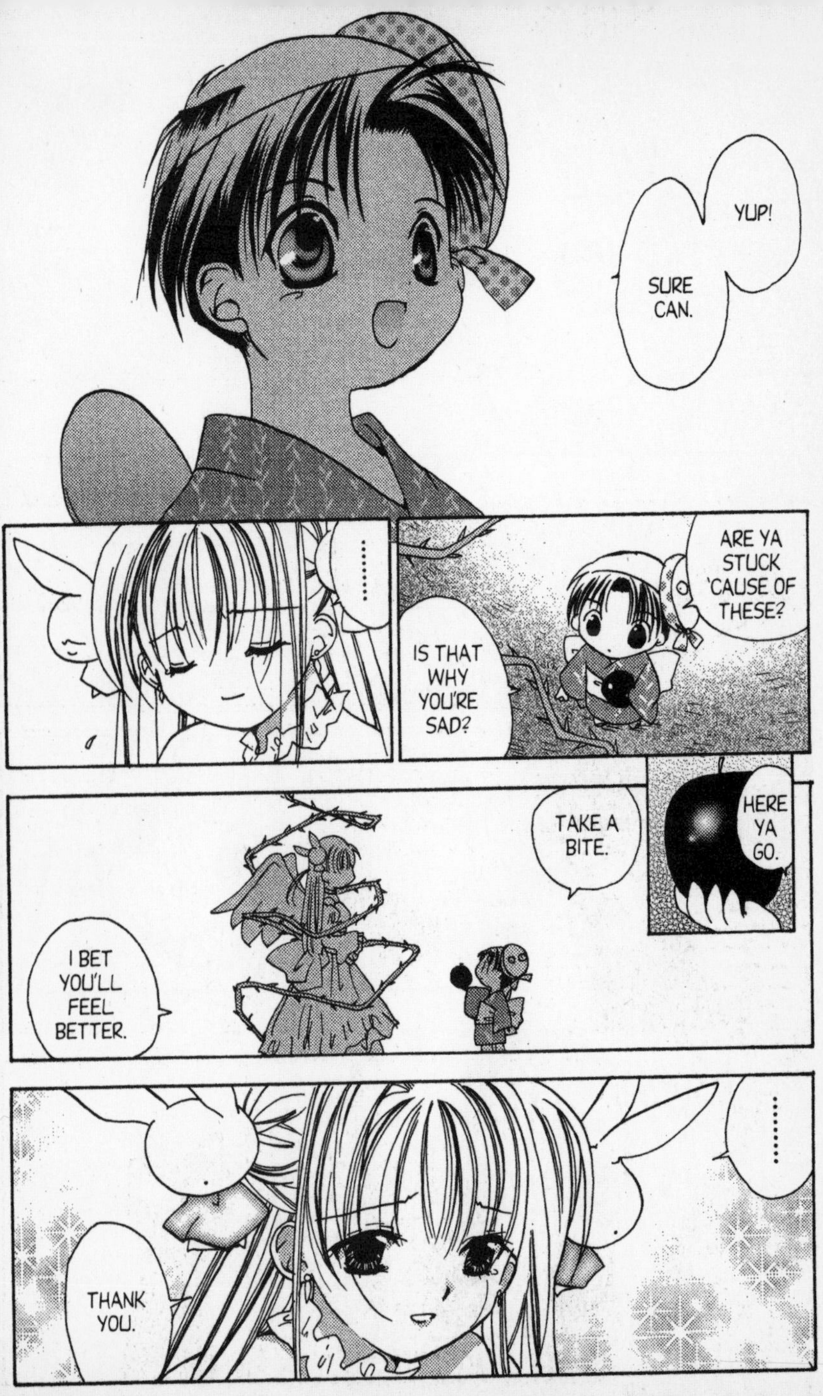
YUP!
SURE CAN.
ARE YA STUCK 'CAUSE OF THESE?
IS THAT WHY YOU'RE SAD?
......
HERE YA GO.
TAKE A BITE.
I BET YOU'LL FEEL BETTER.
......
THANK YOU.

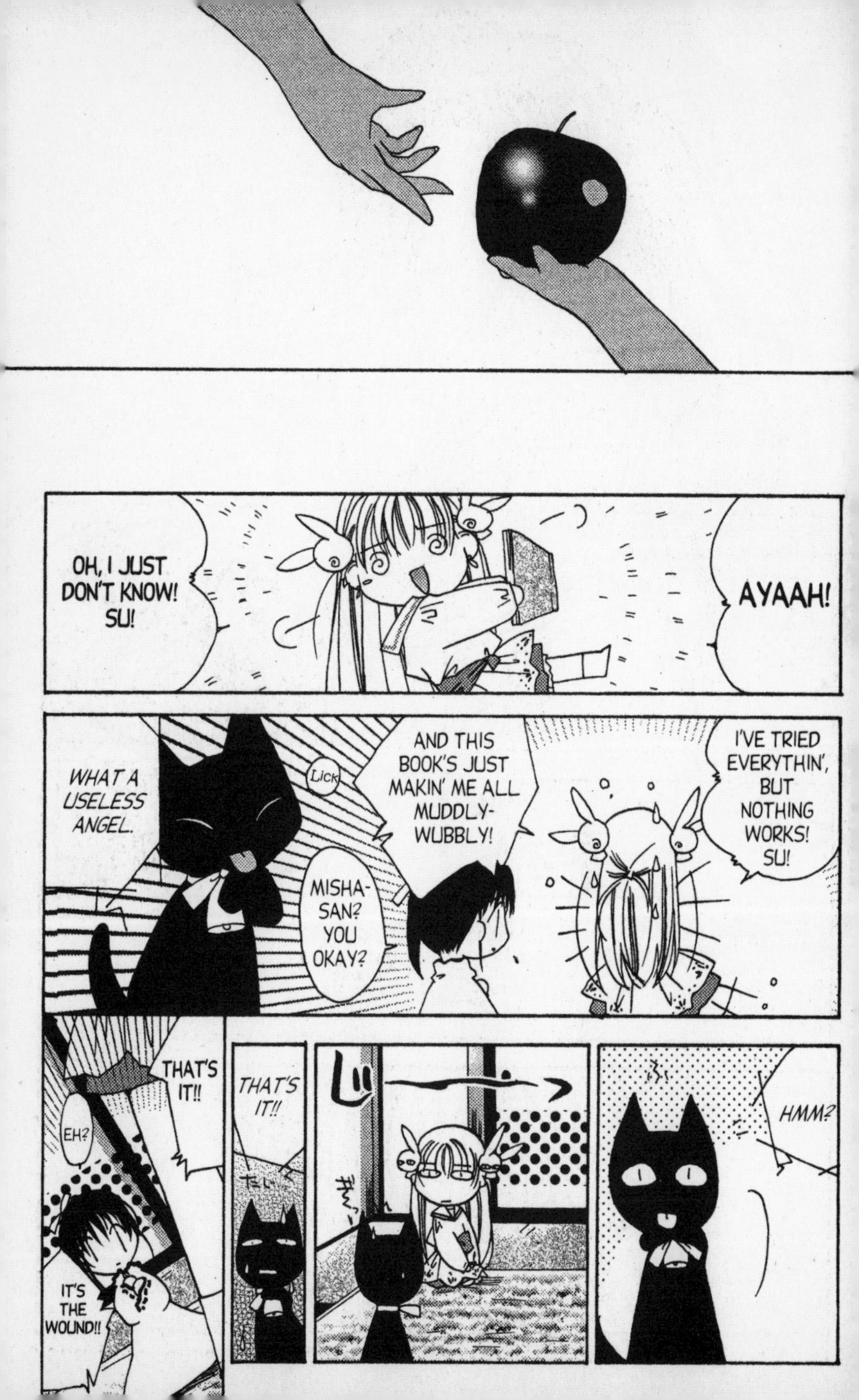
AYAAH!
OH, I JUST DON'T KNOW! SU!
I'VE TRIED EVERYTHIN', BUT NOTHING WORKS! SU!
AND THIS BOOK'S JUST MAKIN' ME ALL MUDDLY-WUBBLY!
MISHA-SAN? YOU OKAY?
LICK
WHAT A USELESS ANGEL.
HMM?
THAT'S IT!!
THAT'S IT!!
EH?
IT'S THE WOUND!!

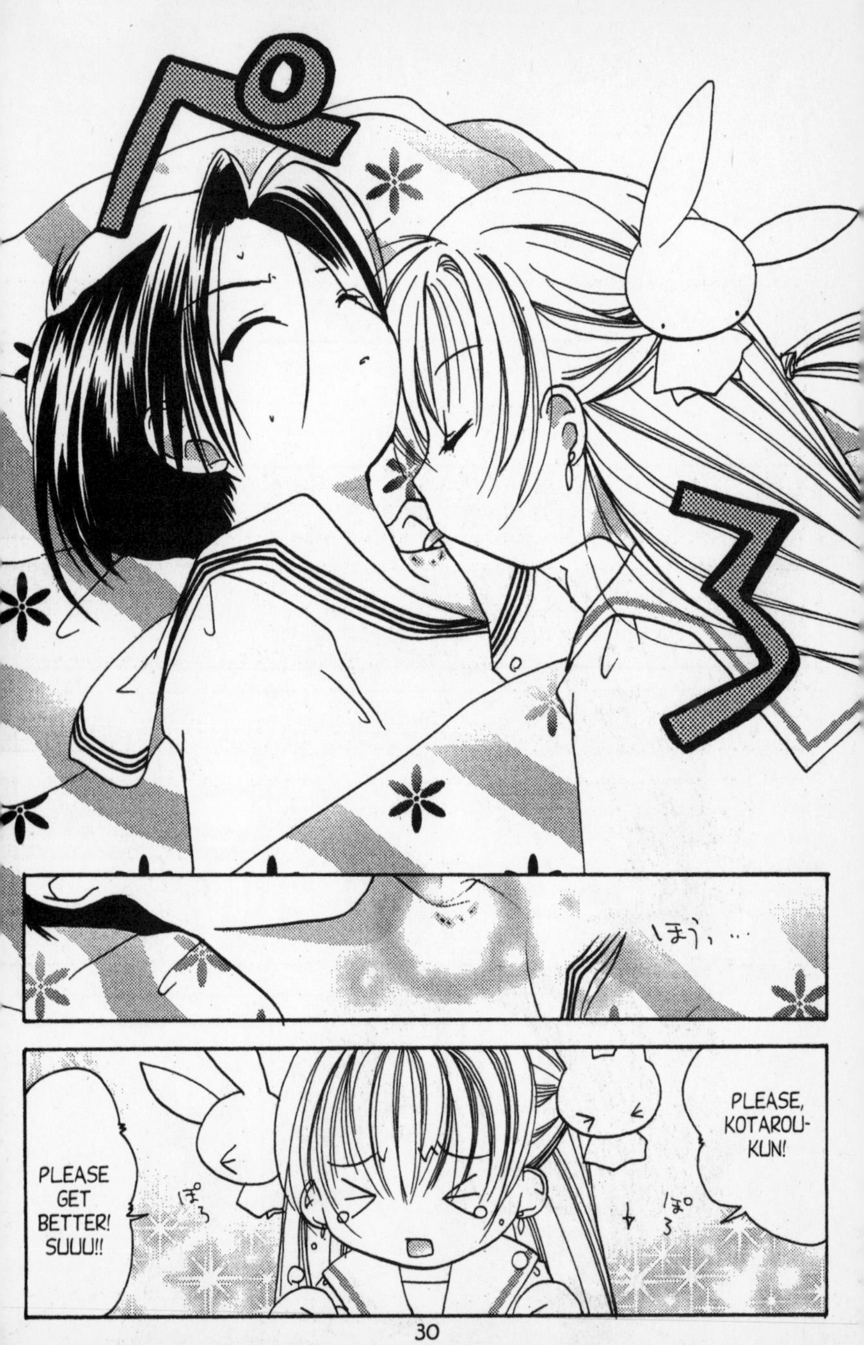
ぺろ
ほぅ…
PLEASE, KOTAROU-KUN!
ぽろ
ぽろ
PLEASE GET BETTER! SUUU!!

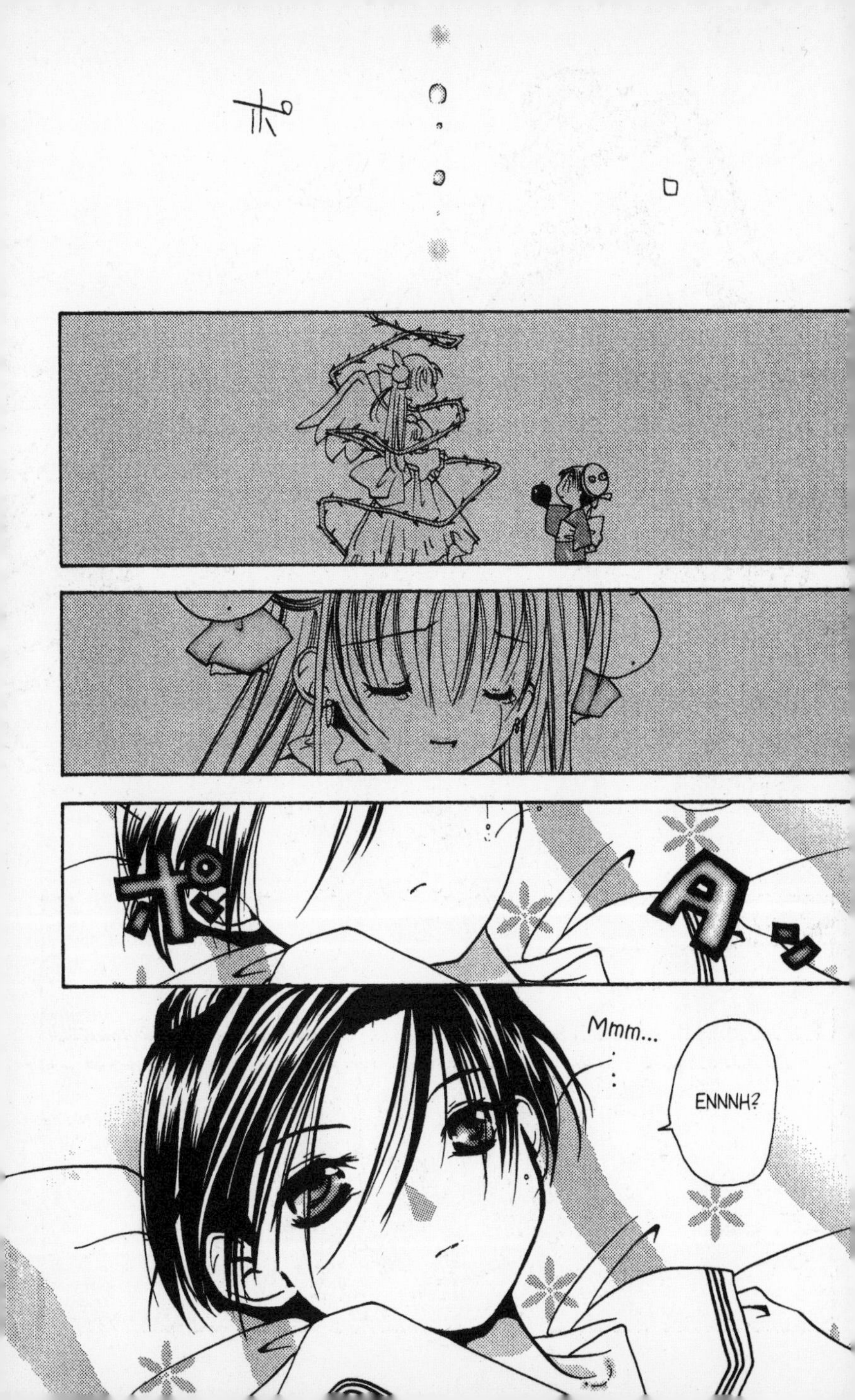
Mmm...
ENNNH?

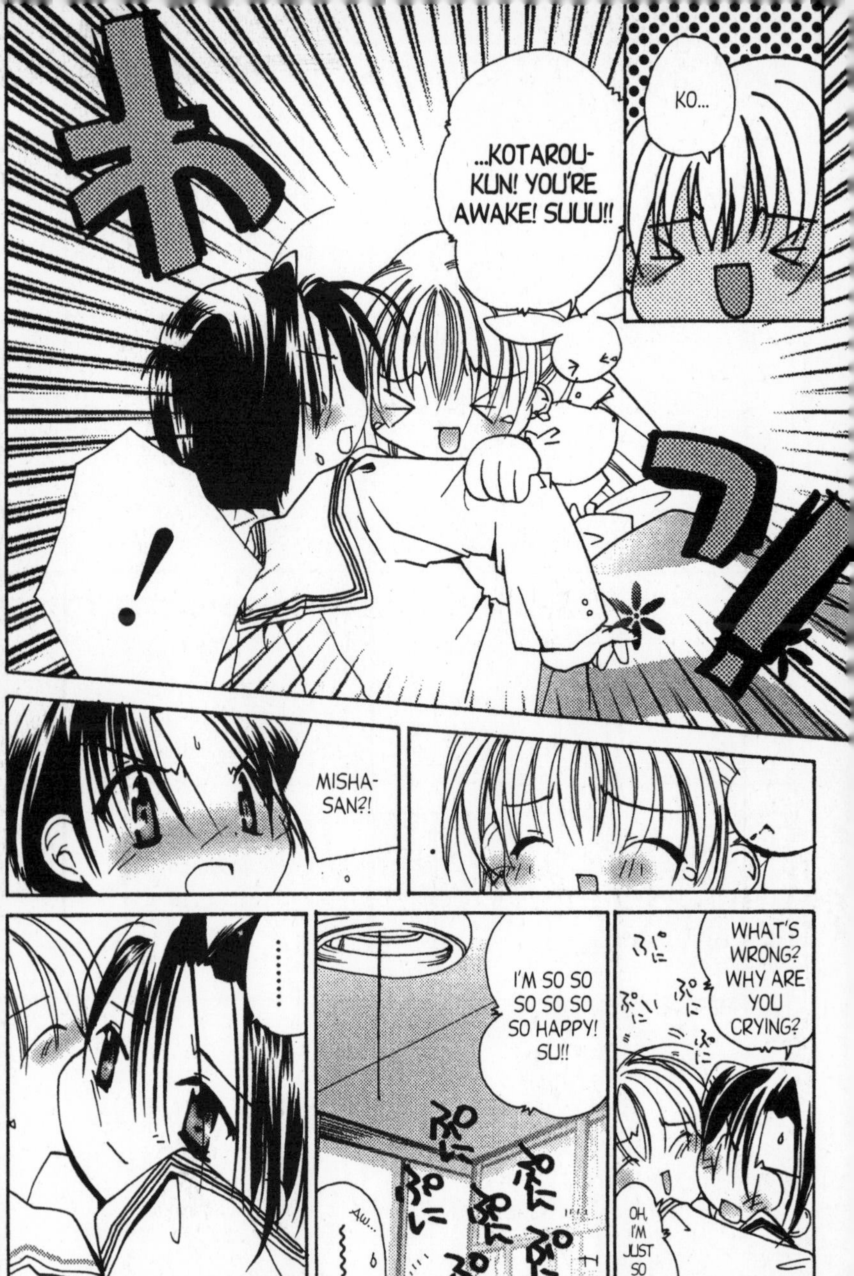
KO...
...KOTAROU-KUN! YOU'RE AWAKE! SUUU!!
!
MISHA-SAN?!
WHAT'S WRONG? WHY ARE YOU CRYING?
ぷに ぷに ぷに ぷに
OH, I'M JUST SO HAPPY-WAPPY!!
I'M SO SO SO SO SO SO HAPPY! SU!!
ぷに ぷに ぷに ぷに ぷに ぷに
Aw...
......

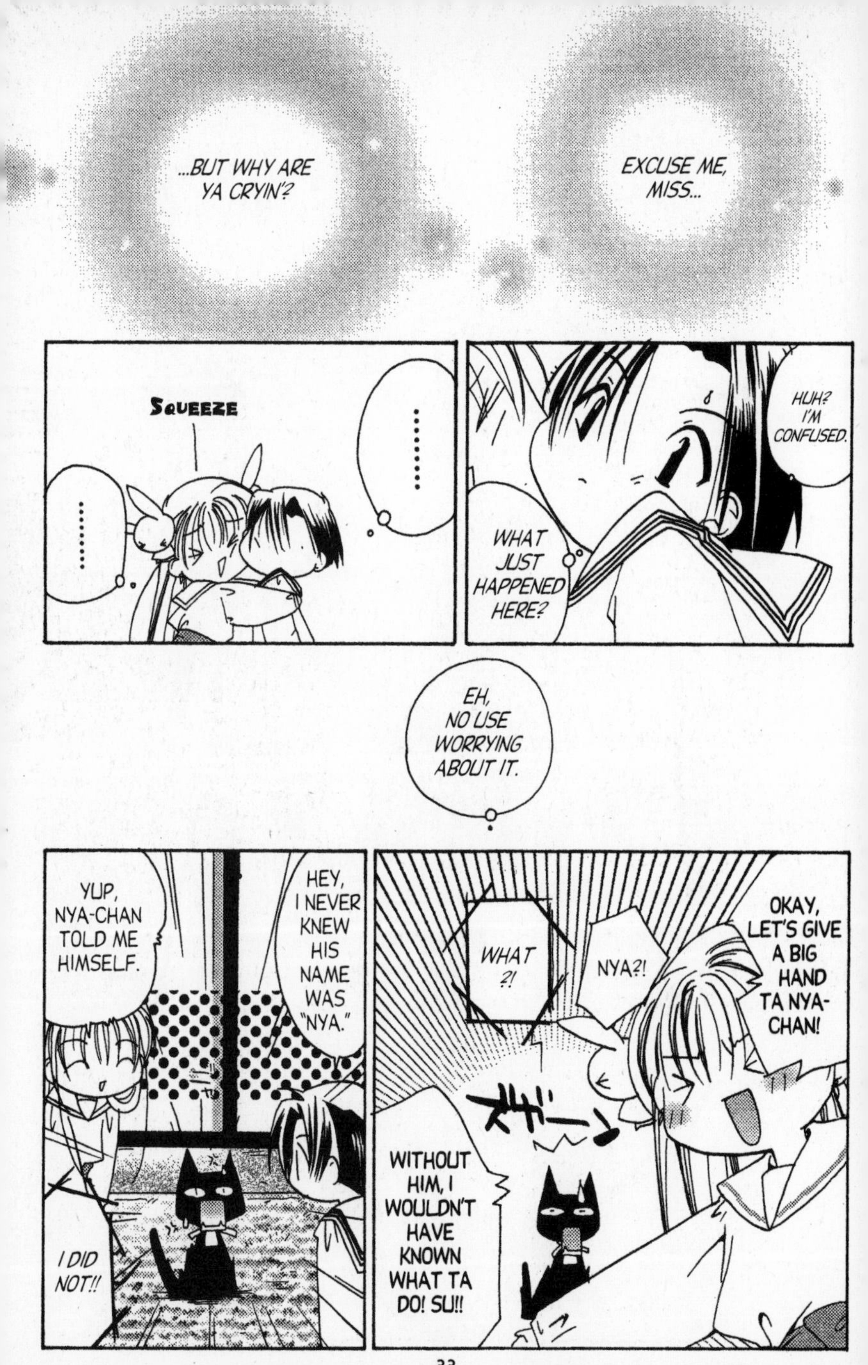
EXCUSE ME, MISS...
...BUT WHY ARE YA CRYIN'?
HUH? I'M CONFUSED.
WHAT JUST HAPPENED HERE?
......
SQUEEZE
......
EH, NO USE WORRYING ABOUT IT.
OKAY, LET'S GIVE A BIG HAND TA NYA-CHAN!
NYA?!
WHAT ?!
WITHOUT HIM, I WOULDN'T HAVE KNOWN WHAT TA DO! SU!!
HEY, I NEVER KNEW HIS NAME WAS "NYA."
YUP, NYA-CHAN TOLD ME HIMSELF.
I DID NOT!!

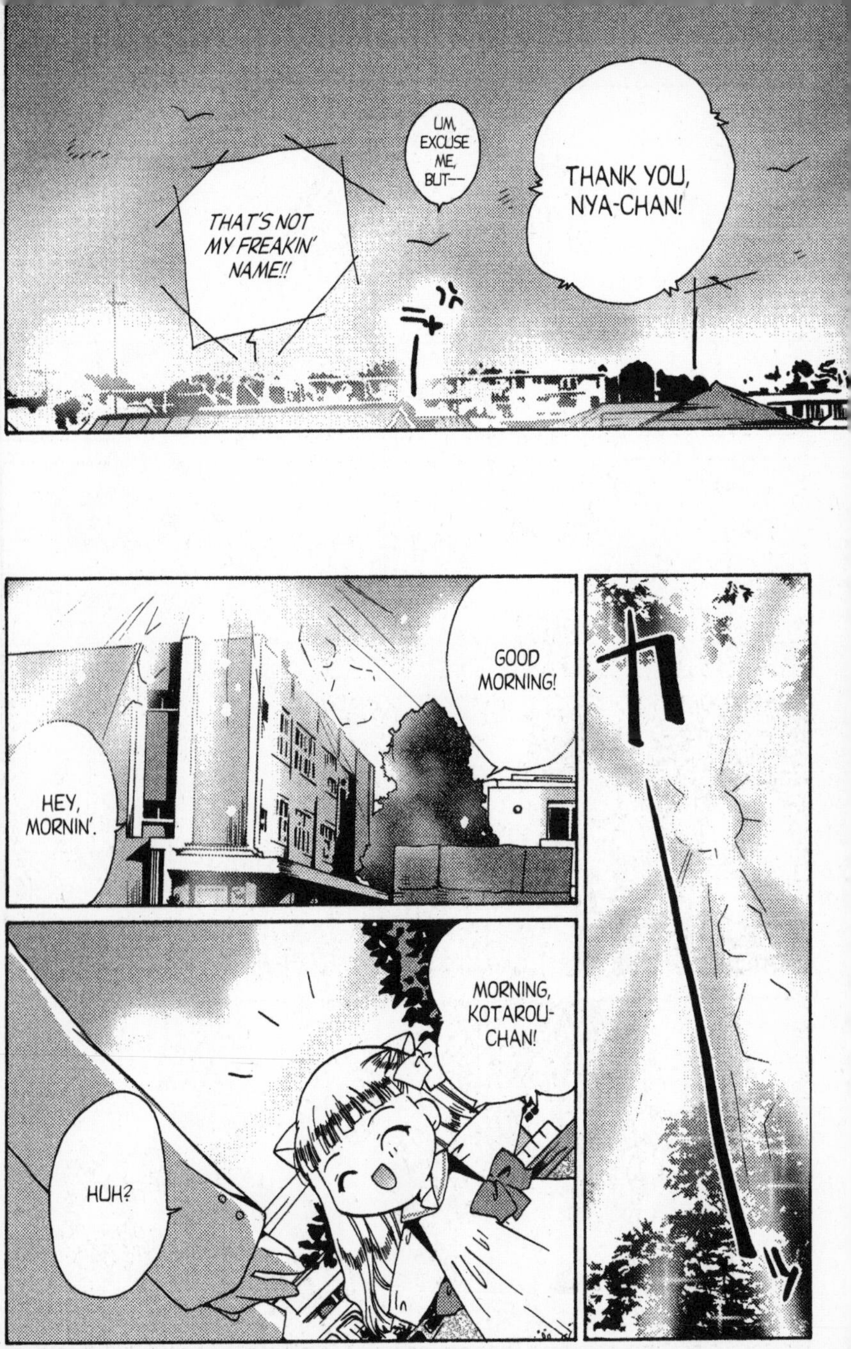
THANK YOU, NYA-CHAN!
UM, EXCUSE ME, BUT--
THAT'S NOT MY FREAKIN' NAME!!
GOOD MORNING!
HEY, MORNIN'.
MORNING, KOTAROU-CHAN!
HUH?

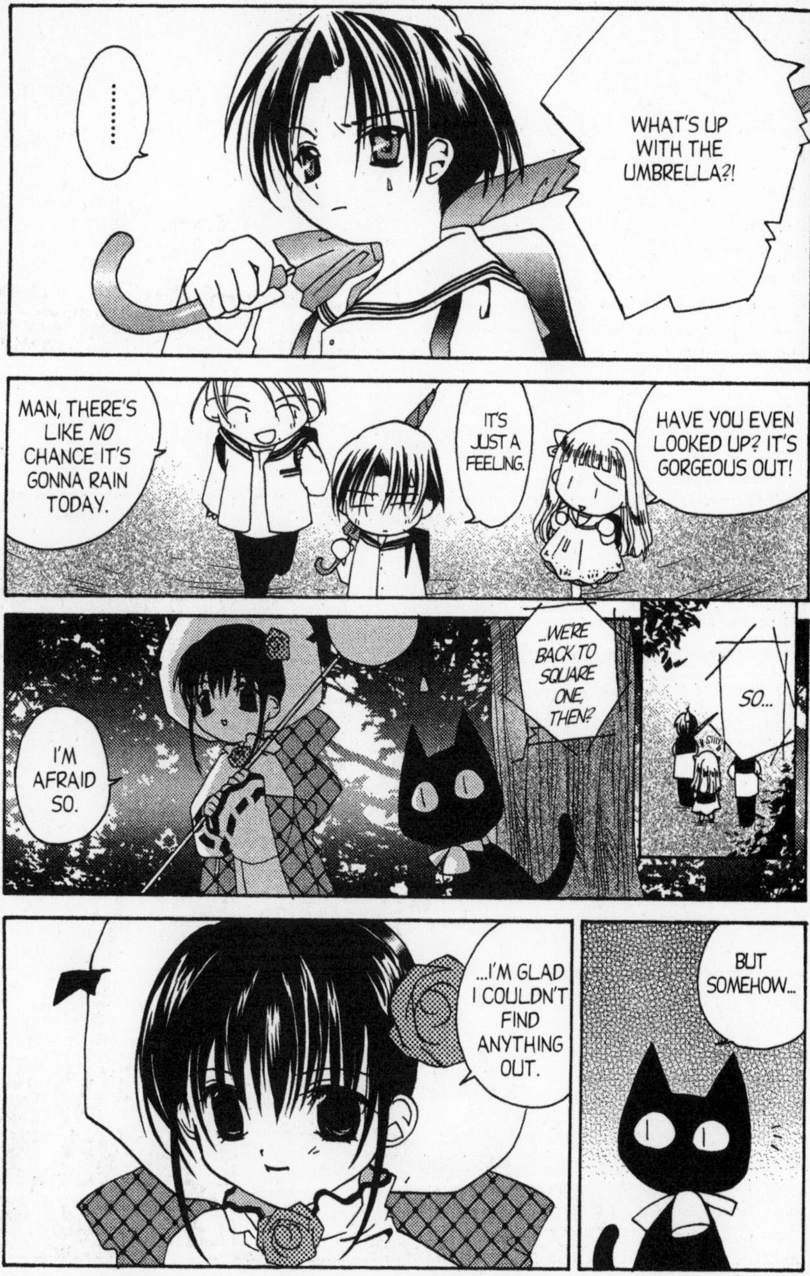
WHAT'S UP WITH THE UMBRELLA?!
......
HAVE YOU EVEN LOOKED UP? IT'S GORGEOUS OUT!
IT'S JUST A FEELING.
MAN, THERE'S LIKE *NO* CHANCE IT'S GONNA RAIN TODAY.
SO...
...WE'RE BACK TO SQUARE ONE, THEN?
I'M AFRAID SO.
BUT SOMEHOW...
...I'M GLAD I COULDN'T FIND ANYTHING OUT.

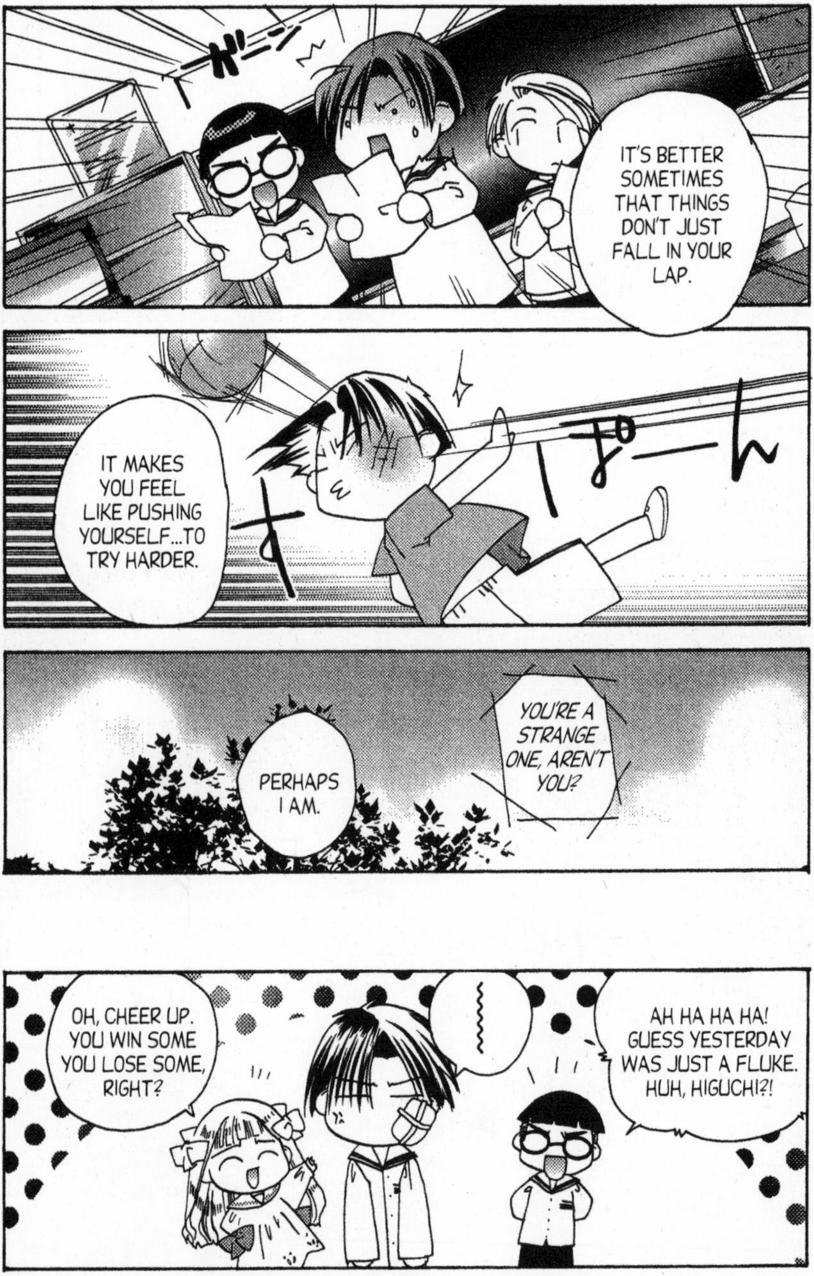
IT'S BETTER SOMETIMES THAT THINGS DON'T JUST FALL IN YOUR LAP.
IT MAKES YOU FEEL LIKE PUSHING YOURSELF...TO TRY HARDER.
YOU'RE A STRANGE ONE, AREN'T YOU?
PERHAPS I AM.
AH HA HA HA! GUESS YESTERDAY WAS JUST A FLUKE. HUH, HIGUCHI!?!
OH, CHEER UP. YOU WIN SOME YOU LOSE SOME, RIGHT?

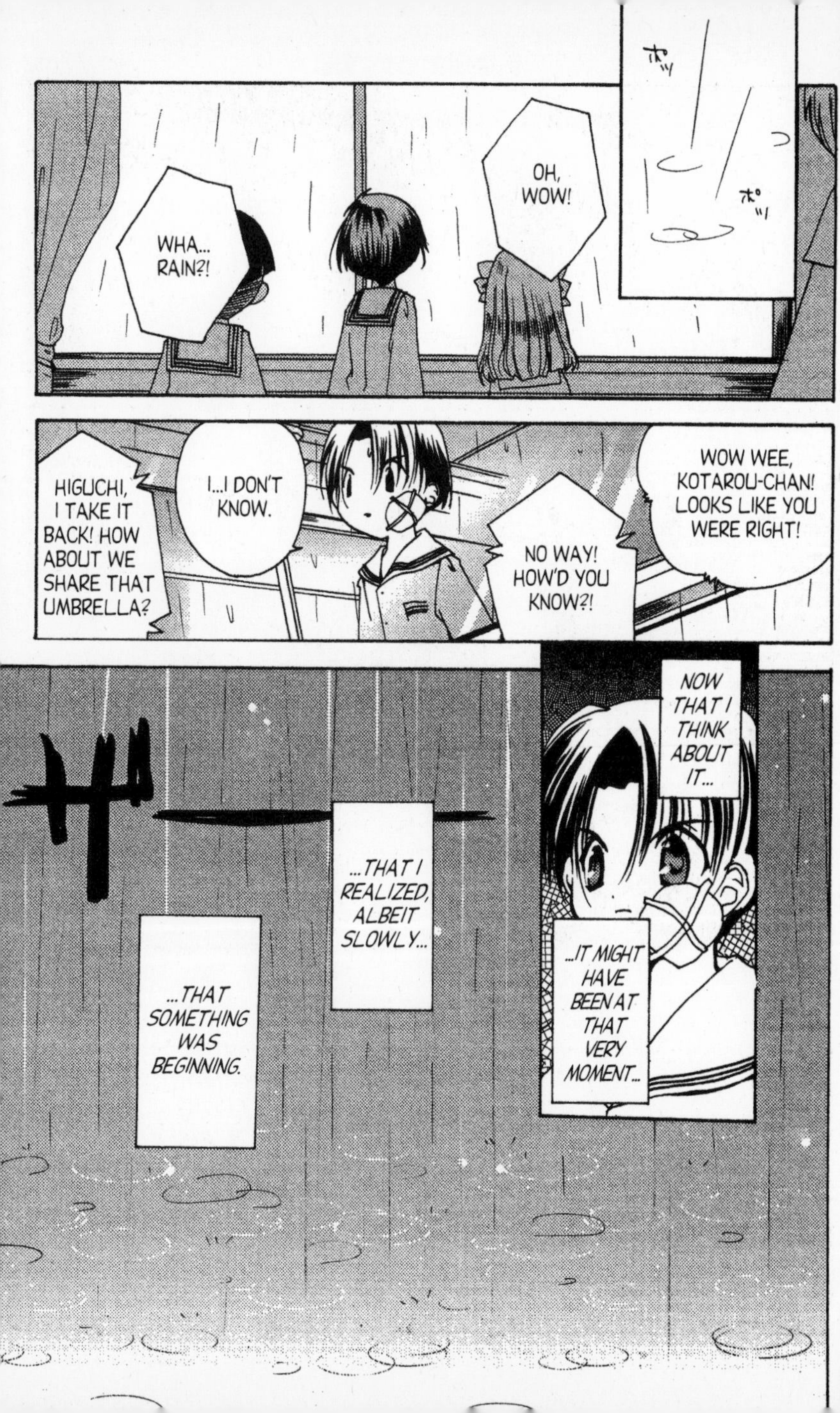
ポッ
ポッ
OH, WOW!
WHA... RAIN?!
WOW WEE, KOTAROU-CHAN! LOOKS LIKE YOU WERE RIGHT!
NO WAY! HOW'D YOU KNOW?!
I...I DON'T KNOW.
HIGUCHI, I TAKE IT BACK! HOW ABOUT WE SHARE THAT UMBRELLA?
NOW THAT I THINK ABOUT IT...
...IT MIGHT HAVE BEEN AT THAT VERY MOMENT...
...THAT I REALIZED, ALBEIT SLOWLY...
...THAT SOMETHING WAS BEGINNING.

Lesson 15

How to Explore a Mansion

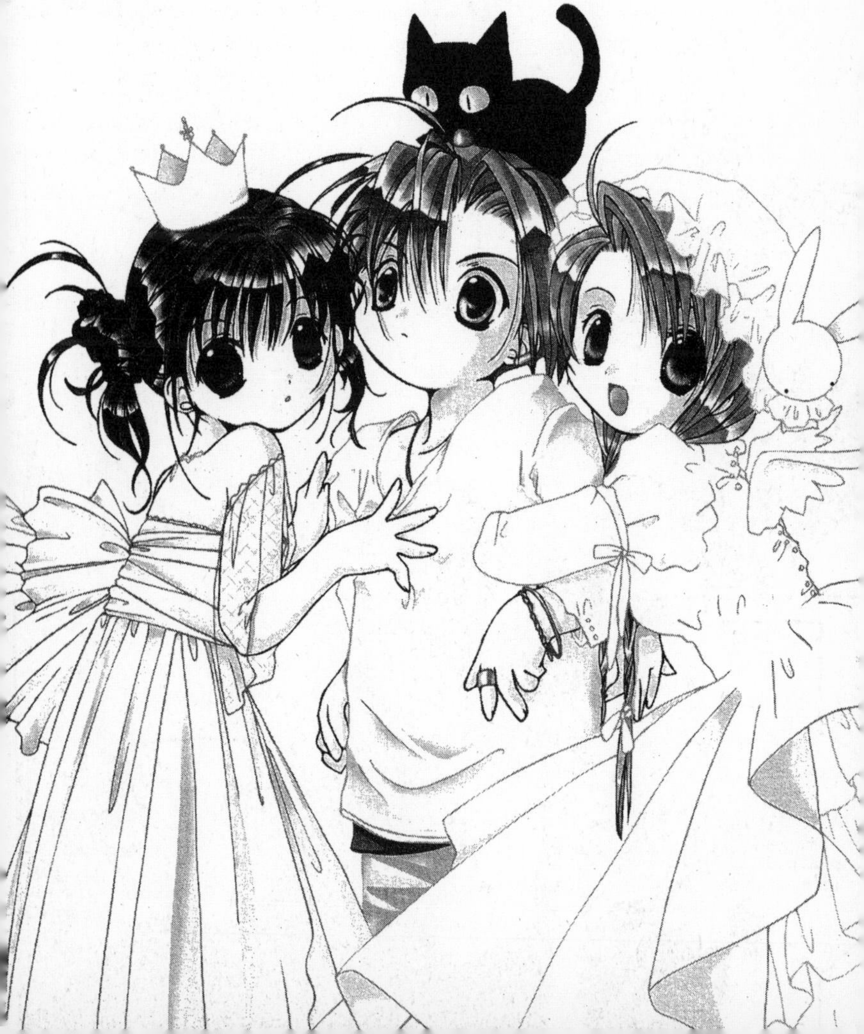

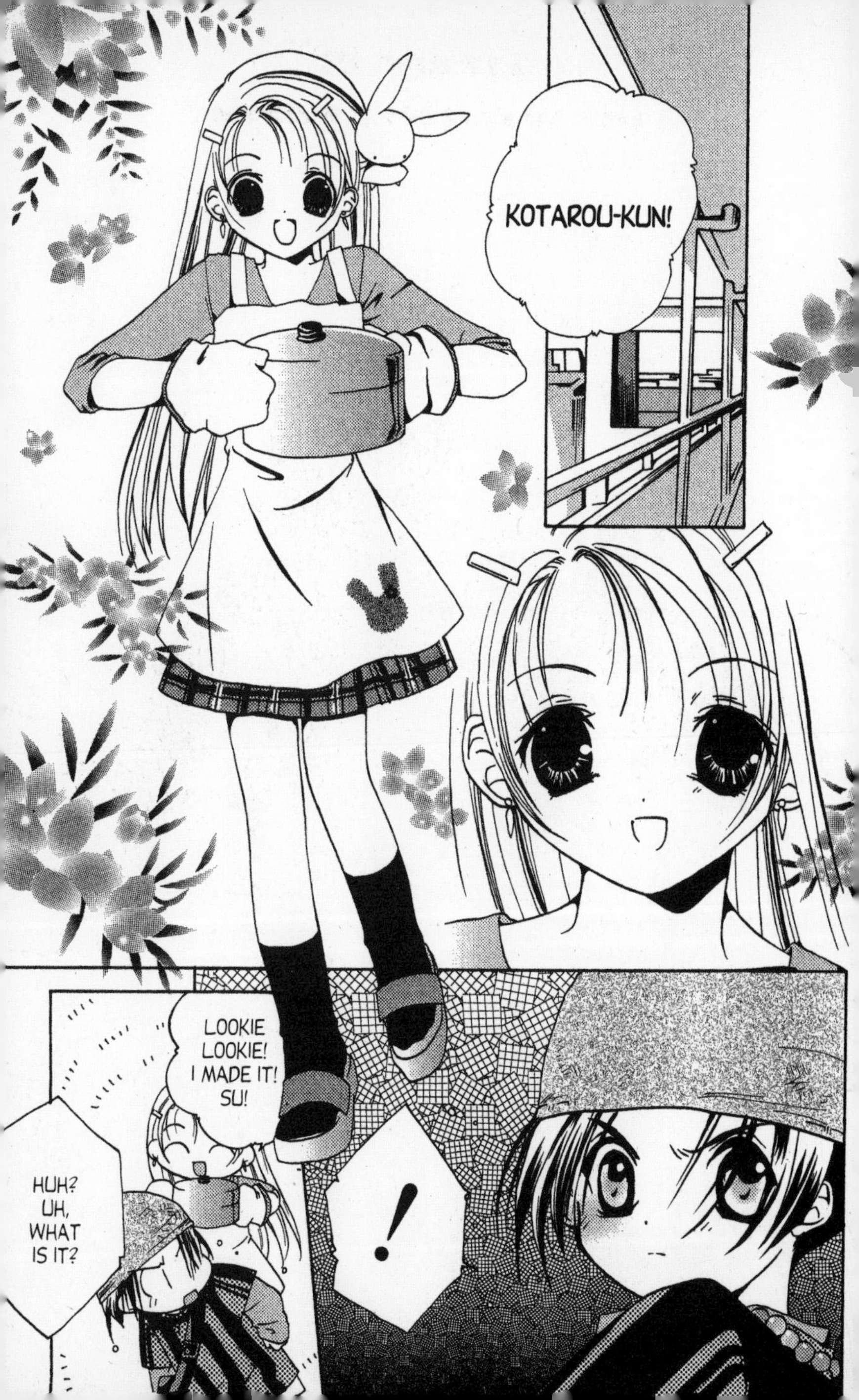
KOTAROU-KUN!
LOOKIE LOOKIE! I MADE IT! SU!
!
HUH? UH, WHAT IS IT?

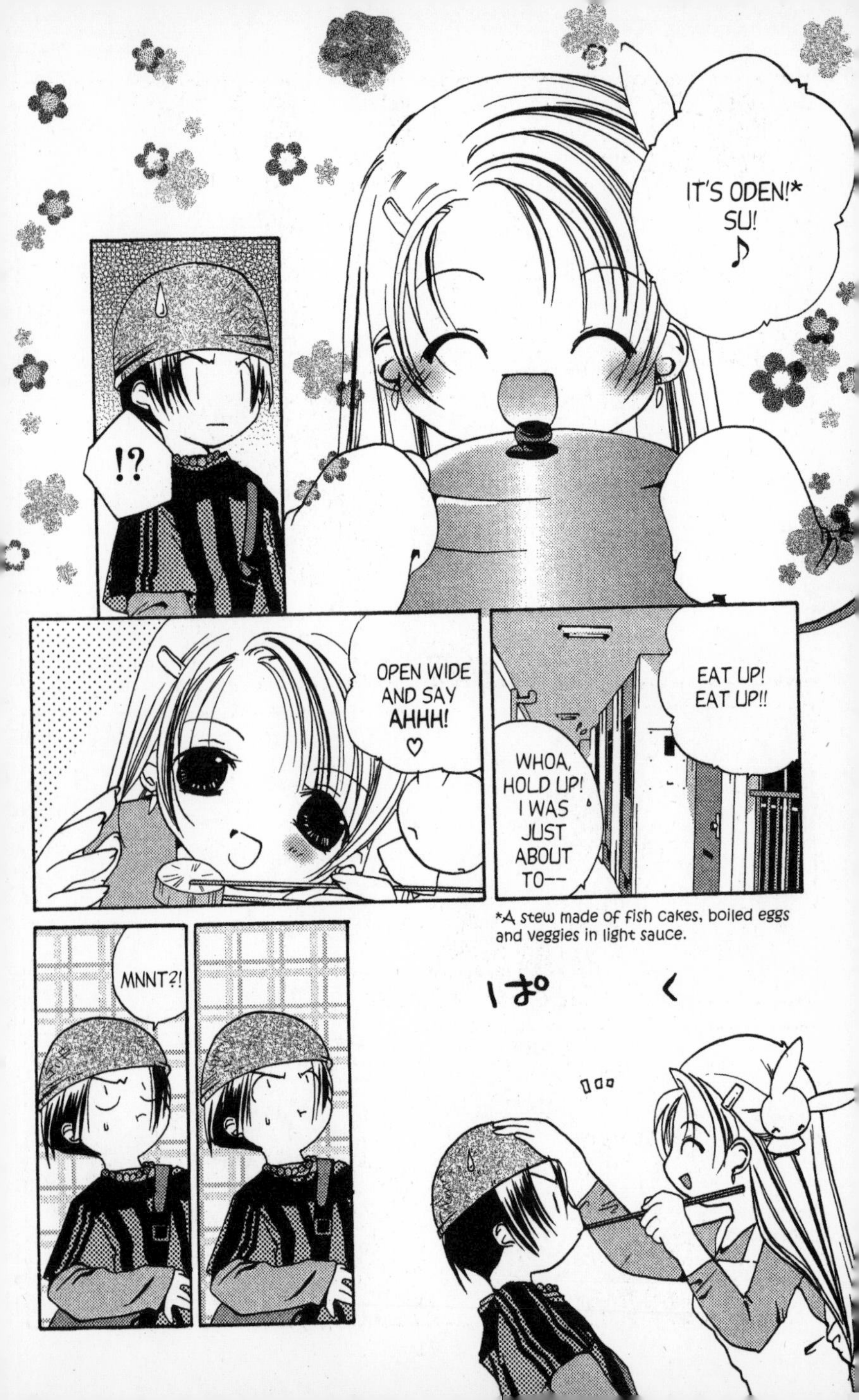
IT'S ODEN!* SU! ♪
!?
EAT UP! EAT UP!!
WHOA, HOLD UP! I WAS JUST ABOUT TO--
OPEN WIDE AND SAY AHHH! ♡
ぱく
MNNT?!

*A stew made of fish cakes, boiled eggs and veggies in light sauce.

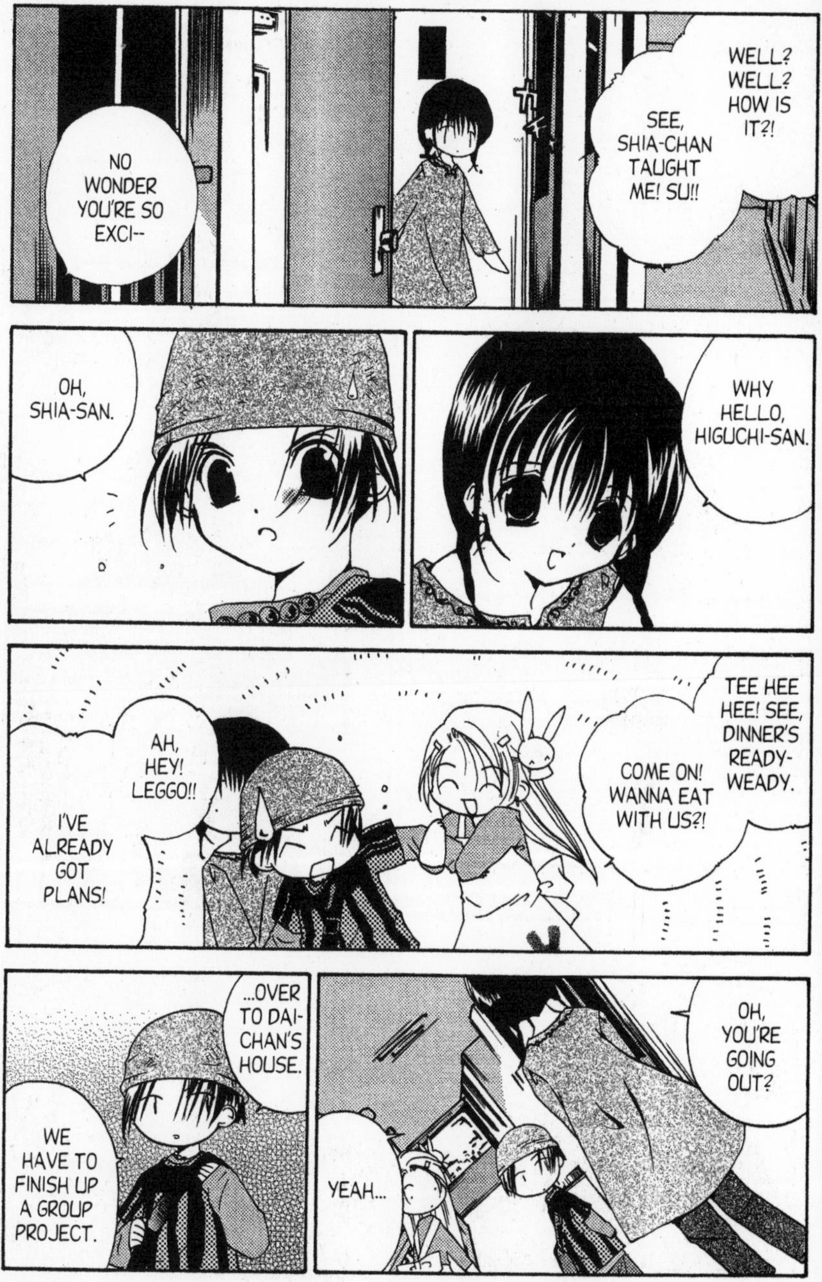
WELL? WELL? HOW IS IT?!
SEE, SHIA-CHAN TAUGHT ME! SU!!
NO WONDER YOU'RE SO EXCI--
WHY HELLO, HIGUCHI-SAN.
OH, SHIA-SAN.
TEE HEE HEE! SEE, DINNER'S READY-WEADY.
COME ON! WANNA EAT WITH US?!
AH, HEY! LEGGO!!
I'VE ALREADY GOT PLANS!
OH, YOU'RE GOING OUT?
YEAH...
...OVER TO DAI-CHAN'S HOUSE.
WE HAVE TO FINISH UP A GROUP PROJECT.

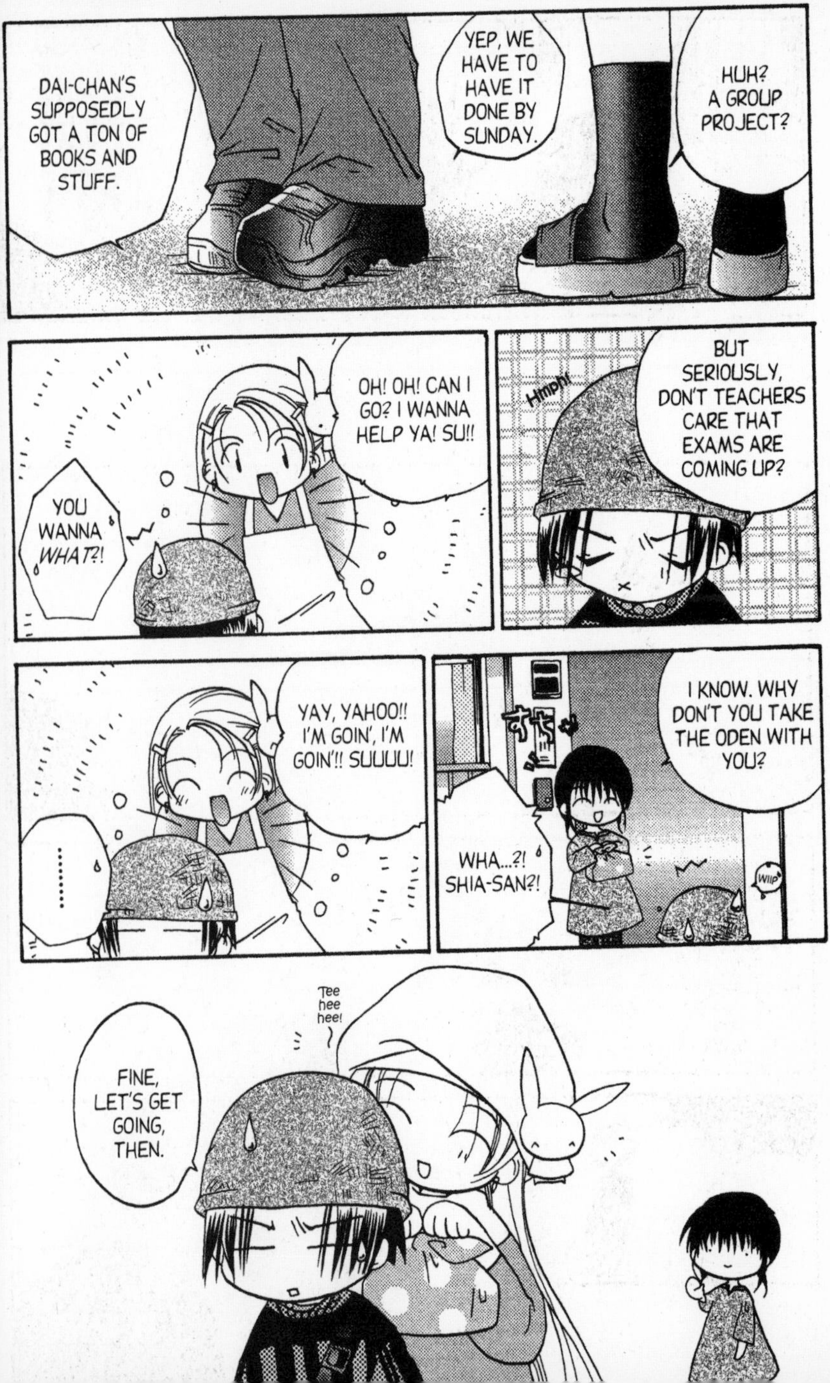
HUH? A GROUP PROJECT?
YEP, WE HAVE TO HAVE IT DONE BY SUNDAY.
DAI-CHAN'S SUPPOSEDLY GOT A TON OF BOOKS AND STUFF.
Hmph!
BUT SERIOUSLY, DON'T TEACHERS CARE THAT EXAMS ARE COMING UP?
OH! OH! CAN I GO? I WANNA HELP YA! SU!!
YOU WANNA *WHAT*?!
I KNOW. WHY DON'T YOU TAKE THE ODEN WITH YOU?
WIIP
WHA...?! SHIA-SAN?!
YAY, YAHOO!! I'M GOIN', I'M GOIN'!! SUUUU!
....
Tee hee hee!
FINE, LET'S GET GOING, THEN.

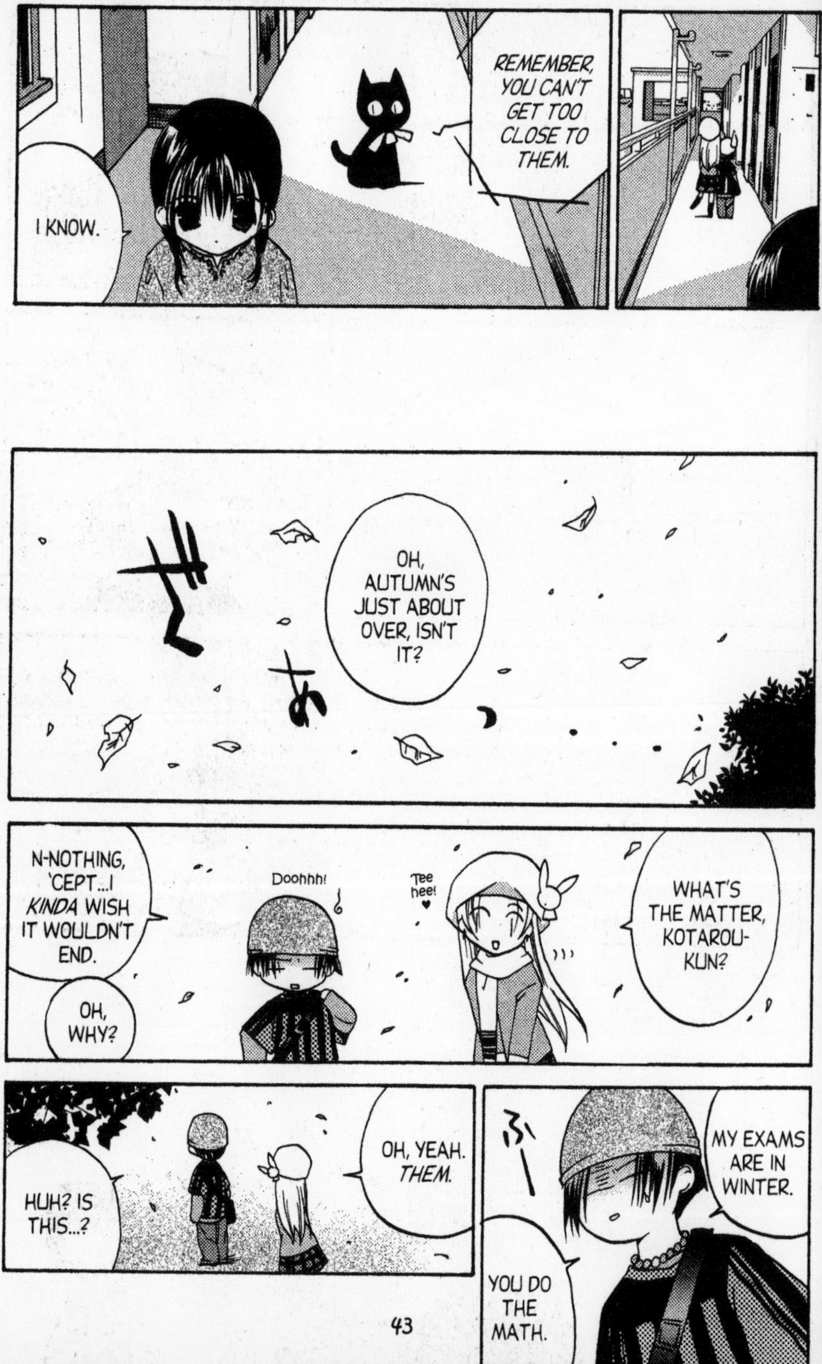
REMEMBER, YOU CAN'T GET TOO CLOSE TO THEM.
I KNOW.
OH, AUTUMN'S JUST ABOUT OVER, ISN'T IT?
WHAT'S THE MATTER, KOTAROU-KUN?
Tee hee! ♥
Doohhh!
N-NOTHING, 'CEPT...I *KINDA* WISH IT WOULDN'T END.
OH, WHY?
ふー
MY EXAMS ARE IN WINTER.
YOU DO THE MATH.
OH, YEAH. *THEM.*
HUH? IS THIS...?

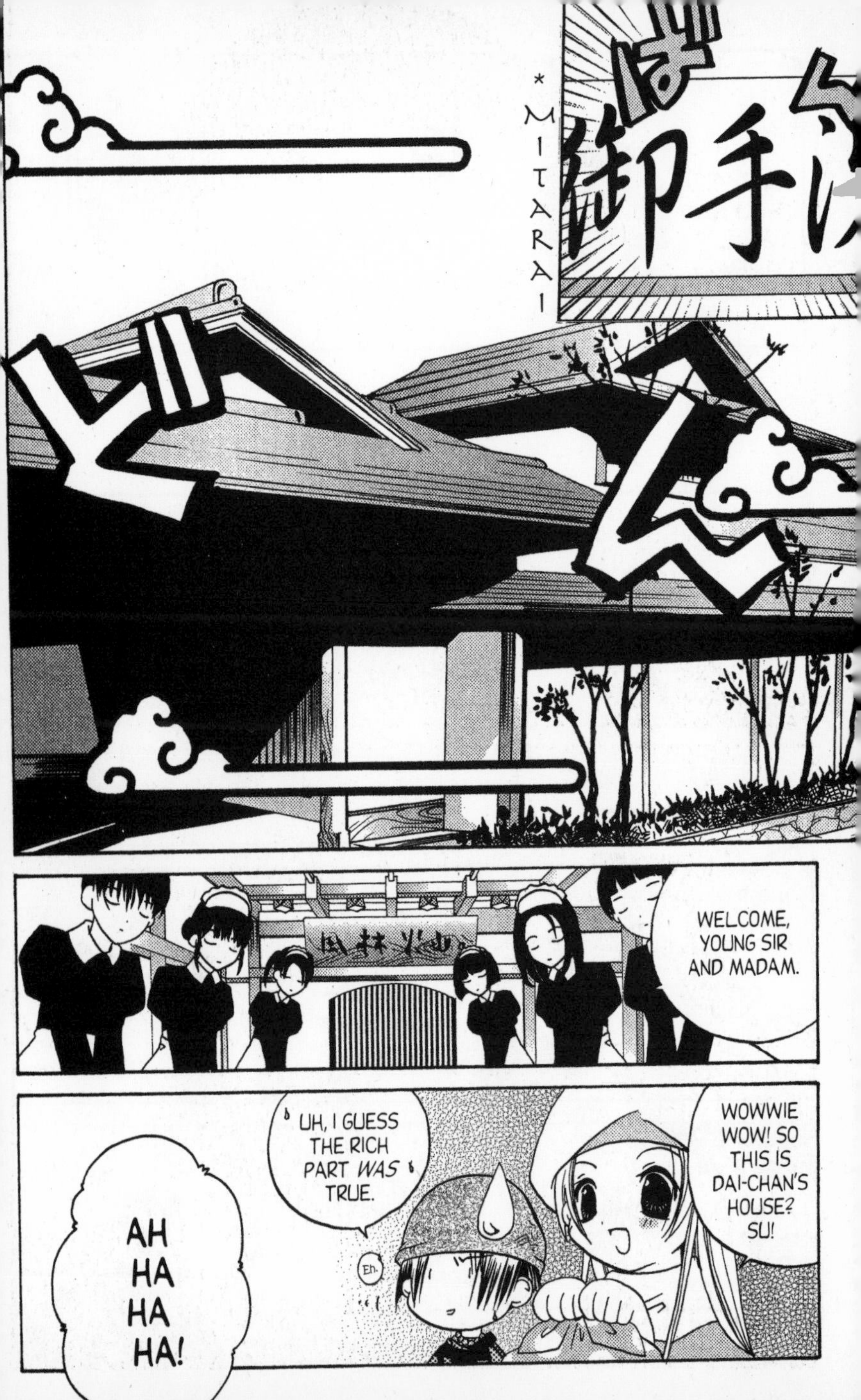
*MITARAI
WELCOME, YOUNG SIR AND MADAM.
WOWWIE WOW! SO THIS IS DAI-CHAN'S HOUSE? SU!
UH, I GUESS THE RICH PART *WAS* TRUE.
Eh.
AH HA HA HA!

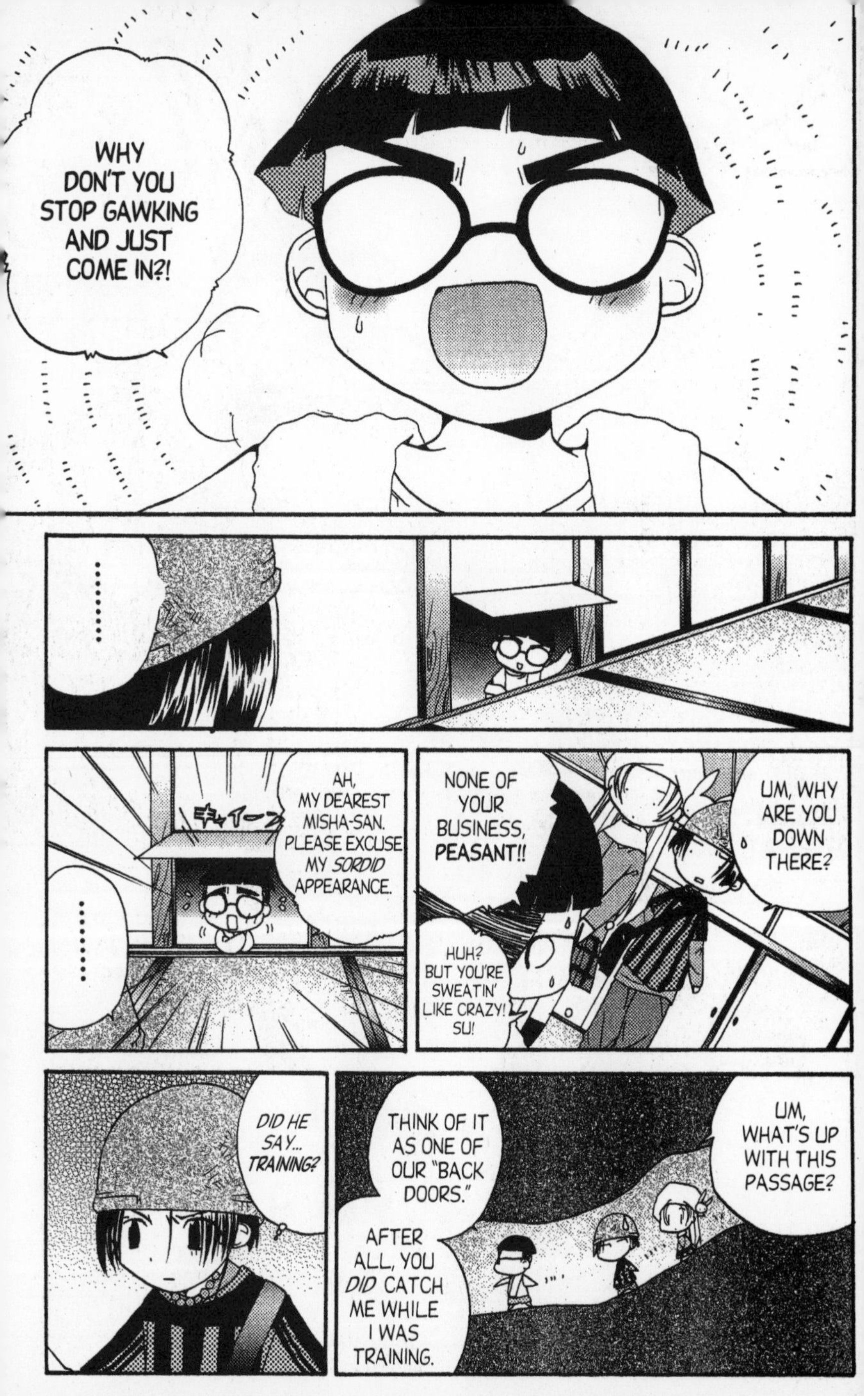
WHY DON'T YOU STOP GAWKING AND JUST COME IN?!
......
UM, WHY ARE YOU DOWN THERE?
NONE OF YOUR BUSINESS, **PEASANT!!**
HUH? BUT YOU'RE SWEATIN' LIKE CRAZY! SU!
AH, MY DEAREST MISHA-SAN. PLEASE EXCUSE MY *SORDID* APPEARANCE.
......
UM, WHAT'S UP WITH THIS PASSAGE?
THINK OF IT AS ONE OF OUR "BACK DOORS."
AFTER ALL, YOU *DID* CATCH ME WHILE I WAS TRAINING.
DID HE SAY... TRAINING?

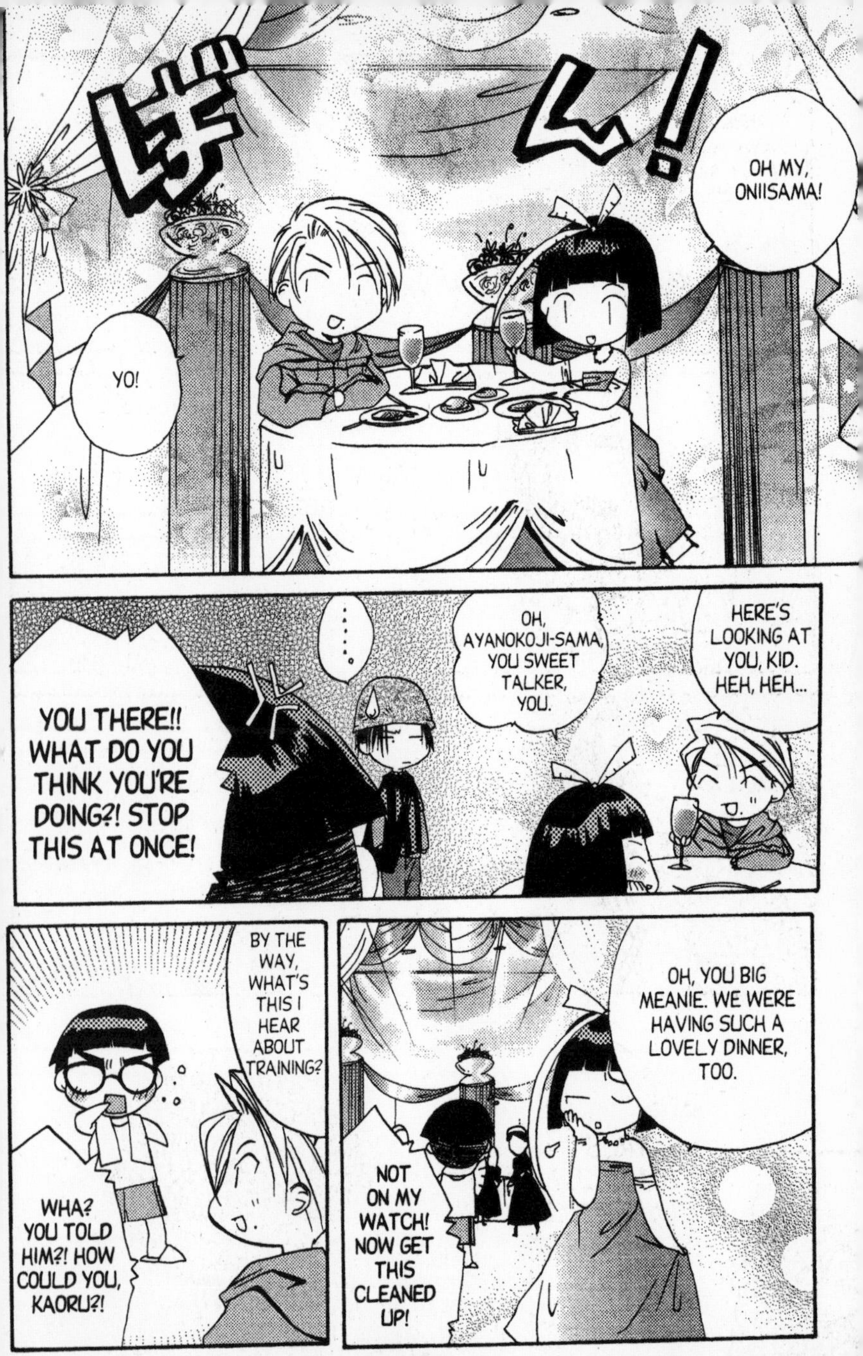
ぎん!
OH MY, ONIISAMA!
YO!
HERE'S LOOKING AT YOU, KID. HEH, HEH...
OH, AYANOKOJI-SAMA, YOU SWEET TALKER, YOU.
......
YOU THERE!! WHAT DO YOU THINK YOU'RE DOING?! STOP THIS AT ONCE!
OH, YOU BIG MEANIE. WE WERE HAVING SUCH A LOVELY DINNER, TOO.
NOT ON MY WATCH! NOW GET THIS CLEANED UP!
BY THE WAY, WHAT'S THIS I HEAR ABOUT TRAINING?
WHA? YOU TOLD HIM?! HOW COULD YOU, KAORU?!

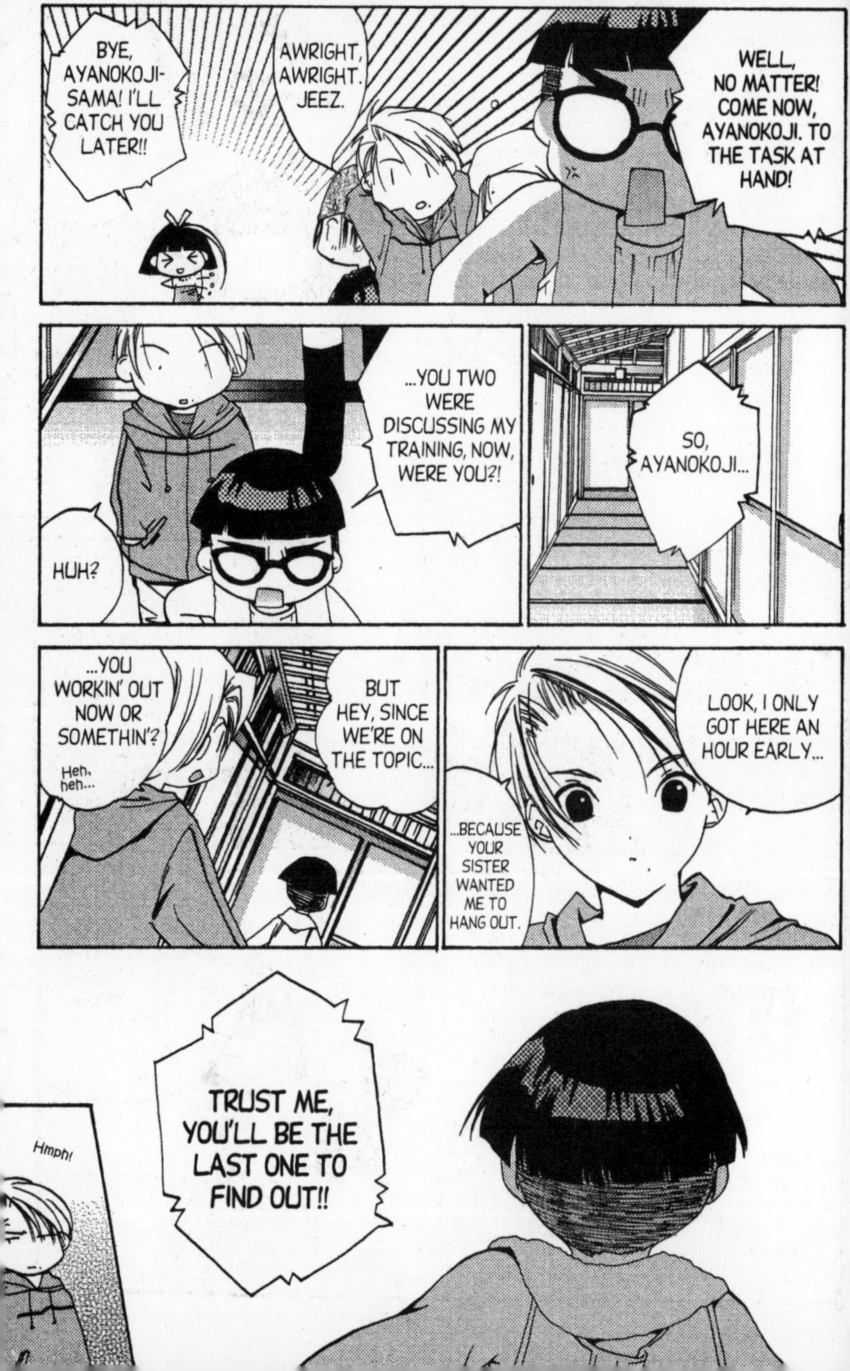
WELL, NO MATTER! COME NOW, AYANOKOJI. TO THE TASK AT HAND!
AWRIGHT, AWRIGHT. JEEZ.
BYE, AYANOKOJI-SAMA! I'LL CATCH YOU LATER!!
SO, AYANOKOJI...
...YOU TWO WERE DISCUSSING MY TRAINING, NOW, WERE YOU?!
HUH?
LOOK, I ONLY GOT HERE AN HOUR EARLY...
...BECAUSE YOUR SISTER WANTED ME TO HANG OUT.
BUT HEY, SINCE WE'RE ON THE TOPIC...
...YOU WORKIN' OUT NOW OR SOMETHIN'?
Heh, heh...
TRUST ME, YOU'LL BE THE LAST ONE TO FIND OUT!!
Hmph!

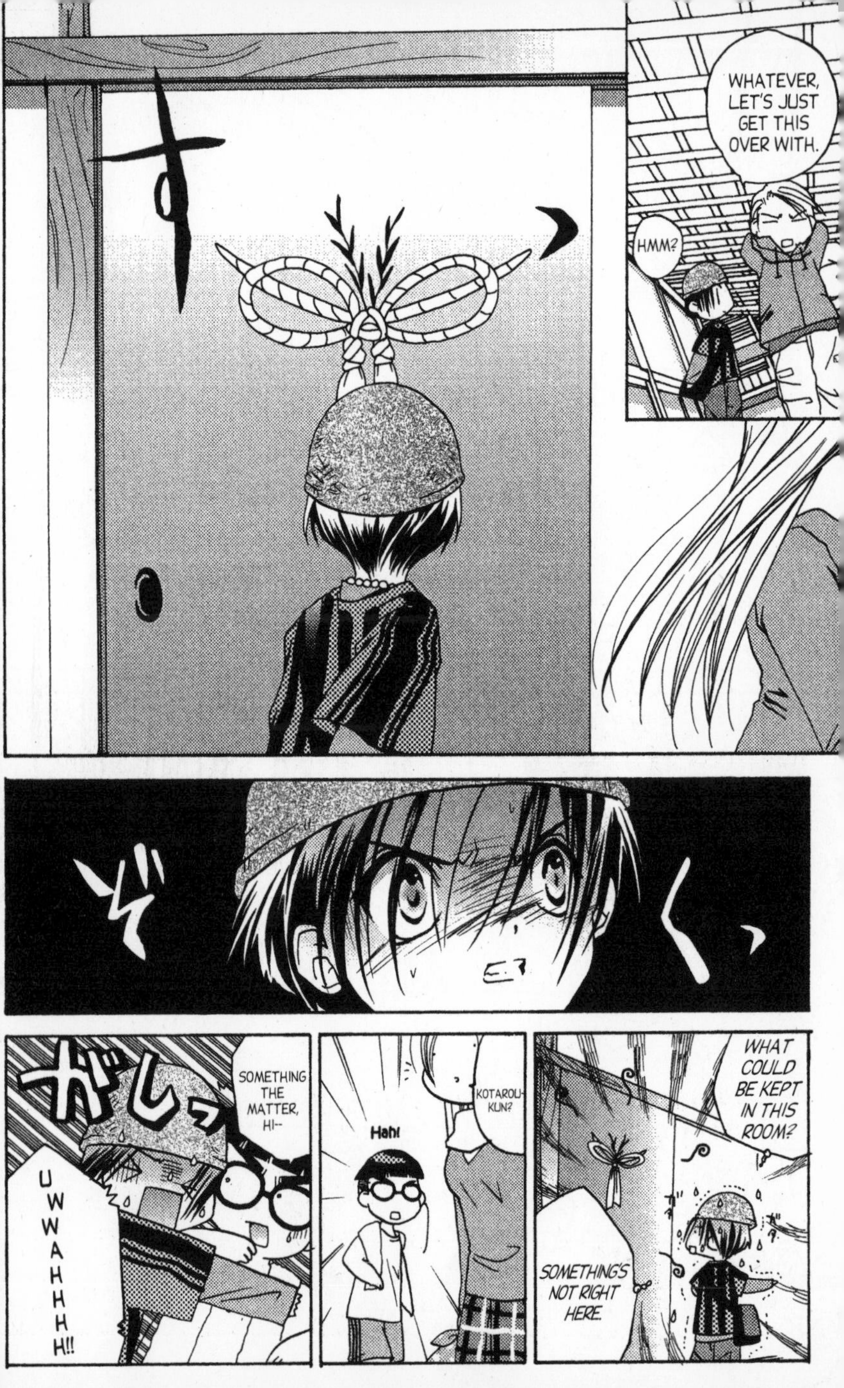
WHATEVER, LET'S JUST GET THIS OVER WITH.
HMM?
す
ぞくっ
WHAT COULD BE KEPT IN THIS ROOM?
SOMETHING'S NOT RIGHT HERE.
KOTAROU-KUN?
Hah!
SOMETHING THE MATTER, HI--
がしっ
UWWAHHHHH!!

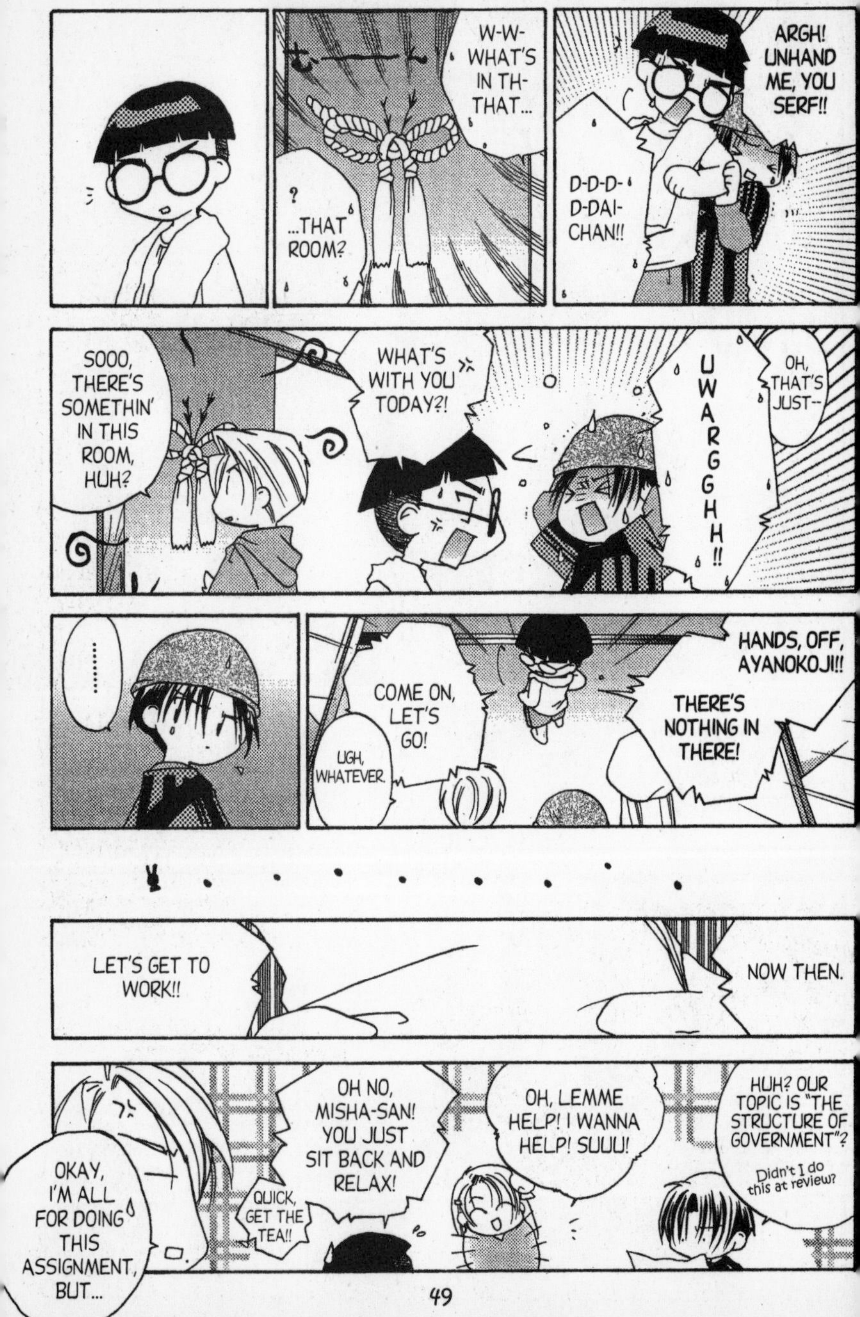
ARGH! UNHAND ME, YOU SERF!!
D-D-D-D-DAI-CHAN!!
W-W-WHAT'S IN TH-THAT...
?
...THAT ROOM?
OH, THAT'S JUST--
UWARGGHH!!
WHAT'S WITH YOU TODAY?!
SOOO, THERE'S SOMETHIN' IN THIS ROOM, HUH?
HANDS, OFF, AYANOKOJI!!
THERE'S NOTHING IN THERE!
COME ON, LET'S GO!
UGH, WHATEVER.
......
NOW THEN.
LET'S GET TO WORK!!
HUH? OUR TOPIC IS "THE STRUCTURE OF GOVERNMENT"?
Didn't I do this at review?
OH, LEMME HELP! I WANNA HELP! SUUU!
OH NO, MISHA-SAN! YOU JUST SIT BACK AND RELAX!
QUICK, GET THE TEA!!
OKAY, I'M ALL FOR DOING THIS ASSIGNMENT, BUT...

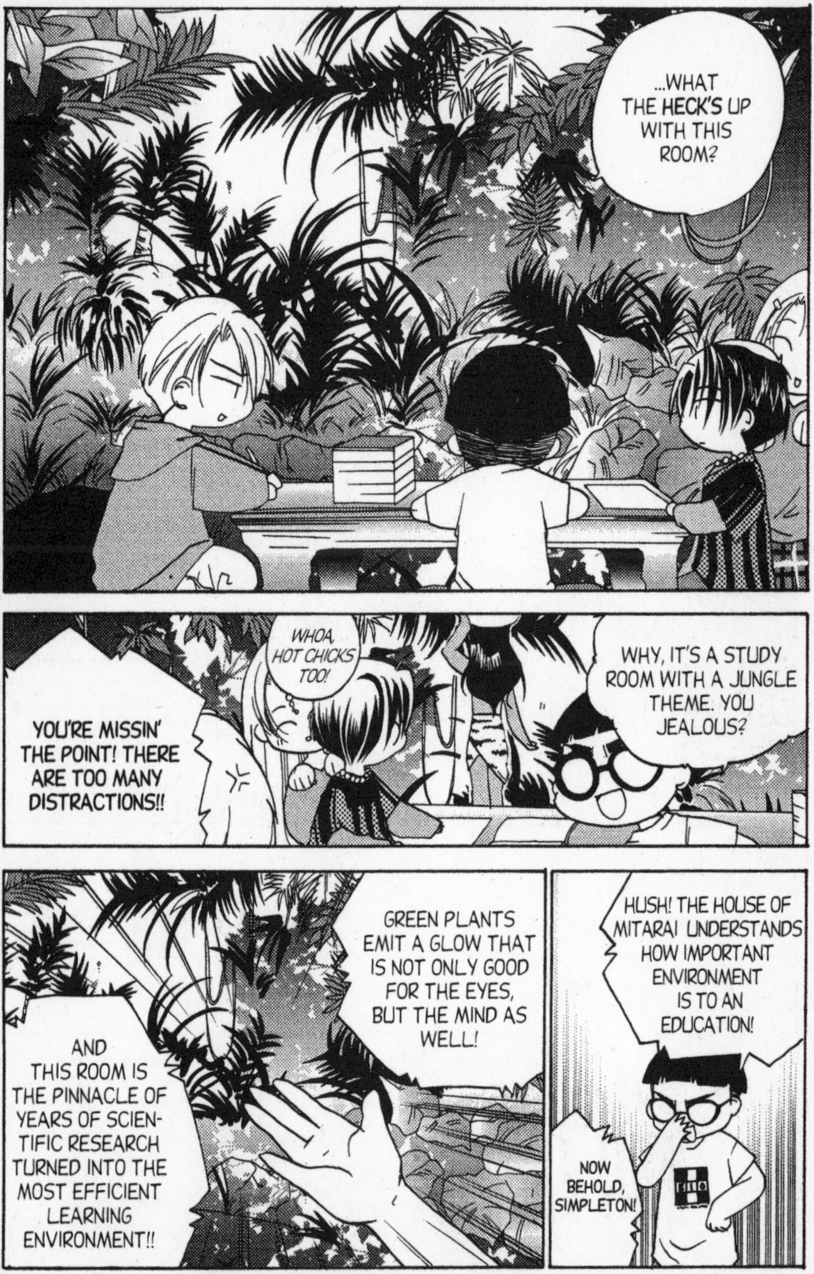
...WHAT THE HECK'S UP WITH THIS ROOM?
WHY, IT'S A STUDY ROOM WITH A JUNGLE THEME. YOU JEALOUS?
WHOA, HOT CHICKS TOO!
YOU'RE MISSIN' THE POINT! THERE ARE TOO MANY DISTRACTIONS!!
HUSH! THE HOUSE OF MITARAI UNDERSTANDS HOW IMPORTANT ENVIRONMENT IS TO AN EDUCATION!
NOW BEHOLD, SIMPLETON!
GREEN PLANTS EMIT A GLOW THAT IS NOT ONLY GOOD FOR THE EYES, BUT THE MIND AS WELL!
AND THIS ROOM IS THE PINNACLE OF YEARS OF SCIEN-TIFIC RESEARCH TURNED INTO THE MOST EFFICIENT LEARNING ENVIRONMENT!!

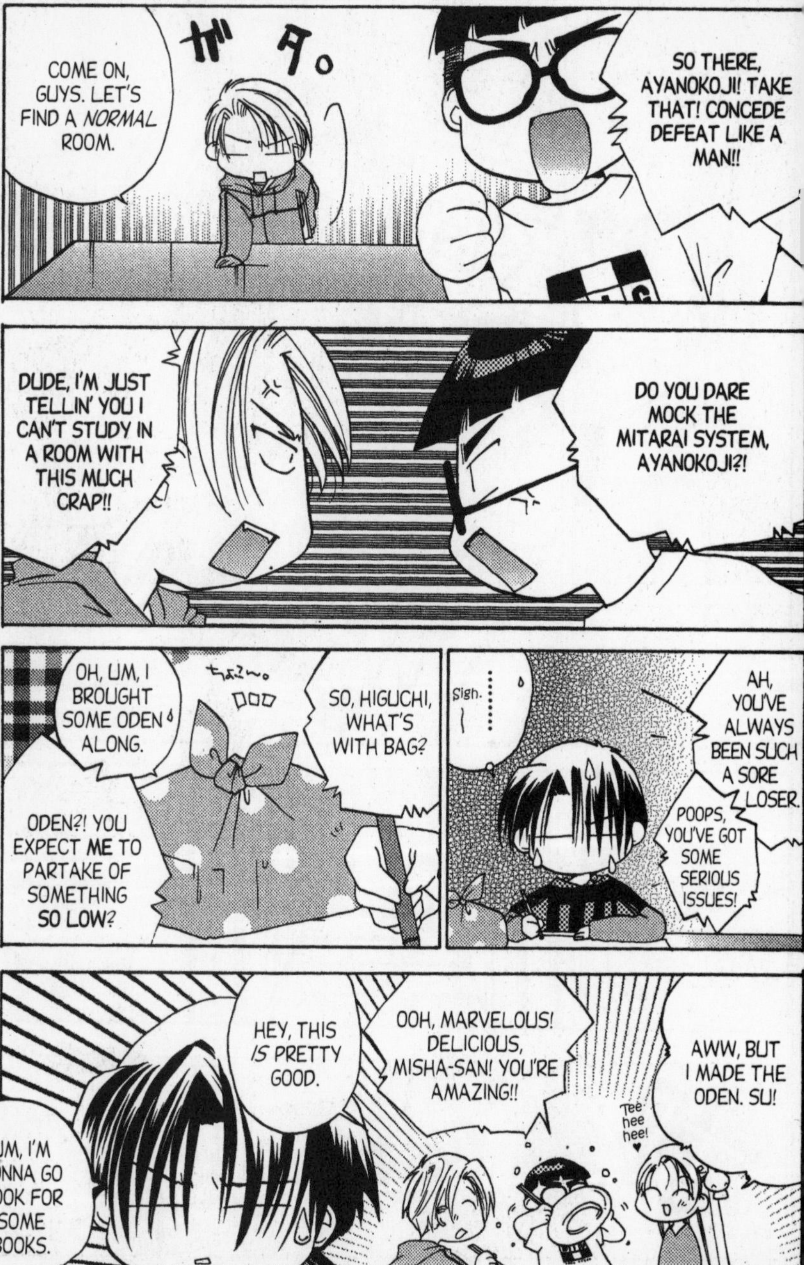
SO THERE, AYANOKOJI! TAKE THAT! CONCEDE DEFEAT LIKE A MAN!!
ガタ。
COME ON, GUYS. LET'S FIND A *NORMAL* ROOM.
DO YOU DARE MOCK THE MITARAI SYSTEM, AYANOKOJI?!
DUDE, I'M JUST TELLIN' YOU I CAN'T STUDY IN A ROOM WITH THIS MUCH CRAP!!
AH, YOU'VE ALWAYS BEEN SUCH A SORE LOSER.
POOPS, YOU'VE GOT SOME SERIOUS ISSUES!
Sigh. ....
SO, HIGUCHI, WHAT'S WITH BAG?
OH, UM, I BROUGHT SOME ODEN ALONG.
ODEN?! YOU EXPECT **ME** TO PARTAKE OF SOMETHING **SO LOW**?
AWW, BUT I MADE THE ODEN. SU!
Tee hee hee! ♥
OOH, MARVELOUS! DELICIOUS, MISHA-SAN! YOU'RE AMAZING!!
HEY, THIS *IS* PRETTY GOOD.
UM, I'M GONNA GO LOOK FOR SOME BOOKS.

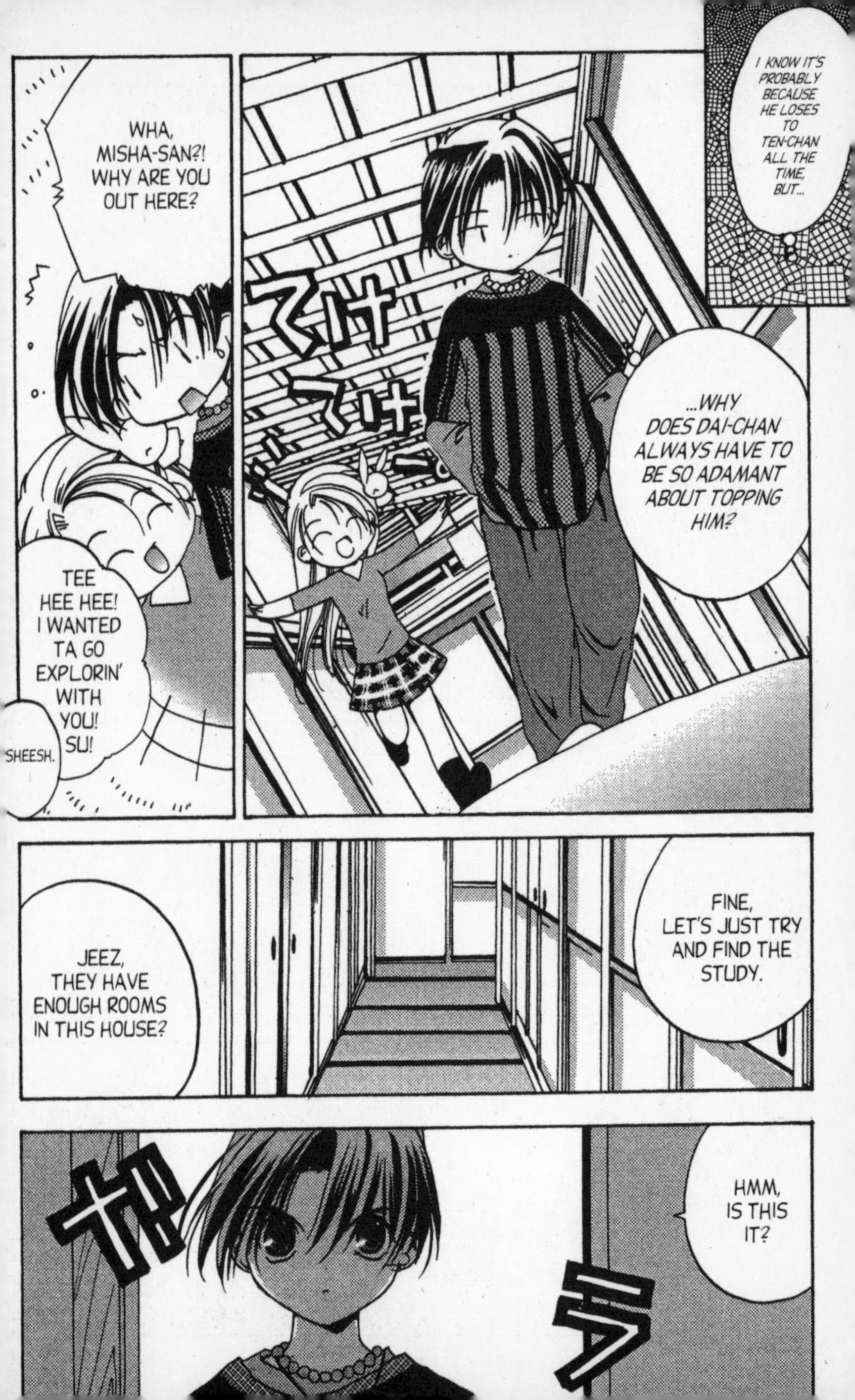
I KNOW IT'S PROBABLY BECAUSE HE LOSES TO TEN-CHAN ALL THE TIME, BUT...
...WHY DOES DAI-CHAN ALWAYS HAVE TO BE SO ADAMANT ABOUT TOPPING HIM?
WHA, MISHA-SAN?! WHY ARE YOU OUT HERE?
TEE HEE HEE! I WANTED TA GO EXPLORIN' WITH YOU! SU!
SHEESH.
FINE, LET'S JUST TRY AND FIND THE STUDY.
JEEZ, THEY HAVE ENOUGH ROOMS IN THIS HOUSE?
HMM, IS THIS IT?

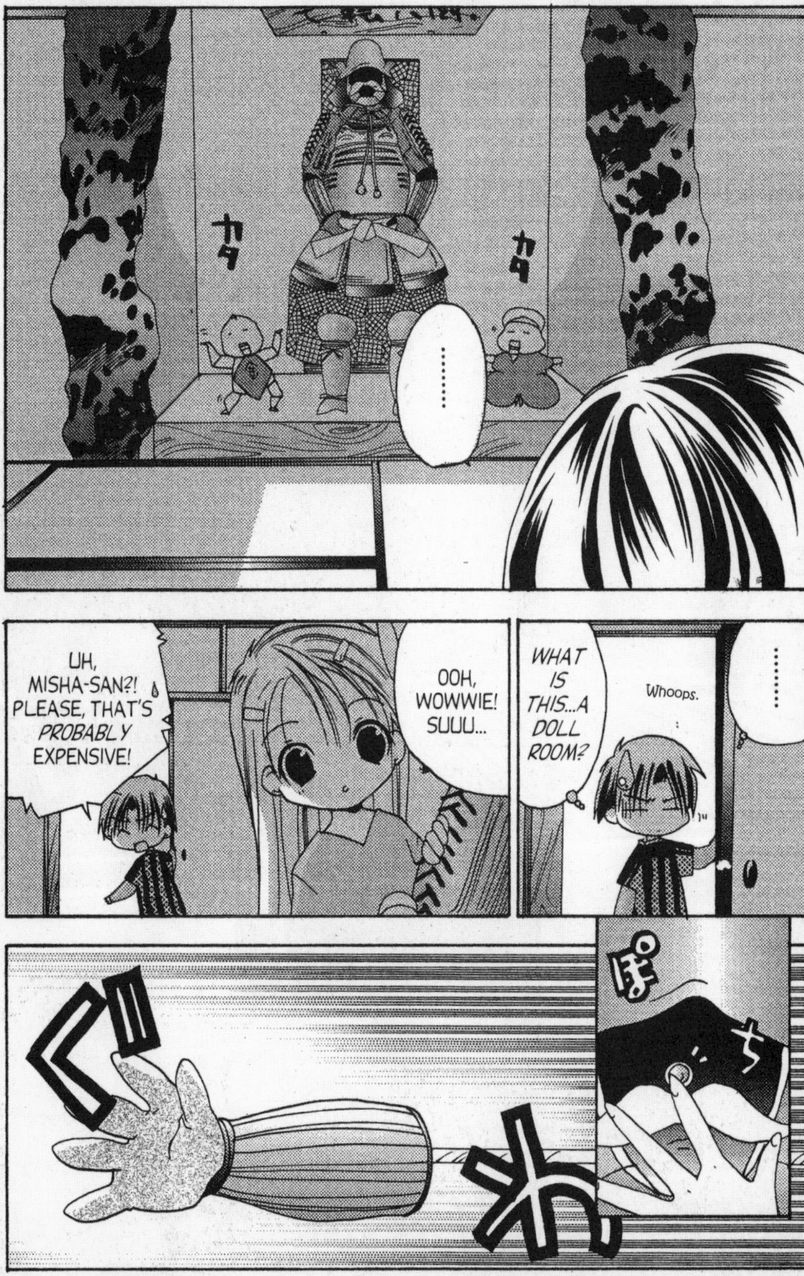
カタ
カタ
......
......
Whoops.
WHAT IS THIS...A DOLL ROOM?
OOH, WOWWIE! SUUU...
UH, MISHA-SAN?! PLEASE, THAT'S *PROBABLY* EXPENSIVE!
ぽち

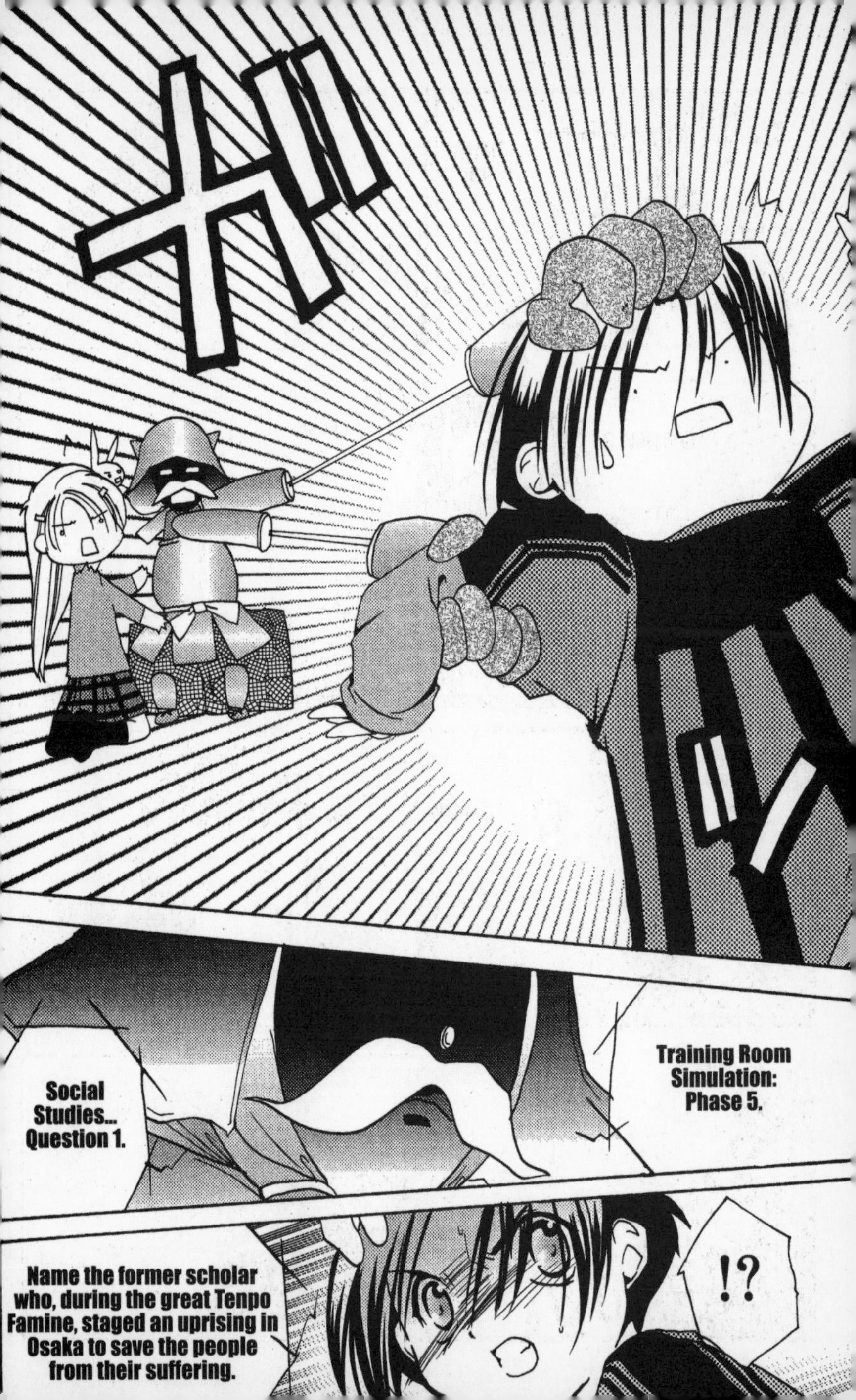
Training Room Simulation: Phase 5.
Social Studies... Question 1.
!?
Name the former scholar who, during the great Tenpo Famine, staged an uprising in Osaka to save the people from their suffering.

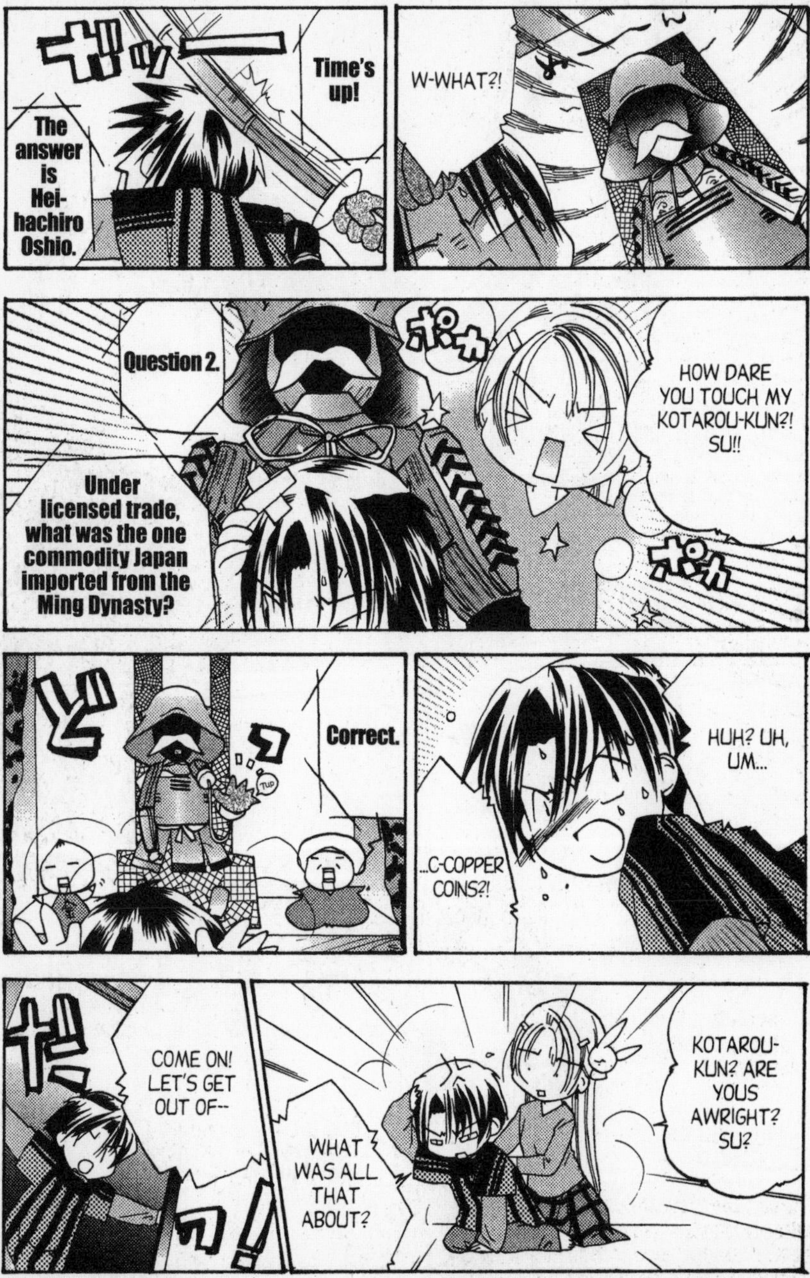

W-WHAT?!
Time's up!
The answer is Hei-hachiro Oshio.
HOW DARE YOU TOUCH MY KOTAROU-KUN?! SU!!
Question 2.
Under licensed trade, what was the one commodity Japan imported from the Ming Dynasty?
HUH? UH, UM...
...C-COPPER COINS?!
Correct.
KOTAROU-KUN? ARE YOUS AWRIGHT? SU?
WHAT WAS ALL THAT ABOUT?
COME ON! LET'S GET OUT OF--

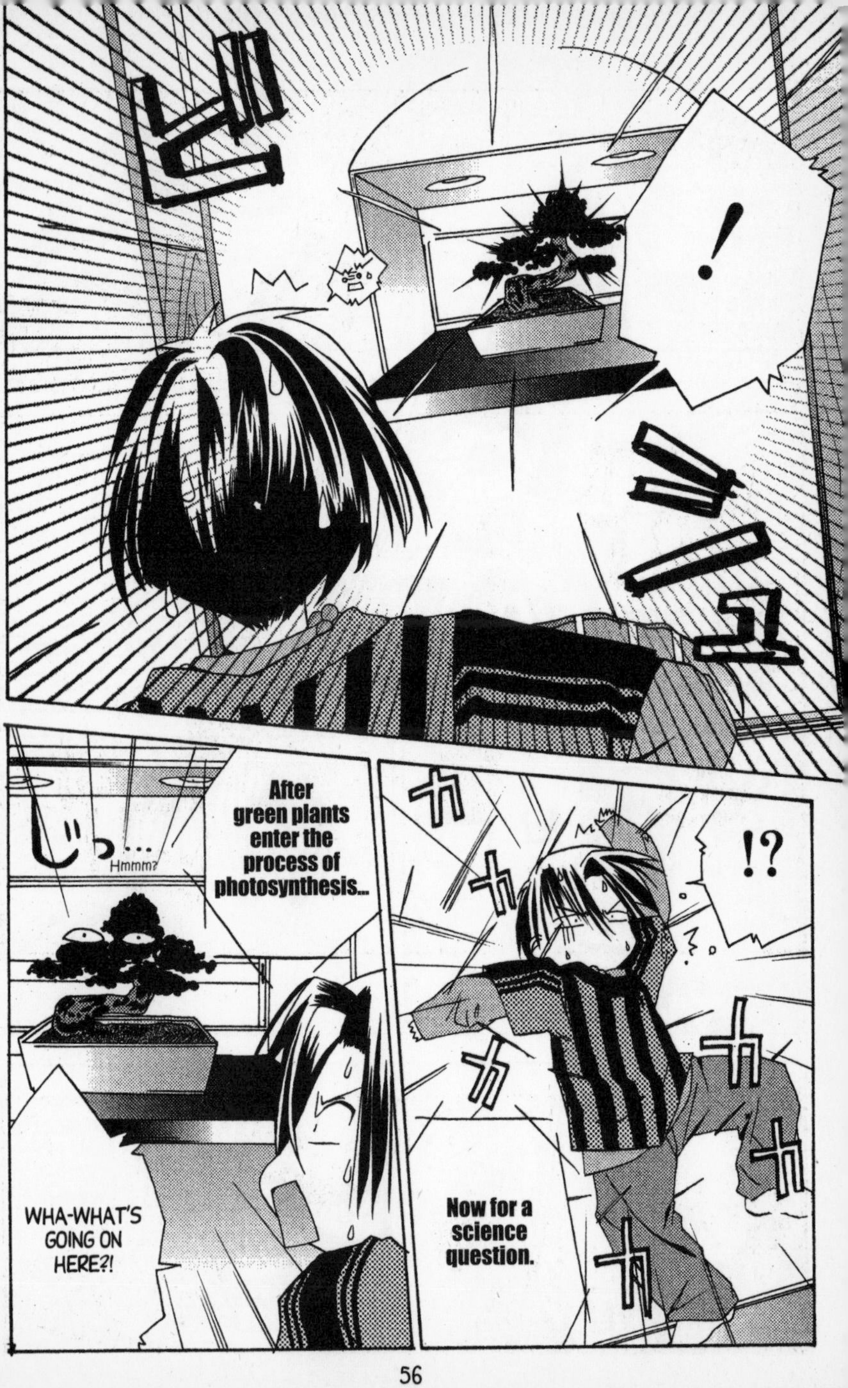
!
!?
Now for a science question.
After green plants enter the process of photosynthesis...
じっ...
Hmmm?
WHA-WHAT'S GOING ON HERE?!

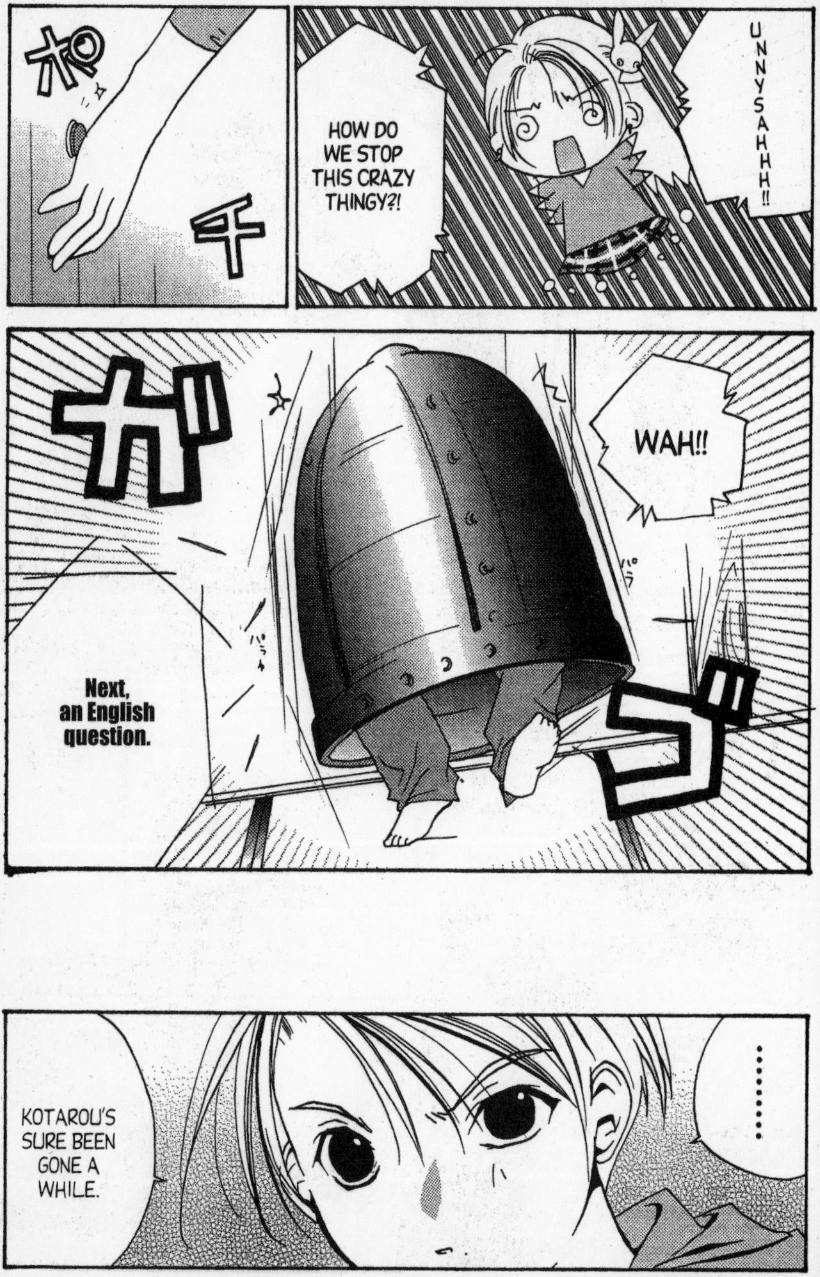
UNNYSAHHH!!
HOW DO WE STOP THIS CRAZY THINGY?!
WAH!!
Next, an English question.
……
KOTAROU'S SURE BEEN GONE A WHILE.

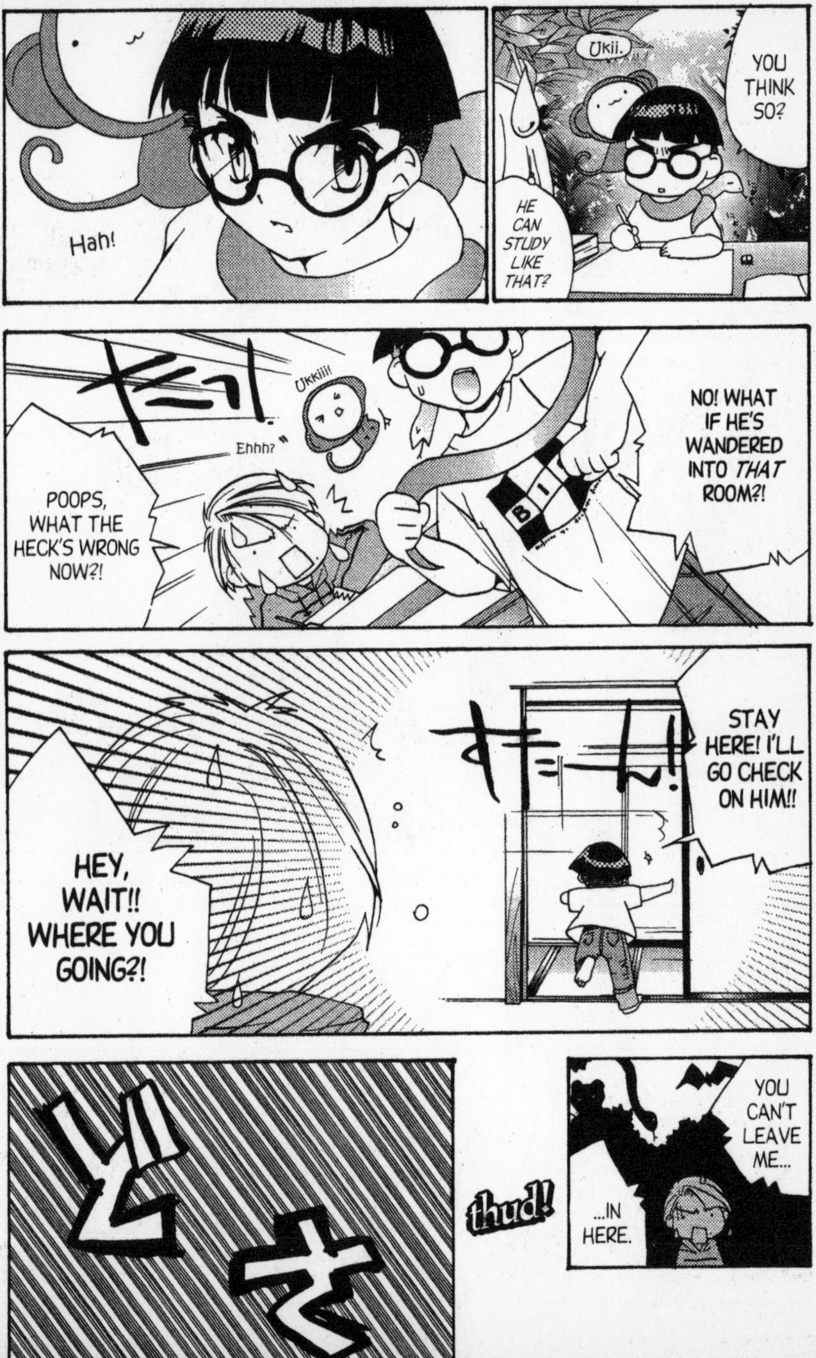
Ukii.
YOU THINK SO?
HE CAN STUDY LIKE THAT?
Hah!
NO! WHAT IF HE'S WANDERED INTO *THAT* ROOM?!
Ukkiii!
Ehhh?
POOPS, WHAT THE HECK'S WRONG NOW?!
STAY HERE! I'LL GO CHECK ON HIM!!
HEY, WAIT!! WHERE YOU GOING?!
YOU CAN'T LEAVE ME...
...IN HERE.
thud!

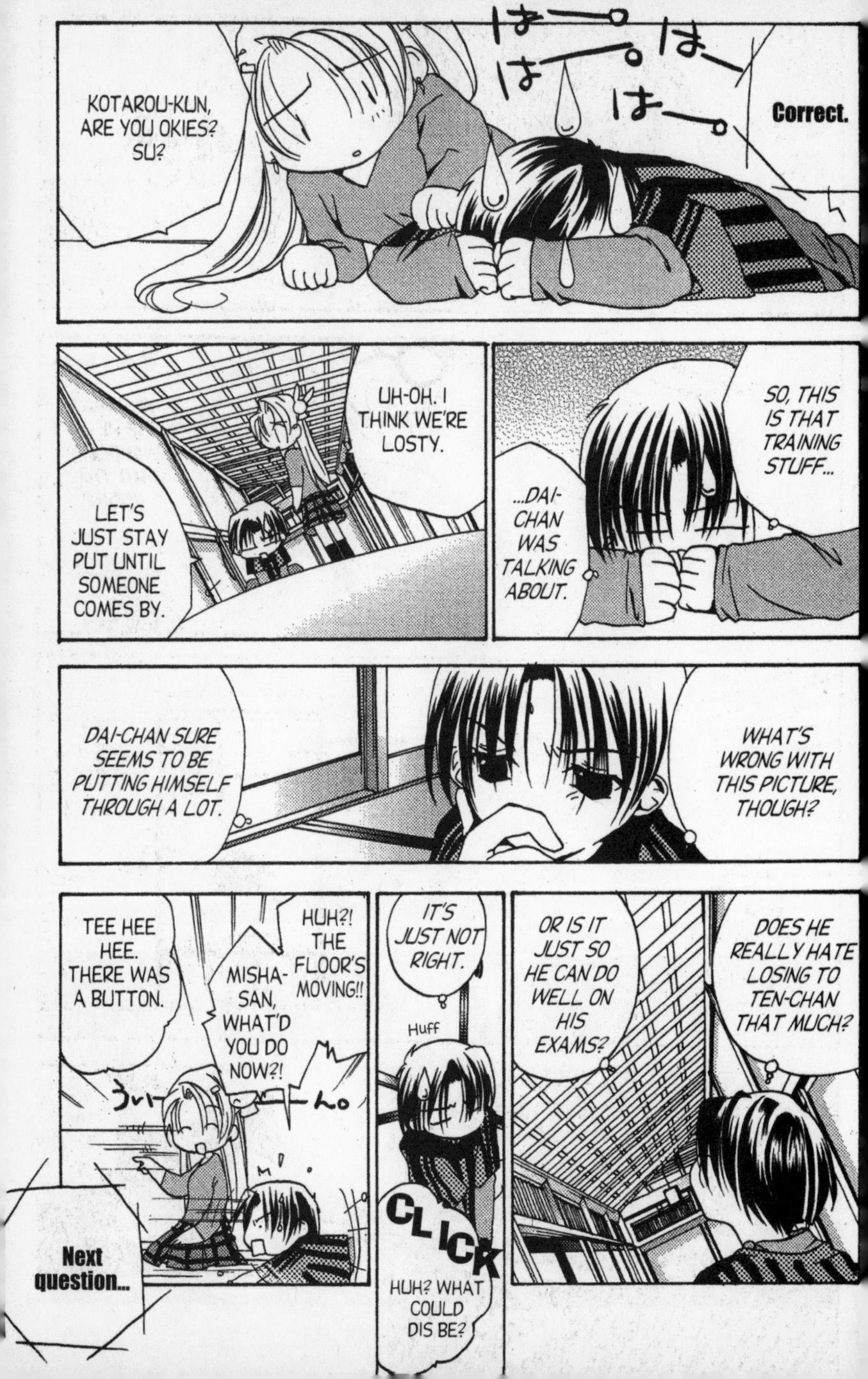
はー。はー
はー はー。
KOTAROU-KUN, ARE YOU OKIES? SU?
Correct.
SO, THIS IS THAT TRAINING STUFF...
...DAI-CHAN WAS TALKING ABOUT.
UH-OH. I THINK WE'RE LOSTY.
LET'S JUST STAY PUT UNTIL SOMEONE COMES BY.
WHAT'S WRONG WITH THIS PICTURE, THOUGH?
DAI-CHAN SURE SEEMS TO BE PUTTING HIMSELF THROUGH A LOT.
DOES HE REALLY HATE LOSING TO TEN-CHAN THAT MUCH?
OR IS IT JUST SO HE CAN DO WELL ON HIS EXAMS?
IT'S JUST NOT RIGHT.
Huff
CLICK
HUH? WHAT COULD DIS BE?
HUH?! THE FLOOR'S MOVING!!
MISHA-SAN, WHAT'D YOU DO NOW?!
TEE HEE HEE. THERE WAS A BUTTON.
うぃーーーん。
Next question...

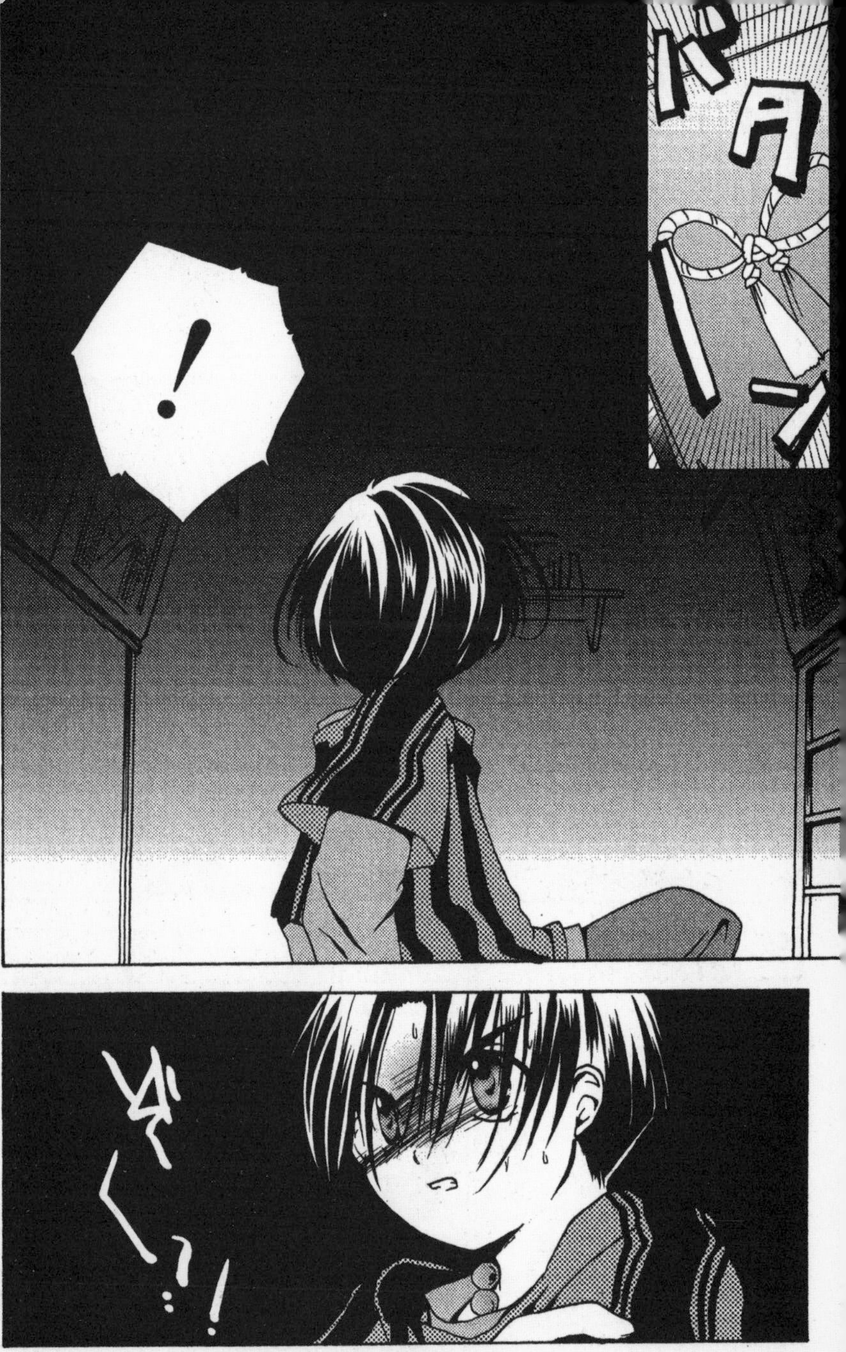
バターン
!
びくっ!!

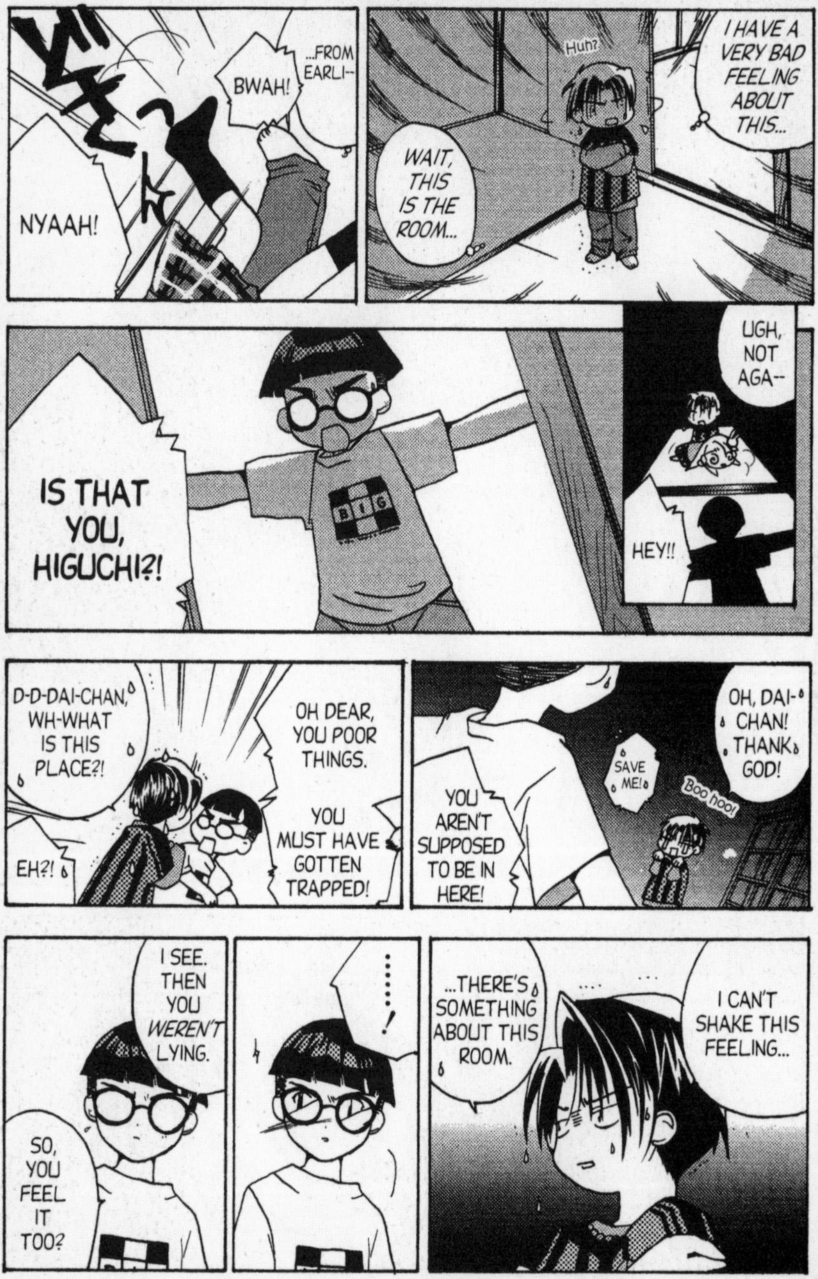
I HAVE A VERY BAD FEELING ABOUT THIS...
Huh?
WAIT, THIS IS THE ROOM...
...FROM EARLI--
BWAH!
NYAAH!
UGH, NOT AGA--
HEY!!
IS THAT YOU, HIGUCHI?!
OH, DAI-CHAN! THANK GOD!
Boo hoo!
SAVE ME!
YOU AREN'T SUPPOSED TO BE IN HERE!
OH DEAR, YOU POOR THINGS.
YOU MUST HAVE GOTTEN TRAPPED!
D-D-DAI-CHAN, WH-WHAT IS THIS PLACE?!
EH?!
I CAN'T SHAKE THIS FEELING...
...
...
...THERE'S SOMETHING ABOUT THIS ROOM.
......!
I SEE. THEN YOU *WEREN'T* LYING.
SO, YOU FEEL IT TOO?

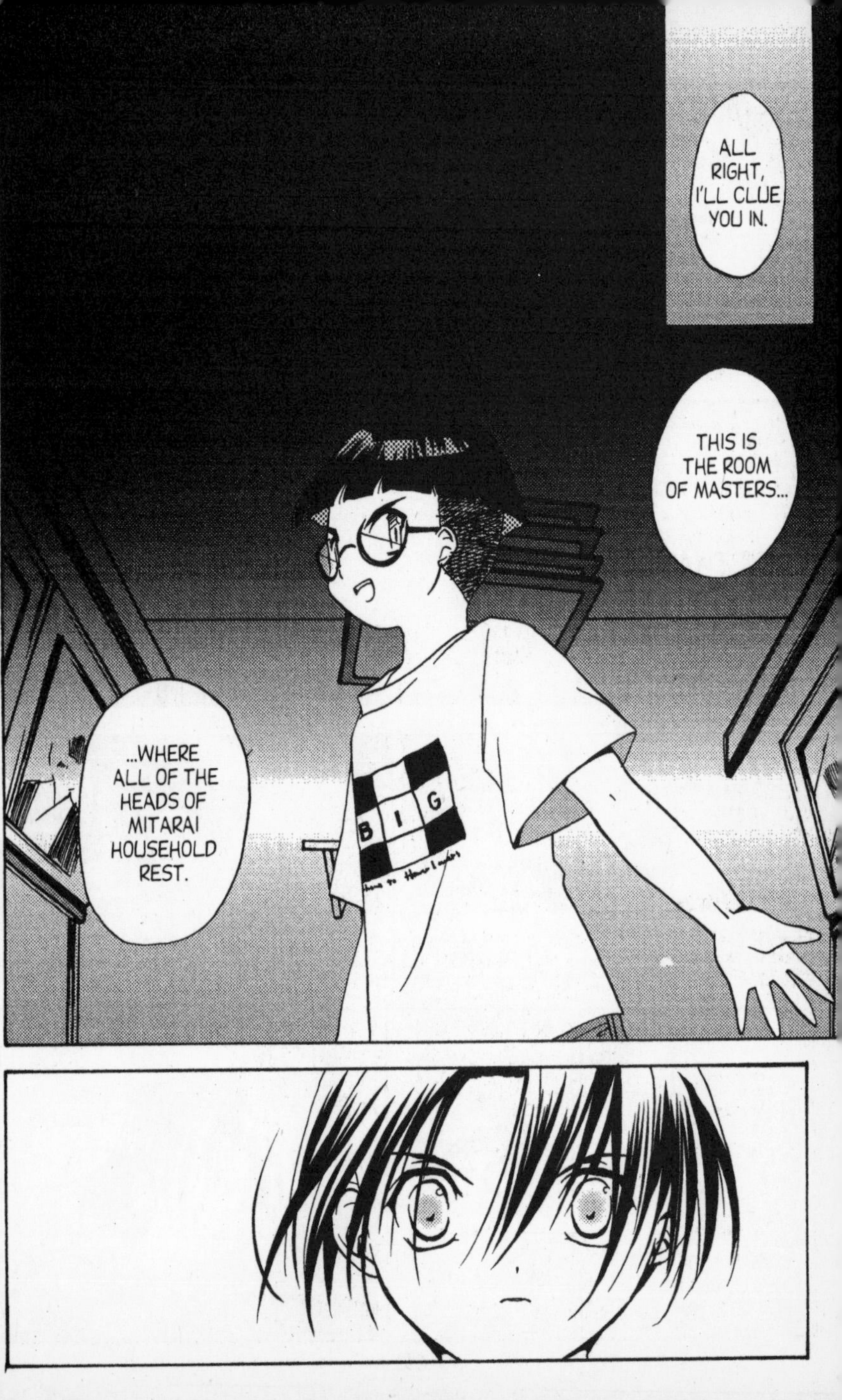
ALL RIGHT, I'LL CLUE YOU IN.
THIS IS THE ROOM OF MASTERS...
BIG
...WHERE ALL OF THE HEADS OF MITARAI HOUSEHOLD REST.

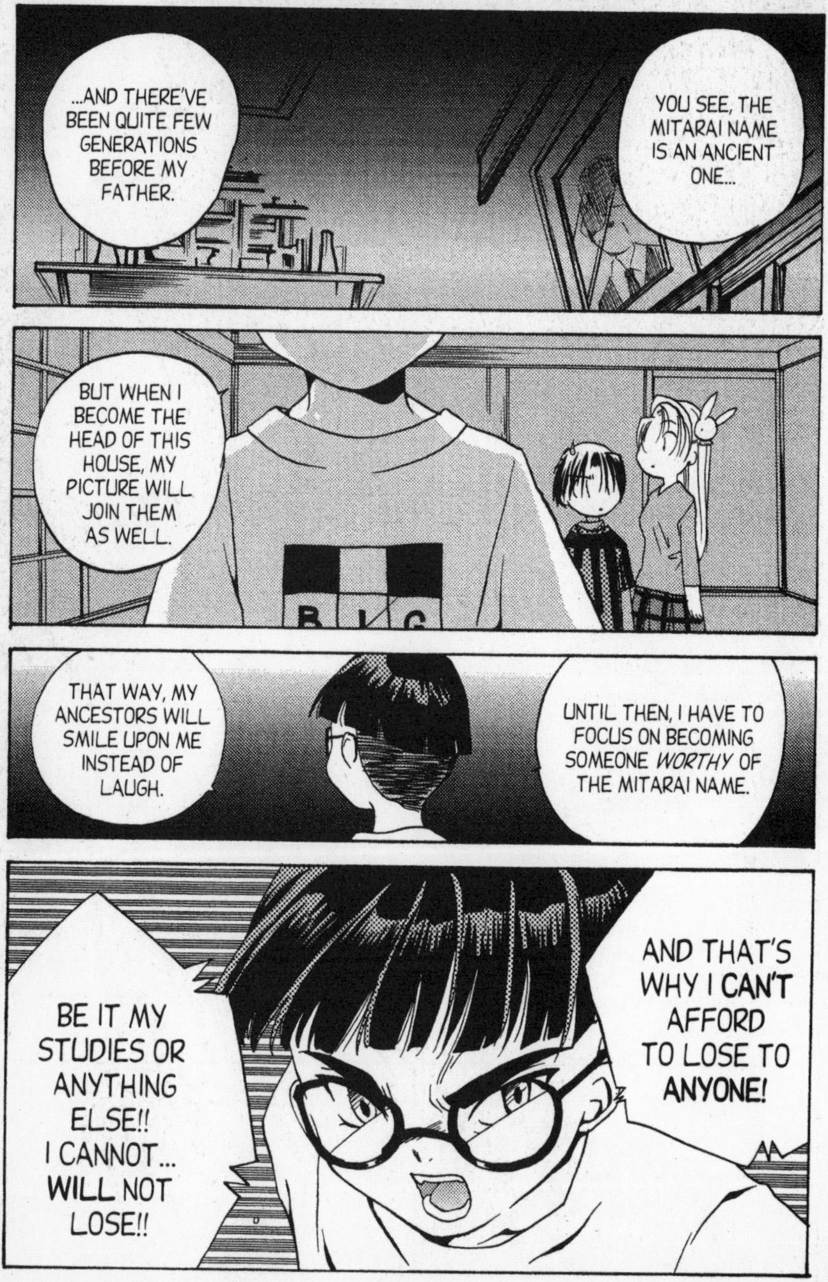
YOU SEE, THE MITARAI NAME IS AN ANCIENT ONE...
...AND THERE'VE BEEN QUITE FEW GENERATIONS BEFORE MY FATHER.
BUT WHEN I BECOME THE HEAD OF THIS HOUSE, MY PICTURE WILL JOIN THEM AS WELL.
UNTIL THEN, I HAVE TO FOCUS ON BECOMING SOMEONE *WORTHY* OF THE MITARAI NAME.
THAT WAY, MY ANCESTORS WILL SMILE UPON ME INSTEAD OF LAUGH.
AND THAT'S WHY I **CAN'T** AFFORD TO LOSE TO **ANYONE!**
BE IT MY STUDIES OR ANYTHING ELSE!! I CANNOT... **WILL** NOT LOSE!!

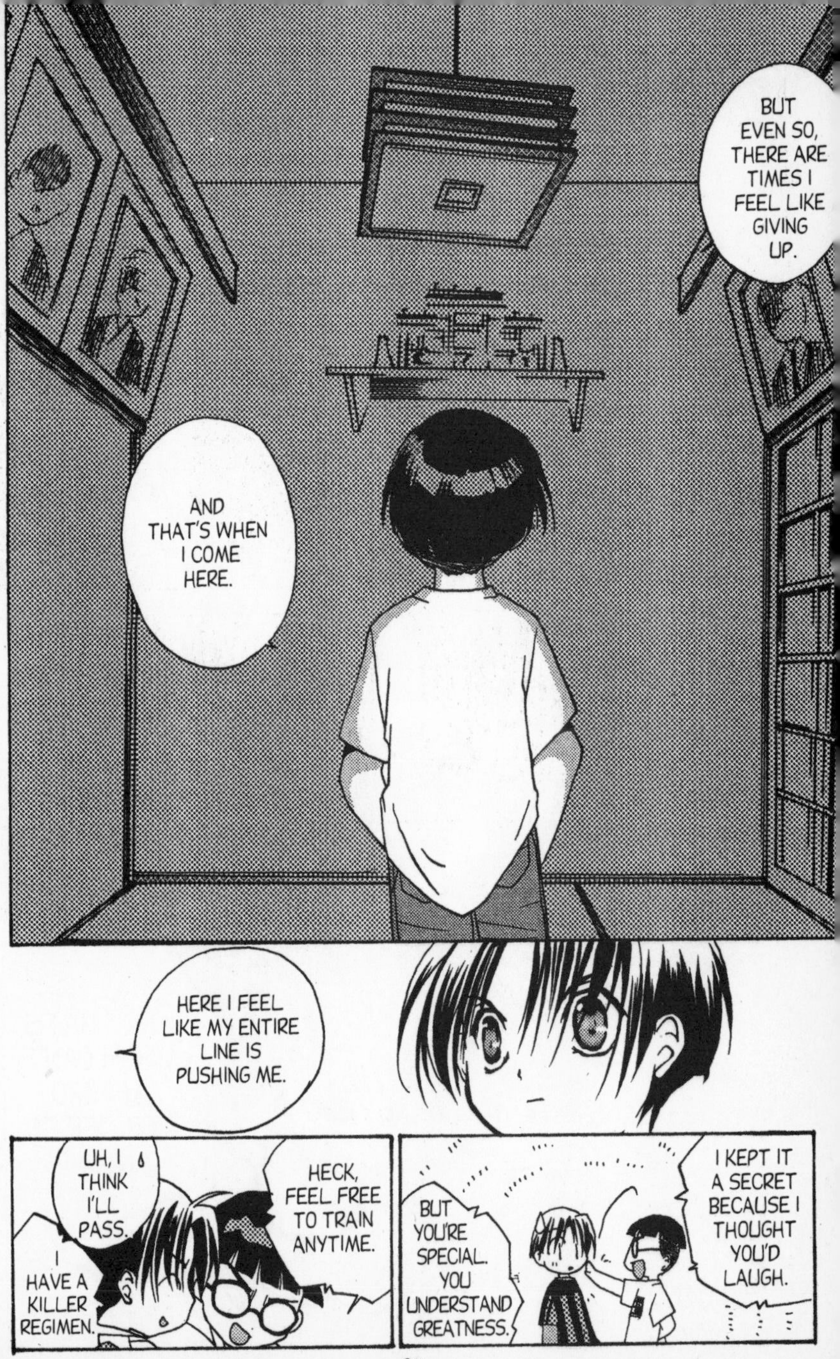
BUT EVEN SO, THERE ARE TIMES I FEEL LIKE GIVING UP.
AND THAT'S WHEN I COME HERE.
HERE I FEEL LIKE MY ENTIRE LINE IS PUSHING ME.
I KEPT IT A SECRET BECAUSE I THOUGHT YOU'D LAUGH.
BUT YOU'RE SPECIAL. YOU UNDERSTAND GREATNESS.
HECK, FEEL FREE TO TRAIN ANYTIME.
UH, I THINK I'LL PASS.
I HAVE A KILLER REGIMEN.

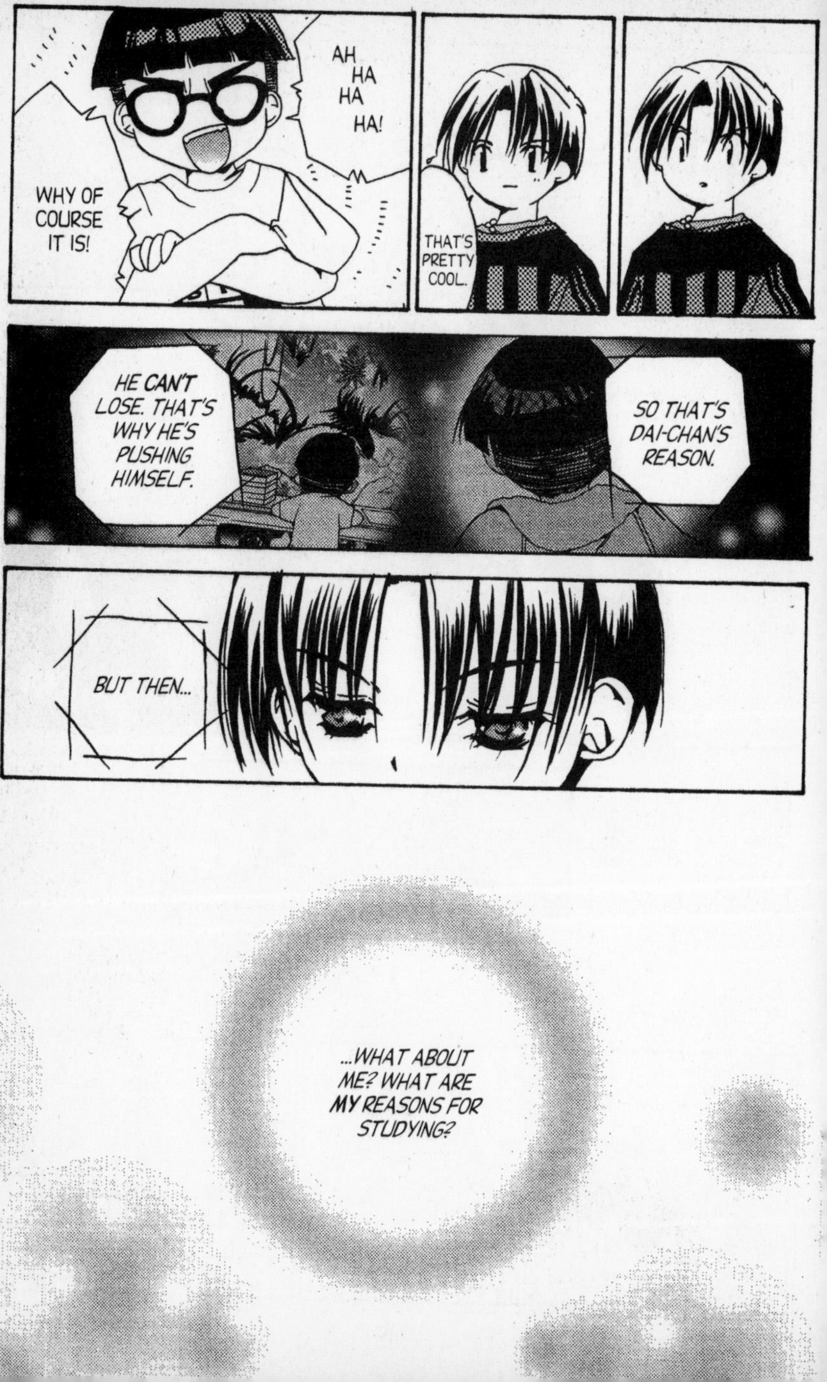
THAT'S PRETTY COOL.
AH HA HA HA!
WHY OF COURSE IT IS!
SO THAT'S DAI-CHAN'S REASON.
HE CAN'T LOSE. THAT'S WHY HE'S PUSHING HIMSELF.
BUT THEN...
...WHAT ABOUT ME? WHAT ARE MY REASONS FOR STUDYING?

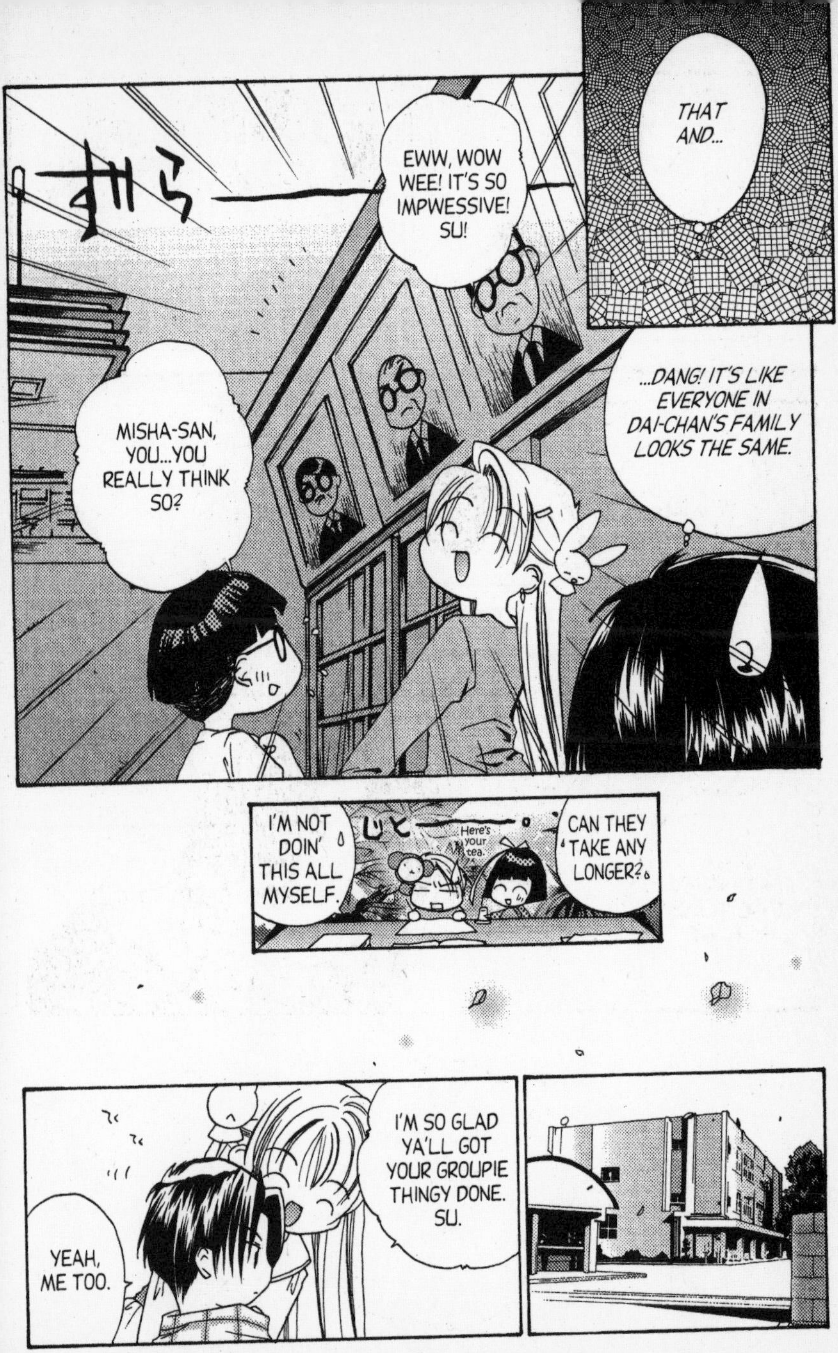
THAT AND...
EWW, WOW WEE! IT'S SO IMPWESSIVE! SU!
...DANG! IT'S LIKE EVERYONE IN DAI-CHAN'S FAMILY LOOKS THE SAME.
すら
MISHA-SAN, YOU...YOU REALLY THINK SO?
CAN THEY TAKE ANY LONGER?
じと
Here's your tea.
I'M NOT DOIN' THIS ALL MYSELF.
I'M SO GLAD YA'LL GOT YOUR GROUPIE THINGY DONE. SU.
YEAH, ME TOO.

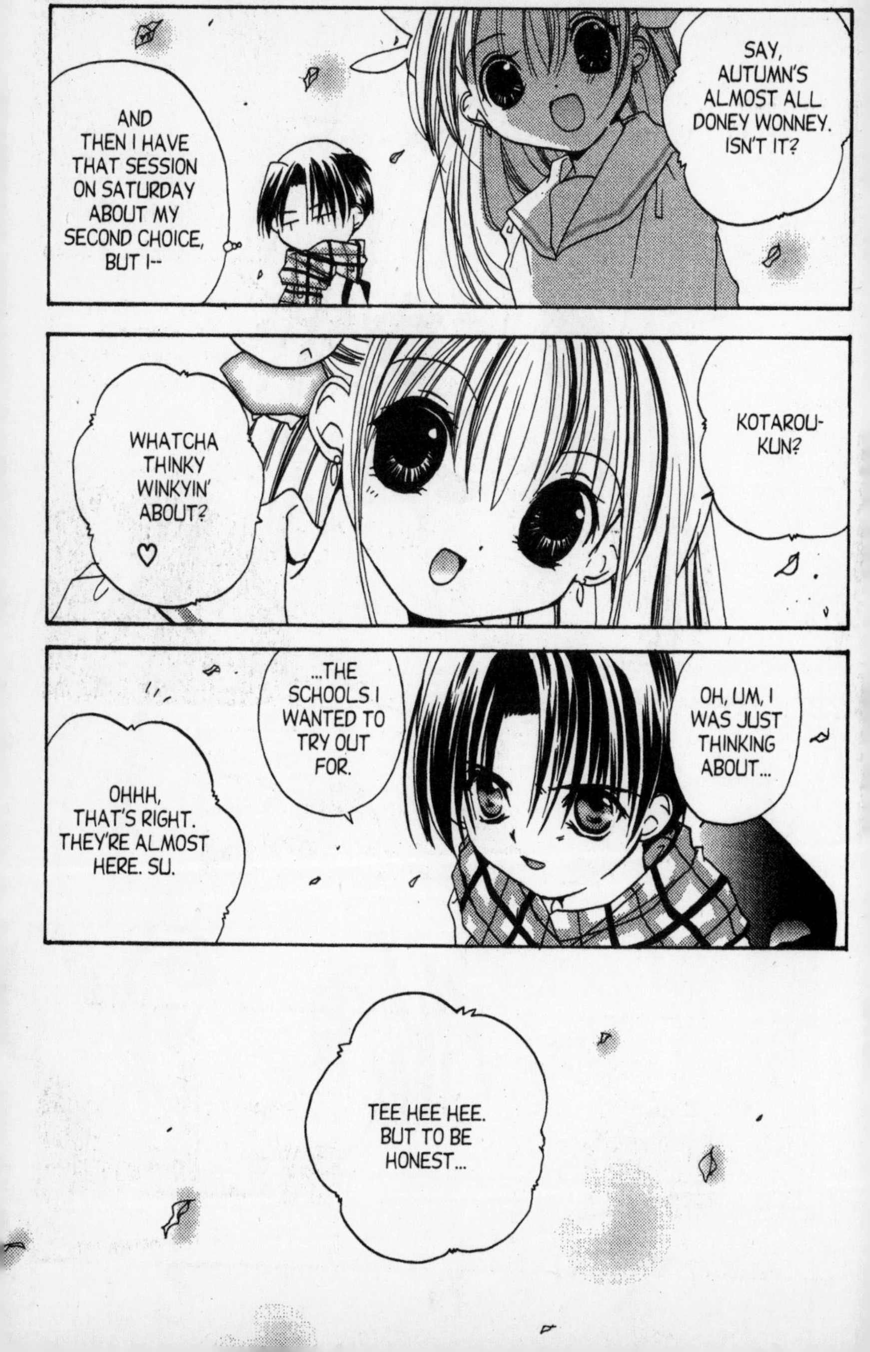
SAY, AUTUMN'S ALMOST ALL DONEY WONNEY. ISN'T IT?
AND THEN I HAVE THAT SESSION ON SATURDAY ABOUT MY SECOND CHOICE, BUT I--
KOTAROU-KUN?
WHATCHA THINKY WINKYIN' ABOUT? ♡
OH, UM, I WAS JUST THINKING ABOUT...
...THE SCHOOLS I WANTED TO TRY OUT FOR.
OHHH, THAT'S RIGHT. THEY'RE ALMOST HERE. SU.
TEE HEE HEE. BUT TO BE HONEST...

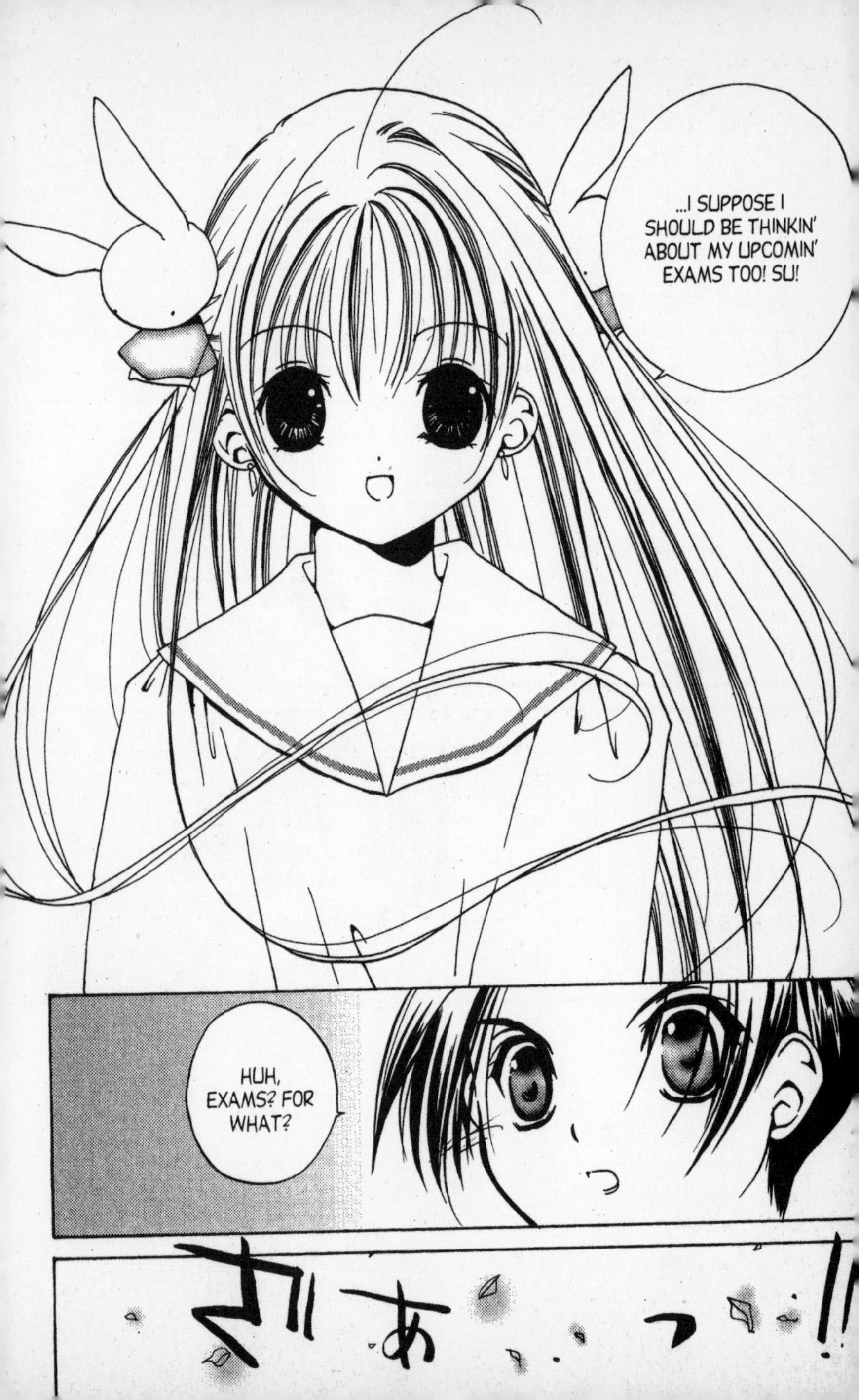
...I SUPPOSE I SHOULD BE THINKIN' ABOUT MY UPCOMIN' EXAMS TOO! SU!
HUH, EXAMS? FOR WHAT?
ざあっ…!!

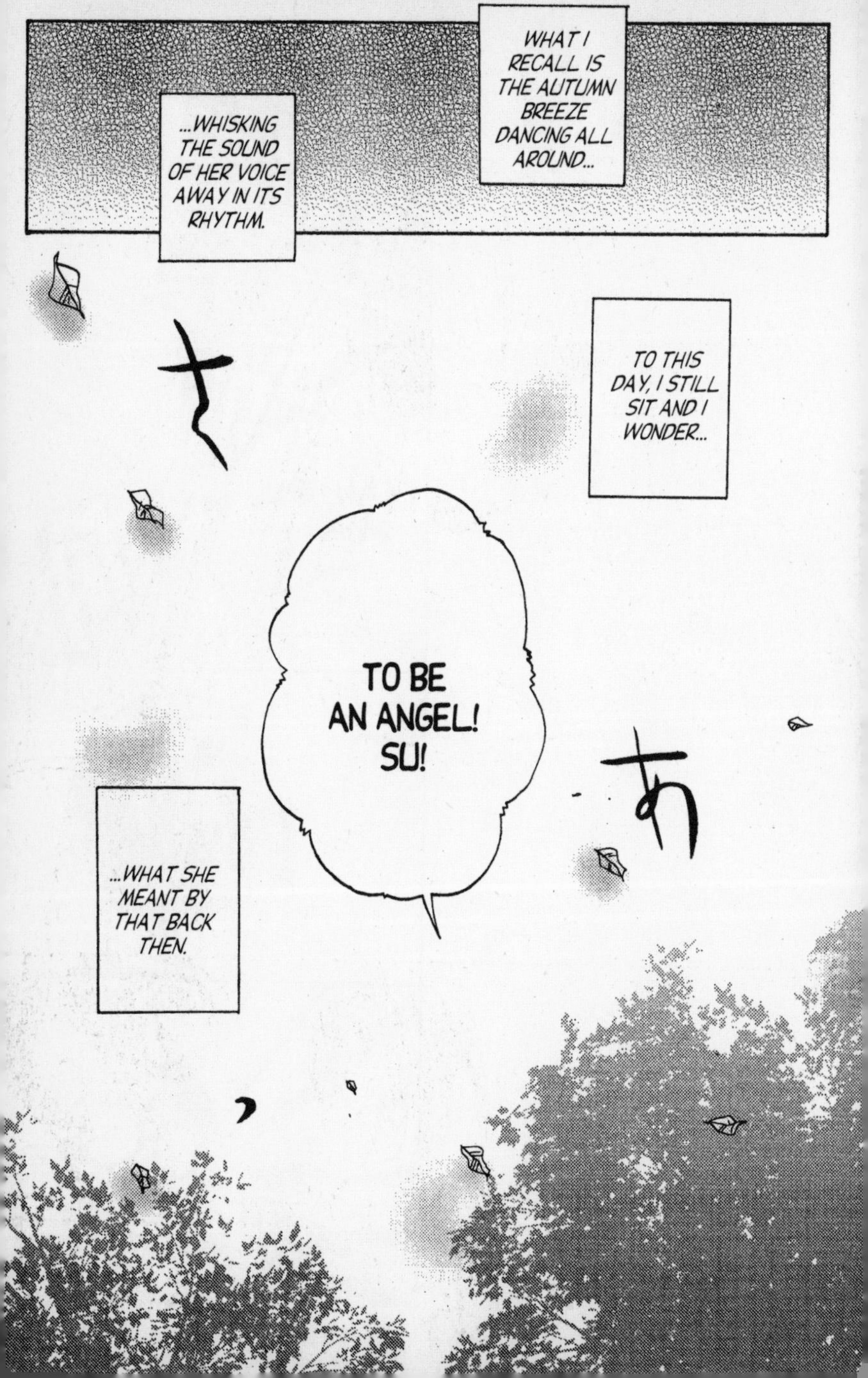
WHAT I RECALL IS THE AUTUMN BREEZE DANCING ALL AROUND...
...WHISKING THE SOUND OF HER VOICE AWAY IN ITS RHYTHM.
TO THIS DAY, I STILL SIT AND I WONDER...
TO BE AN ANGEL! SU!
さあっ
...WHAT SHE MEANT BY THAT BACK THEN.

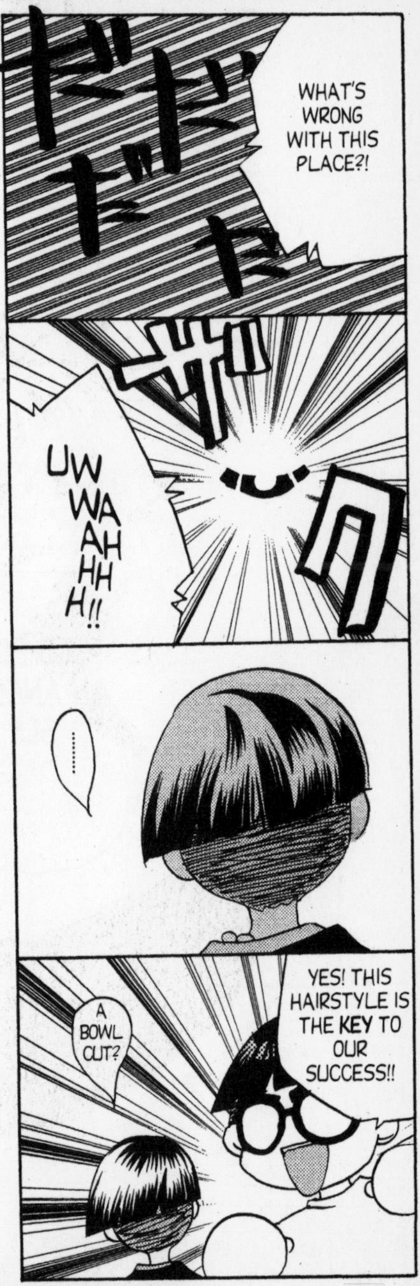
WHAT'S WRONG WITH THIS PLACE?!
UWWAAHHHH!!
......
YES! THIS HAIRSTYLE IS THE KEY TO OUR SUCCESS!!
A BOWL CUT?

Lesson 16

How to Truly Feel Happy

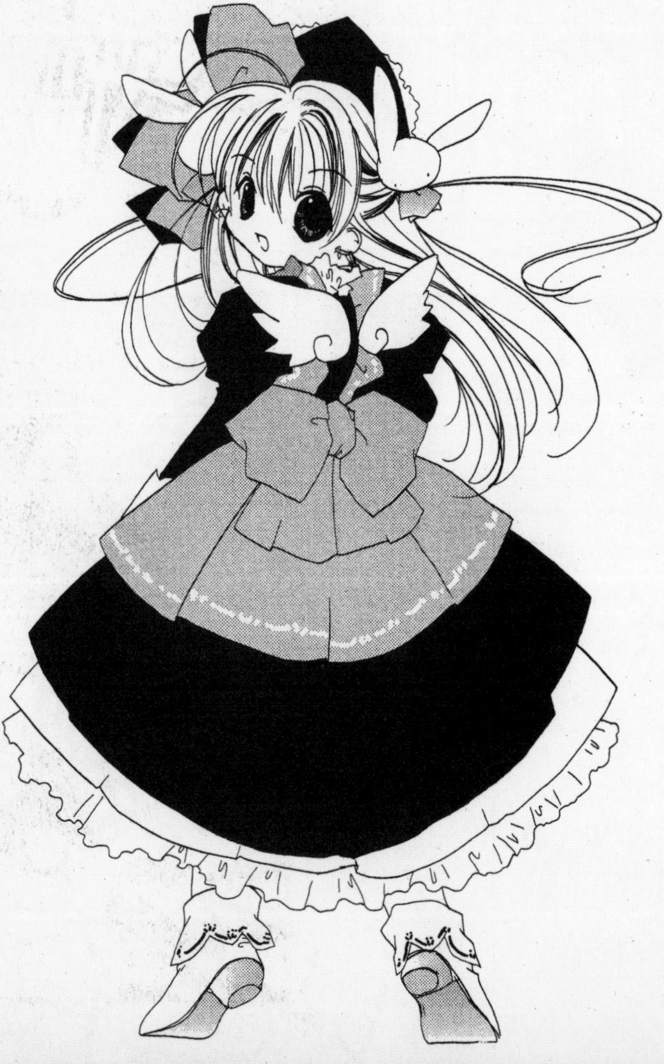

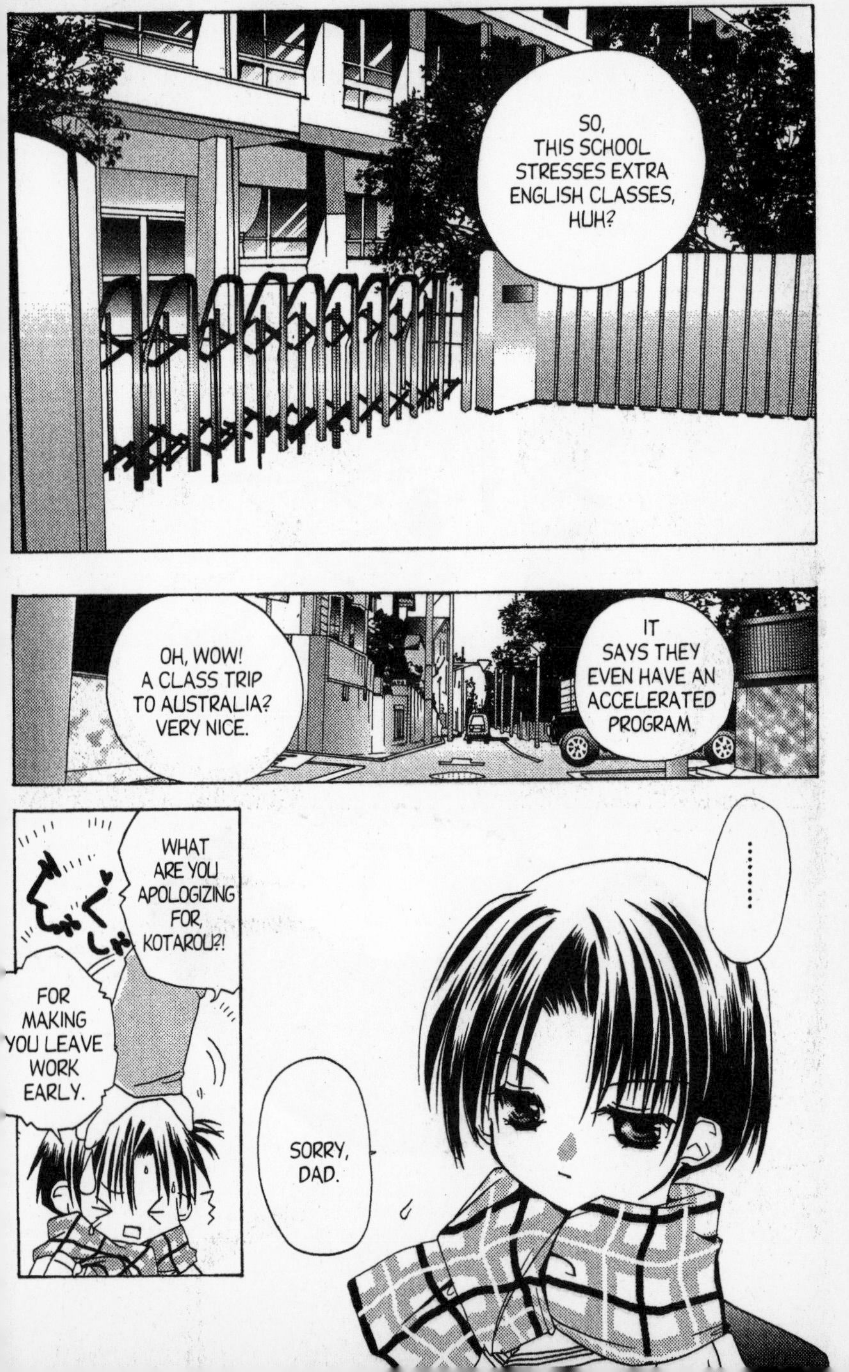
SO, THIS SCHOOL STRESSES EXTRA ENGLISH CLASSES, HUH?
IT SAYS THEY EVEN HAVE AN ACCELERATED PROGRAM.
OH, WOW! A CLASS TRIP TO AUSTRALIA? VERY NICE.
......
SORRY, DAD.
WHAT ARE YOU APOLOGIZING FOR, KOTAROU?!
FOR MAKING YOU LEAVE WORK EARLY.

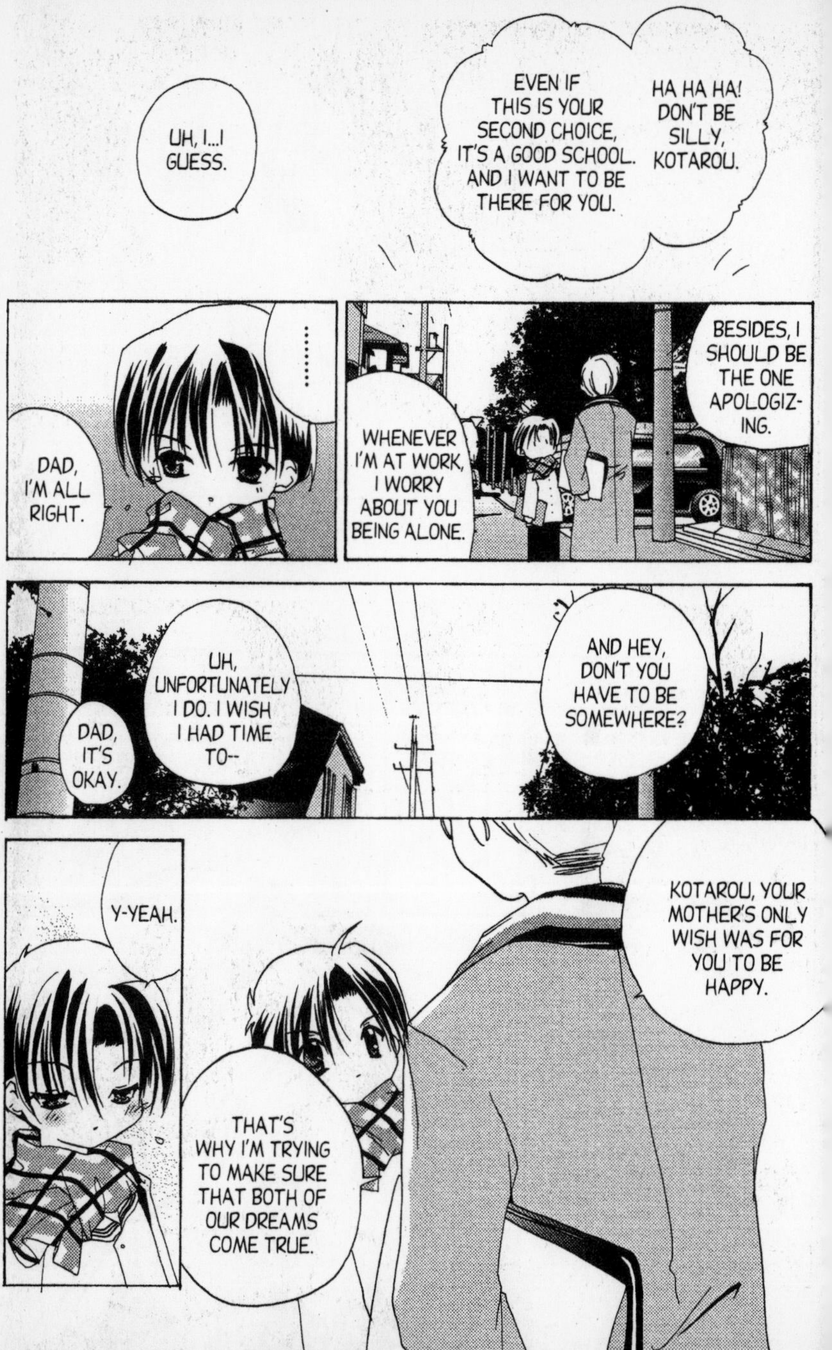
HA HA HA! DON'T BE SILLY, KOTAROU.
EVEN IF THIS IS YOUR SECOND CHOICE, IT'S A GOOD SCHOOL. AND I WANT TO BE THERE FOR YOU.
UH, I...I GUESS.
BESIDES, I SHOULD BE THE ONE APOLOGIZ-ING.
WHENEVER I'M AT WORK, I WORRY ABOUT YOU BEING ALONE.
......
DAD, I'M ALL RIGHT.
AND HEY, DON'T YOU HAVE TO BE SOMEWHERE?
UH, UNFORTUNATELY I DO. I WISH I HAD TIME TO--
DAD, IT'S OKAY.
KOTAROU, YOUR MOTHER'S ONLY WISH WAS FOR YOU TO BE HAPPY.
THAT'S WHY I'M TRYING TO MAKE SURE THAT BOTH OF OUR DREAMS COME TRUE.
Y-YEAH.

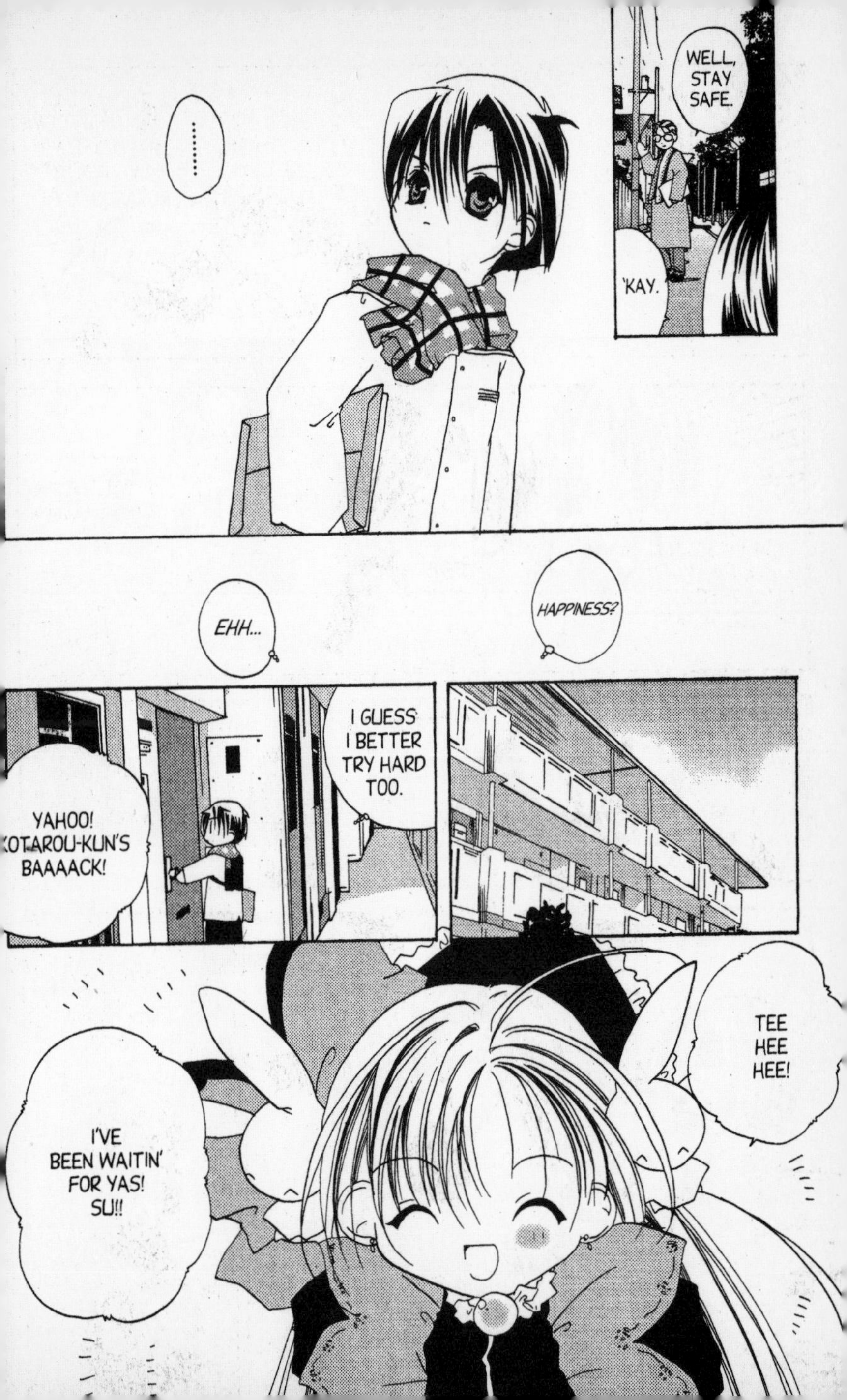
WELL, STAY SAFE.
'KAY.
....
HAPPINESS?
EHH...
I GUESS I BETTER TRY HARD TOO.
YAHOO! KOTAROU-KUN'S BAAAACK!
TEE HEE HEE!
I'VE BEEN WAITIN' FOR YAS! SU!!

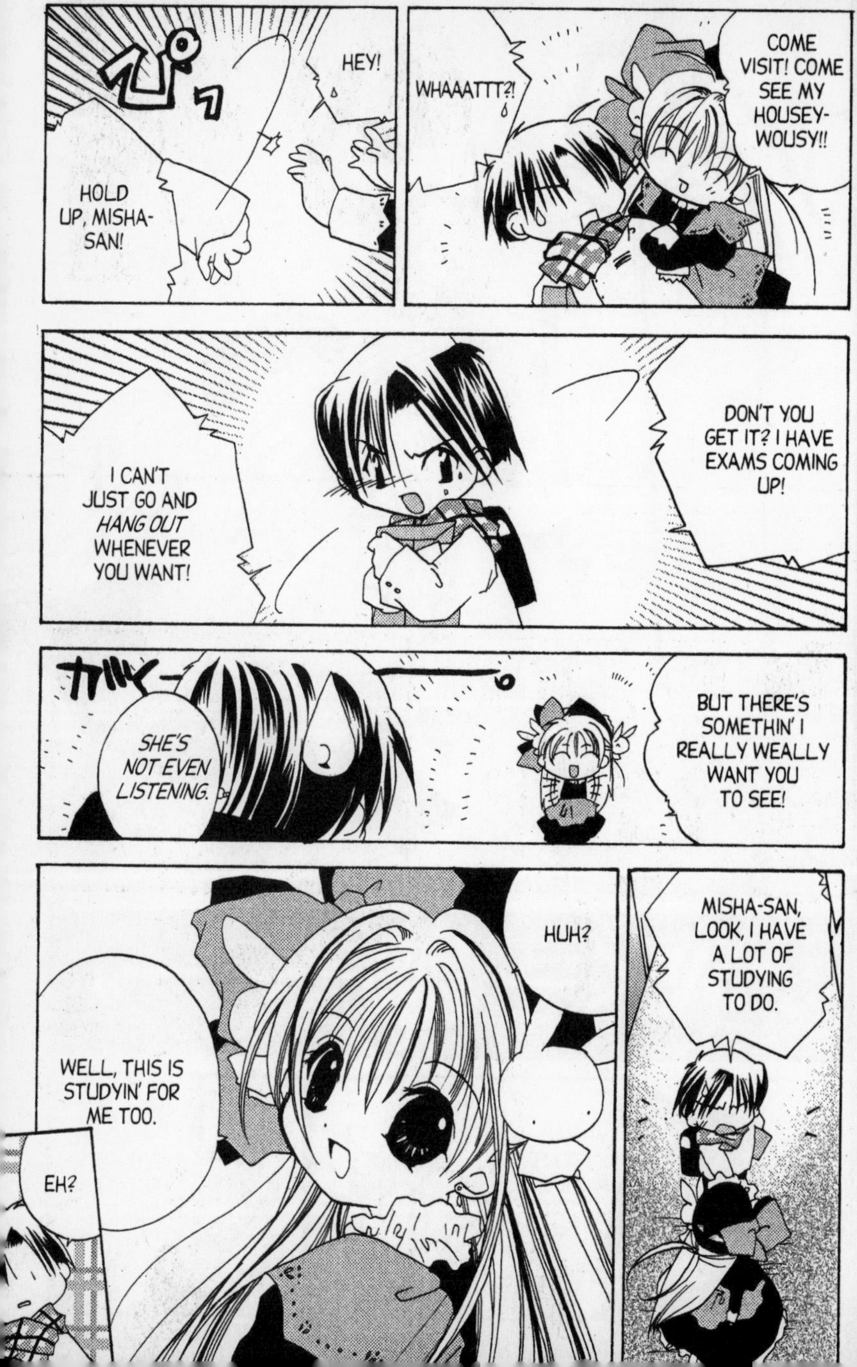
COME VISIT! COME SEE MY HOUSEY-WOUSY!!
WHAAATTT?!
HEY!
HOLD UP, MISHA-SAN!
DON'T YOU GET IT? I HAVE EXAMS COMING UP!
I CAN'T JUST GO AND *HANG OUT* WHENEVER YOU WANT!
BUT THERE'S SOMETHIN' I REALLY WEALLY WANT YOU TO SEE!
SHE'S NOT EVEN LISTENING.
MISHA-SAN, LOOK, I HAVE A LOT OF STUDYING TO DO.
HUH?
WELL, THIS IS STUDYIN' FOR ME TOO.
EH?

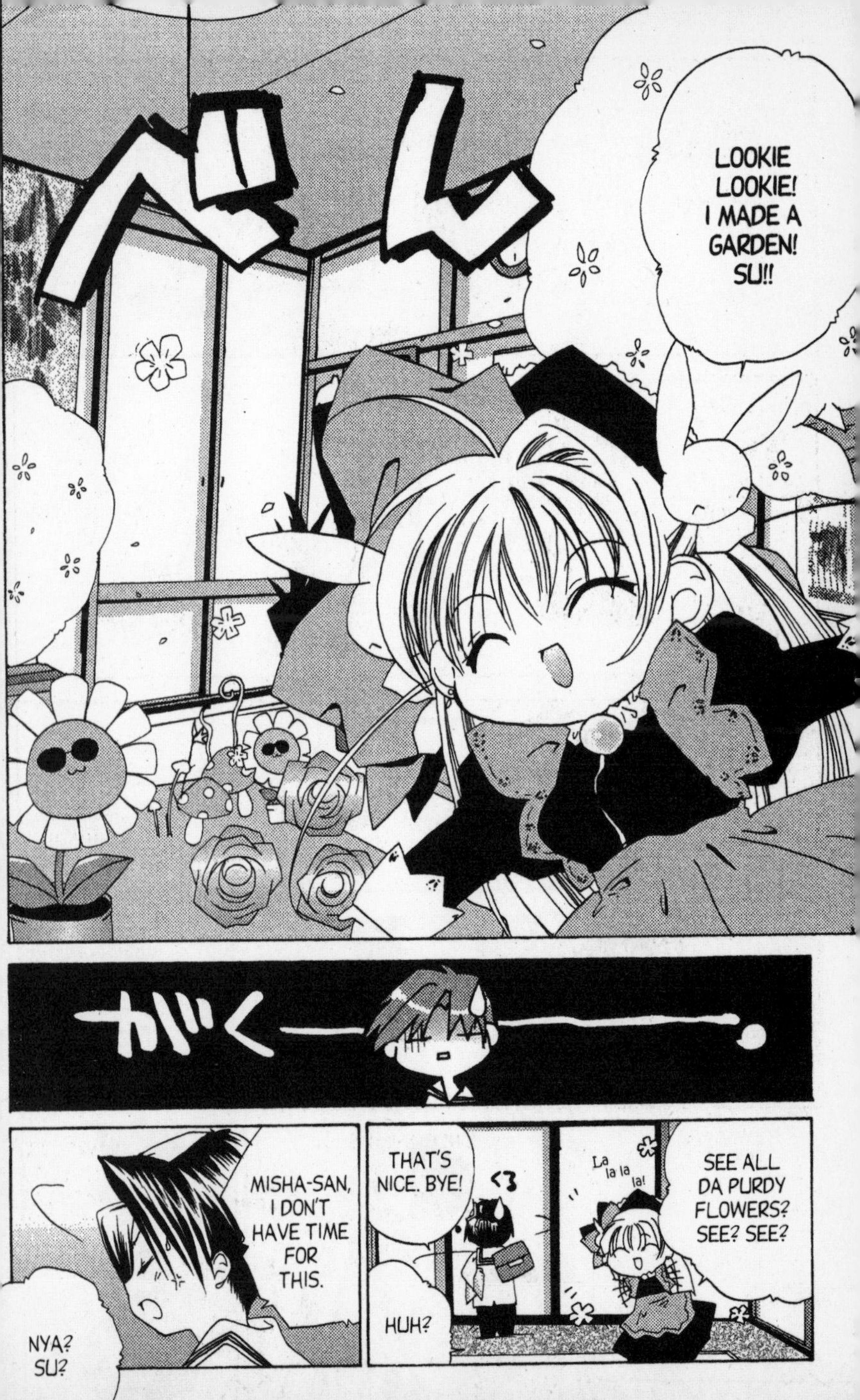
LOOKIE LOOKIE! I MADE A GARDEN! SU!!
SEE ALL DA PURDY FLOWERS? SEE? SEE?
La la la la!
THAT'S NICE. BYE!
HUH?
MISHA-SAN, I DON'T HAVE TIME FOR THIS.
NYA? SU?

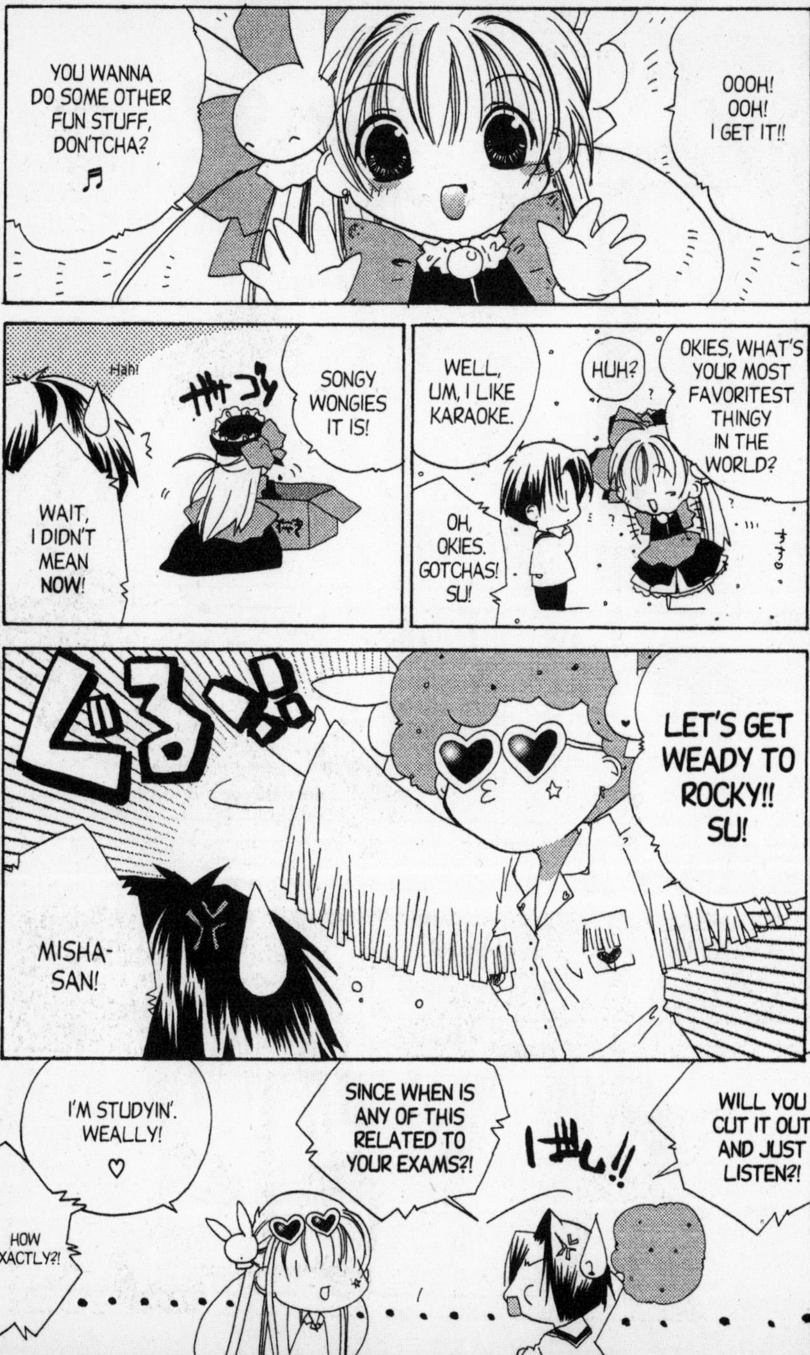
OOOH! OOH! I GET IT!!
YOU WANNA DO SOME OTHER FUN STUFF, DON'TCHA? ♪
OKIES, WHAT'S YOUR MOST FAVORITEST THINGY IN THE WORLD?
HUH?
WELL, UM, I LIKE KARAOKE.
OH, OKIES. GOTCHAS! SU!
SONGY WONGIES IT IS!
Hah!
WAIT, I DIDN'T MEAN NOW!
LET'S GET WEADY TO ROCKY!! SU!
MISHA-SAN!
WILL YOU CUT IT OUT AND JUST LISTEN?!
SINCE WHEN IS ANY OF THIS RELATED TO YOUR EXAMS?!
I'M STUDYIN'. WEALLY! ♡
HOW EXACTLY?!

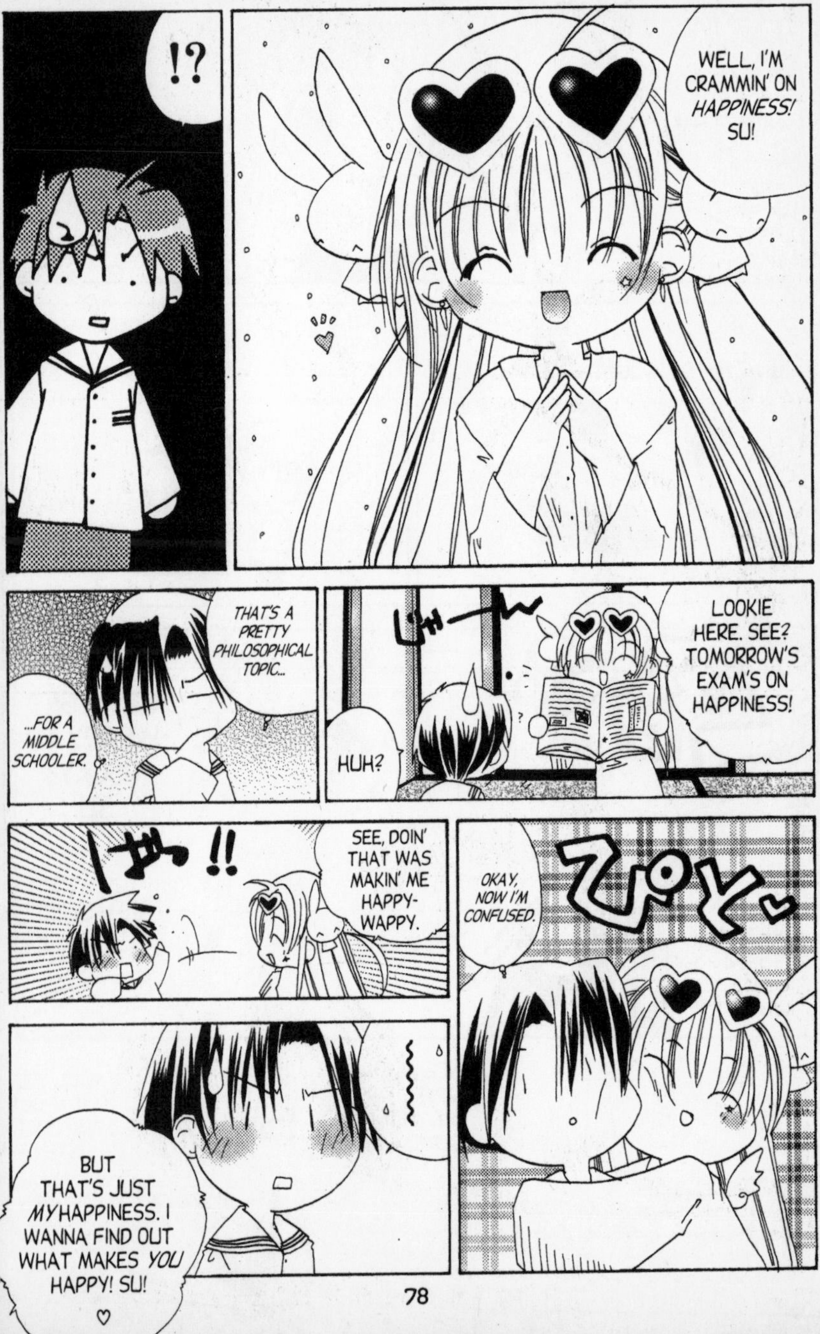

WELL, I'M CRAMMIN' ON *HAPPINESS!* SU!
!?
LOOKIE HERE. SEE? TOMORROW'S EXAM'S ON HAPPINESS!
じゃーん
HUH?
THAT'S A PRETTY PHILOSOPHICAL TOPIC...
...FOR A MIDDLE SCHOOLER.
ぴと
OKAY, NOW I'M CONFUSED.
SEE, DOIN' THAT WAS MAKIN' ME HAPPY-WAPPY.
ばっ!!
BUT THAT'S JUST *MY* HAPPINESS. I WANNA FIND OUT WHAT MAKES *YOU* HAPPY! SU!

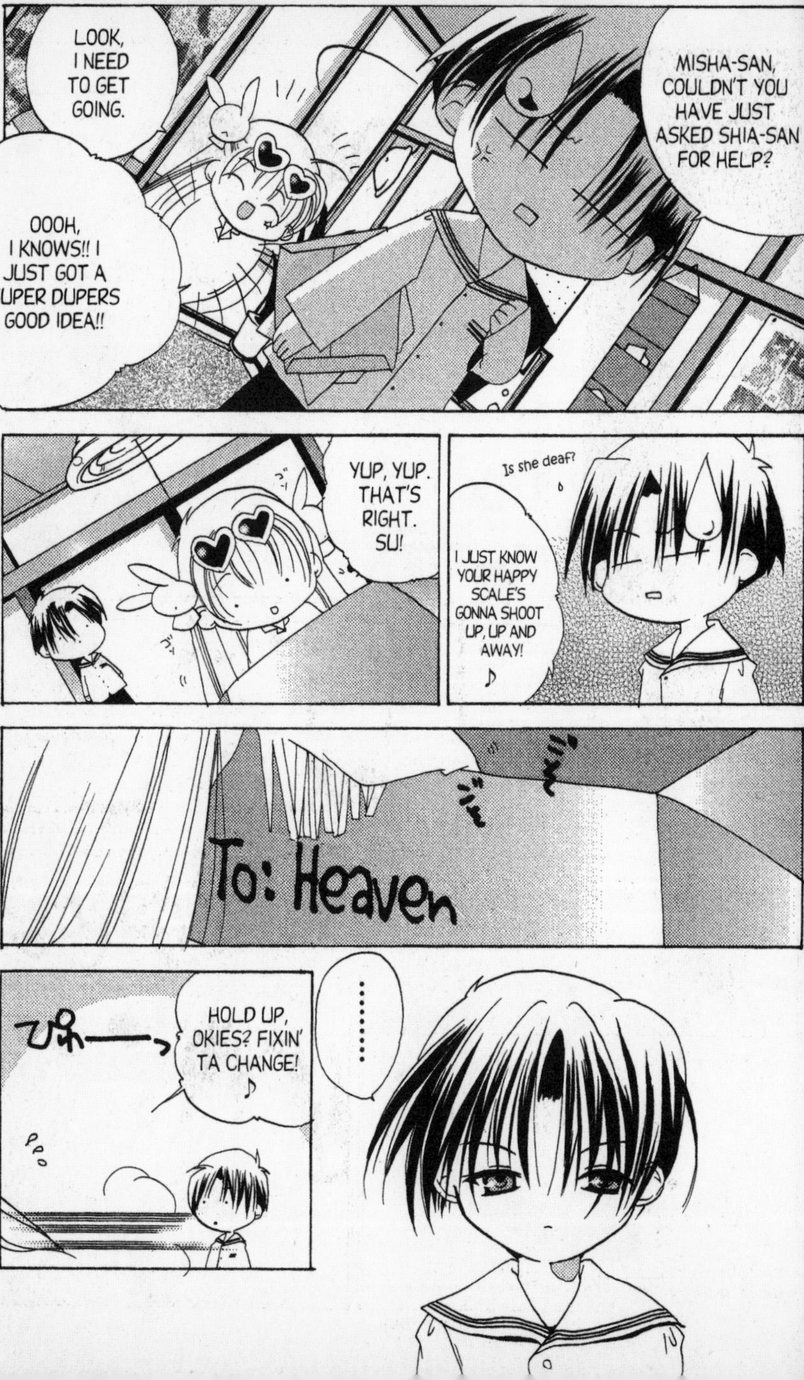
MISHA-SAN, COULDN'T YOU HAVE JUST ASKED SHIA-SAN FOR HELP?
LOOK, I NEED TO GET GOING.
OOOH, I KNOWS!! I JUST GOT A SUPER DUPERS GOOD IDEA!!
Is she deaf?
I JUST KNOW YOUR HAPPY SCALE'S GONNA SHOOT UP, UP AND AWAY! ♪
YUP, YUP. THAT'S RIGHT. SU!
To: Heaven
....
HOLD UP, OKIES? FIXIN' TA CHANGE! ♪
ぴゅー―っ

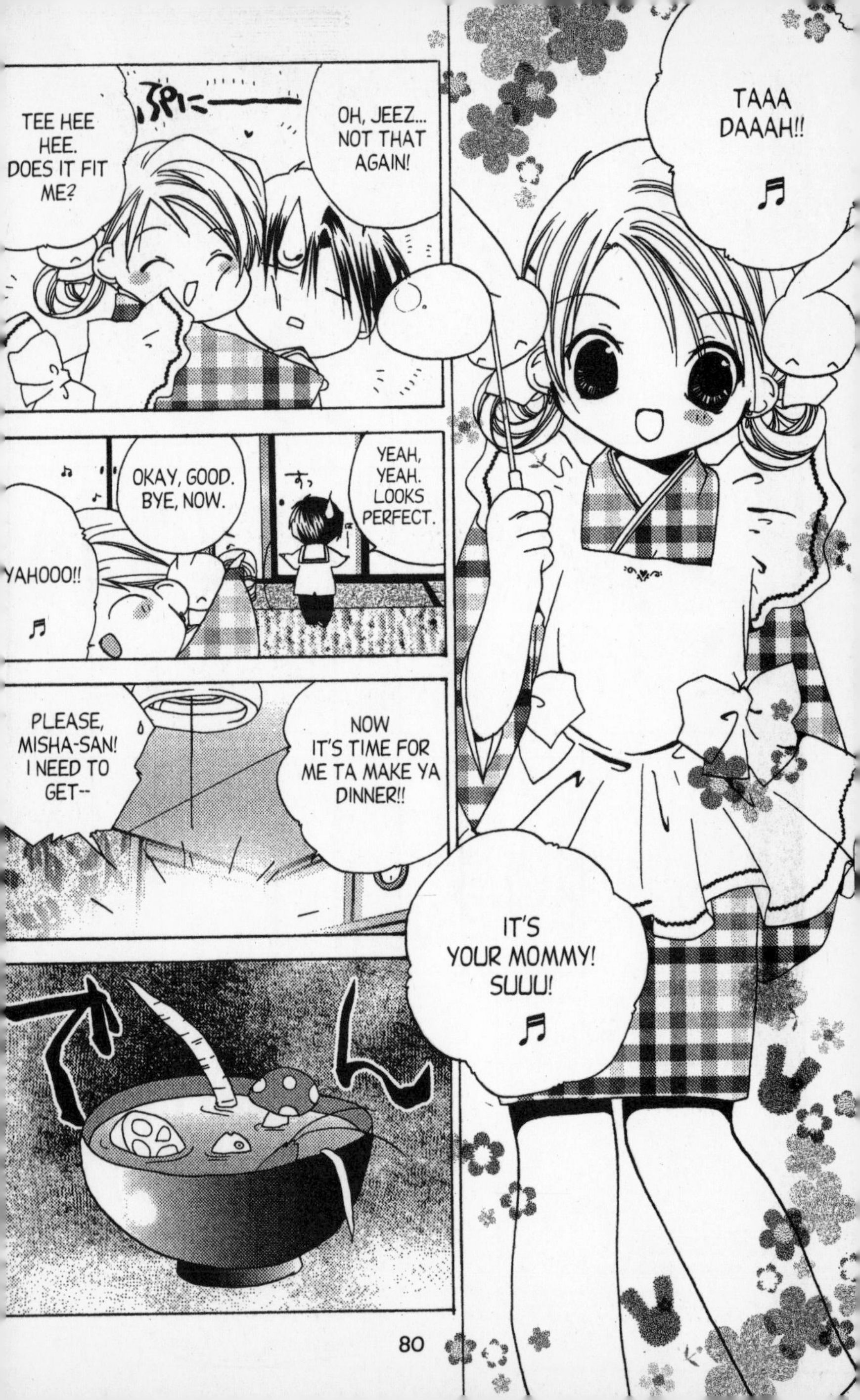
TAAA DAAAH!!
IT'S YOUR MOMMY! SUUU!
OH, JEEZ... NOT THAT AGAIN!
TEE HEE HEE. DOES IT FIT ME?
YEAH, YEAH. LOOKS PERFECT.
OKAY, GOOD. BYE, NOW.
YAHOOO!!
NOW IT'S TIME FOR ME TA MAKE YA DINNER!!
PLEASE, MISHA-SAN! I NEED TO GET--

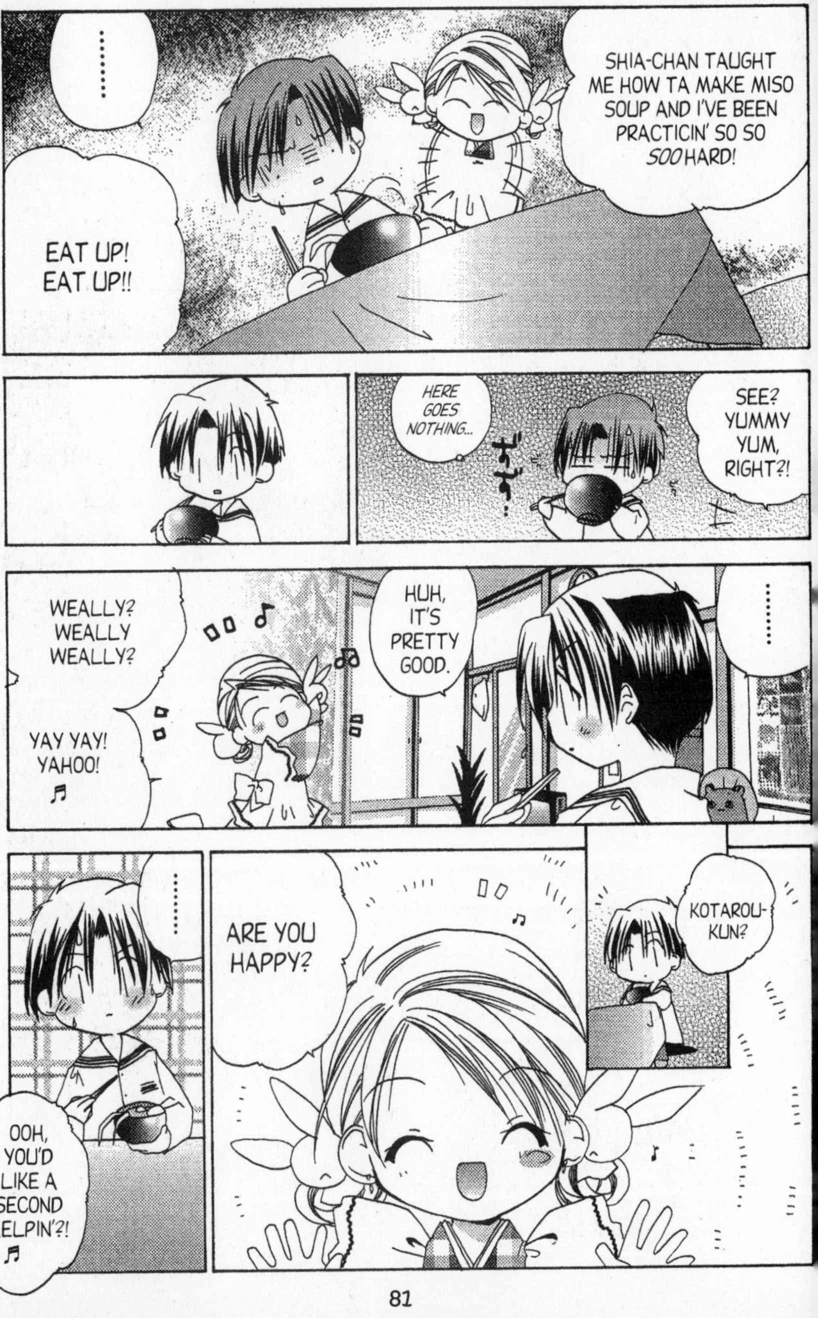
SHIA-CHAN TAUGHT ME HOW TA MAKE MISO SOUP AND I'VE BEEN PRACTICIN' SO SO *SOO* HARD!
......
EAT UP! EAT UP!!
SEE? YUMMY YUM, RIGHT?!
HERE GOES NOTHING...
......
HUH, IT'S PRETTY GOOD.
WEALLY? WEALLY WEALLY?
YAY YAY! YAHOO! ♬
KOTAROU-KUN?
ARE YOU HAPPY?
......
OOH, YOU'D LIKE A SECOND HELPIN'?! ♬

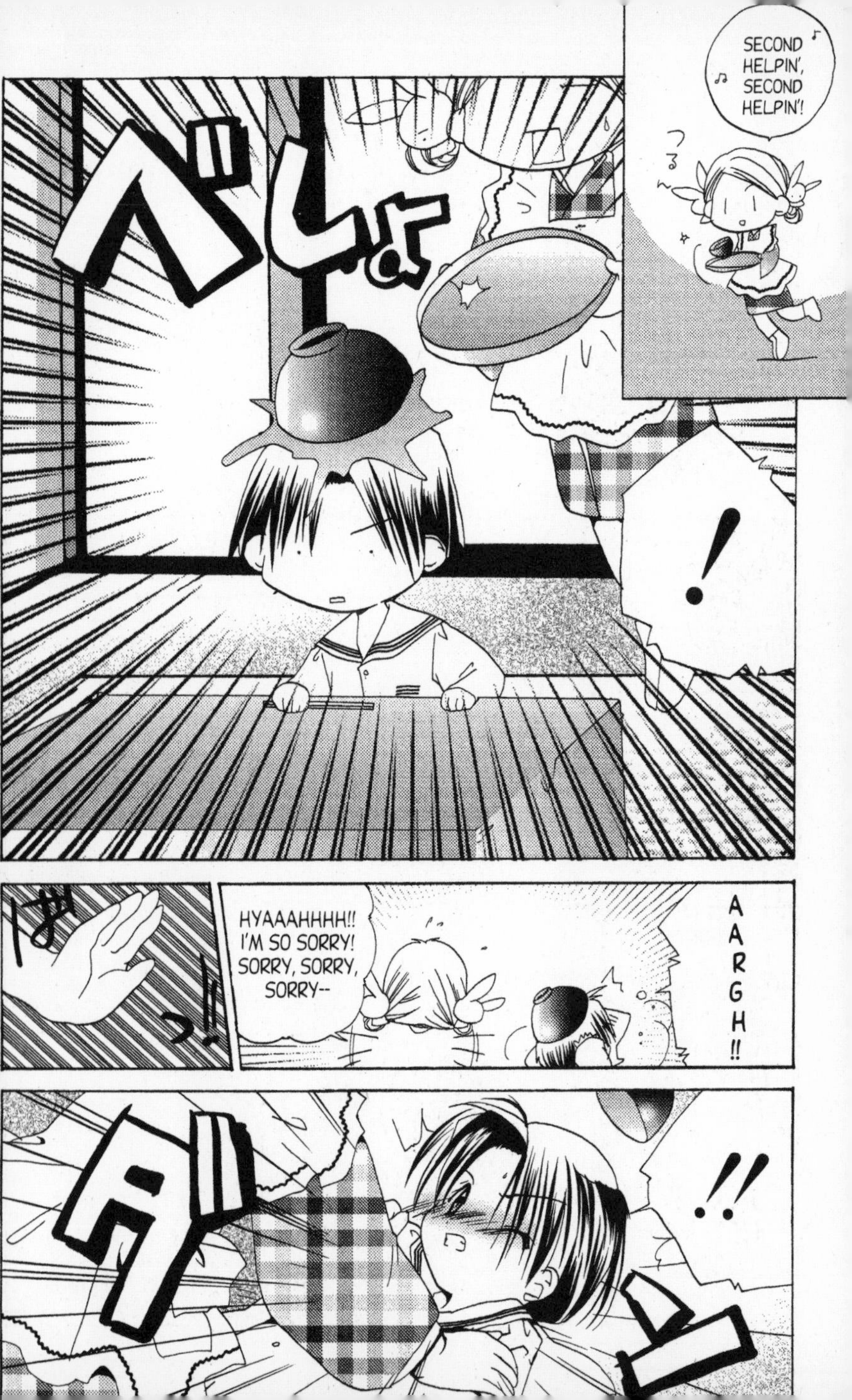
SECOND HELPIN', SECOND HELPIN'!
!
AARGH!!
HYAAAHHHH!! I'M SO SORRY! SORRY, SORRY, SORRY--
!!

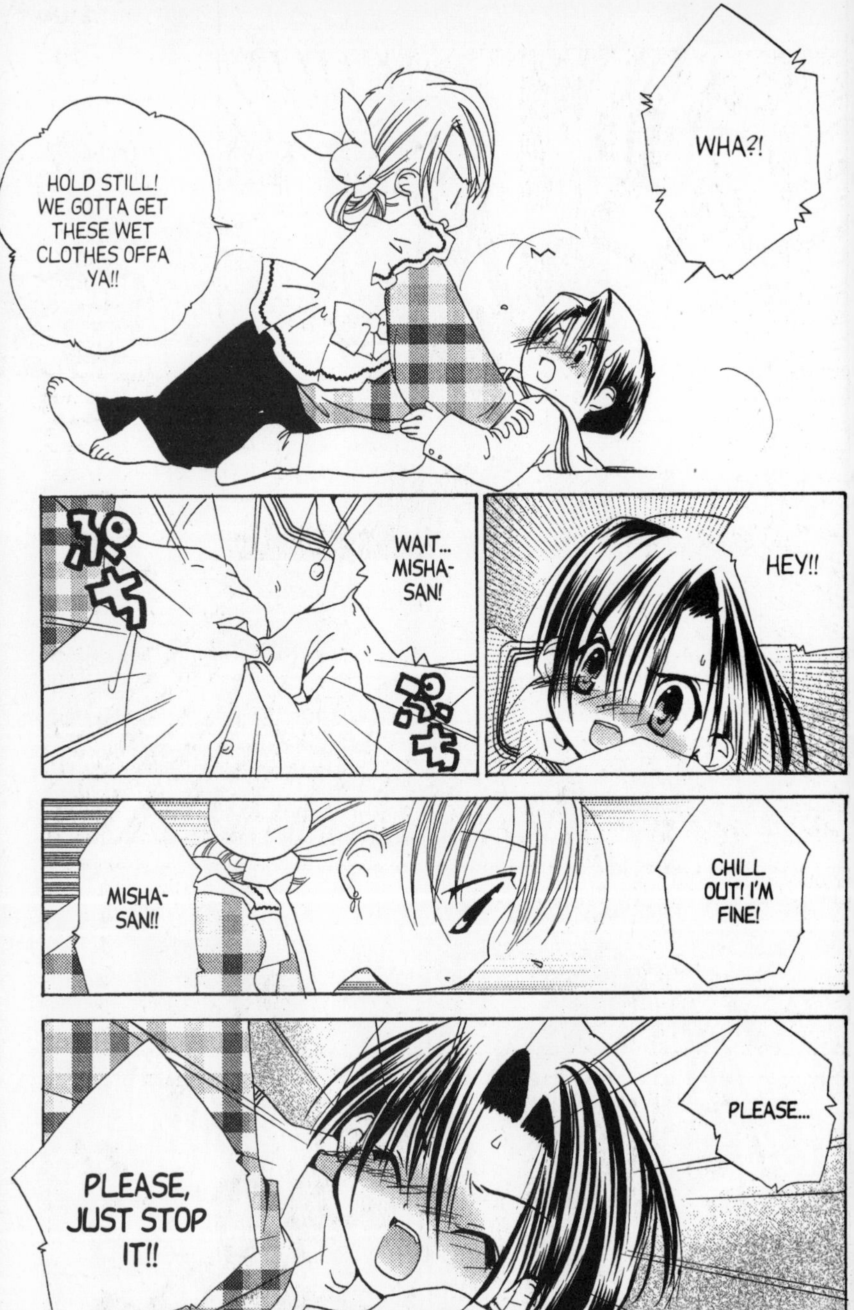
WHA?!
HOLD STILL! WE GOTTA GET THESE WET CLOTHES OFFA YA!!
HEY!!
WAIT... MISHA-SAN!
CHILL OUT! I'M FINE!
MISHA-SAN!!
PLEASE...
PLEASE, JUST STOP IT!!

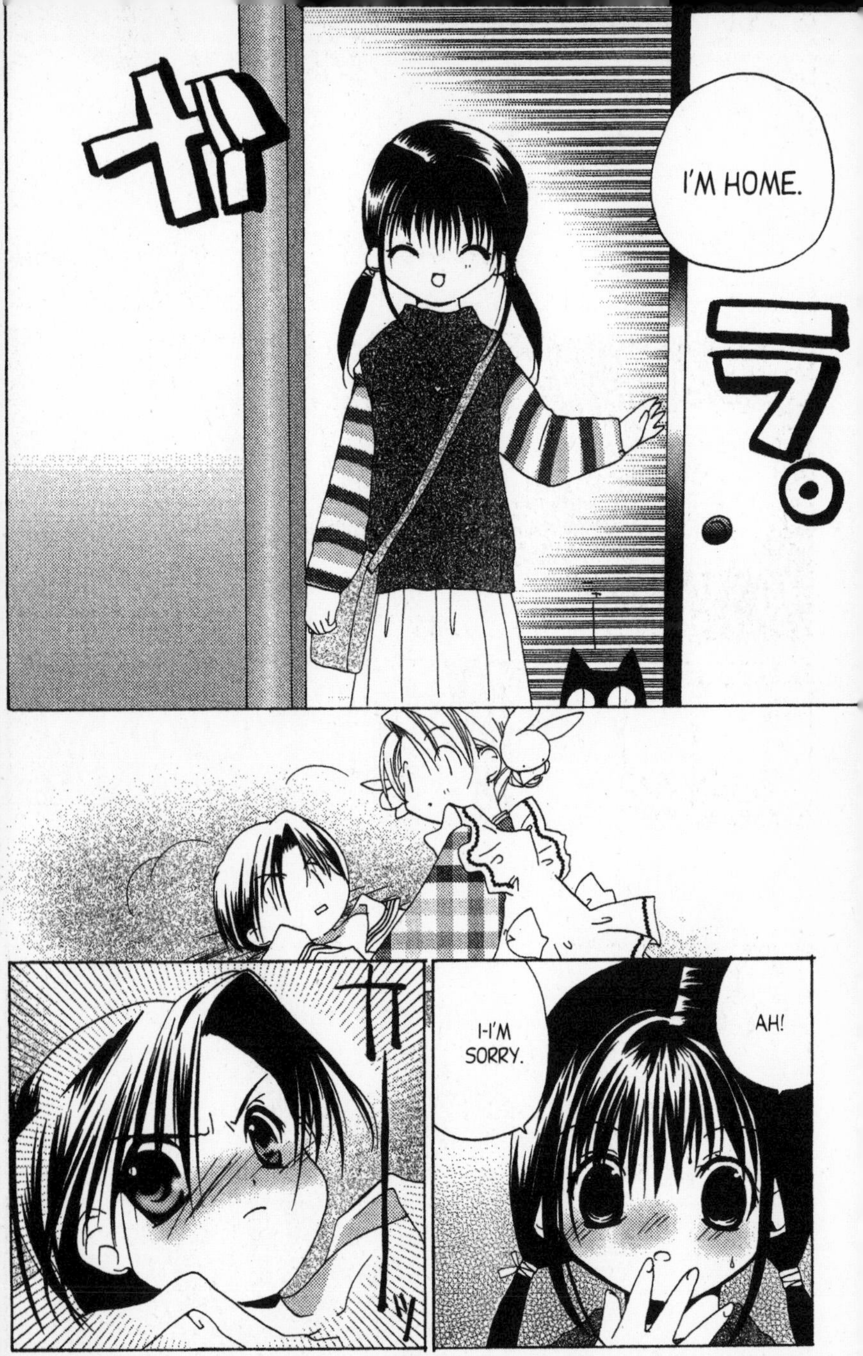
I'M HOME.
AH!
I-I'M SORRY.

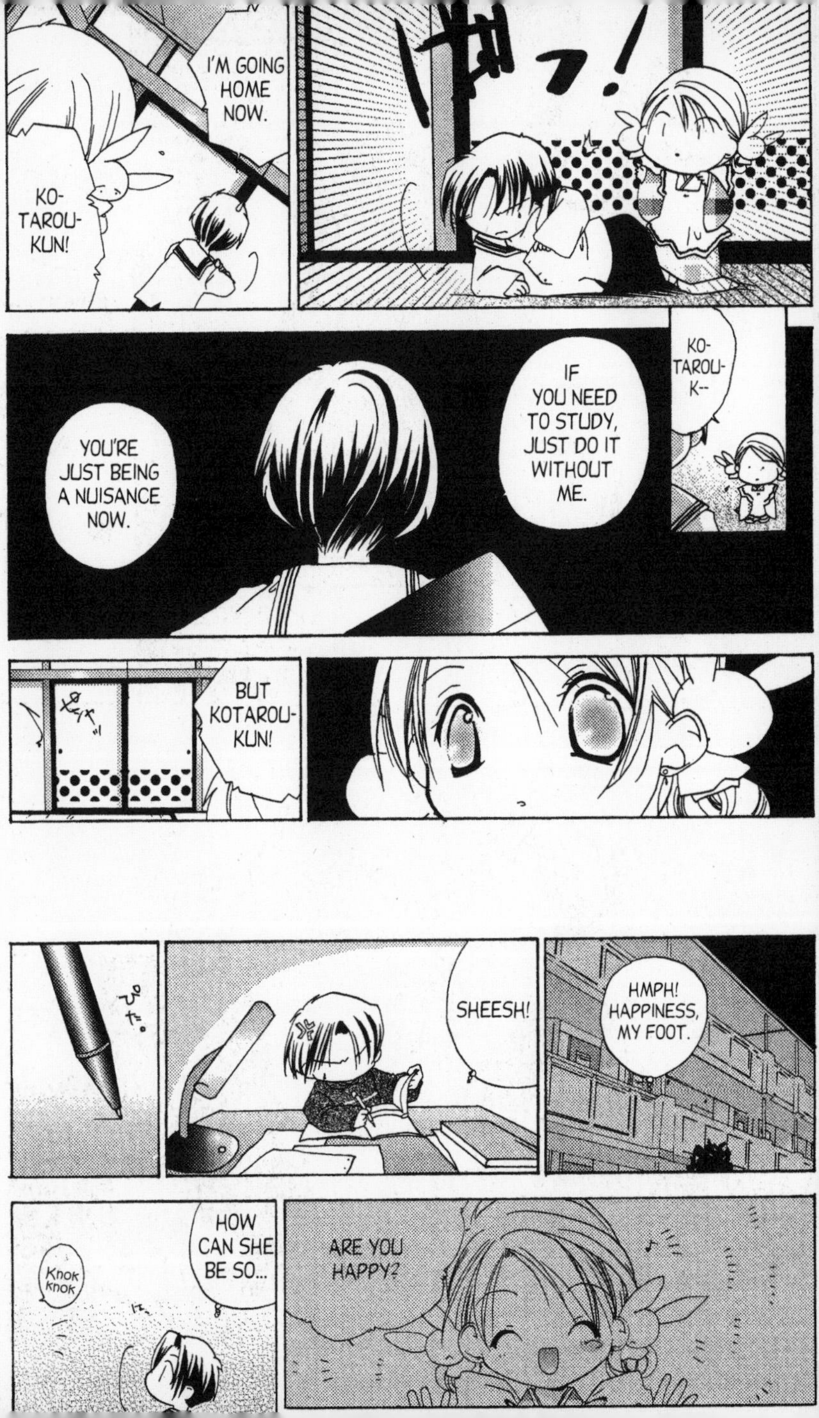
I'M GOING HOME NOW.
KO-TAROU-KUN!
KO-TAROU-K--
IF YOU NEED TO STUDY, JUST DO IT WITHOUT ME.
YOU'RE JUST BEING A NUISANCE NOW.
BUT KOTAROU-KUN!
HMPH! HAPPINESS, MY FOOT.
SHEESH!
ARE YOU HAPPY?
HOW CAN SHE BE SO...
Knok knok

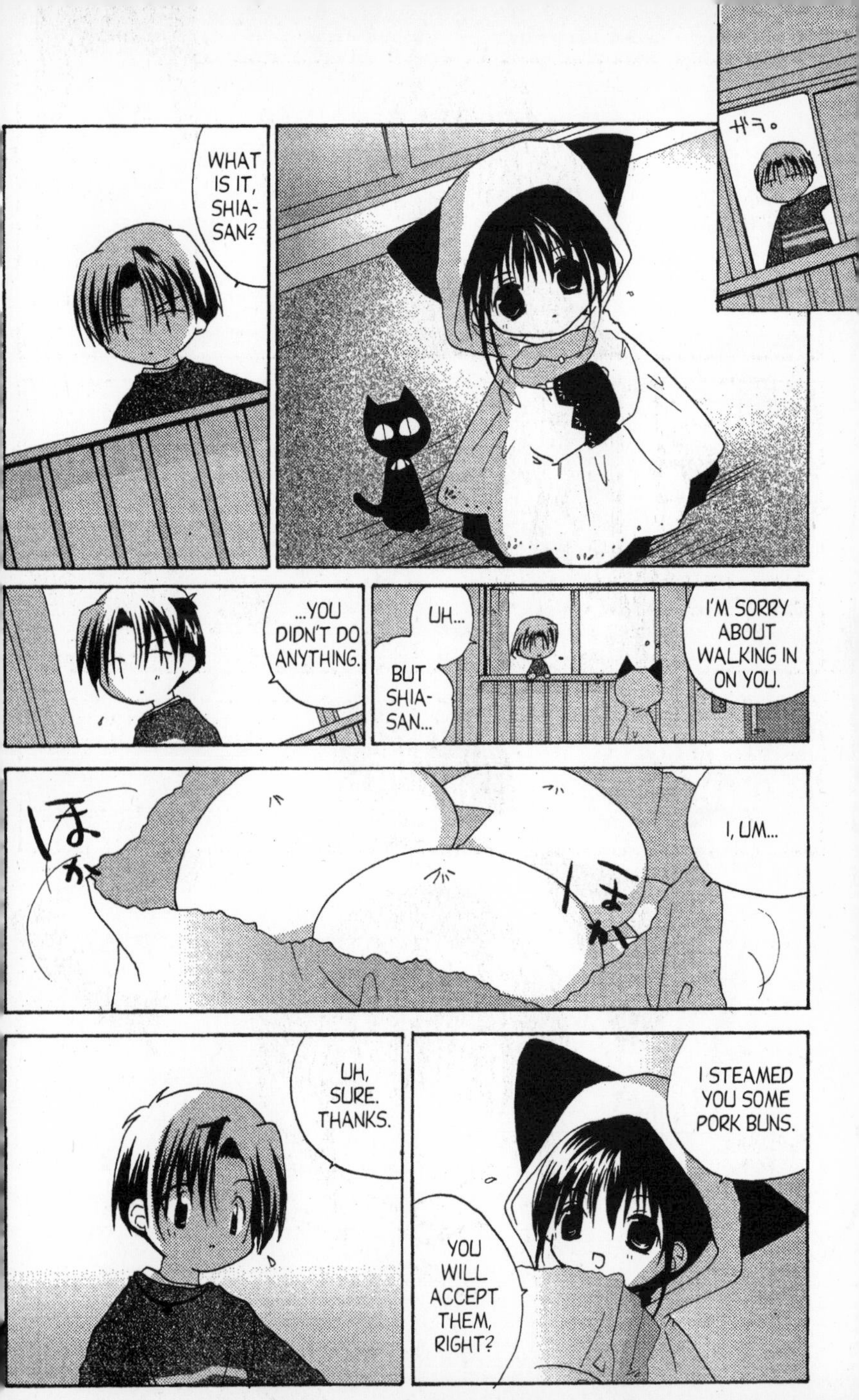
ガラ。
WHAT IS IT, SHIA-SAN?
I'M SORRY ABOUT WALKING IN ON YOU.
UH... BUT SHIA-SAN...
...YOU DIDN'T DO ANYTHING.
I, UM...
ほか
ほか
I STEAMED YOU SOME PORK BUNS.
YOU WILL ACCEPT THEM, RIGHT?
UH, SURE. THANKS.

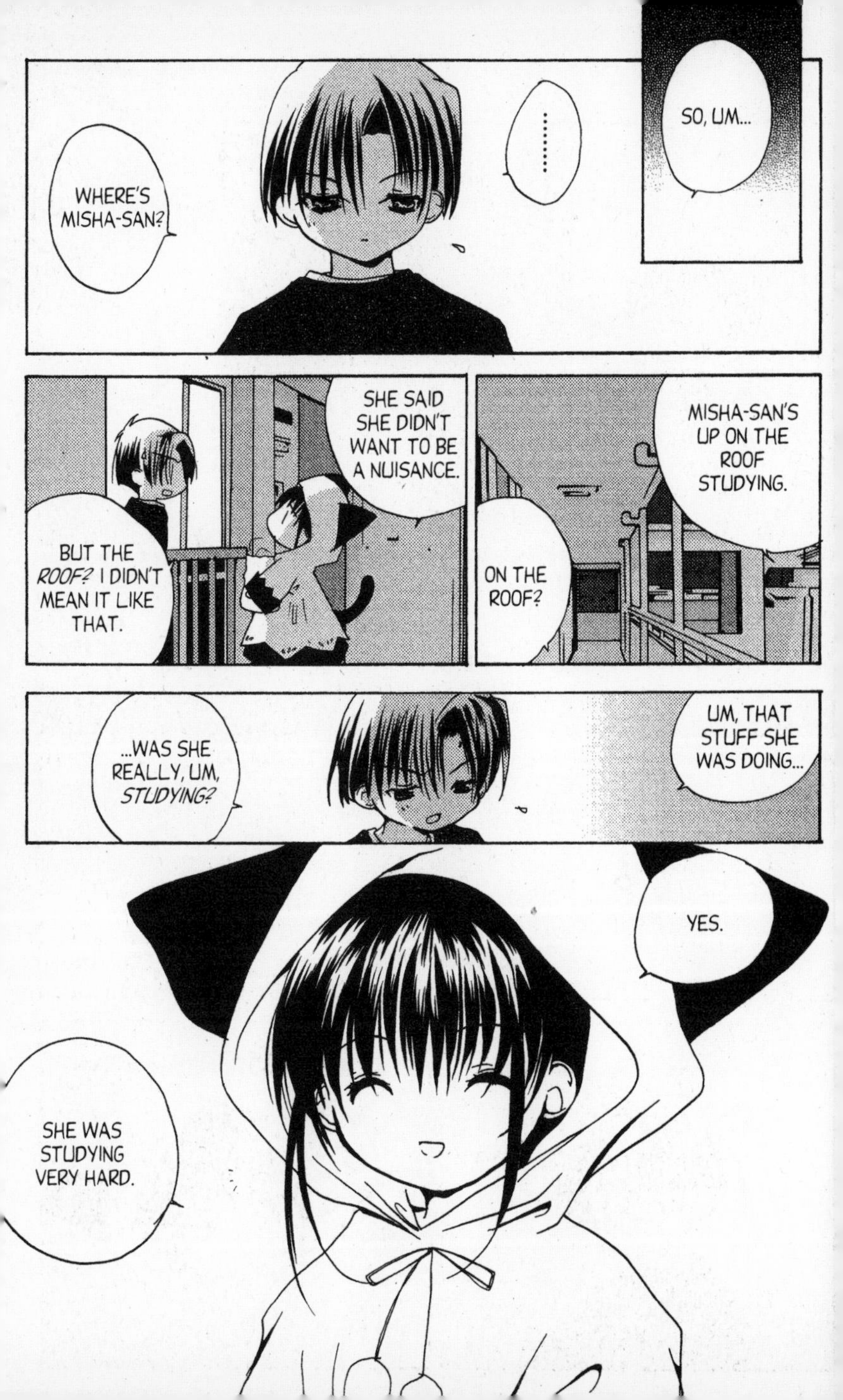
SO, UM...
......
WHERE'S MISHA-SAN?
MISHA-SAN'S UP ON THE ROOF STUDYING.
ON THE ROOF?
SHE SAID SHE DIDN'T WANT TO BE A NUISANCE.
BUT THE *ROOF?* I DIDN'T MEAN IT LIKE THAT.
UM, THAT STUFF SHE WAS DOING...
...WAS SHE REALLY, UM, *STUDYING?*
YES.
SHE WAS STUDYING VERY HARD.

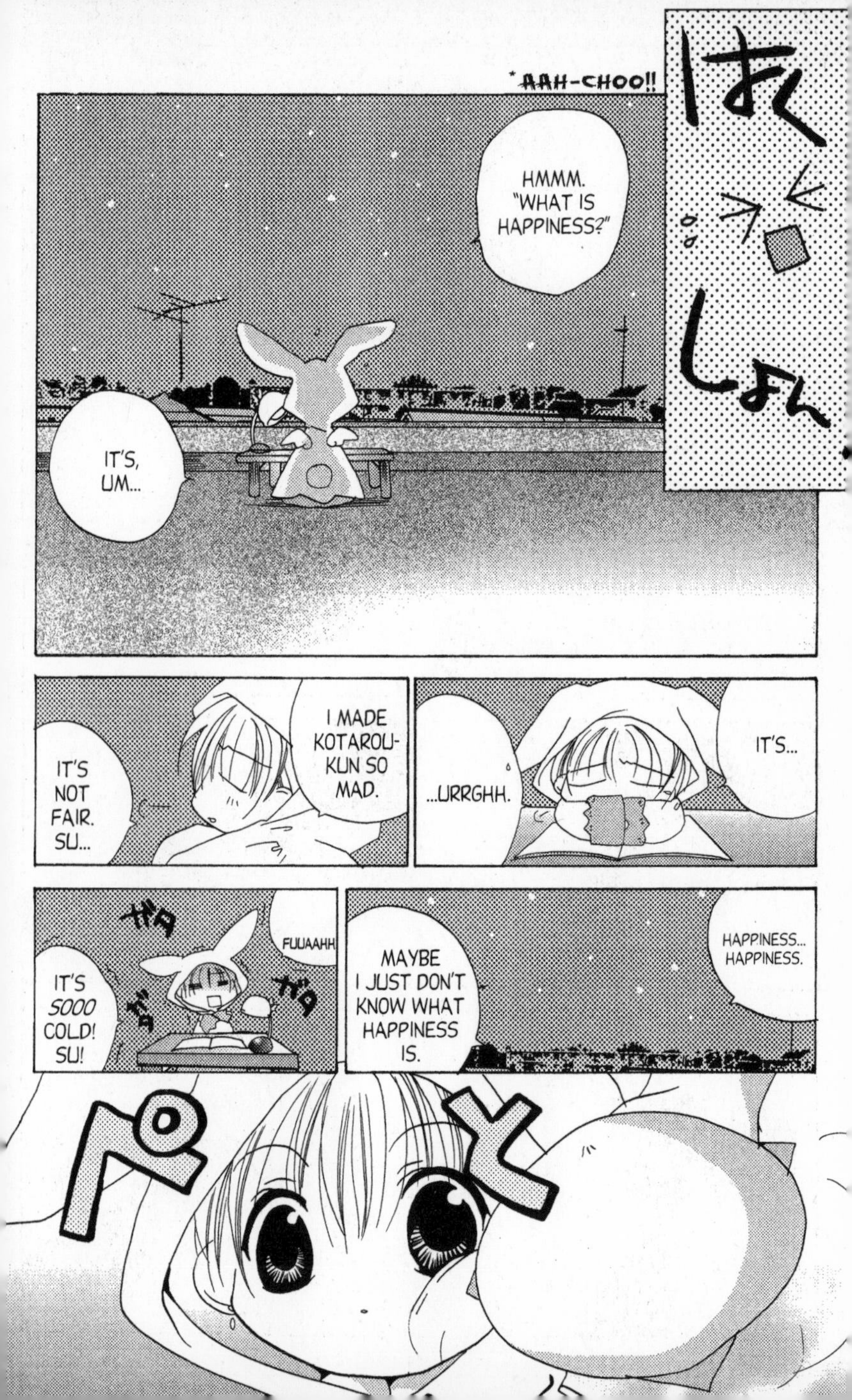
はくしょん
*AAH-CHOO!!
HMMM. "WHAT IS HAPPINESS?"
IT'S, UM...
IT'S...
...URRGHH.
I MADE KOTAROU-KUN SO MAD.
IT'S NOT FAIR. SU...
HAPPINESS... HAPPINESS.
MAYBE I JUST DON'T KNOW WHAT HAPPINESS IS.
FUUAAHH
IT'S *SOOO* COLD! SU!

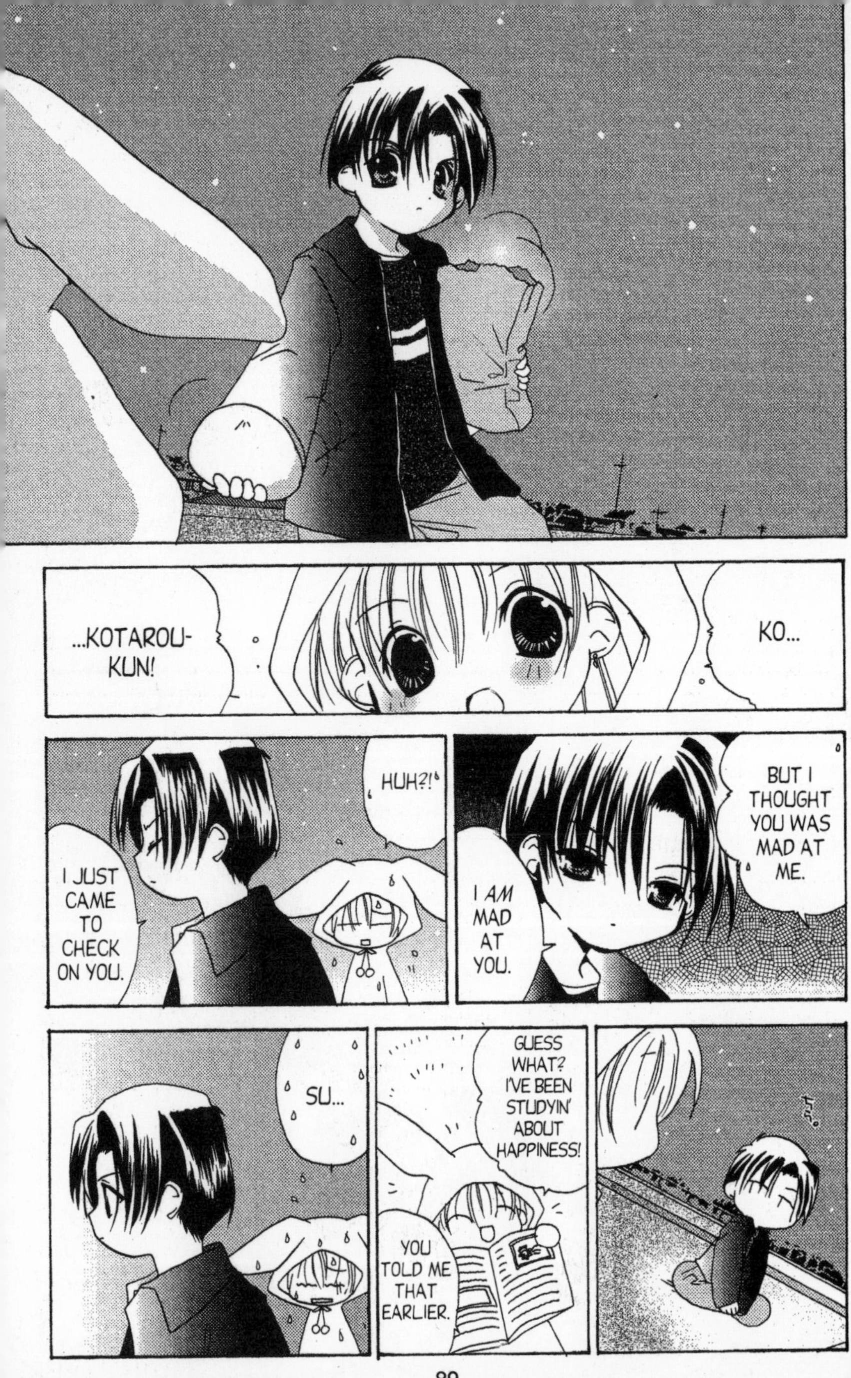

KO...
...KOTAROU-KUN!
BUT I THOUGHT YOU WAS MAD AT ME.
I *AM* MAD AT YOU.
HUH?!
I JUST CAME TO CHECK ON YOU.
GUESS WHAT? I'VE BEEN STUDYIN' ABOUT HAPPINESS!
YOU TOLD ME THAT EARLIER.
SU...

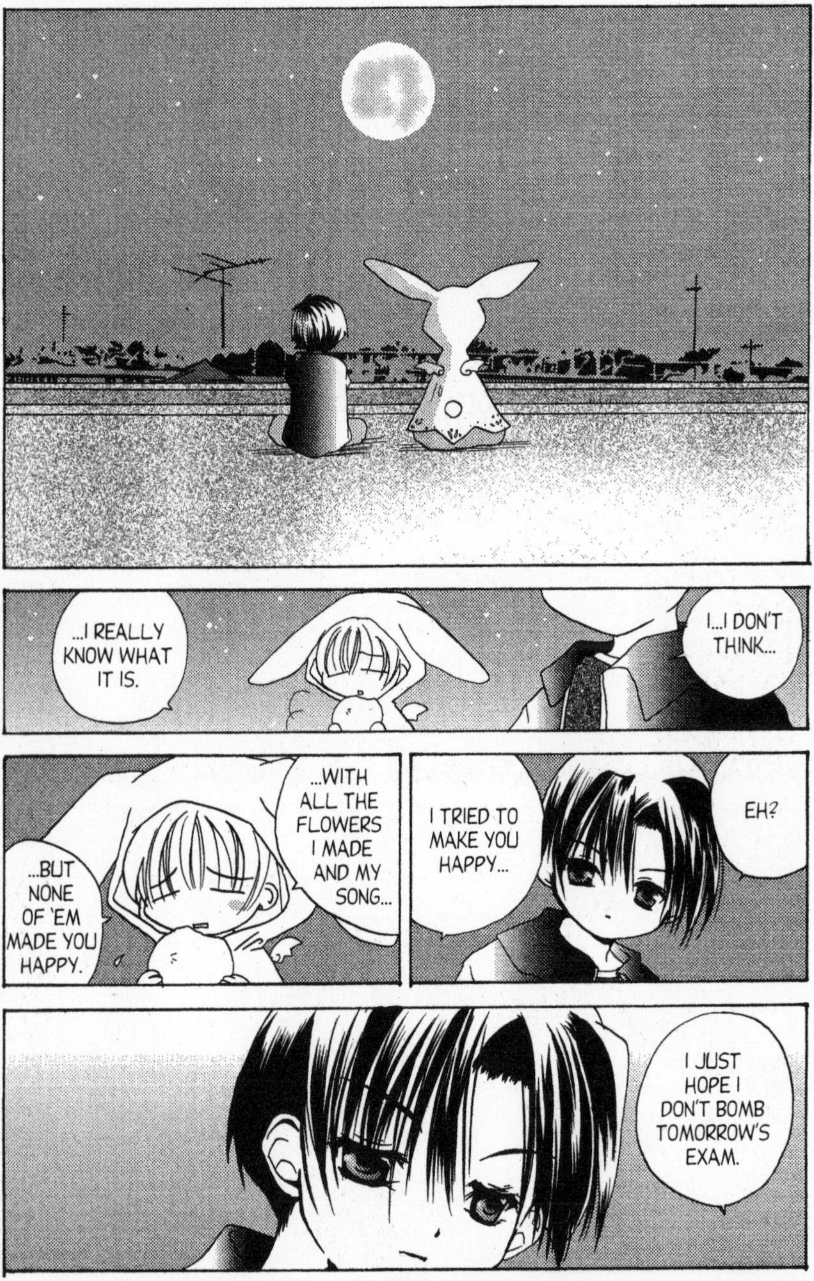
I...I DON'T THINK...
...I REALLY KNOW WHAT IT IS.
EH?
I TRIED TO MAKE YOU HAPPY...
...WITH ALL THE FLOWERS I MADE AND MY SONG...
...BUT NONE OF 'EM MADE YOU HAPPY.
I JUST HOPE I DON'T BOMB TOMORROW'S EXAM.

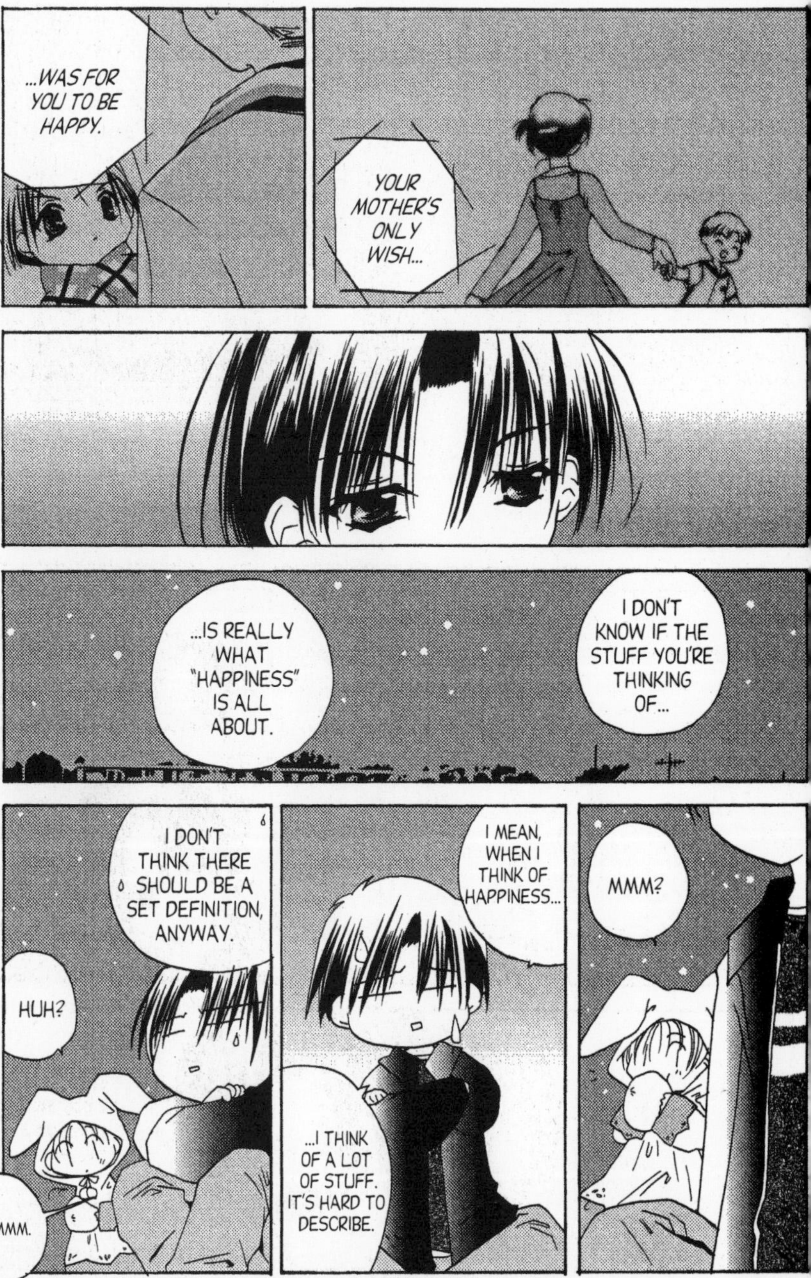
YOUR MOTHER'S ONLY WISH...
...WAS FOR YOU TO BE HAPPY.
I DON'T KNOW IF THE STUFF YOU'RE THINKING OF...
...IS REALLY WHAT "HAPPINESS" IS ALL ABOUT.
MMM?
I MEAN, WHEN I THINK OF HAPPINESS...
...I THINK OF A LOT OF STUFF. IT'S HARD TO DESCRIBE.
I DON'T THINK THERE SHOULD BE A SET DEFINITION, ANYWAY.
HUH?
HMMM.

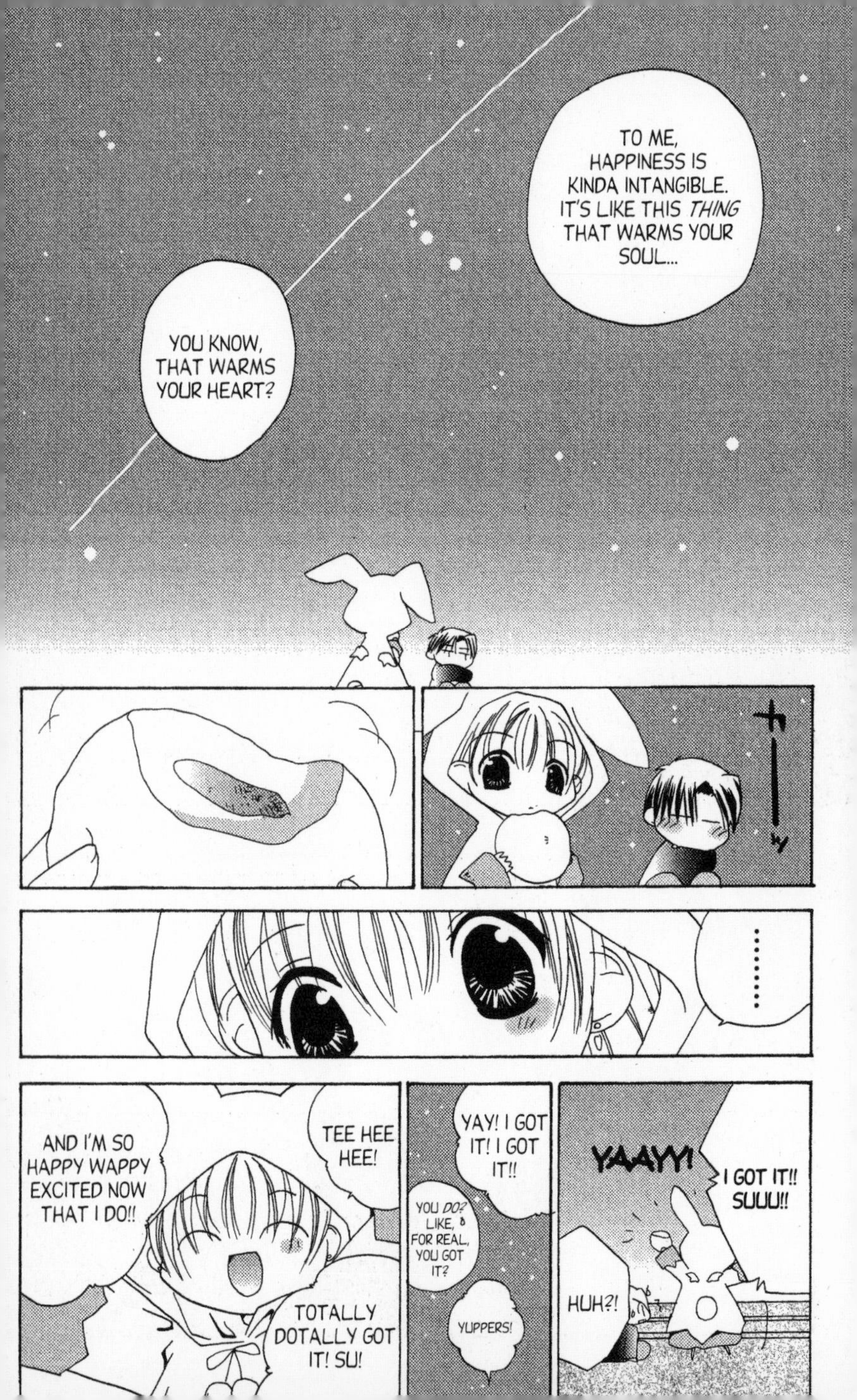
TO ME, HAPPINESS IS KINDA INTANGIBLE. IT'S LIKE THIS *THING* THAT WARMS YOUR SOUL...
YOU KNOW, THAT WARMS YOUR HEART?
....
YAAYY!
I GOT IT!! SUUU!!
HUH?!
YAY! I GOT IT! I GOT IT!!
YOU *DO?* LIKE, FOR REAL, YOU GOT IT?
YUPPERS!
TEE HEE HEE!
AND I'M SO HAPPY WAPPY EXCITED NOW THAT I DO!!
TOTALLY DOTALLY GOT IT! SU!

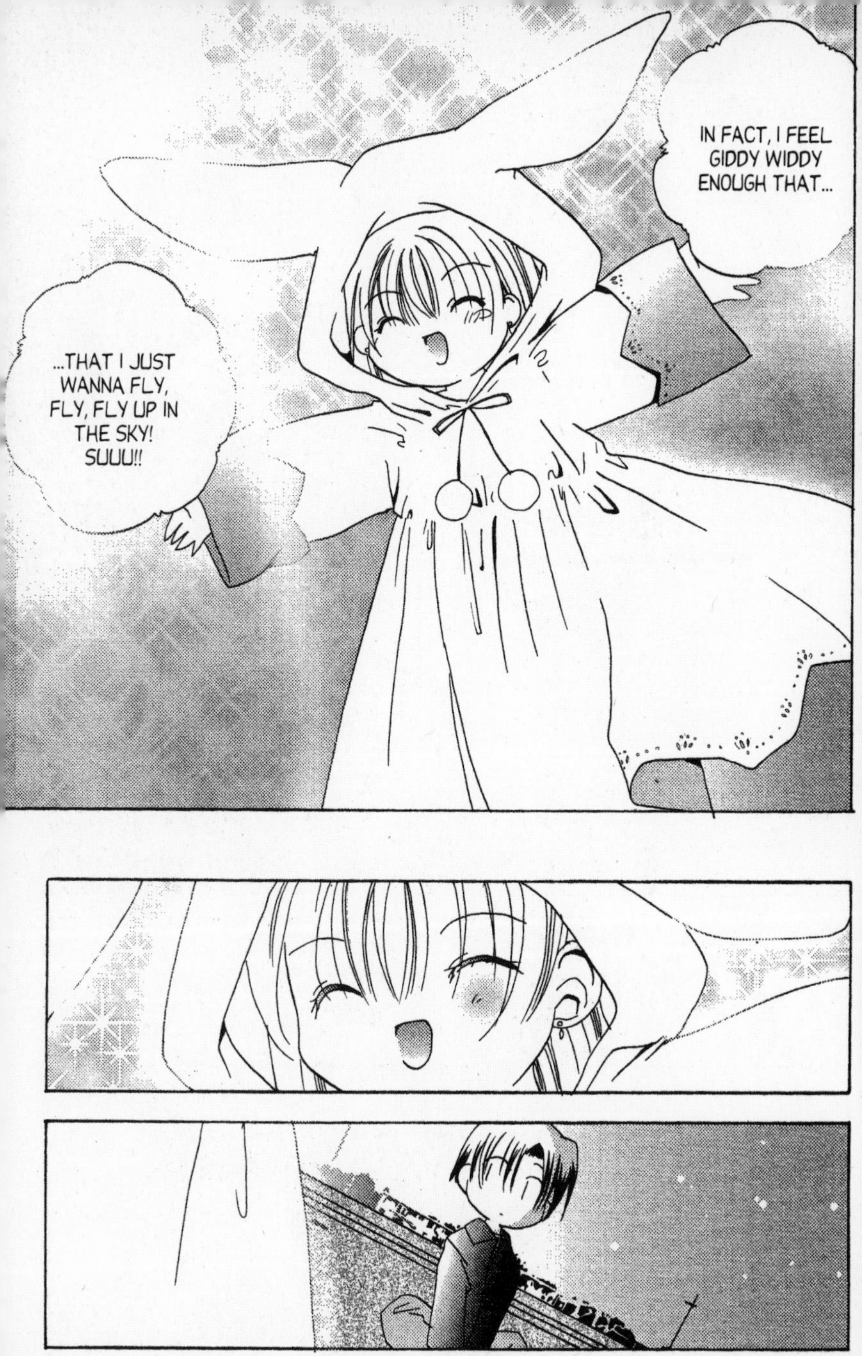
IN FACT, I FEEL GIDDY WIDDY ENOUGH THAT...
...THAT I JUST WANNA FLY, FLY, FLY UP IN THE SKY! SUUU!!

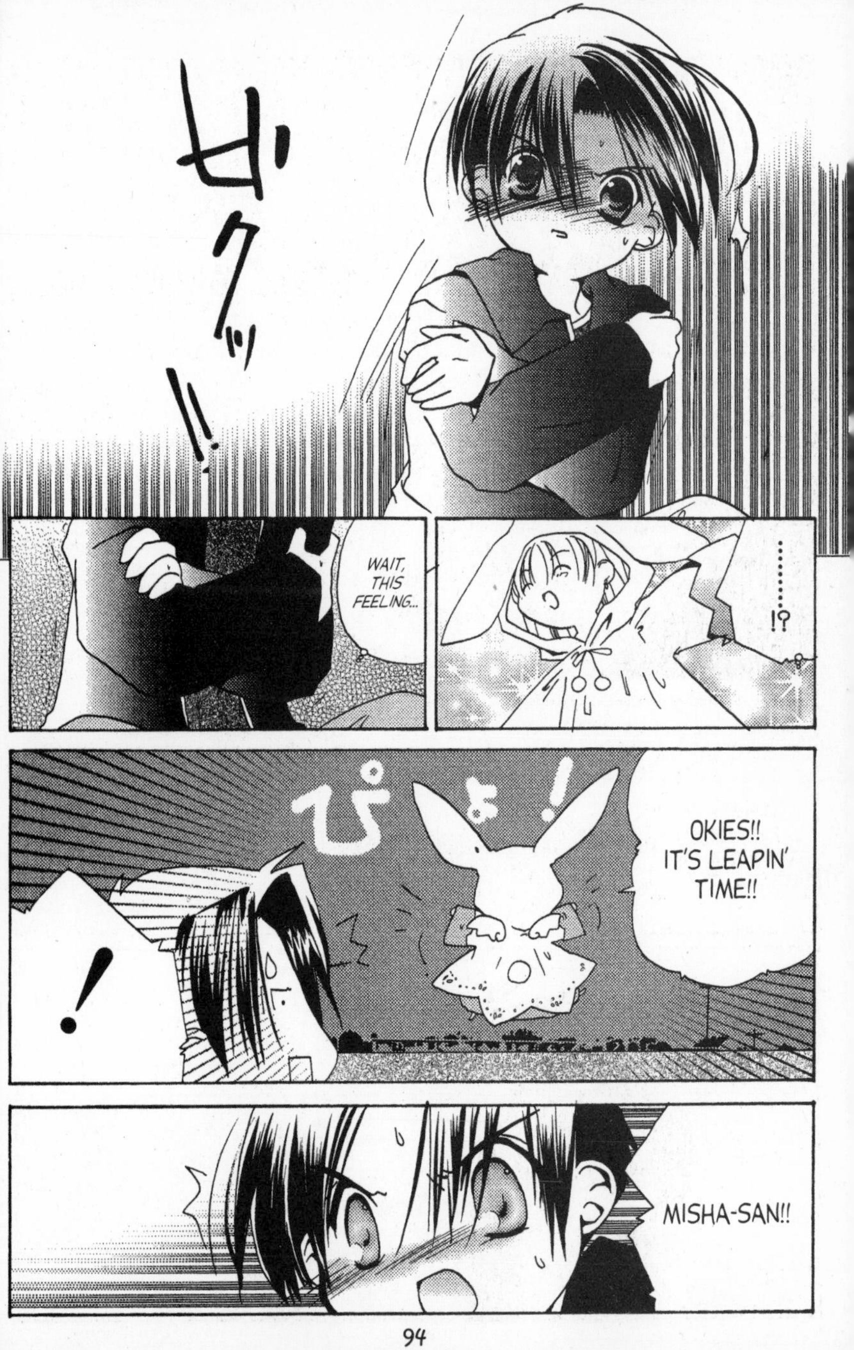
ビクッ!!
......!?
WAIT, THIS FEELING...
OKIES!! IT'S LEAPIN' TIME!!
ぴょ!
!
MISHA-SAN!!

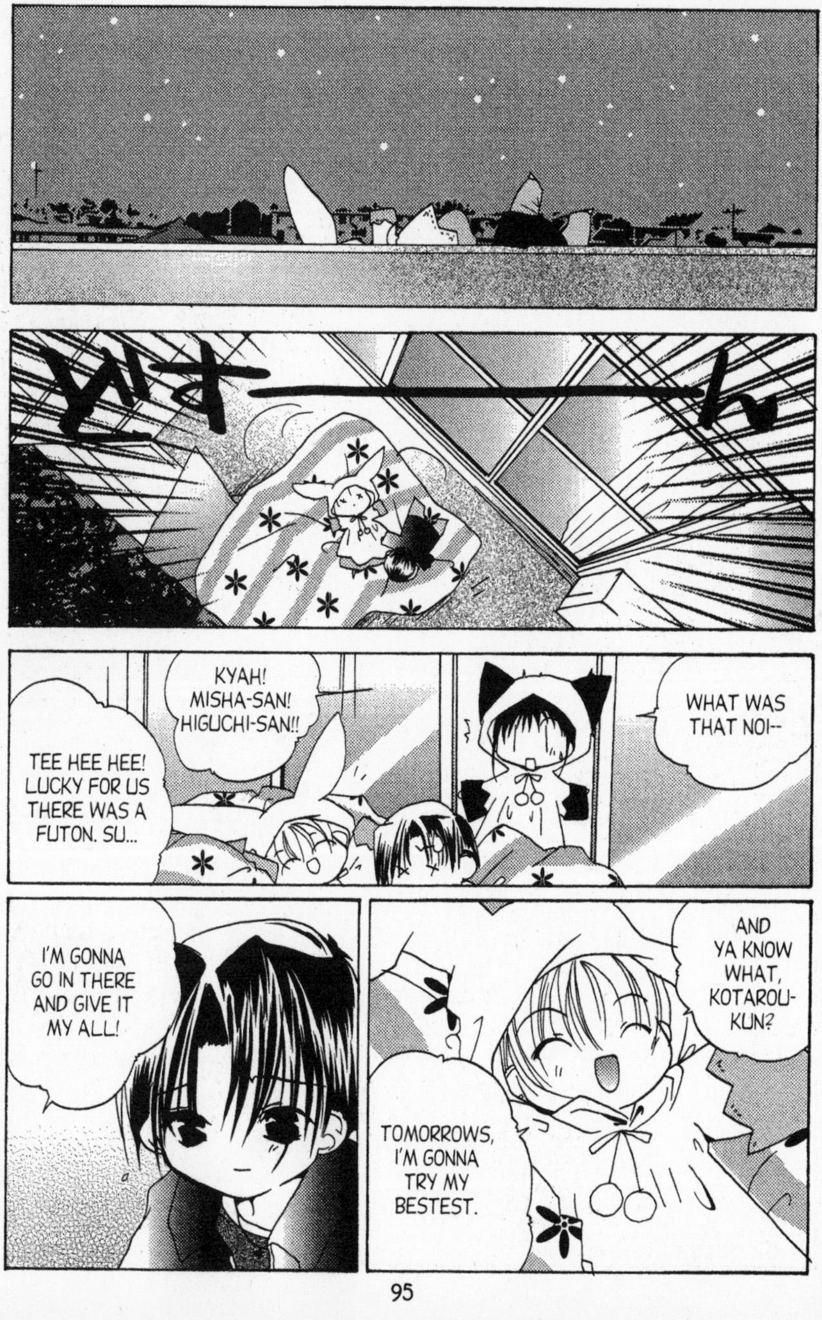
WHAT WAS THAT NOI--
KYAH! MISHA-SAN! HIGUCHI-SAN!!
TEE HEE HEE! LUCKY FOR US THERE WAS A FUTON. SU...
AND YA KNOW WHAT, KOTAROU-KUN?
TOMORROWS, I'M GONNA TRY MY BESTEST.
I'M GONNA GO IN THERE AND GIVE IT MY ALL!

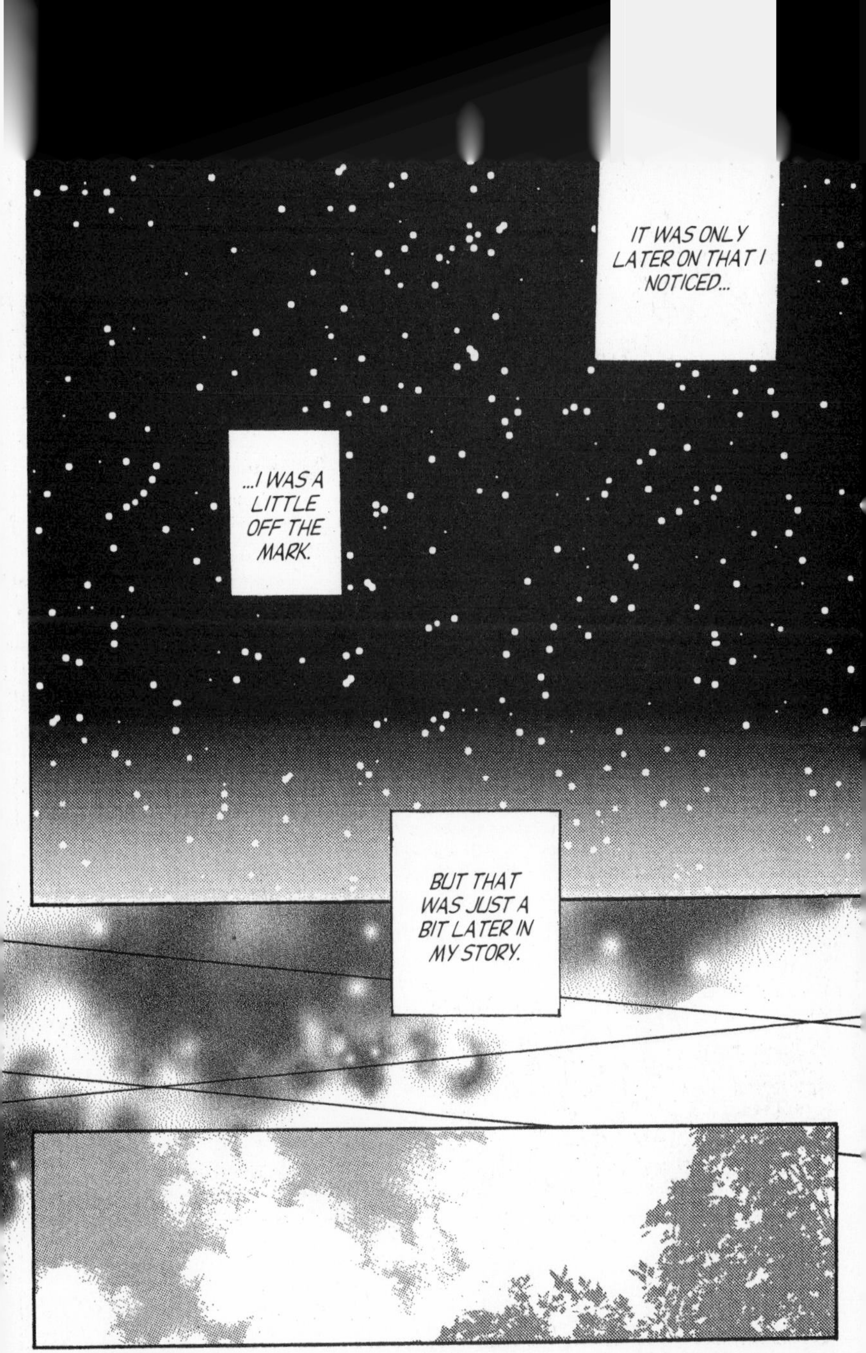
IT WAS ONLY LATER ON THAT I NOTICED...
...I WAS A LITTLE OFF THE MARK.
BUT THAT WAS JUST A BIT LATER IN MY STORY.

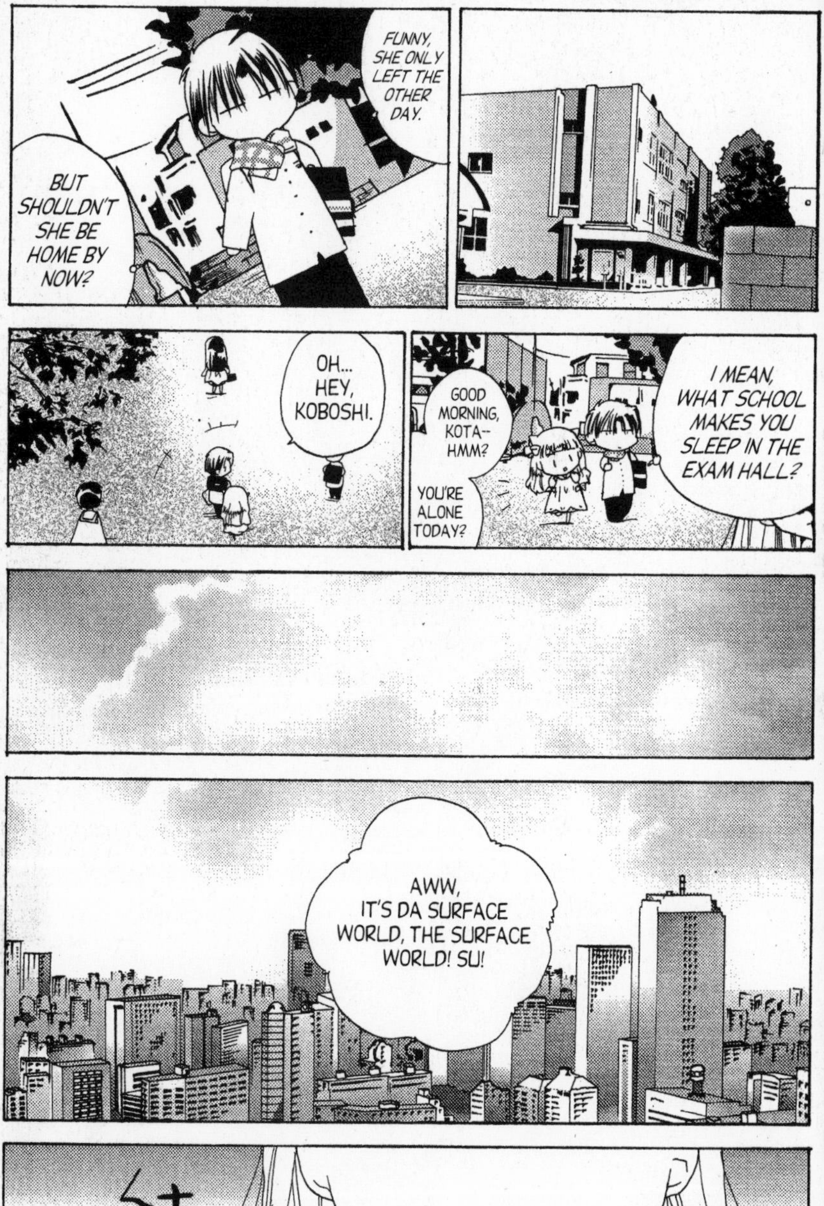
FUNNY, SHE ONLY LEFT THE OTHER DAY.
BUT SHOULDN'T SHE BE HOME BY NOW?
I MEAN, WHAT SCHOOL MAKES YOU SLEEP IN THE EXAM HALL?
GOOD MORNING, KOTA-- HMM?
YOU'RE ALONE TODAY?
OH... HEY, KOBOSHI.
AWW, IT'S DA SURFACE WORLD, THE SURFACE WORLD! SU!

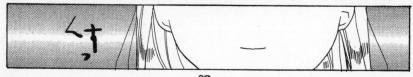

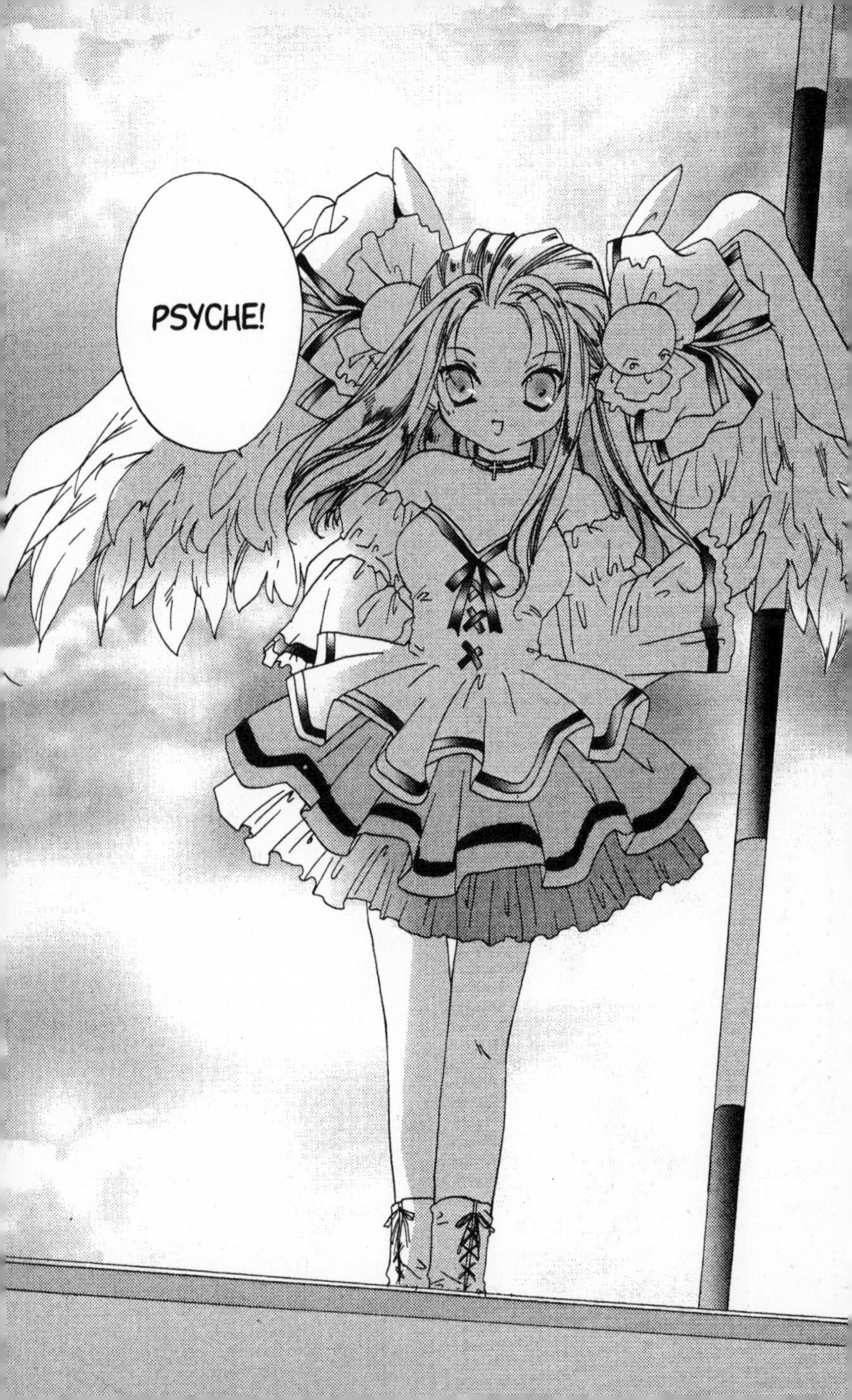
PSYCHE!

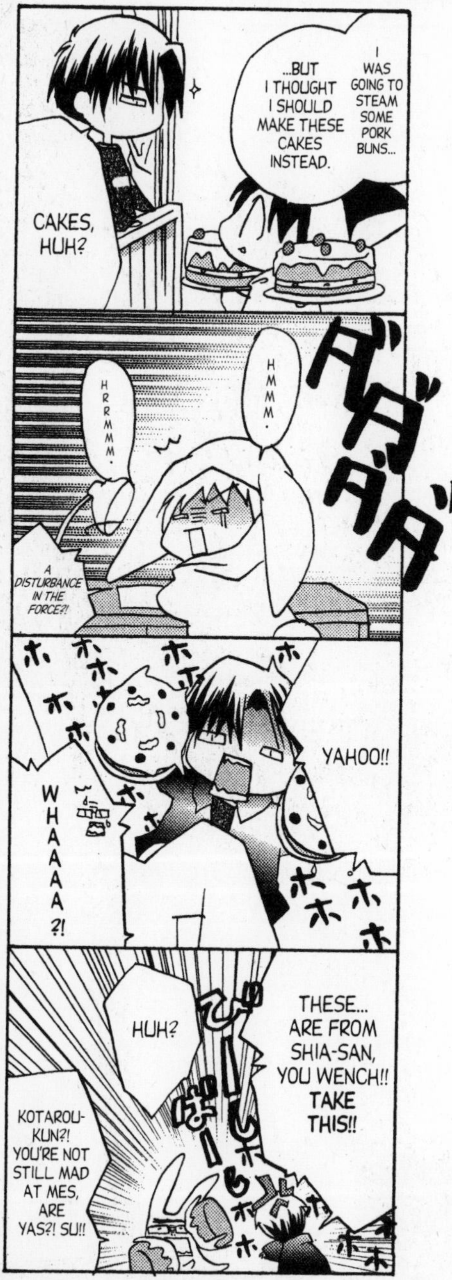
I WAS GOING TO STEAM SOME PORK BUNS...
...BUT I THOUGHT I SHOULD MAKE THESE CAKES INSTEAD.
CAKES, HUH?
ダダダダ
HMMM.
HRRMMM.
A DISTURBANCE IN THE FORCE?!
YAHOO!!
WHAAAAA?!
THESE... ARE FROM SHIA-SAN, YOU WENCH!! TAKE THIS!!
HUH?
KOTAROU-KUN?! YOU'RE NOT STILL MAD AT MES, ARE YAS?! SU!!

Lesson 19 How to Enjoy the World Below: Part 1

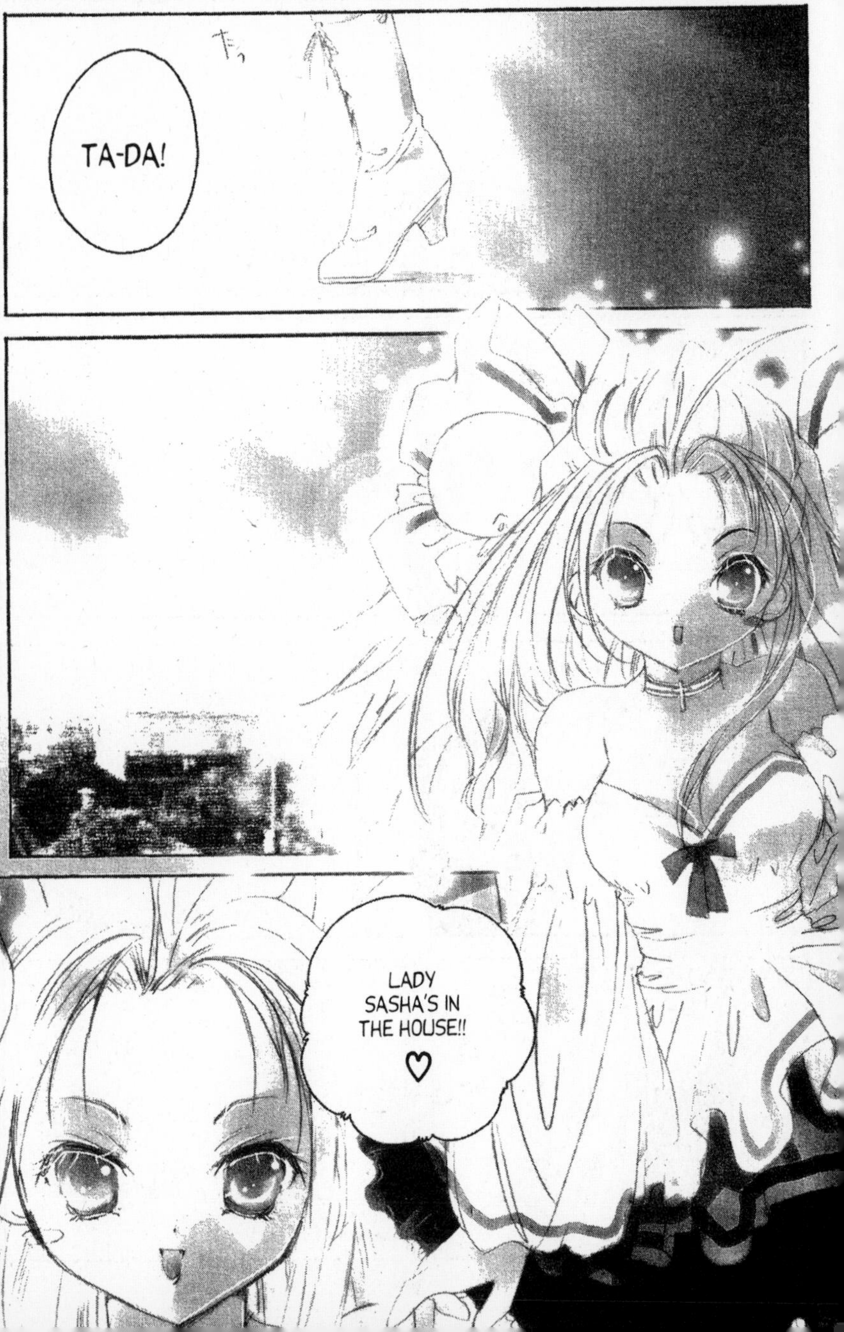
TA-DA!
LADY SASHA'S IN THE HOUSE!! ♡

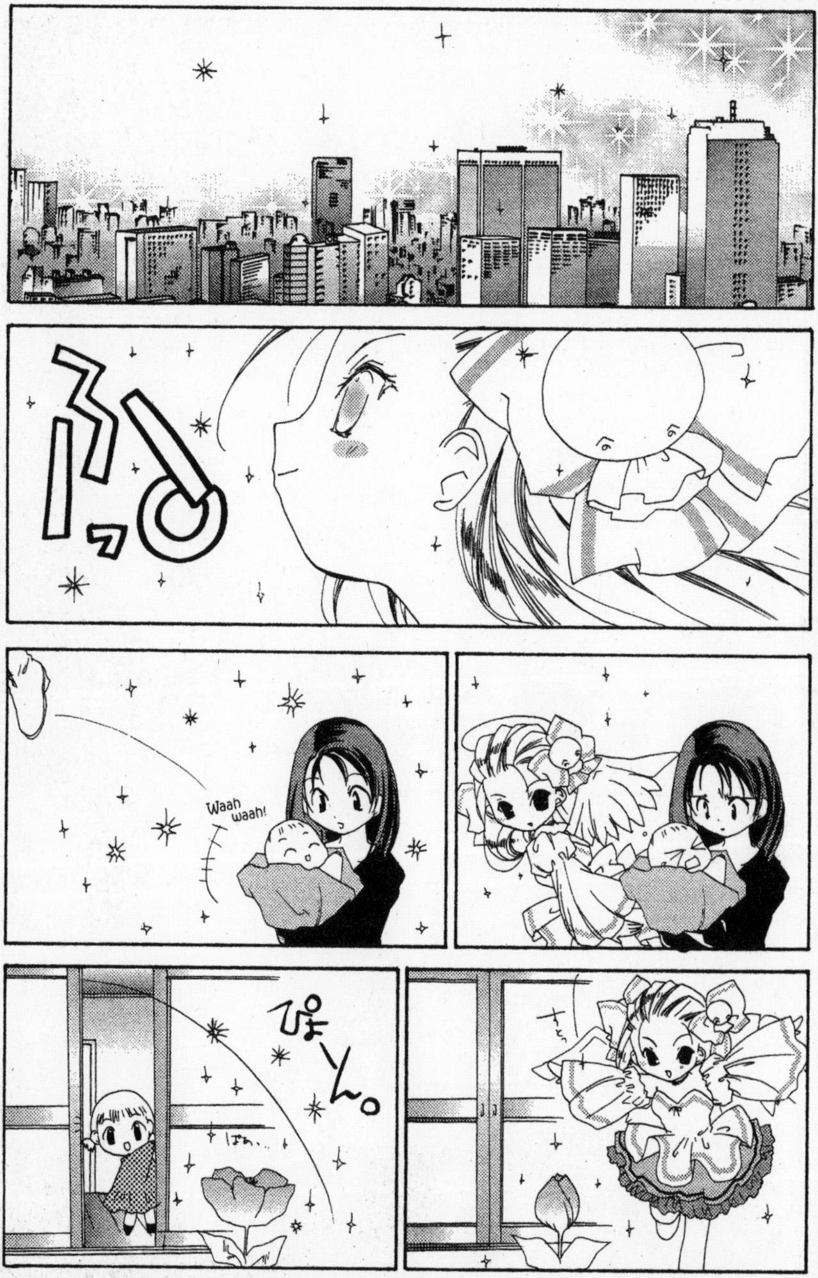
ふっ
Waah waah!
すとっ
ぴょ〜ん。
ぱぁ…

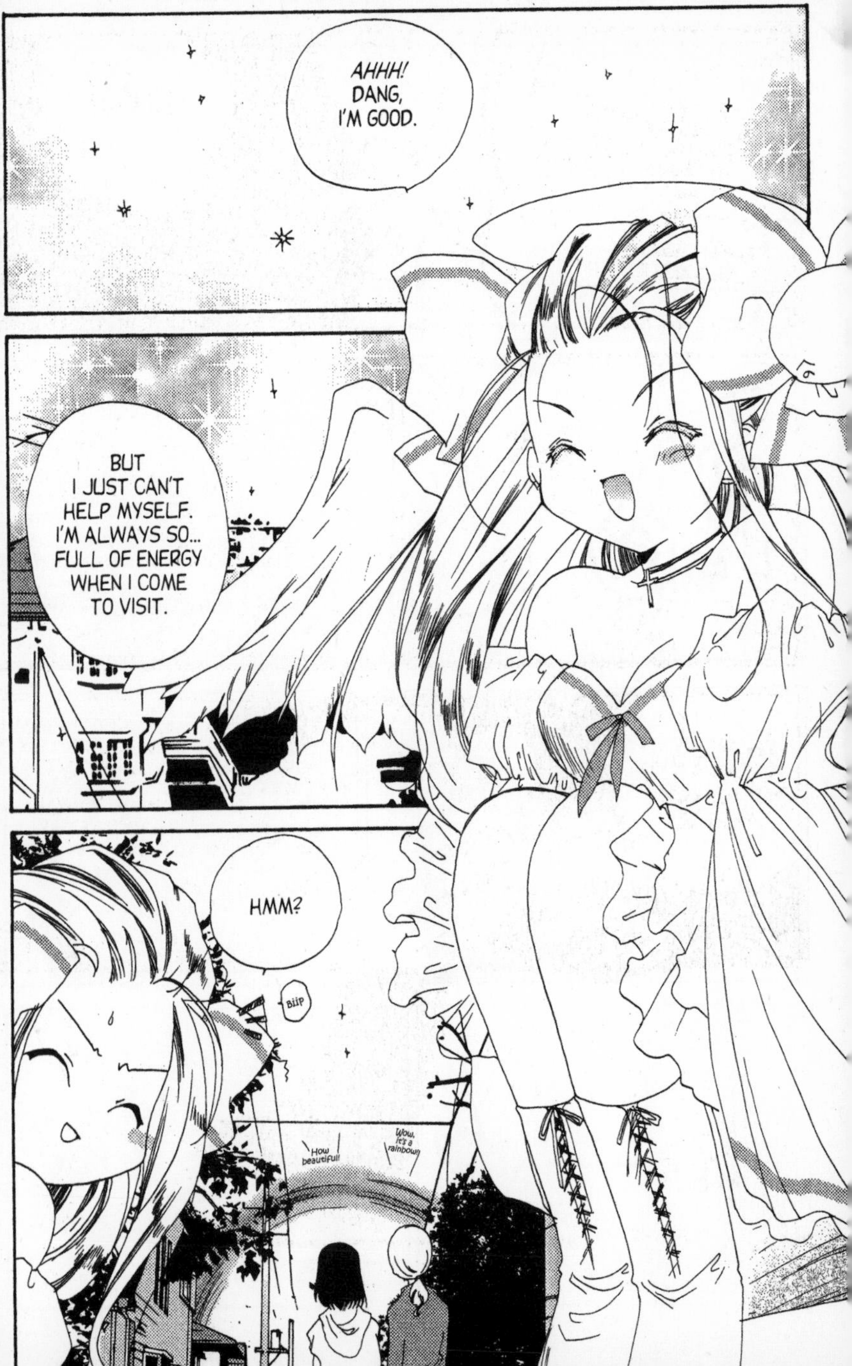
AHHH! DANG, I'M GOOD.
BUT I JUST CAN'T HELP MYSELF. I'M ALWAYS SO... FULL OF ENERGY WHEN I COME TO VISIT.
HMM?
Biip
Wow, it's a rainbow!
How beautiful!

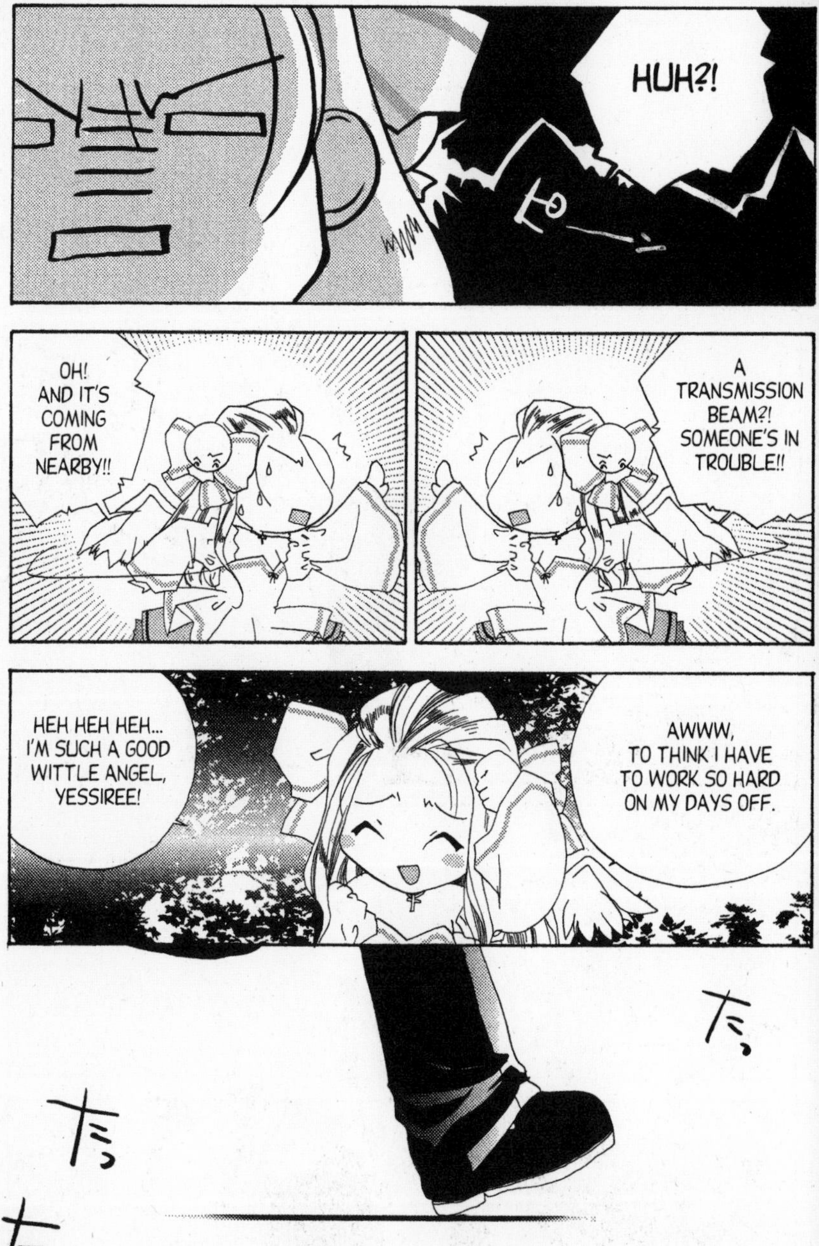
HUH?!
A TRANSMISSION BEAM?! SOMEONE'S IN TROUBLE!!
OH! AND IT'S COMING FROM NEARBY!!
AWWW, TO THINK I HAVE TO WORK SO HARD ON MY DAYS OFF.
HEH HEH HEH... I'M SUCH A GOOD WITTLE ANGEL, YESSIREE!
たっ
たっ
たっ

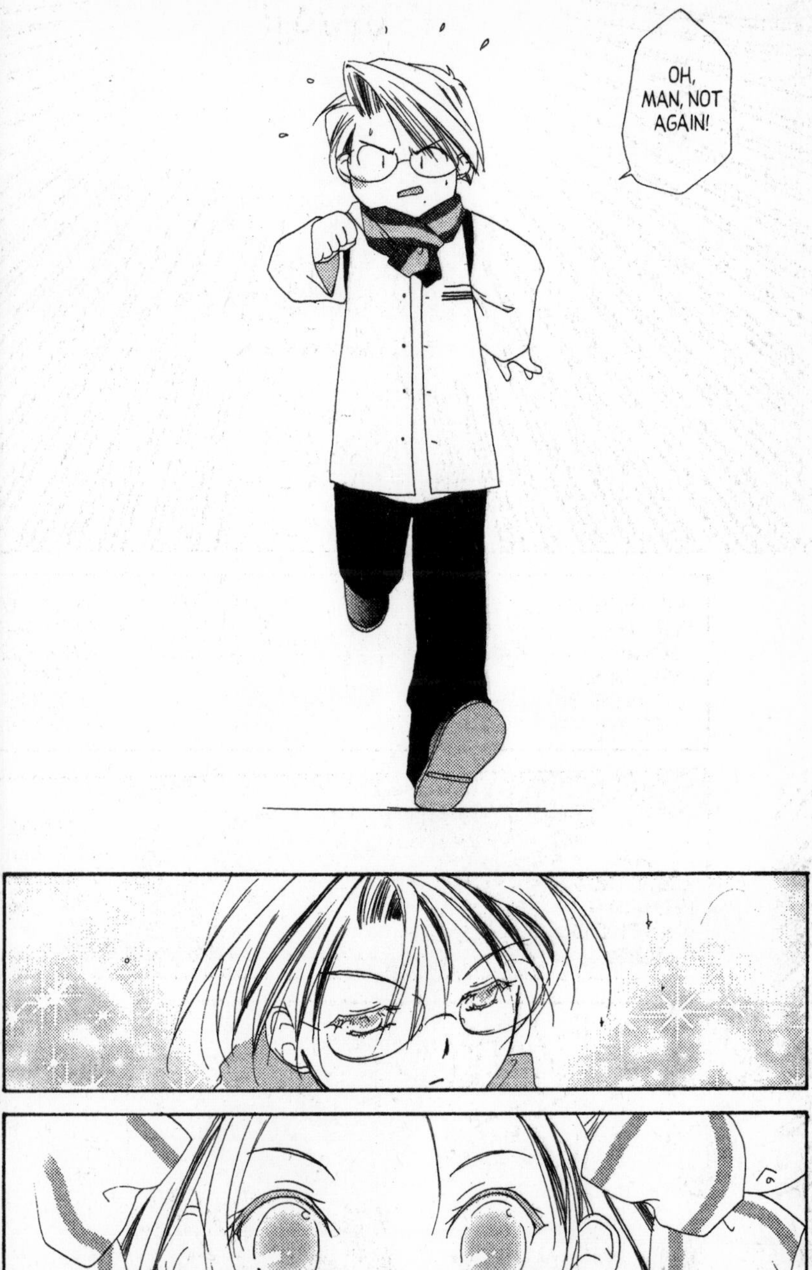
OH, MAN, NOT AGAIN!

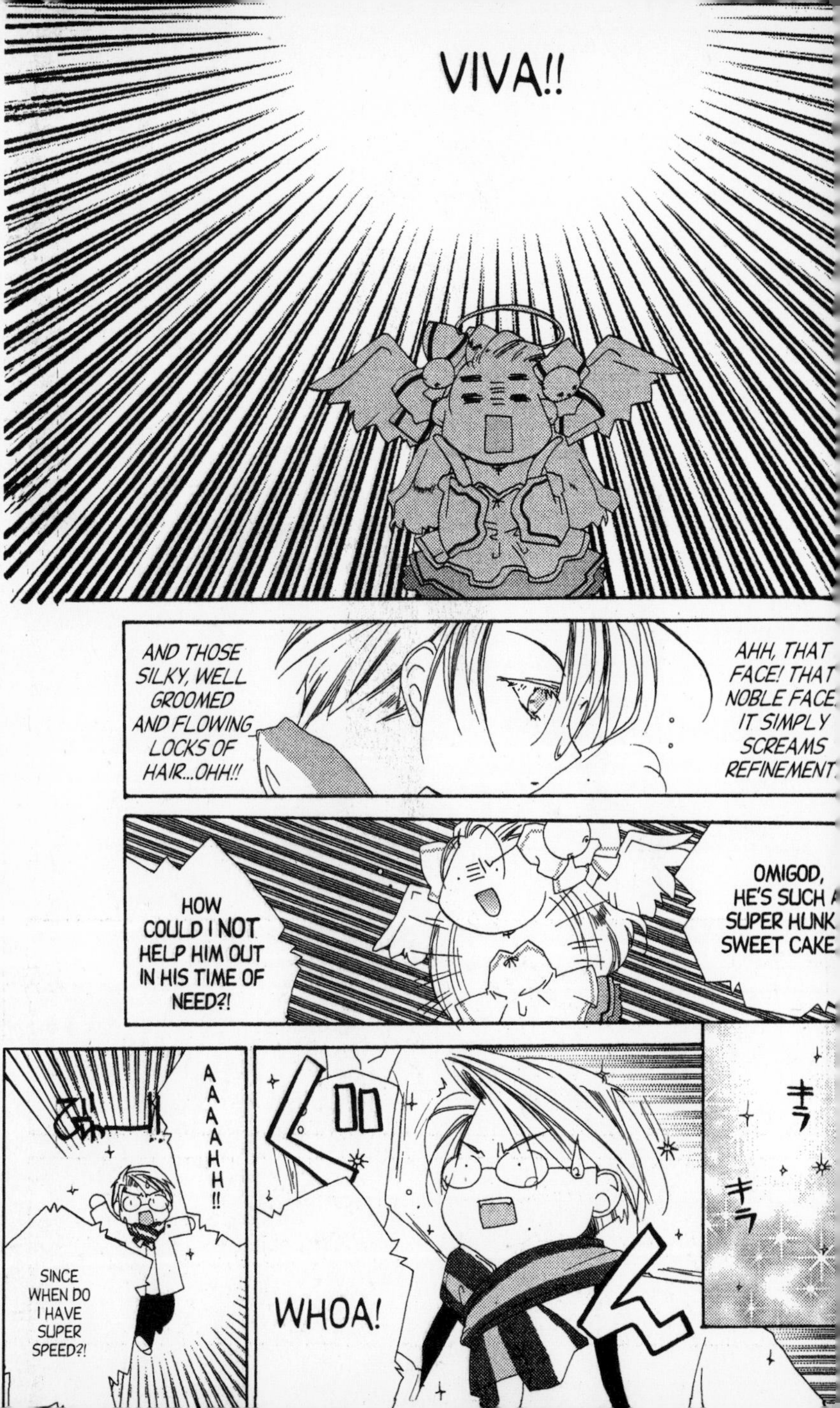
VIVA!!
AHH, THAT FACE! THAT NOBLE FACE. IT SIMPLY SCREAMS REFINEMENT.
AND THOSE SILKY, WELL GROOMED AND FLOWING LOCKS OF HAIR...OHH!!
OMIGOD, HE'S SUCH A SUPER HUNK SWEET CAKE
HOW COULD I NOT HELP HIM OUT IN HIS TIME OF NEED?!
キラ
キラ
WHOA!
AAAAAHH!!
SINCE WHEN DO I HAVE SUPER SPEED?!

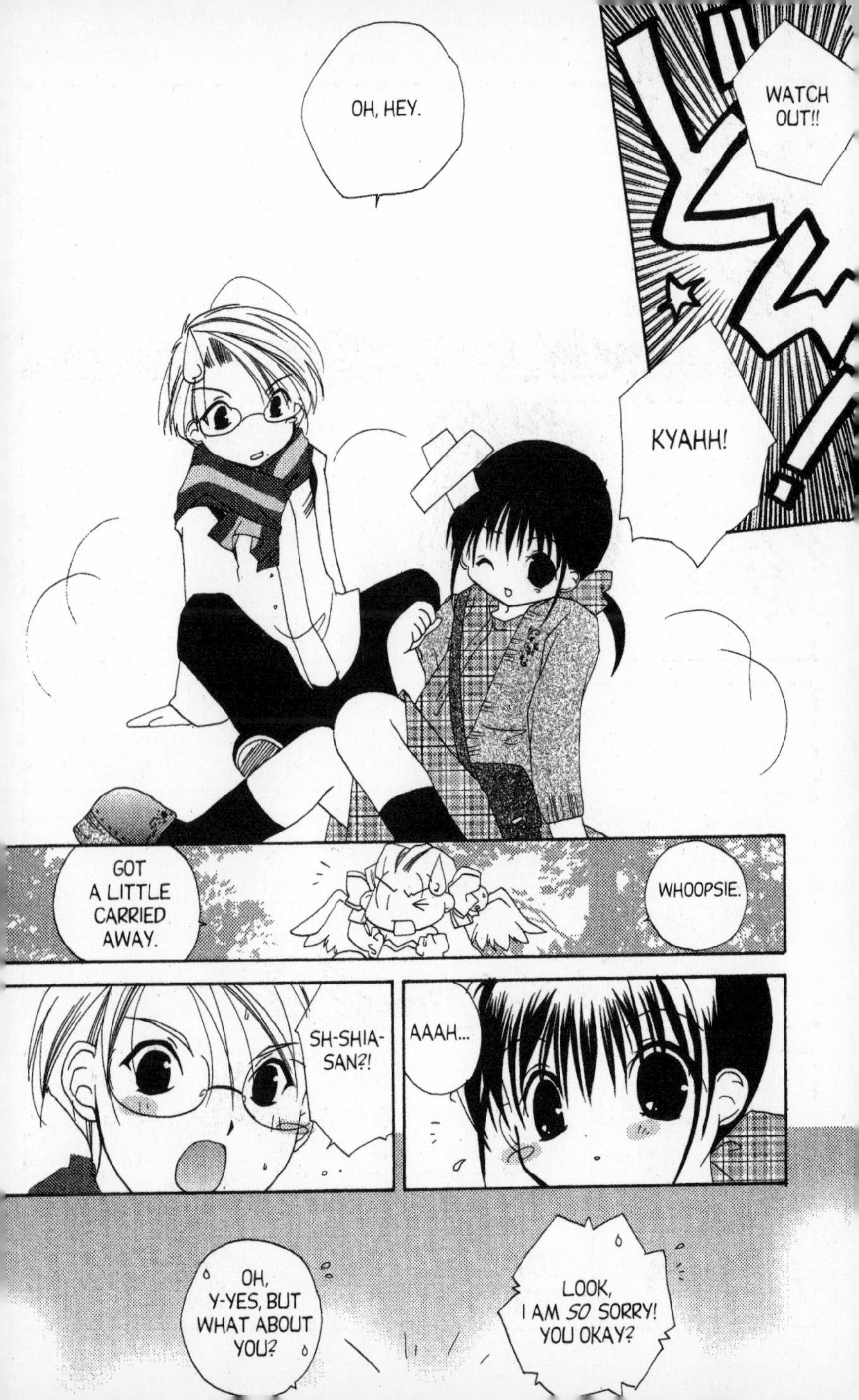
WATCH OUT!!
KYAHH!
OH, HEY.
WHOOPSIE.
GOT A LITTLE CARRIED AWAY.
AAAH...
SH-SHIA-SAN?!
LOOK, I AM *SO* SORRY! YOU OKAY?
OH, Y-YES, BUT WHAT ABOUT YOU?

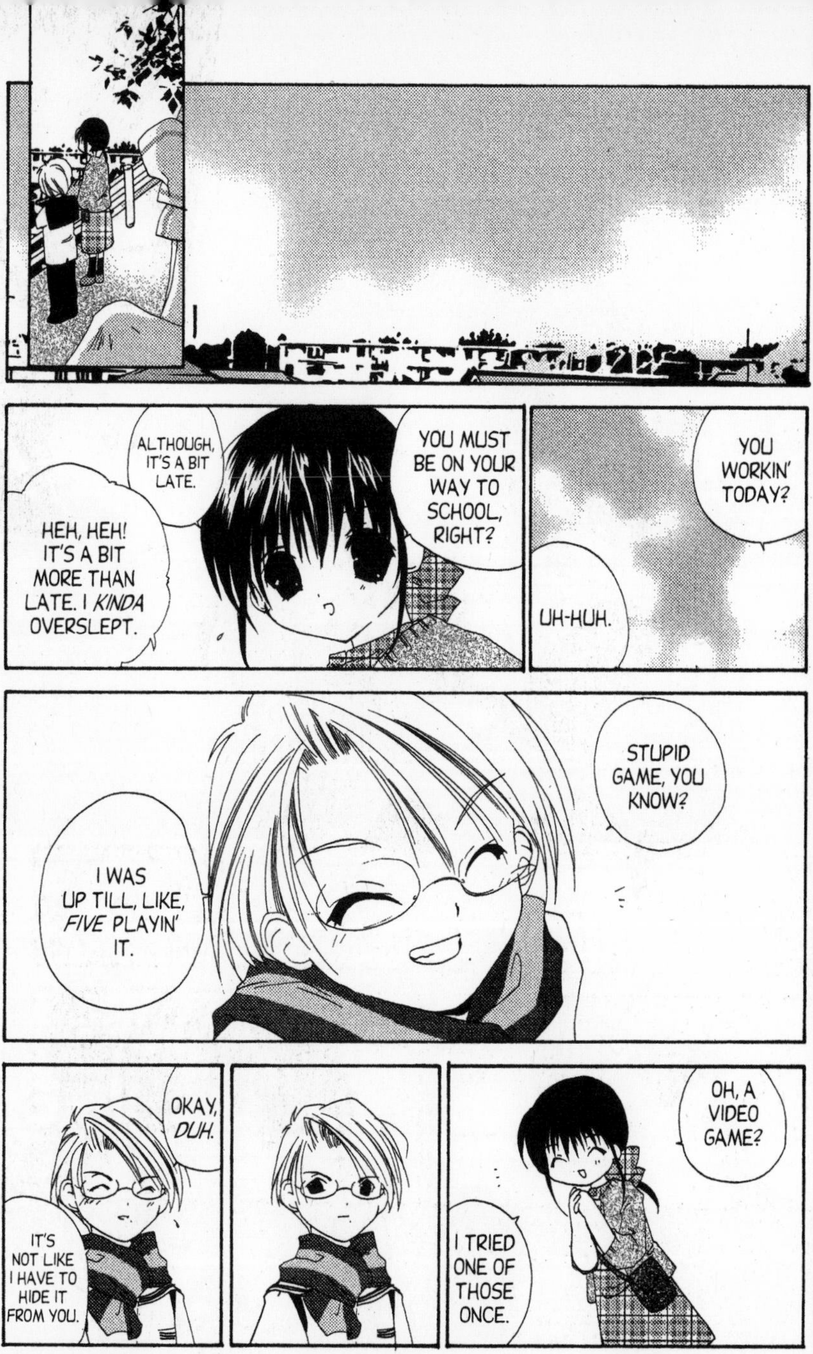
YOU WORKIN' TODAY?
UH-HUH.
YOU MUST BE ON YOUR WAY TO SCHOOL, RIGHT?
ALTHOUGH, IT'S A BIT LATE.
HEH, HEH! IT'S A BIT MORE THAN LATE. I *KINDA* OVERSLEPT.
STUPID GAME, YOU KNOW?
I WAS UP TILL, LIKE, *FIVE* PLAYIN' IT.
OH, A VIDEO GAME?
I TRIED ONE OF THOSE ONCE.
OKAY, *DUH*.
IT'S NOT LIKE I HAVE TO HIDE IT FROM YOU.

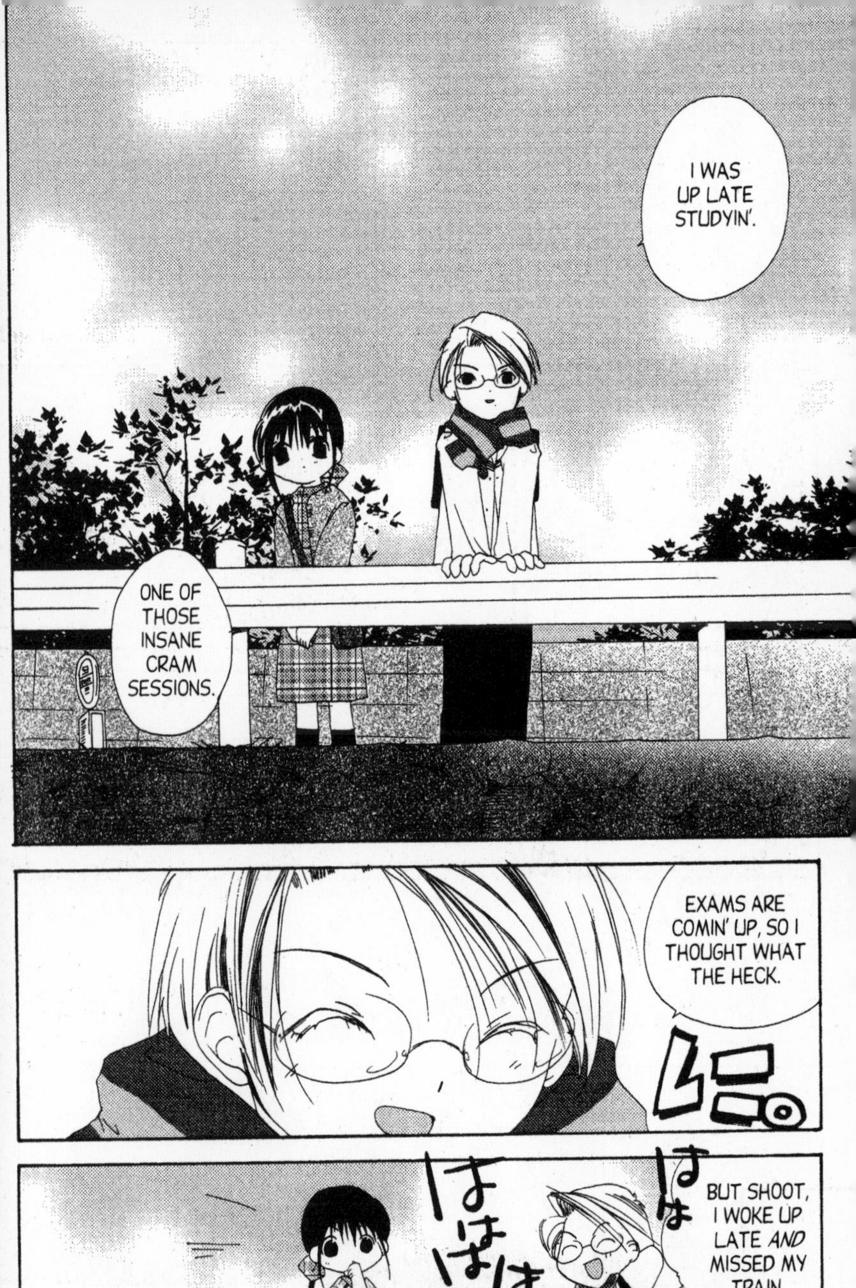
I WAS UP LATE STUDYIN'.
ONE OF THOSE INSANE CRAM SESSIONS.
EXAMS ARE COMIN' UP, SO I THOUGHT WHAT THE HECK.
BUT SHOOT, I WOKE UP LATE *AND* MISSED MY TRAIN.

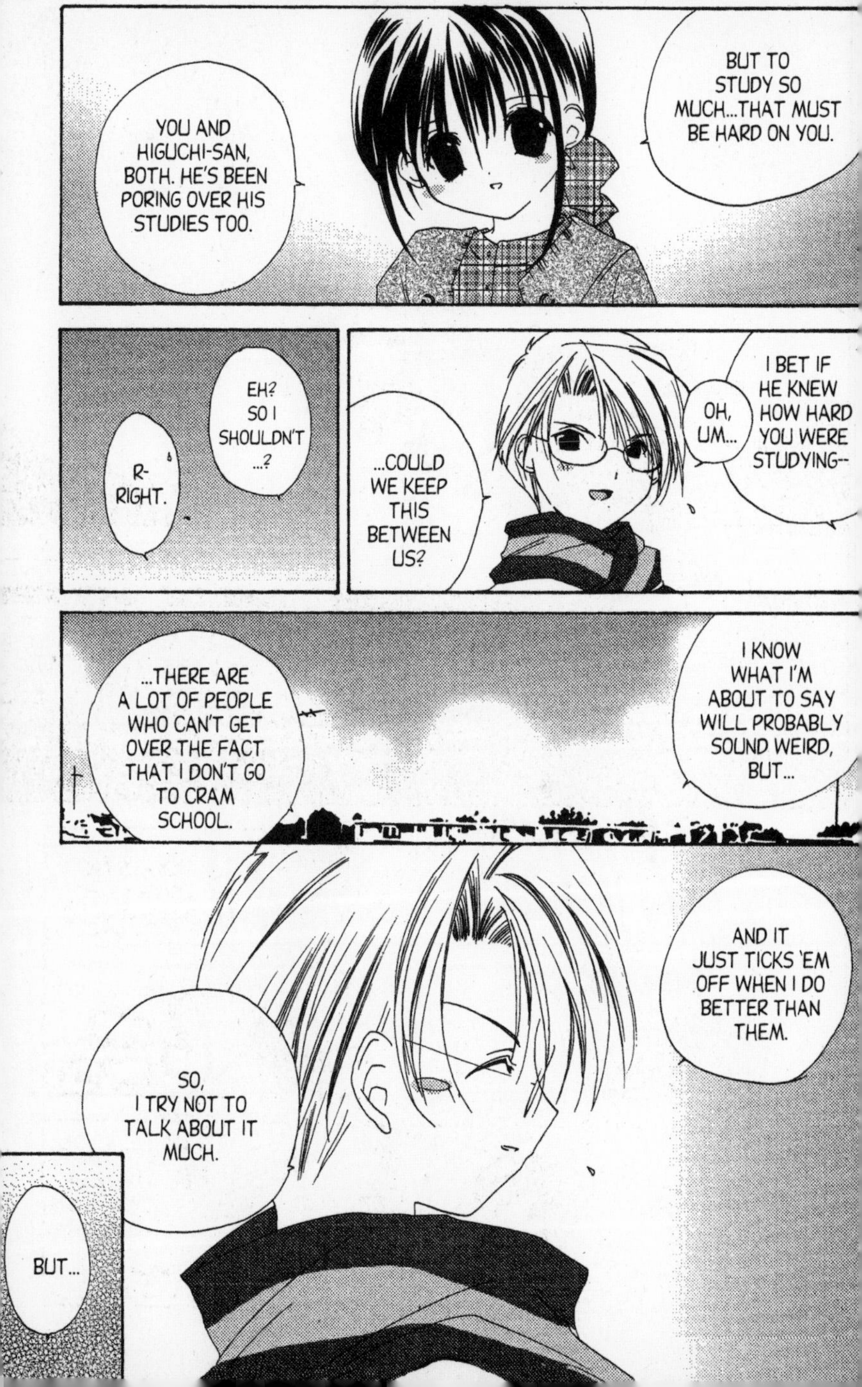
BUT TO STUDY SO MUCH...THAT MUST BE HARD ON YOU.
YOU AND HIGUCHI-SAN, BOTH. HE'S BEEN PORING OVER HIS STUDIES TOO.
I BET IF HE KNEW HOW HARD YOU WERE STUDYING--
OH, UM...
...COULD WE KEEP THIS BETWEEN US?
EH? SO I SHOULDN'T ...?
R-RIGHT.
I KNOW WHAT I'M ABOUT TO SAY WILL PROBABLY SOUND WEIRD, BUT...
...THERE ARE A LOT OF PEOPLE WHO CAN'T GET OVER THE FACT THAT I DON'T GO TO CRAM SCHOOL.
AND IT JUST TICKS 'EM OFF WHEN I DO BETTER THAN THEM.
SO, I TRY NOT TO TALK ABOUT IT MUCH.
BUT...

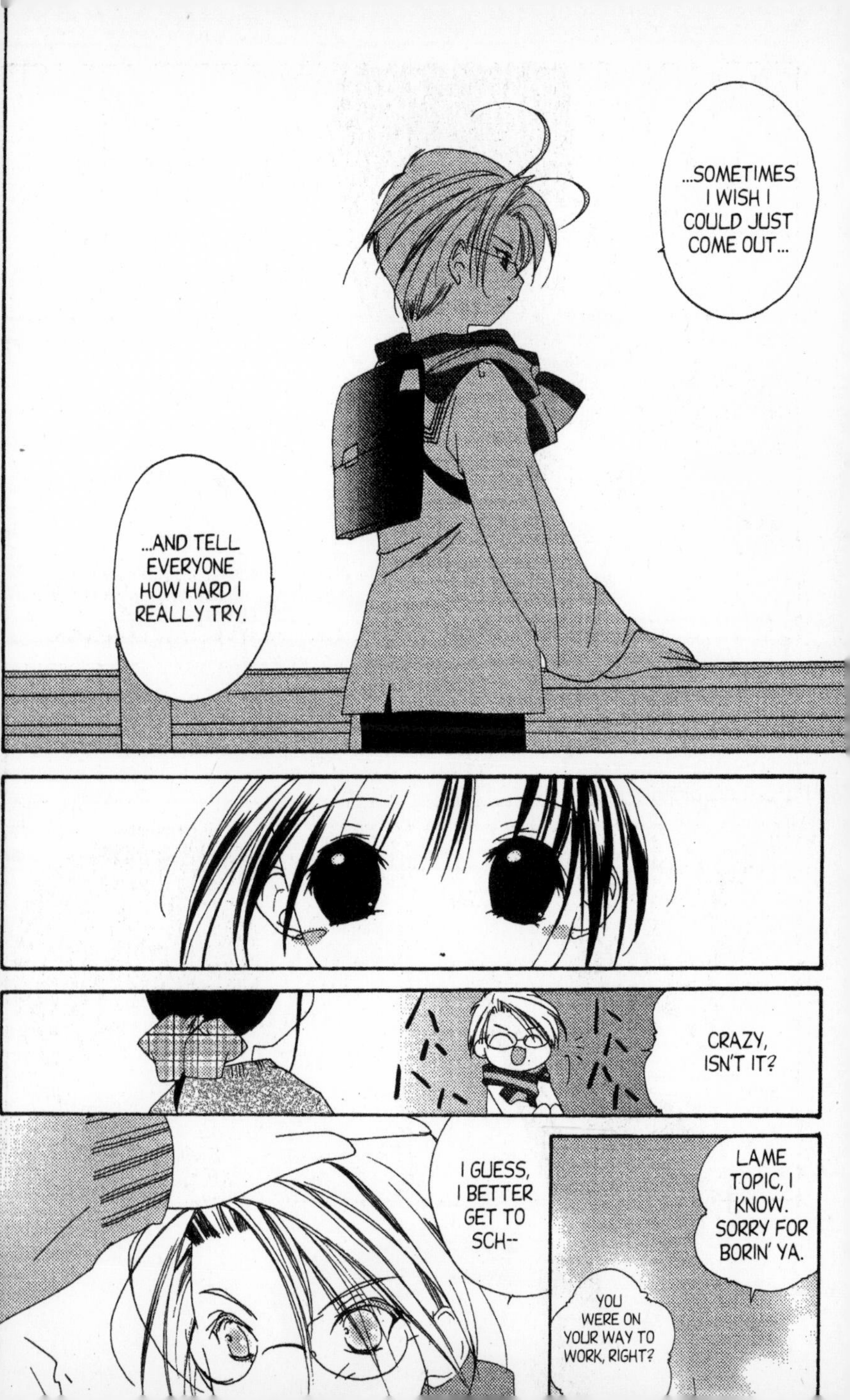
...SOMETIMES I WISH I COULD JUST COME OUT...
...AND TELL EVERYONE HOW HARD I REALLY TRY.
CRAZY, ISN'T IT?
LAME TOPIC, I KNOW. SORRY FOR BORIN' YA.
YOU WERE ON YOUR WAY TO WORK, RIGHT?
I GUESS, I BETTER GET TO SCH--

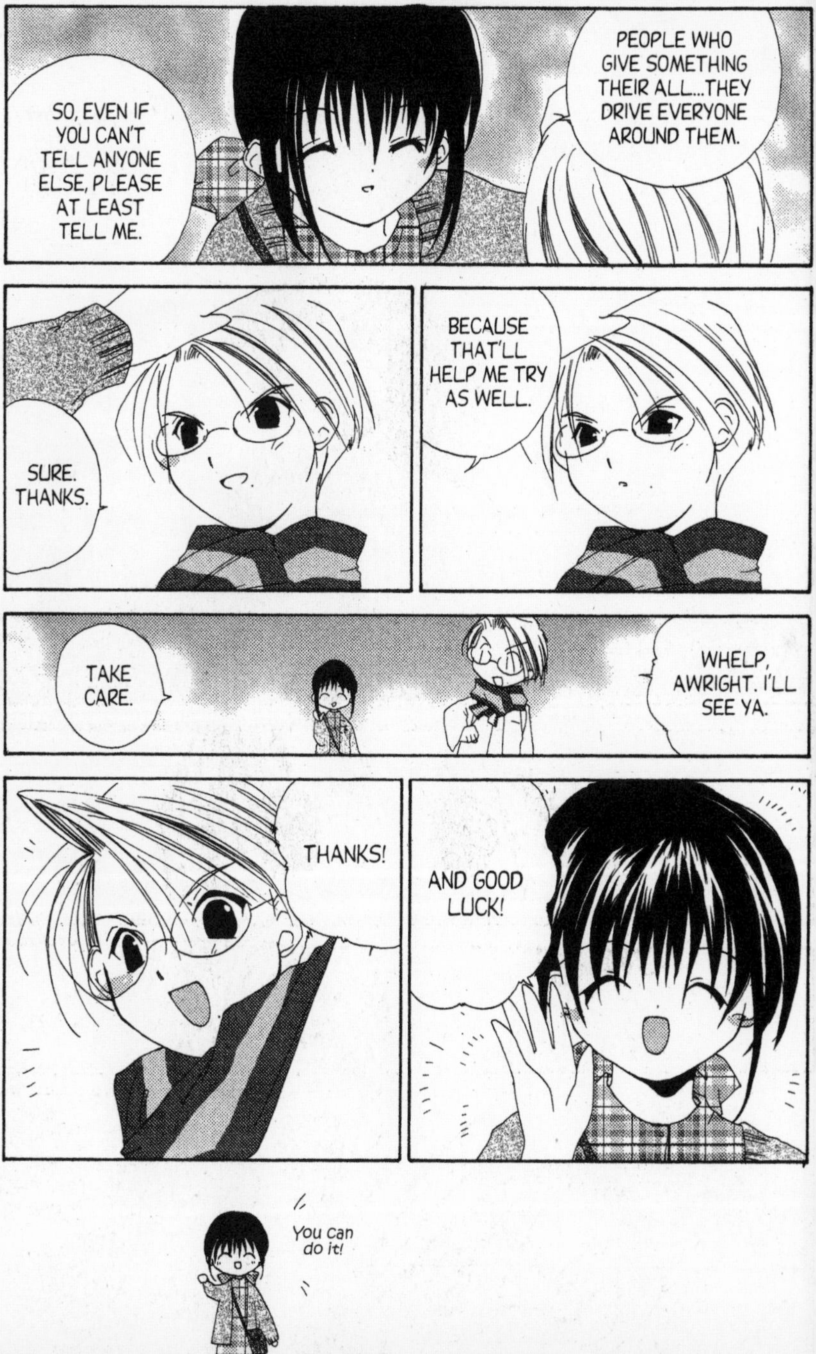
PEOPLE WHO GIVE SOMETHING THEIR ALL...THEY DRIVE EVERYONE AROUND THEM.
SO, EVEN IF YOU CAN'T TELL ANYONE ELSE, PLEASE AT LEAST TELL ME.
BECAUSE THAT'LL HELP ME TRY AS WELL.
SURE. THANKS.
WHELP, AWRIGHT. I'LL SEE YA.
TAKE CARE.
AND GOOD LUCK!
THANKS!
You can do it!

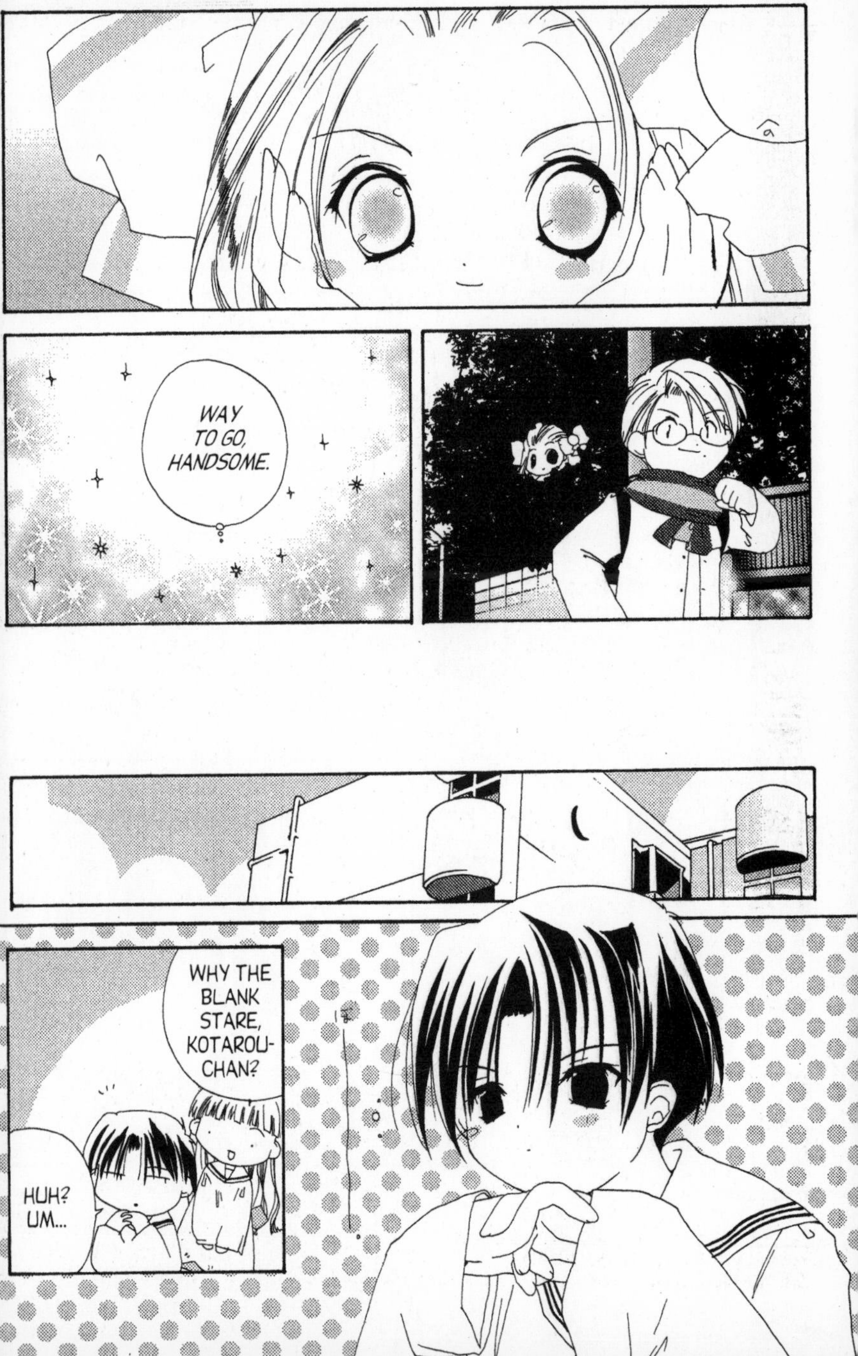
WAY TO GO, HANDSOME.
WHY THE BLANK STARE, KOTAROU-CHAN?
HUH? UM...

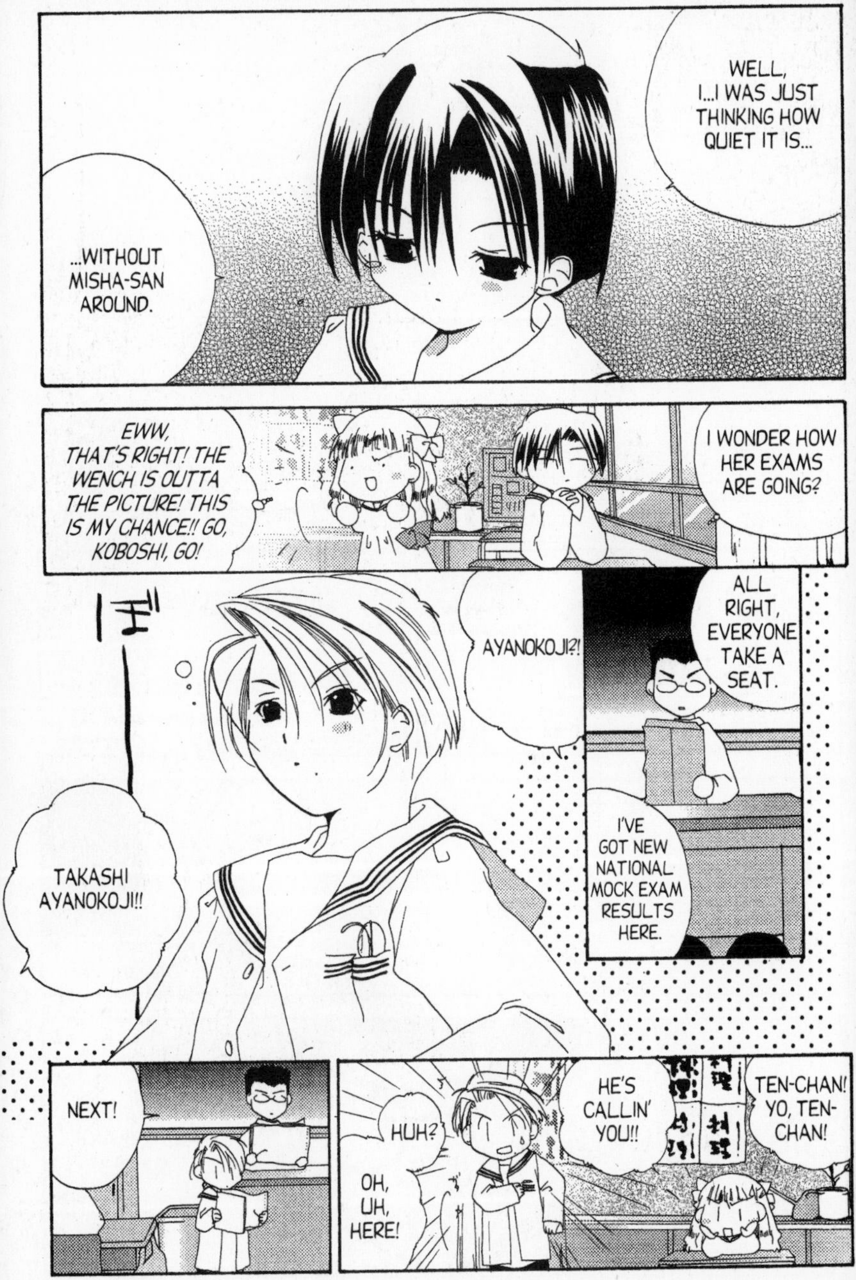
WELL, I...I WAS JUST THINKING HOW QUIET IT IS...
...WITHOUT MISHA-SAN AROUND.
I WONDER HOW HER EXAMS ARE GOING?
EWW, THAT'S RIGHT! THE WENCH IS OUTTA THE PICTURE! THIS IS MY CHANCE!! GO, KOBOSHI, GO!
ALL RIGHT, EVERYONE TAKE A SEAT.
I'VE GOT NEW NATIONAL MOCK EXAM RESULTS HERE.
AYANOKOJI?!
ぼー
TAKASHI AYANOKOJI!!
TEN-CHAN! YO, TEN-CHAN!
HE'S CALLIN' YOU!!
HUH?
OH, UH, HERE!
NEXT!

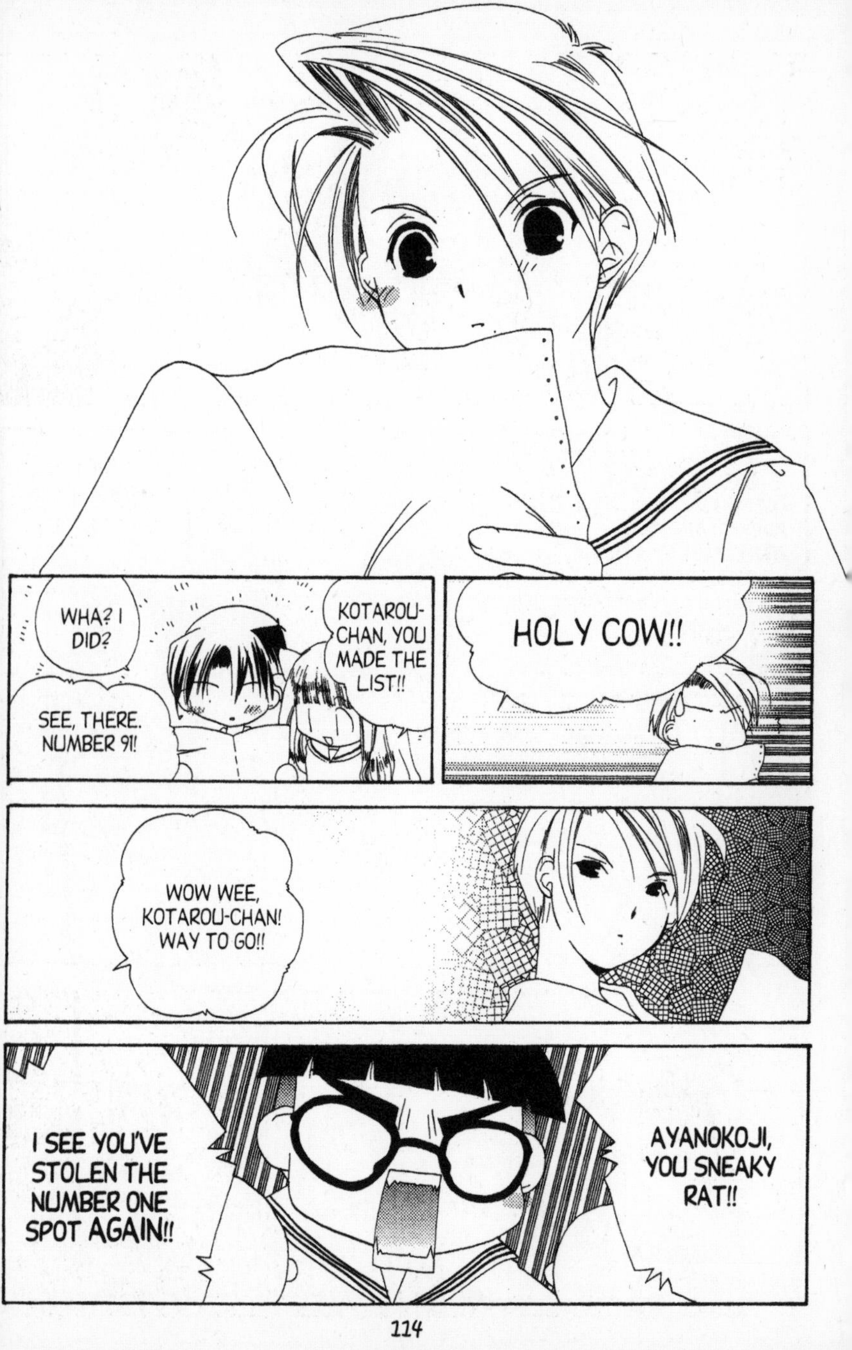
HOLY COW!!
KOTAROU-CHAN, YOU MADE THE LIST!!
WHA? I DID?
SEE, THERE. NUMBER 91!
WOW WEE, KOTAROU-CHAN! WAY TO GO!!
AYANOKOJI, YOU SNEAKY RAT!!
I SEE YOU'VE STOLEN THE NUMBER ONE SPOT AGAIN!!

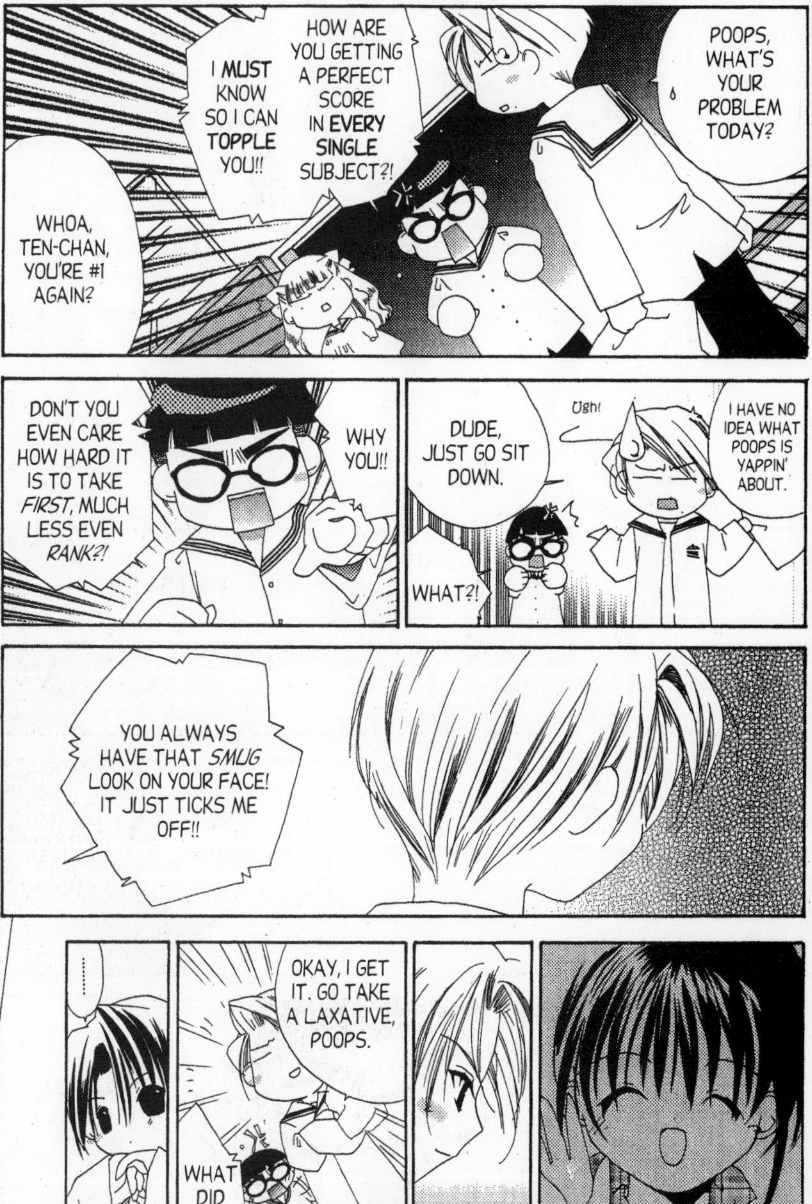
POOPS, WHAT'S YOUR PROBLEM TODAY?
HOW ARE YOU GETTING A PERFECT SCORE IN EVERY SINGLE SUBJECT?!
I MUST KNOW SO I CAN TOPPLE YOU!!
WHOA, TEN-CHAN, YOU'RE #1 AGAIN?
I HAVE NO IDEA WHAT POOPS IS YAPPIN' ABOUT.
Ugh!
DUDE, JUST GO SIT DOWN.
WHAT?!
WHY YOU!!
DON'T YOU EVEN CARE HOW HARD IT IS TO TAKE FIRST, MUCH LESS EVEN RANK?!
YOU ALWAYS HAVE THAT SMUG LOOK ON YOUR FACE! IT JUST TICKS ME OFF!!
OKAY, I GET IT. GO TAKE A LAXATIVE, POOPS.
WHAT DID YOU SAY?!
....

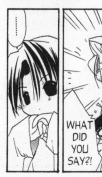

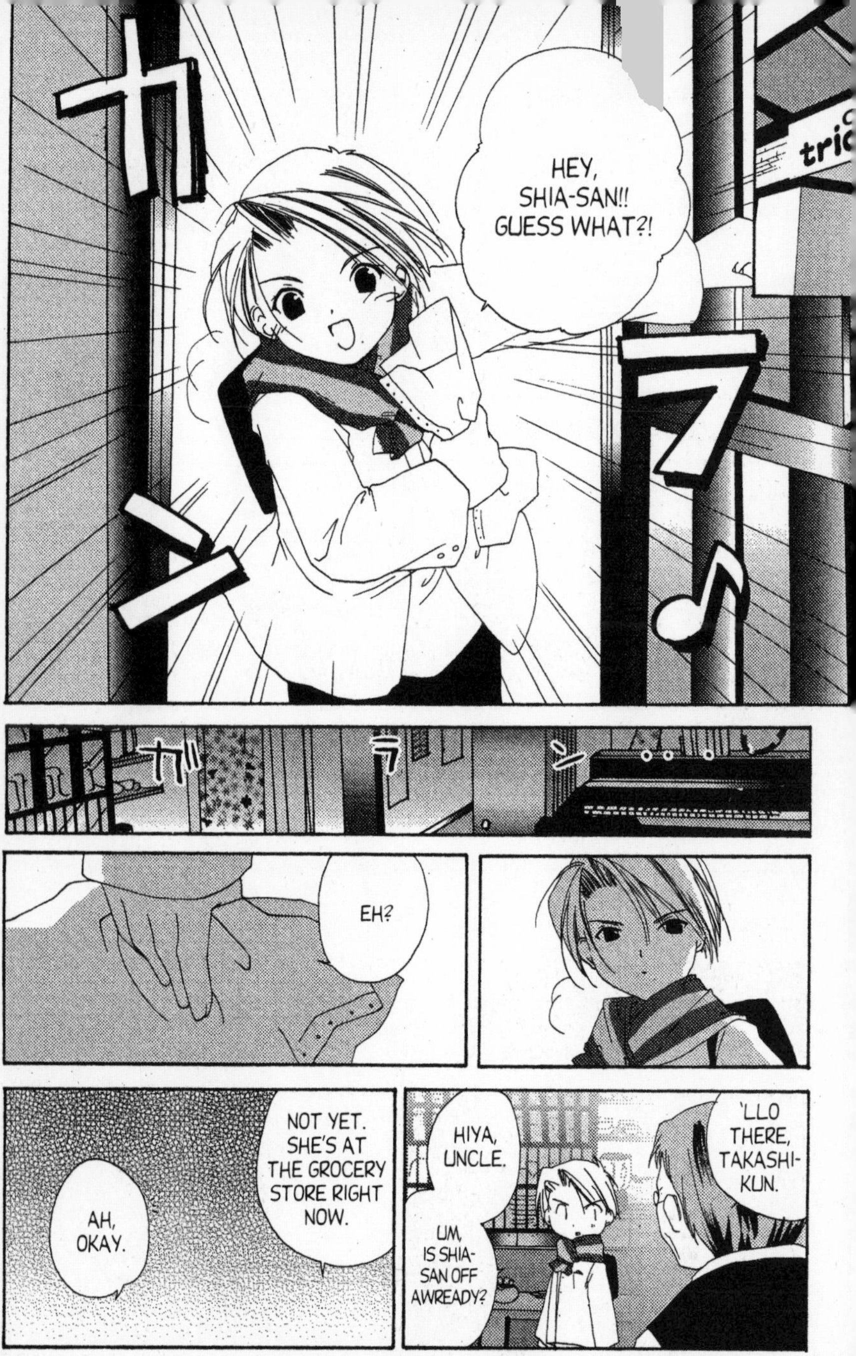
HEY, SHIA-SAN!! GUESS WHAT?!
カラン♪
EH?
'LLO THERE, TAKASHI-KUN.
HIYA, UNCLE.
UM, IS SHIA-SAN OFF AWREADY?
NOT YET. SHE'S AT THE GROCERY STORE RIGHT NOW.
AH, OKAY.

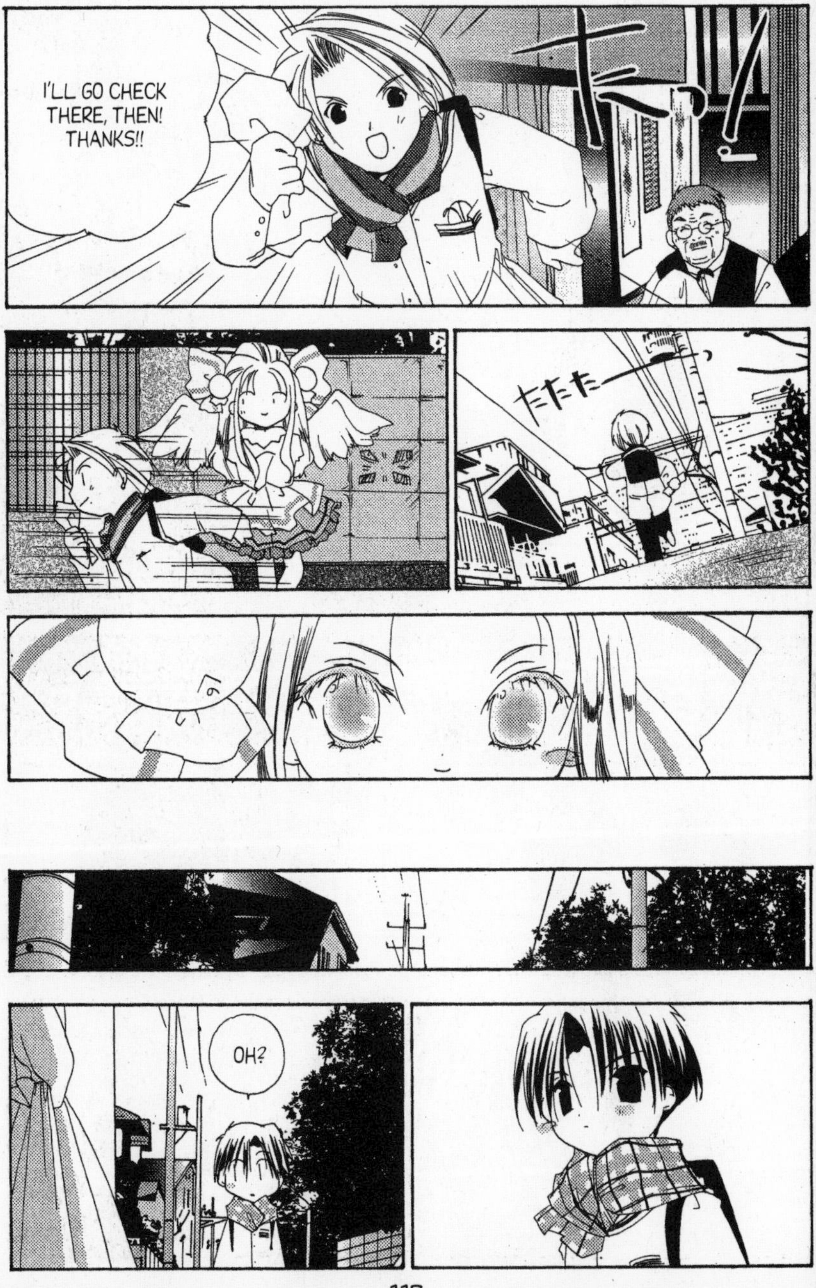
I'LL GO CHECK THERE, THEN! THANKS!!
たたた―
OH?

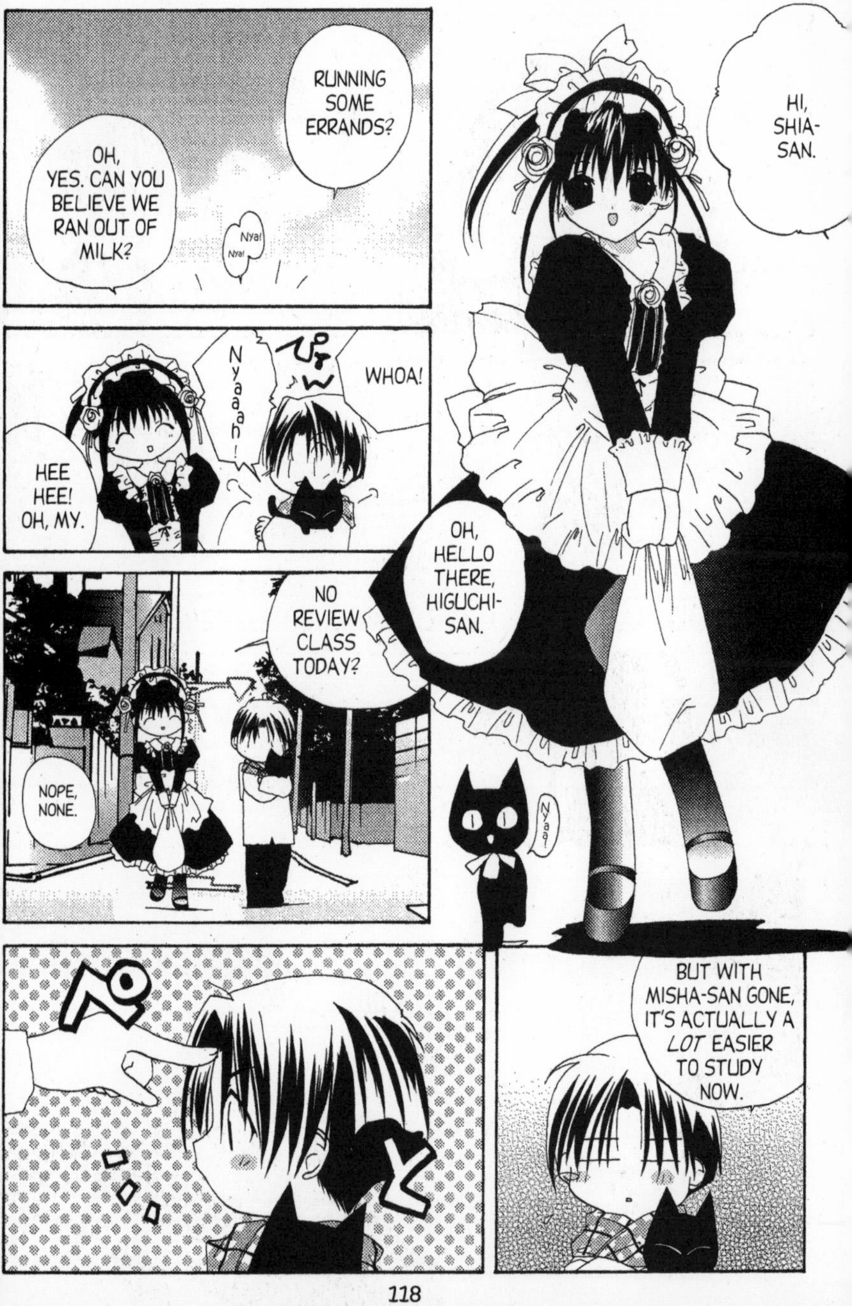
HI, SHIA-SAN.
OH, HELLO THERE, HIGUCHI-SAN.
Nyaa!
RUNNING SOME ERRANDS?
OH, YES. CAN YOU BELIEVE WE RAN OUT OF MILK?
Nya! Nya!
WHOA!
Nyaaaah!
HEE HEE! OH, MY.
NO REVIEW CLASS TODAY?
NOPE, NONE.
BUT WITH MISHA-SAN GONE, IT'S ACTUALLY A *LOT* EASIER TO STUDY NOW.

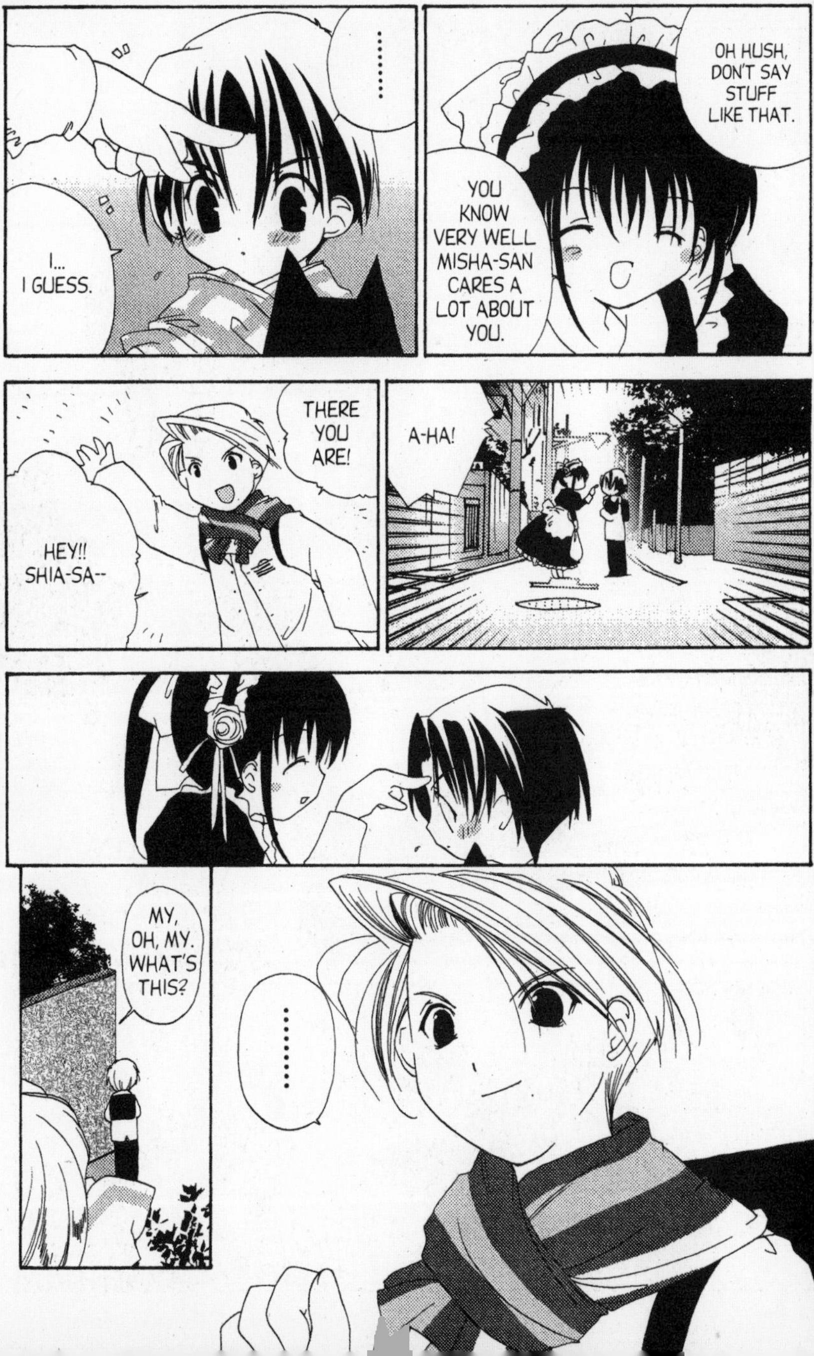
OH HUSH, DON'T SAY STUFF LIKE THAT.
YOU KNOW VERY WELL MISHA-SAN CARES A LOT ABOUT YOU.
......
I... I GUESS.
A-HA!
THERE YOU ARE!
HEY!! SHIA-SA--
......
MY, OH, MY. WHAT'S THIS?

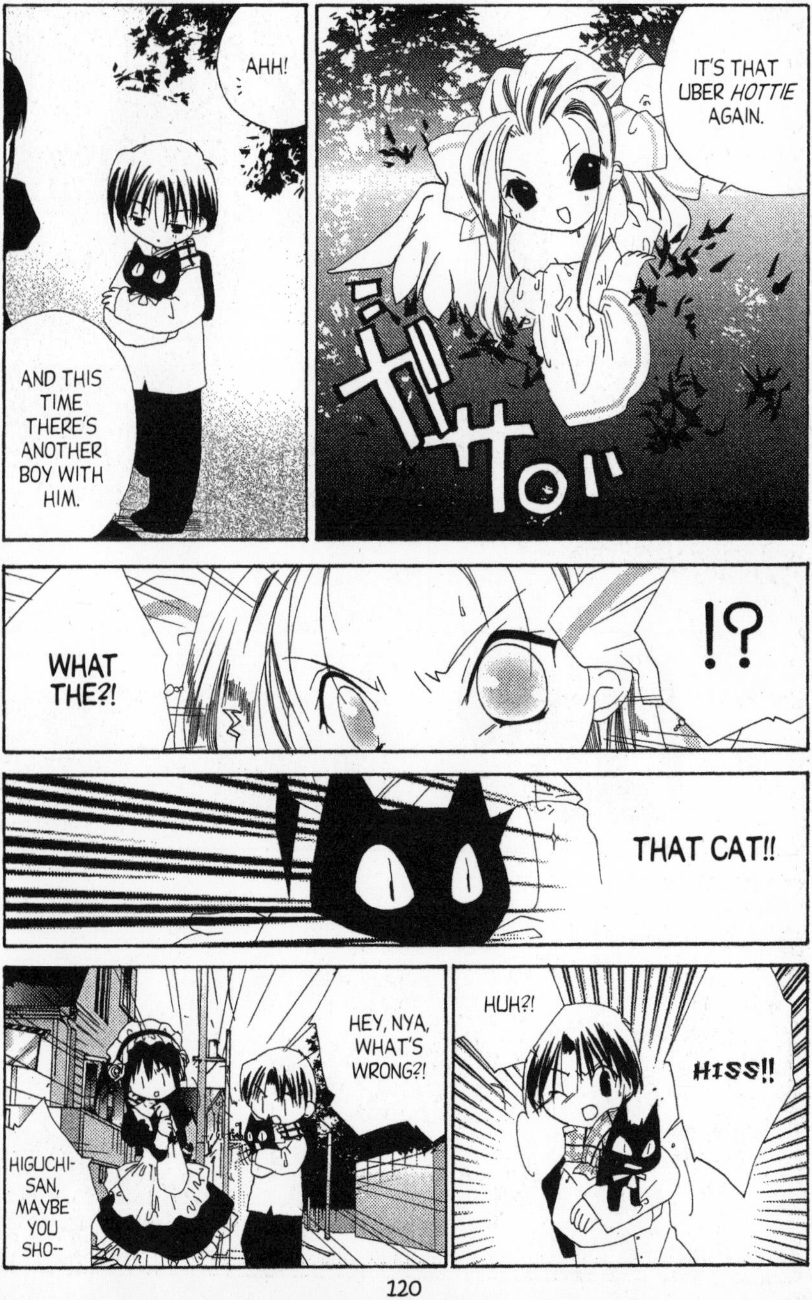
IT'S THAT UBER HOTTIE AGAIN.
AHH!
AND THIS TIME THERE'S ANOTHER BOY WITH HIM.
!?
WHAT THE?!
THAT CAT!!
HISS!!
HUH?!
HEY, NYA, WHAT'S WRONG?!
HIGUCHI-SAN, MAYBE YOU SHO--

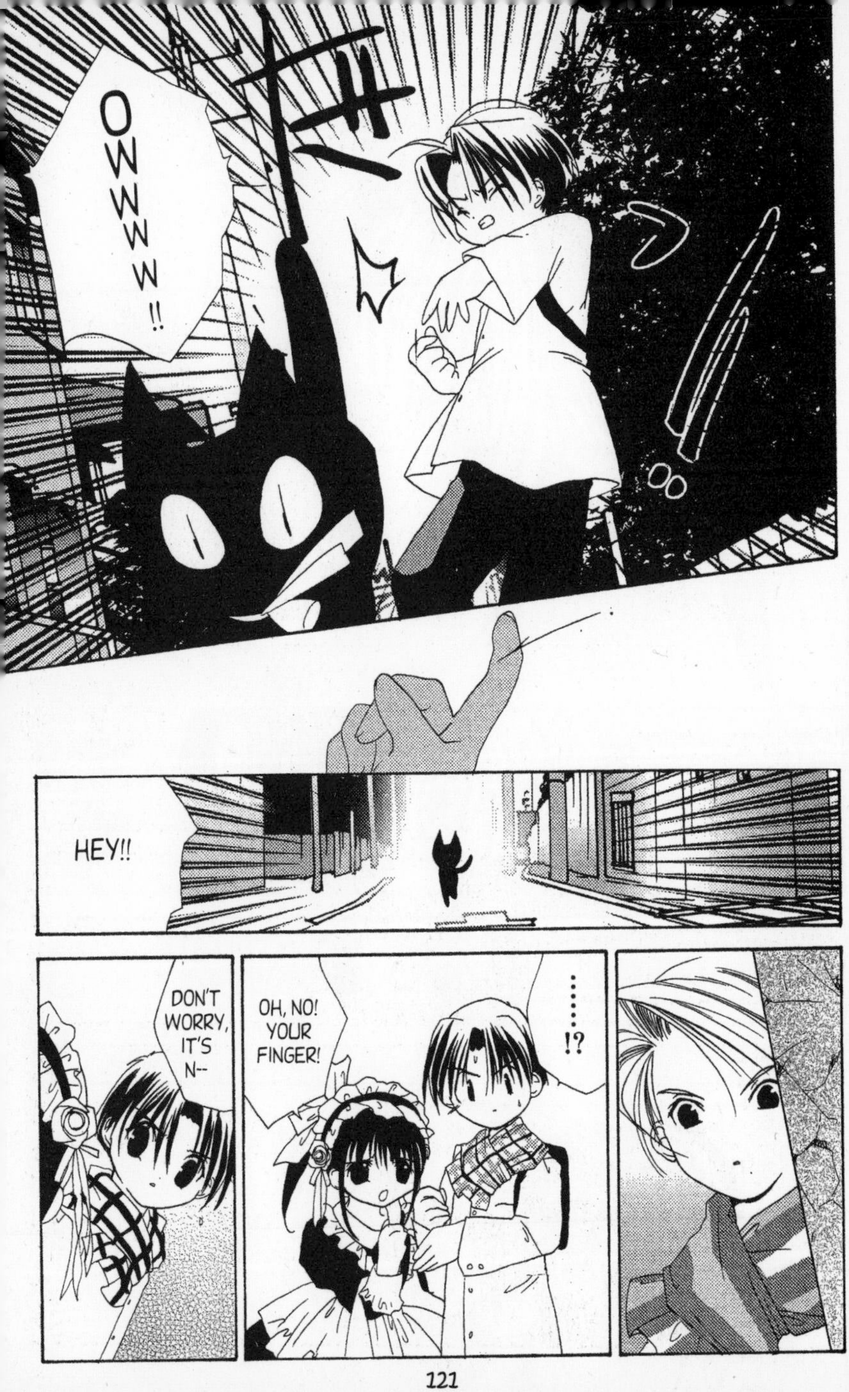
OWWWW!!
HEY!!
......!?
OH, NO! YOUR FINGER!
DON'T WORRY, IT'S N--

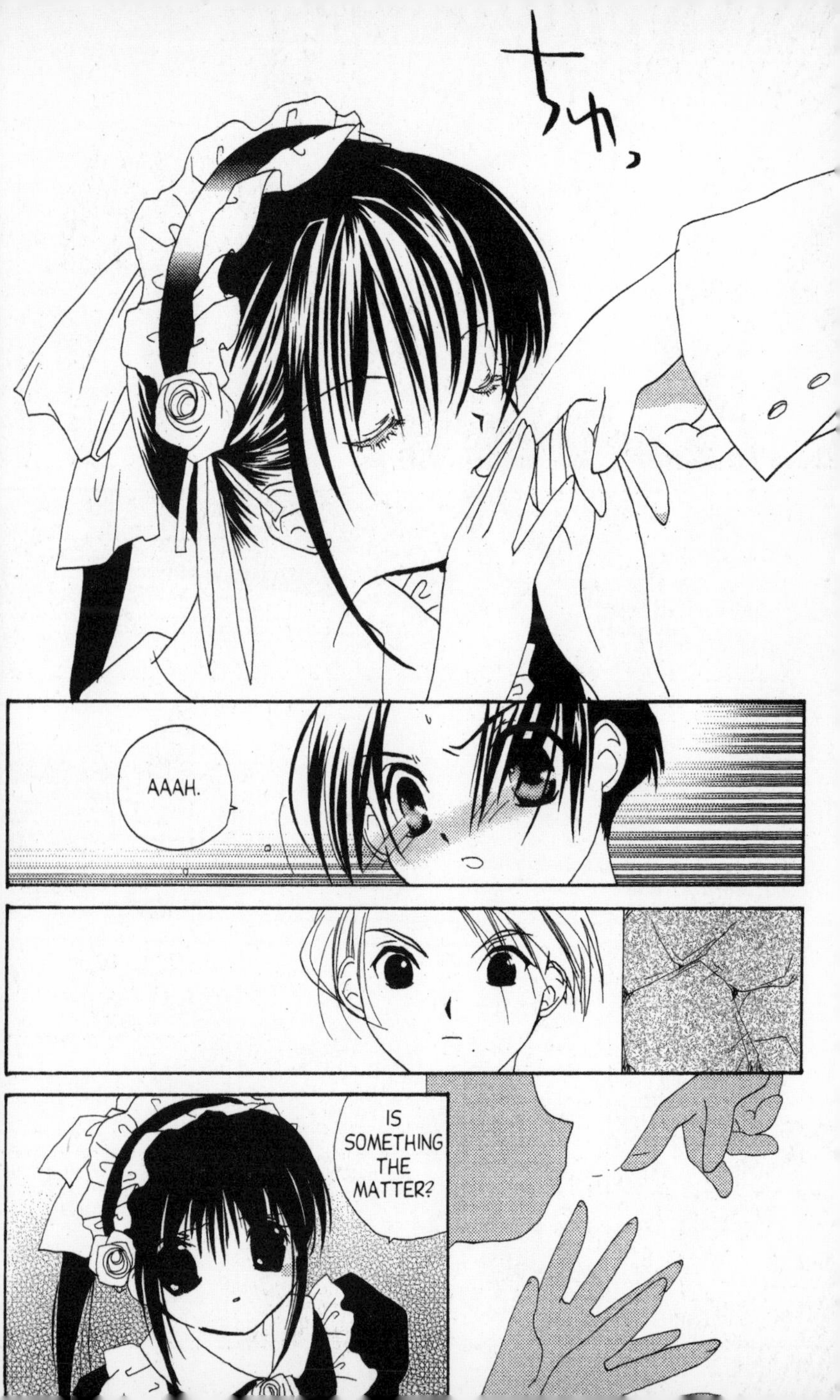
AAAH.
IS SOMETHING THE MATTER?

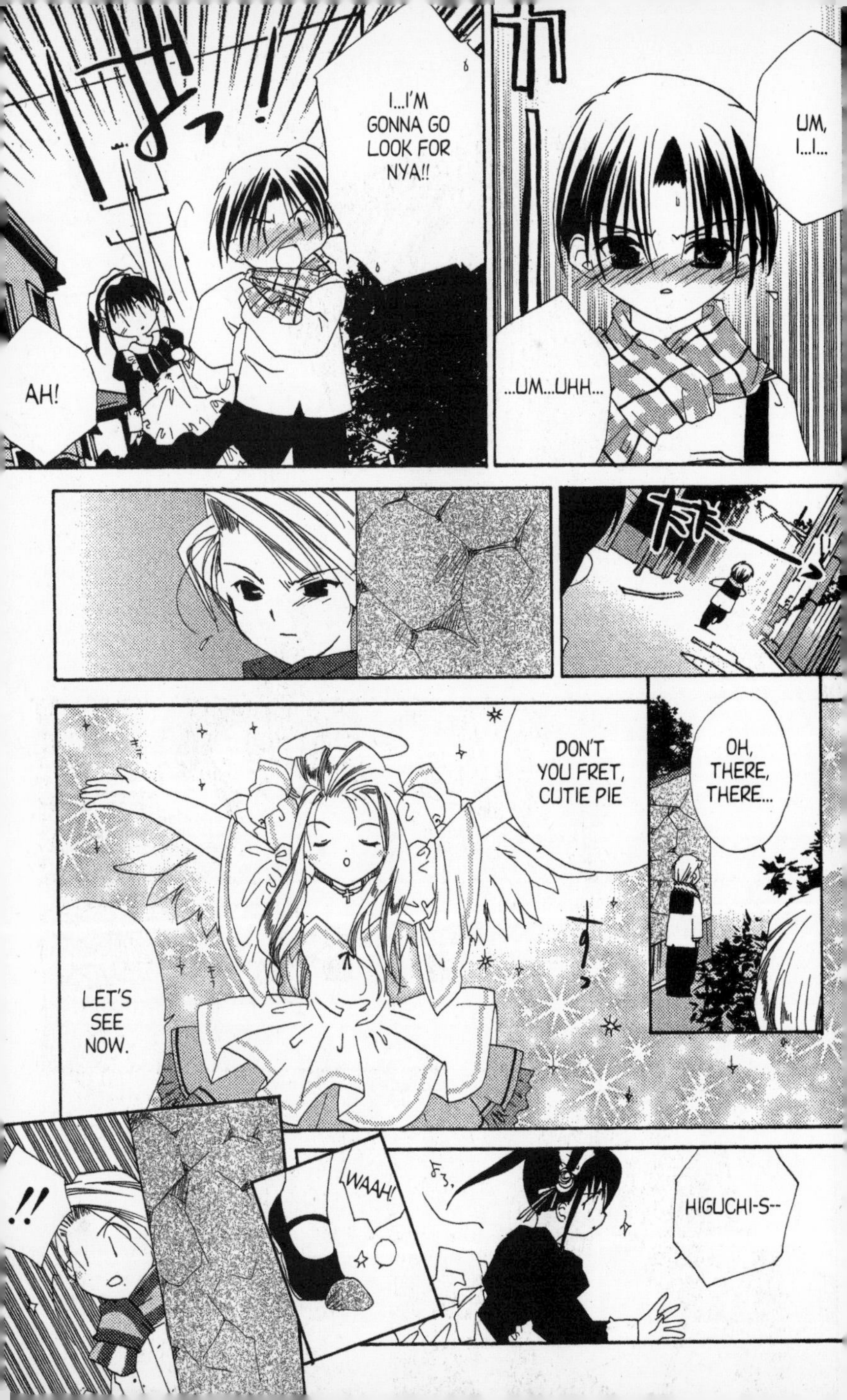
UM, I...I...
...UM...UHH...
I...I'M GONNA GO LOOK FOR NYA!!
AH!
OH, THERE, THERE...
DON'T YOU FRET, CUTIE PIE
LET'S SEE NOW.
HIGUCHI-S--
WAAH!
!!

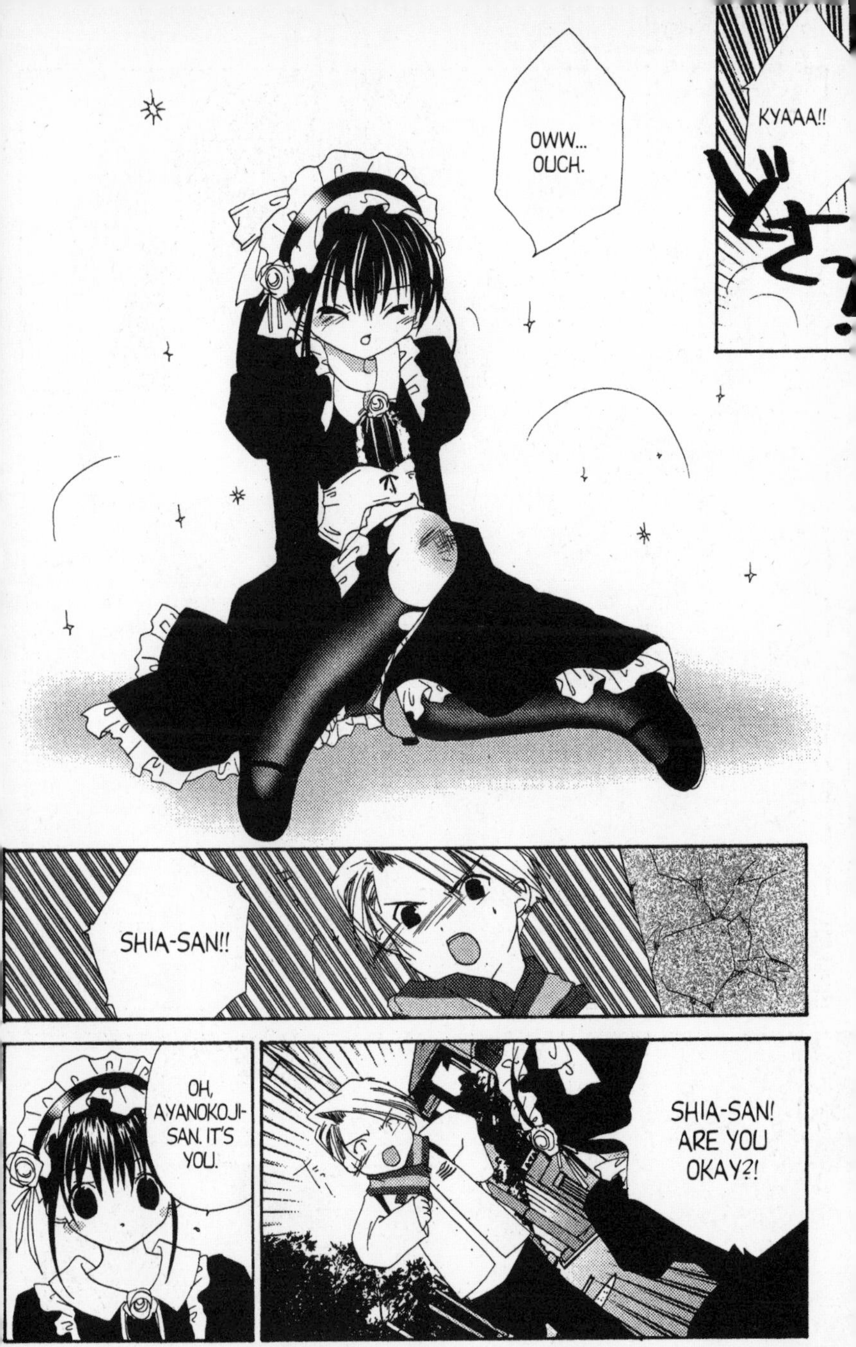
KYAAA!!
どさっ
OWW... OUCH.
SHIA-SAN!!
SHIA-SAN! ARE YOU OKAY?!
OH, AYANOKOJI-SAN. IT'S YOU.

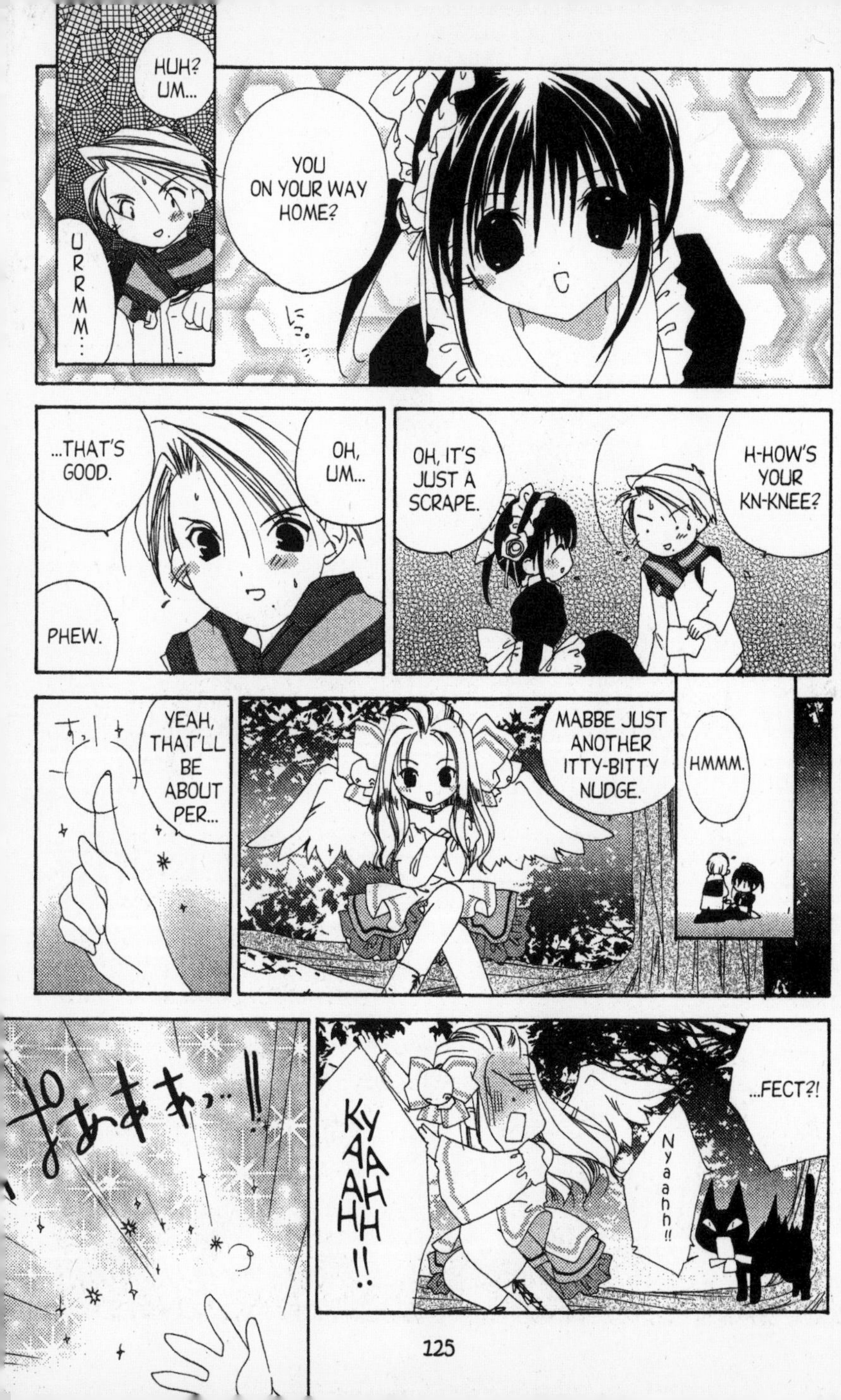
YOU ON YOUR WAY HOME?
HUH? UM...
URRMM...
H-HOW'S YOUR KN-KNEE?
OH, IT'S JUST A SCRAPE.
OH, UM...
...THAT'S GOOD.
PHEW.
HMMM.
MABBE JUST ANOTHER ITTY-BITTY NUDGE.
YEAH, THAT'LL BE ABOUT PER...
...FECT?!
Nyaahh!!
KYAAAHHH!!

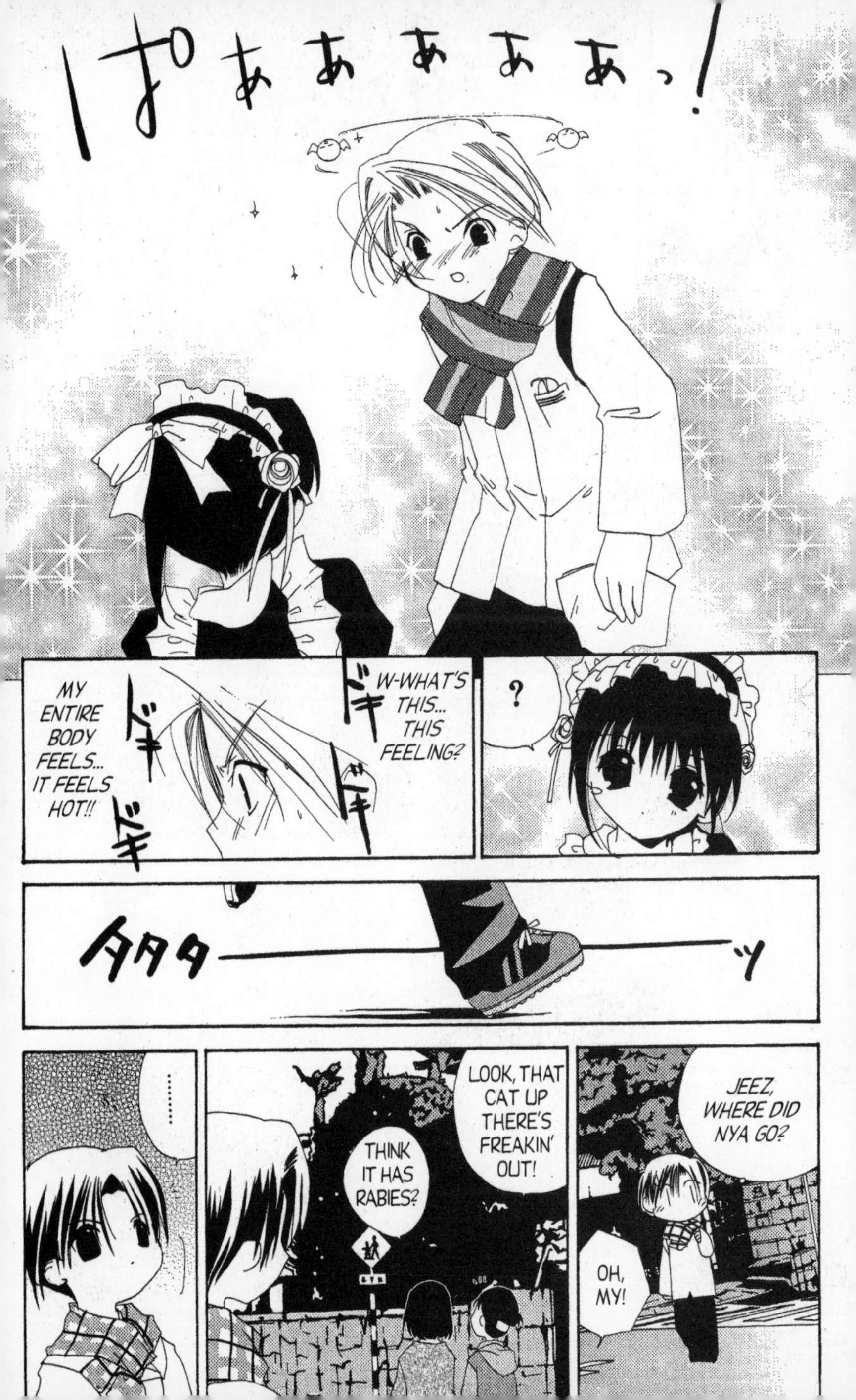
ぱあああああっ!
?
W-WHAT'S THIS... THIS FEELING?
ドキ
ドキ
ドキ
ドキ
MY ENTIRE BODY FEELS... IT FEELS HOT!!
タタタ――ッ
JEEZ, WHERE DID NYA GO?
OH, MY!
LOOK, THAT CAT UP THERE'S FREAKIN' OUT!
THINK IT HAS RABIES?
......

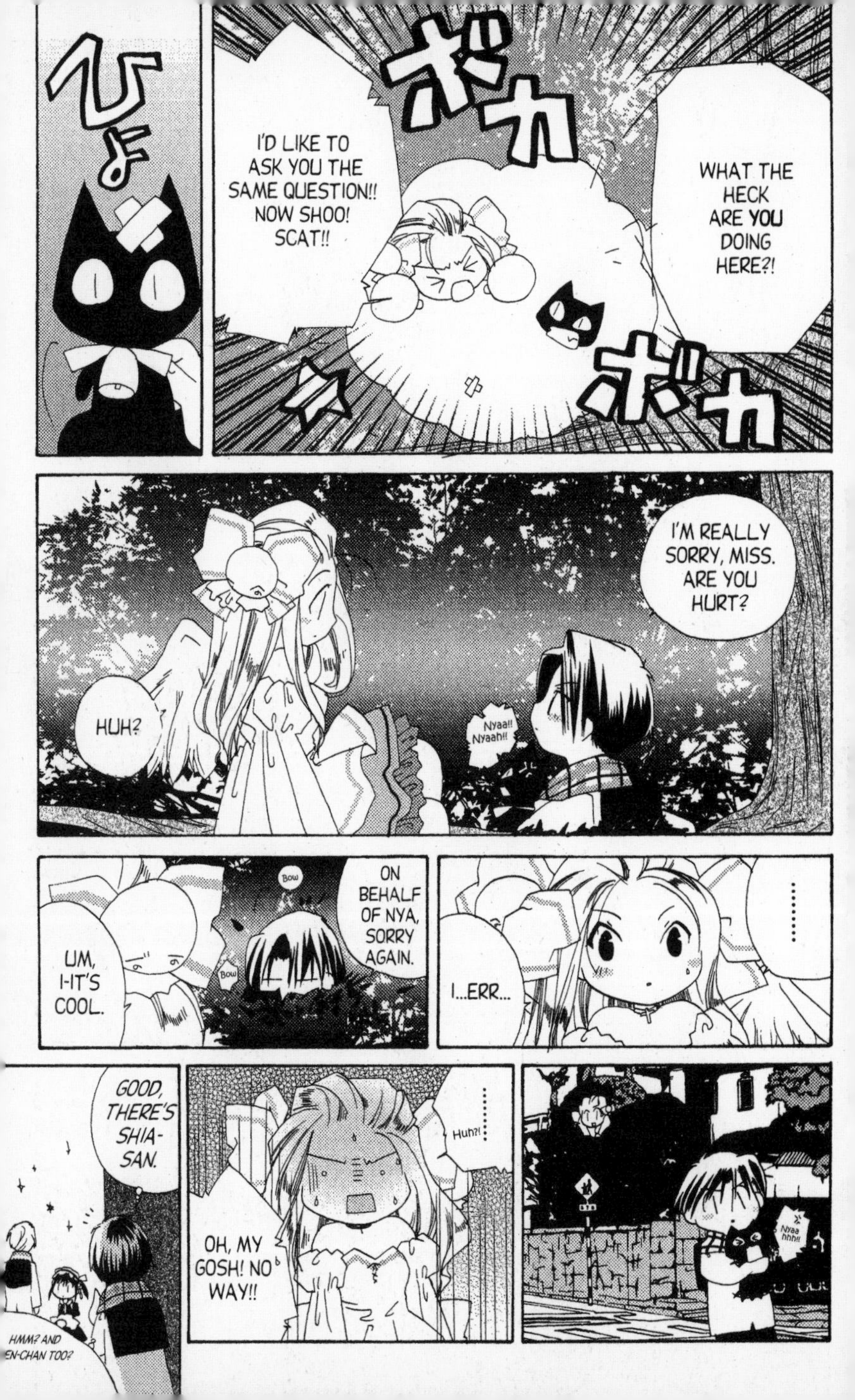

ボカ
WHAT THE HECK ARE YOU DOING HERE?!
I'D LIKE TO ASK YOU THE SAME QUESTION!! NOW SHOO! SCAT!!
ボカ
ひょ
I'M REALLY SORRY, MISS. ARE YOU HURT?
Nyaa!! Nyaah!!
HUH?
......
I...ERR...
Bow
ON BEHALF OF NYA, SORRY AGAIN.
Bow
UM, I-IT'S COOL.
Nyaa hhh!!
......
Huh?!
OH, MY GOSH! NO WAY!!
GOOD, THERE'S SHIA-SAN.
HMM? AND EN-CHAN TOO?

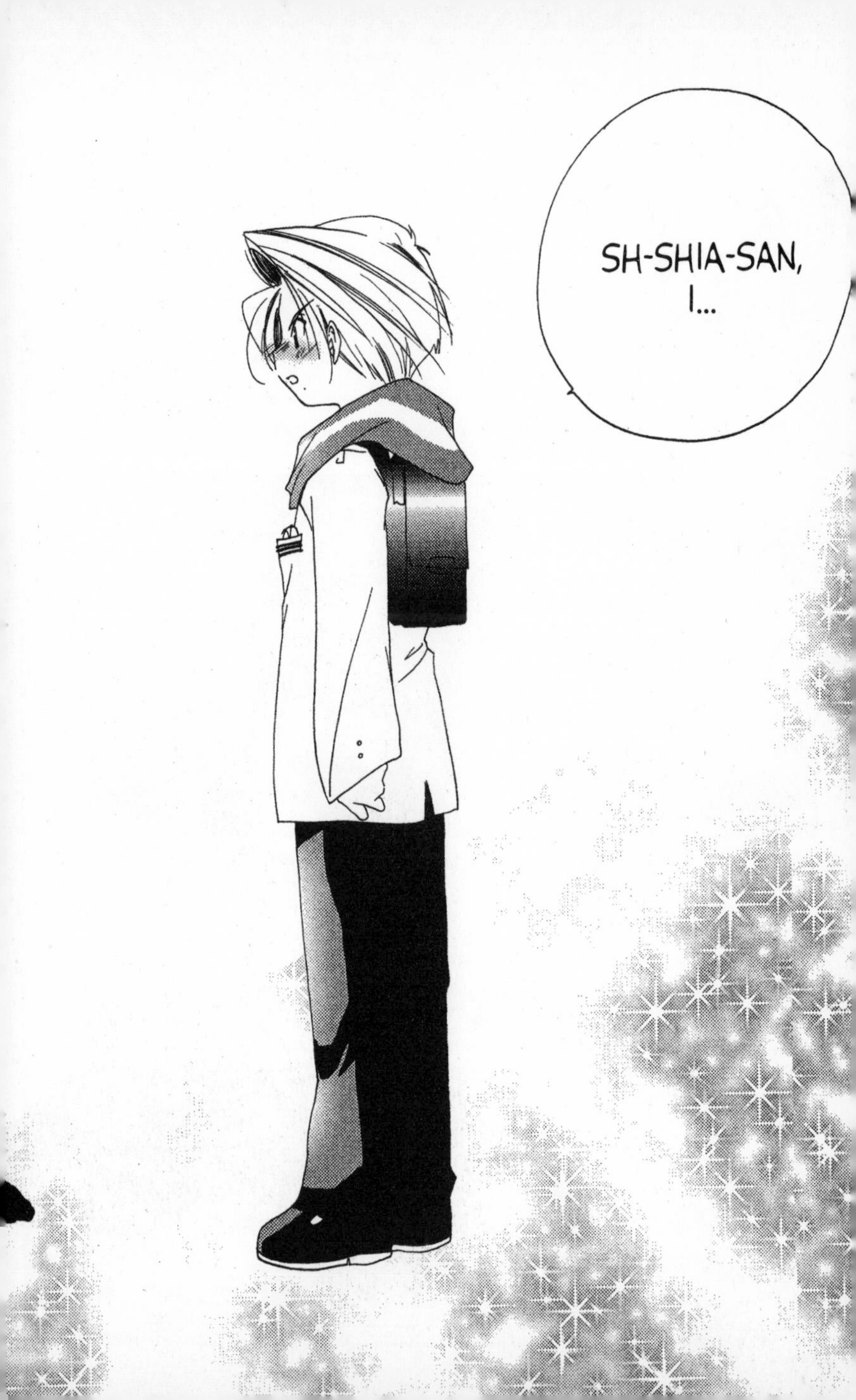
SH-SHIA-SAN, I...

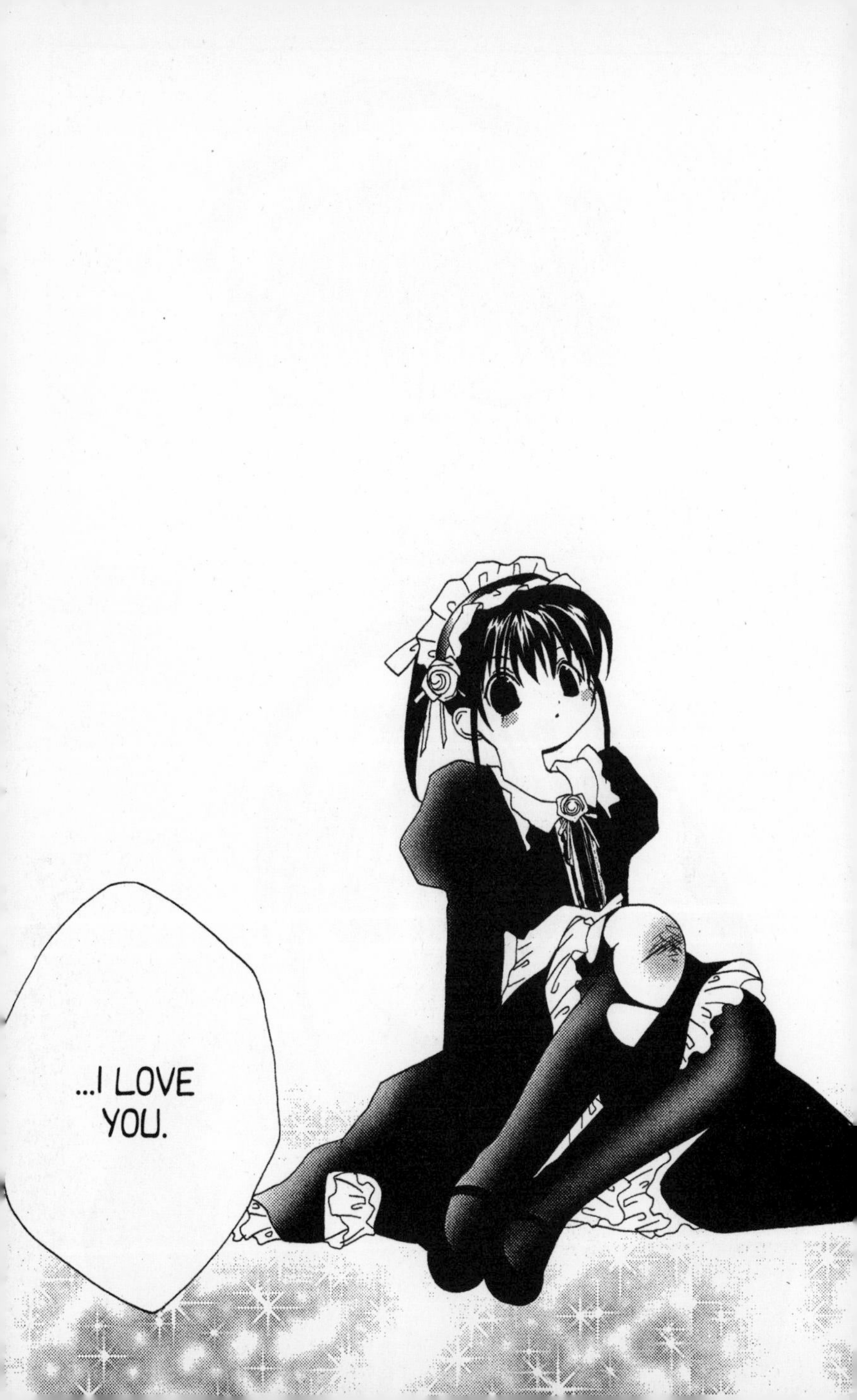
...I LOVE YOU.

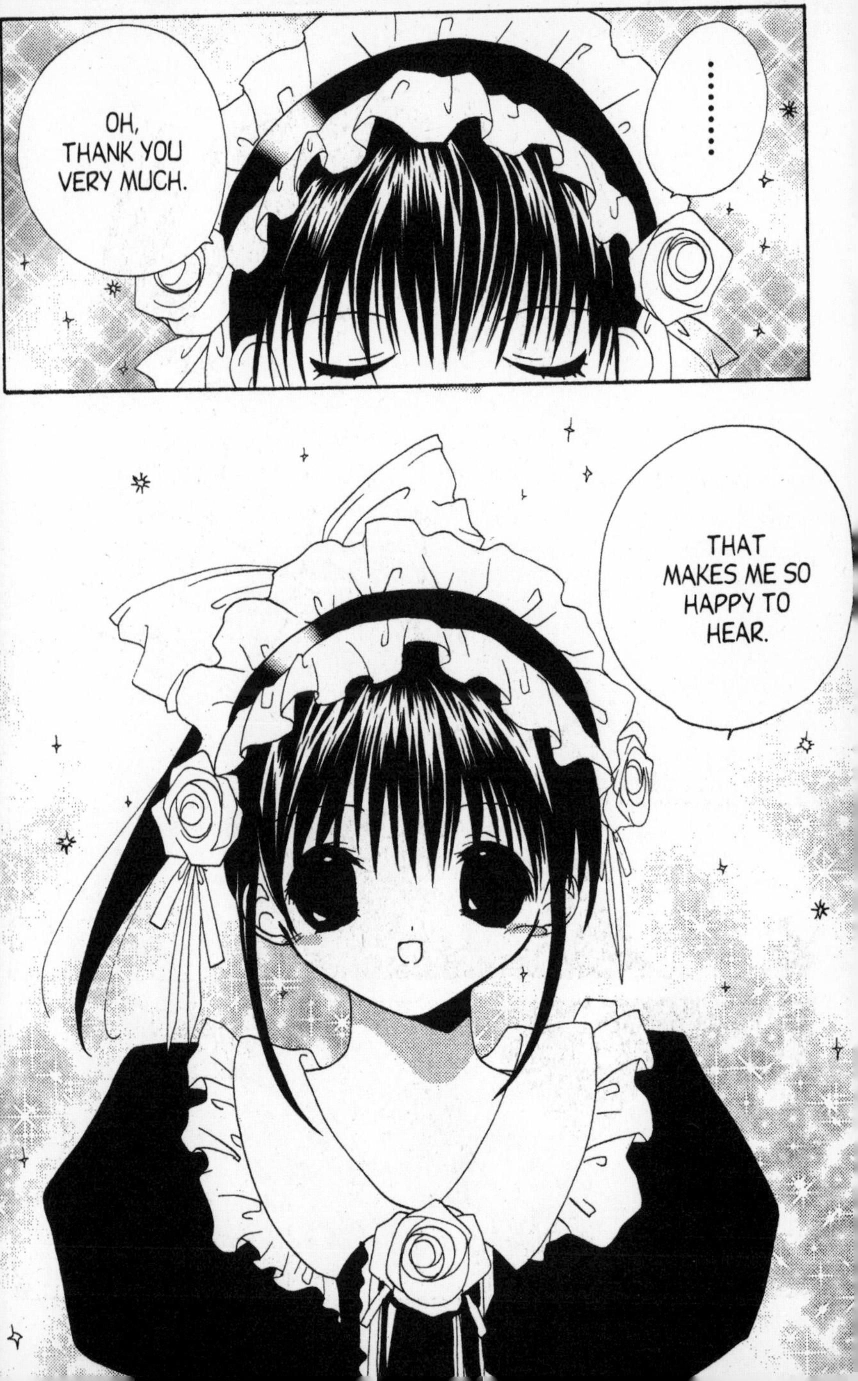
......
OH, THANK YOU VERY MUCH.
THAT MAKES ME SO HAPPY TO HEAR.

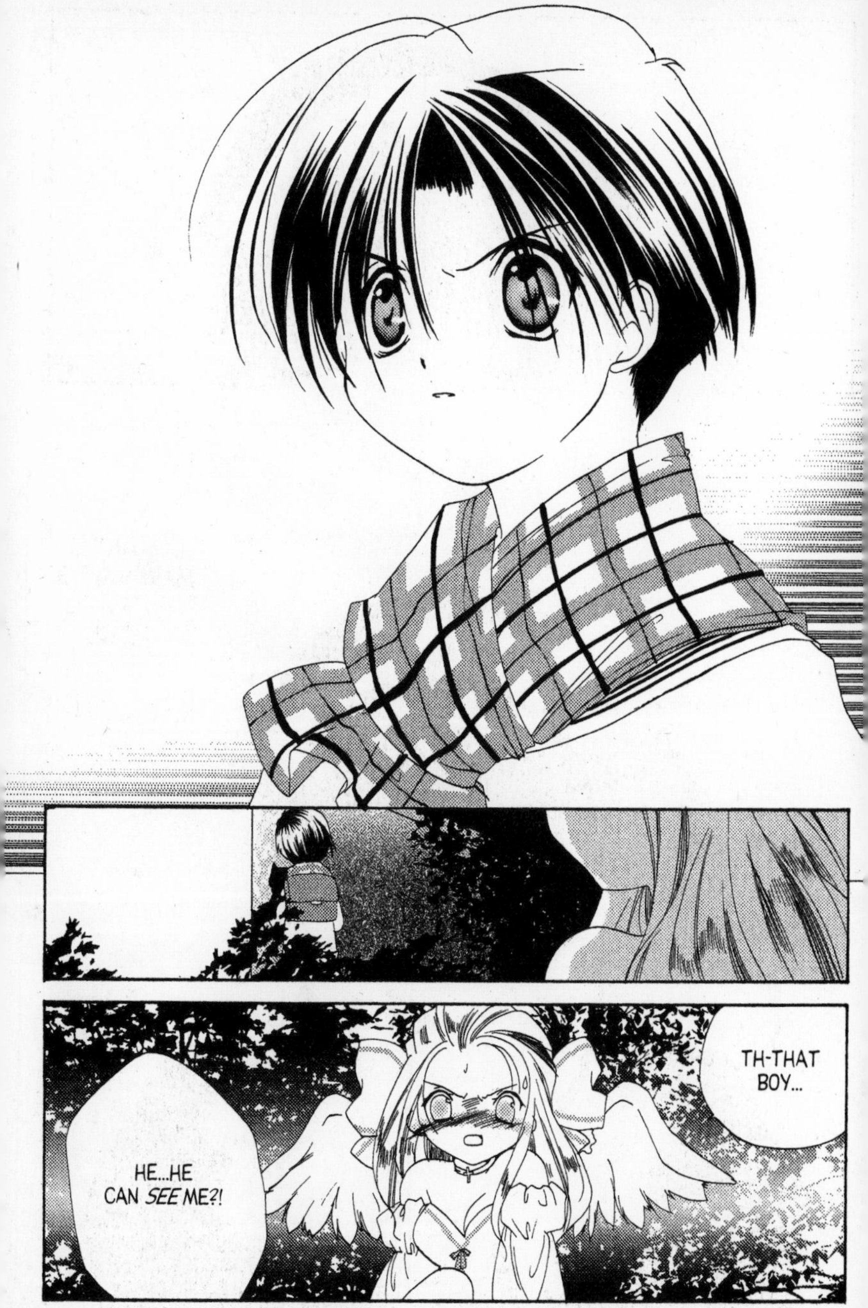
TH-THAT BOY...
HE...HE CAN *SEE* ME?!

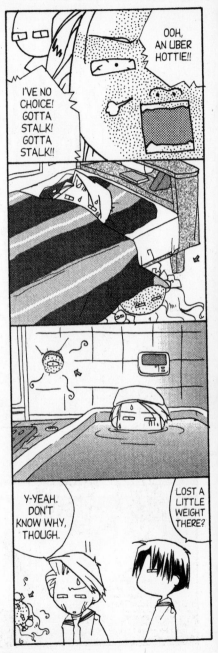

OOH, AN UBER HOTTIE!!
I'VE NO CHOICE! GOTTA STALK! GOTTA STALK!!
LOST A LITTLE WEIGHT THERE?
Y-YEAH. DON'T KNOW WHY, THOUGH.

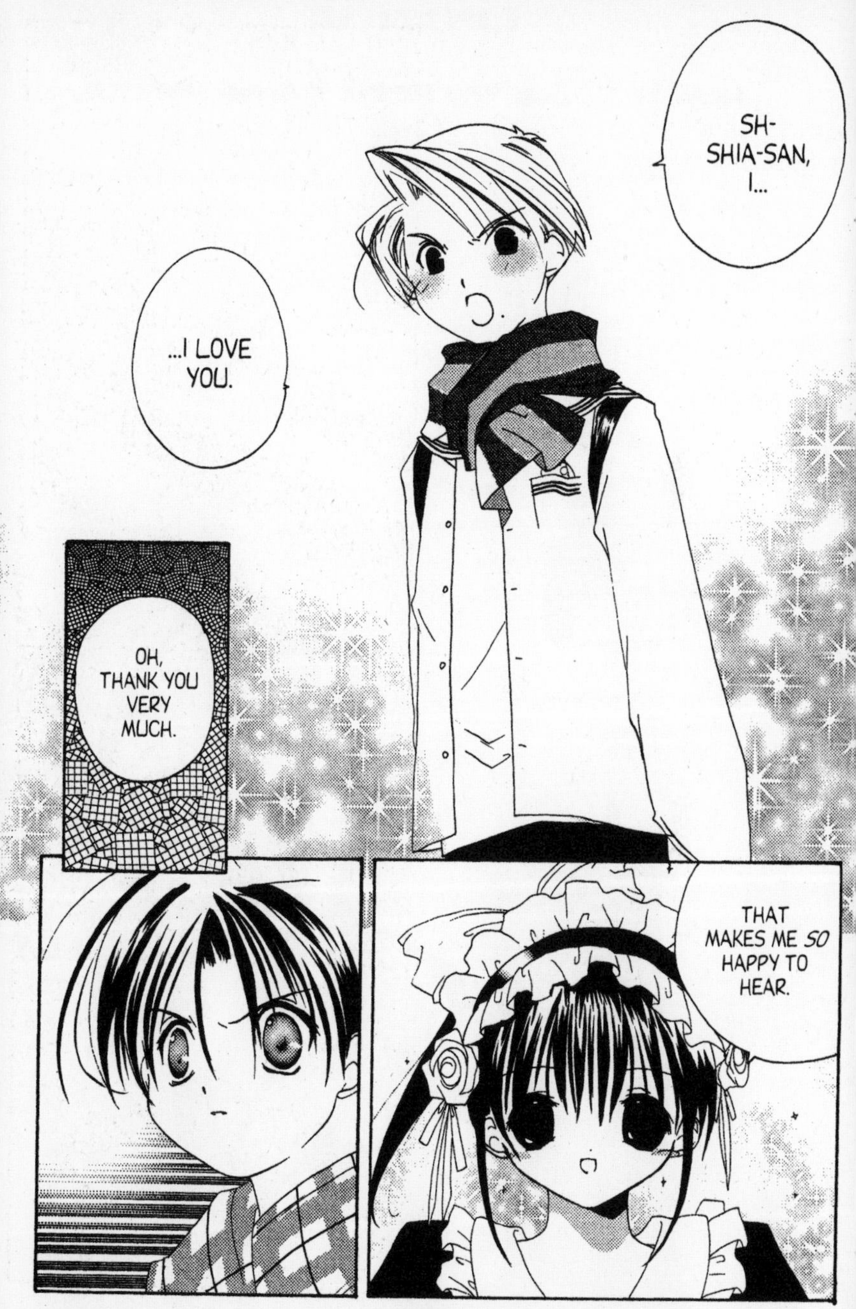
SH- SHIA-SAN, I...
...I LOVE YOU.
OH, THANK YOU VERY MUCH.
THAT MAKES ME *SO* HAPPY TO HEAR.

Lesson 18

How to Enjoy the World Below: Part II

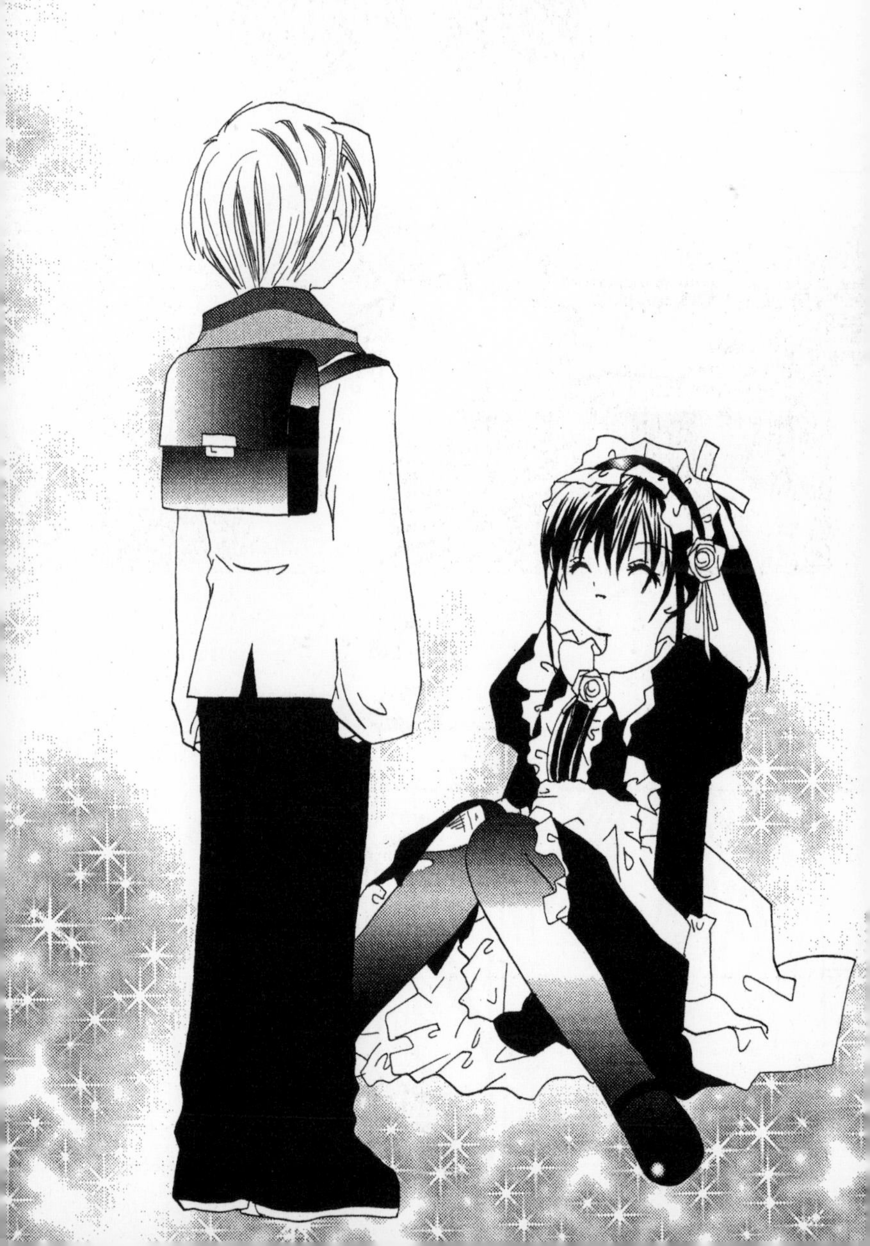

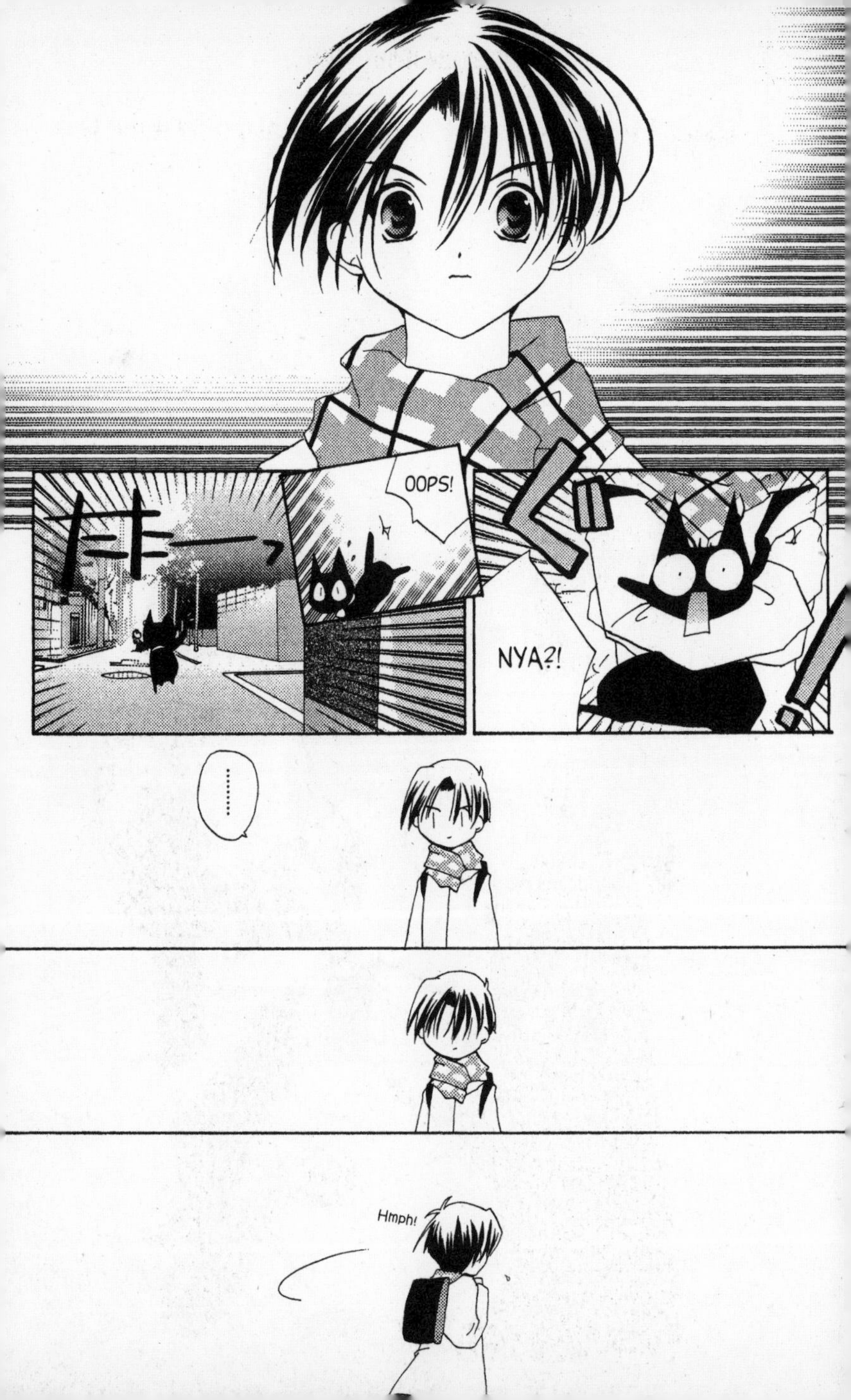
NYA?!
OOPS!
....
Hmph!

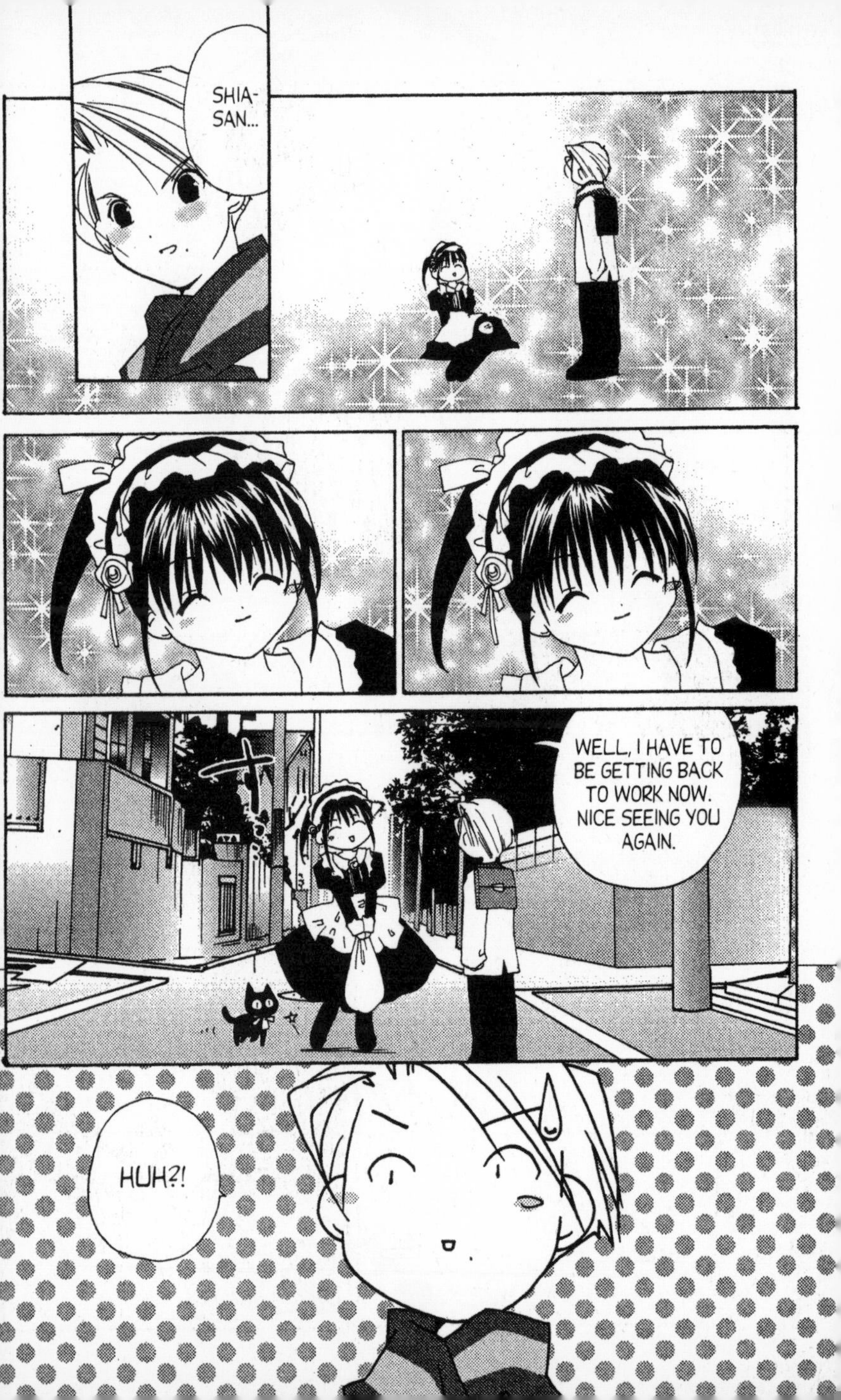
SHIA-SAN...
WELL, I HAVE TO BE GETTING BACK TO WORK NOW. NICE SEEING YOU AGAIN.
HUH?!

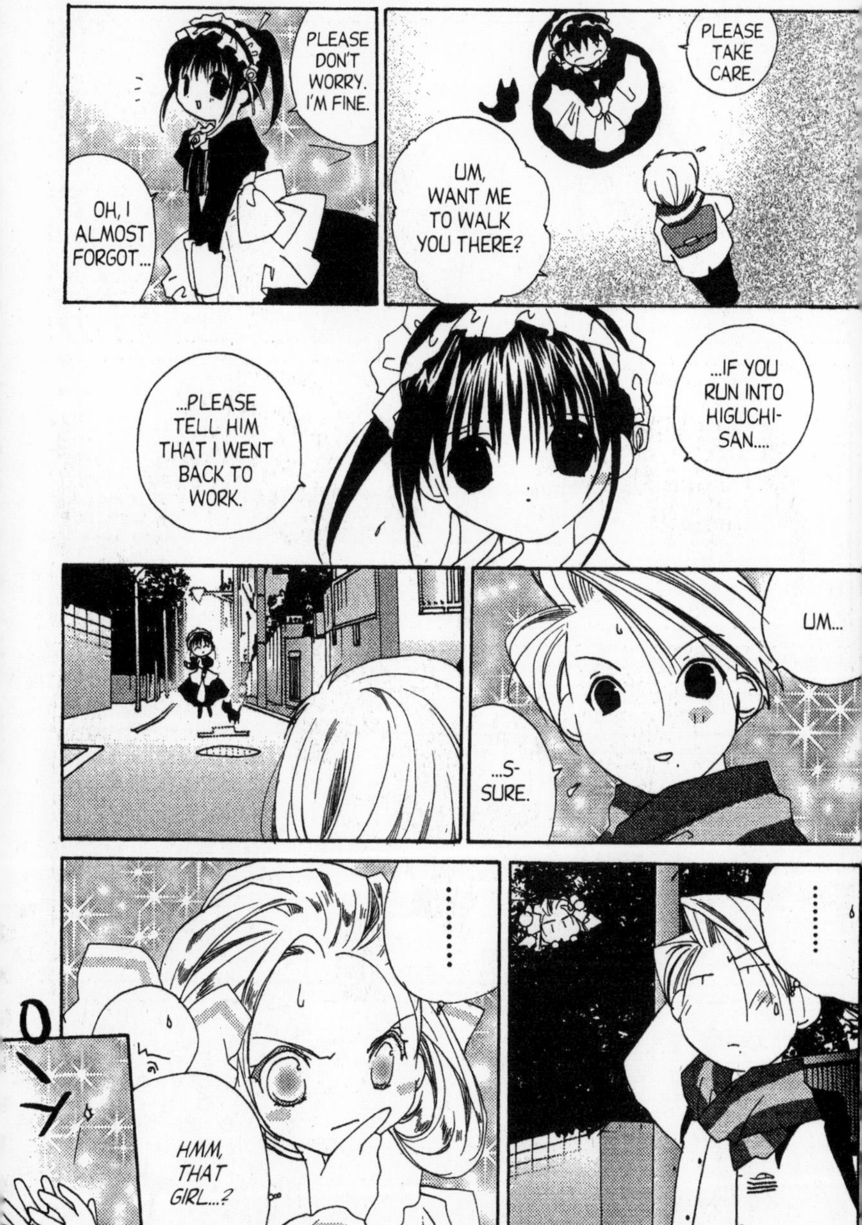
PLEASE TAKE CARE.
UM, WANT ME TO WALK YOU THERE?
PLEASE DON'T WORRY. I'M FINE.
OH, I ALMOST FORGOT...
...IF YOU RUN INTO HIGUCHI-SAN....
...PLEASE TELL HIM THAT I WENT BACK TO WORK.
UM...
...S-SURE.
......
......
HMM, THAT GIRL...?

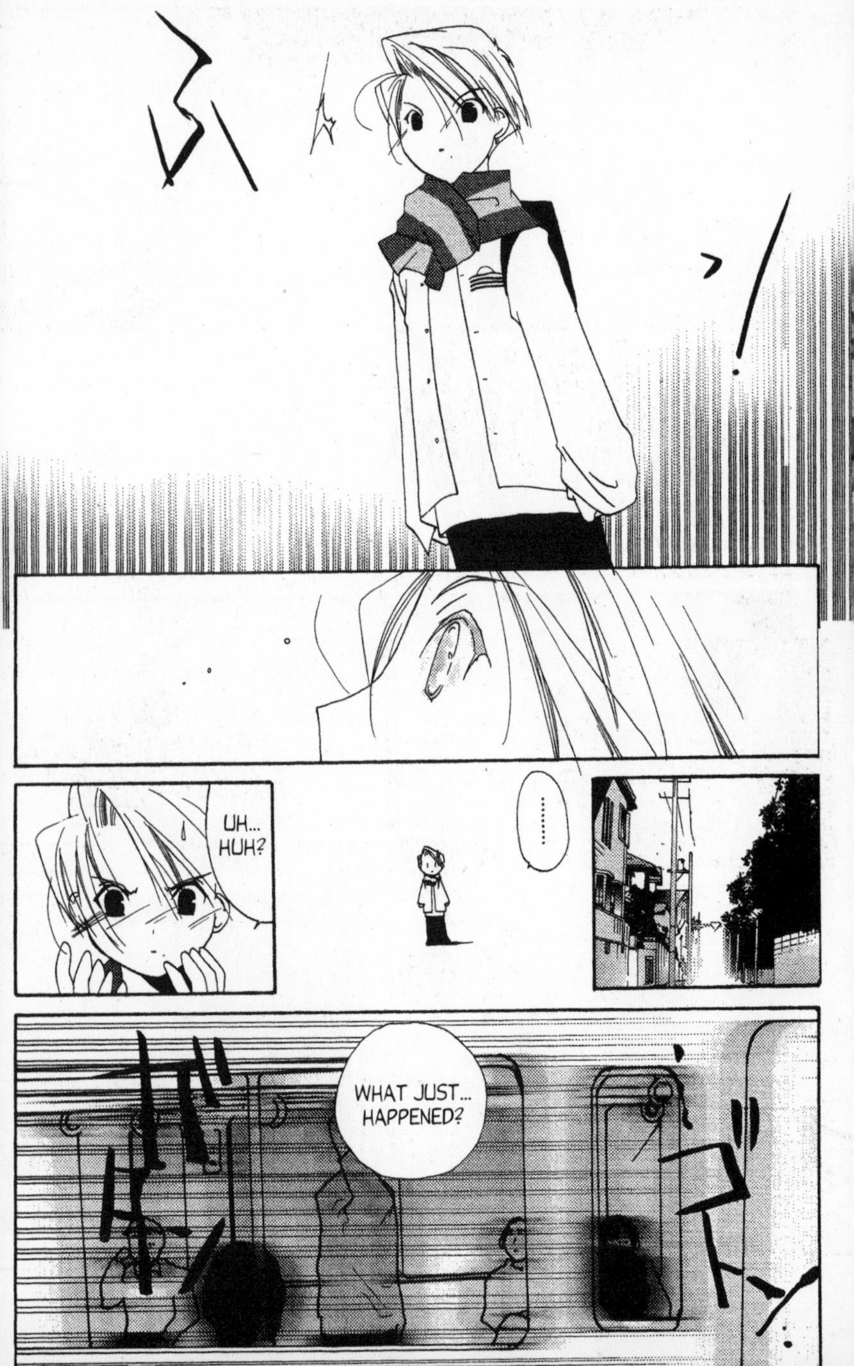
......
UH... HUH?
WHAT JUST... HAPPENED?

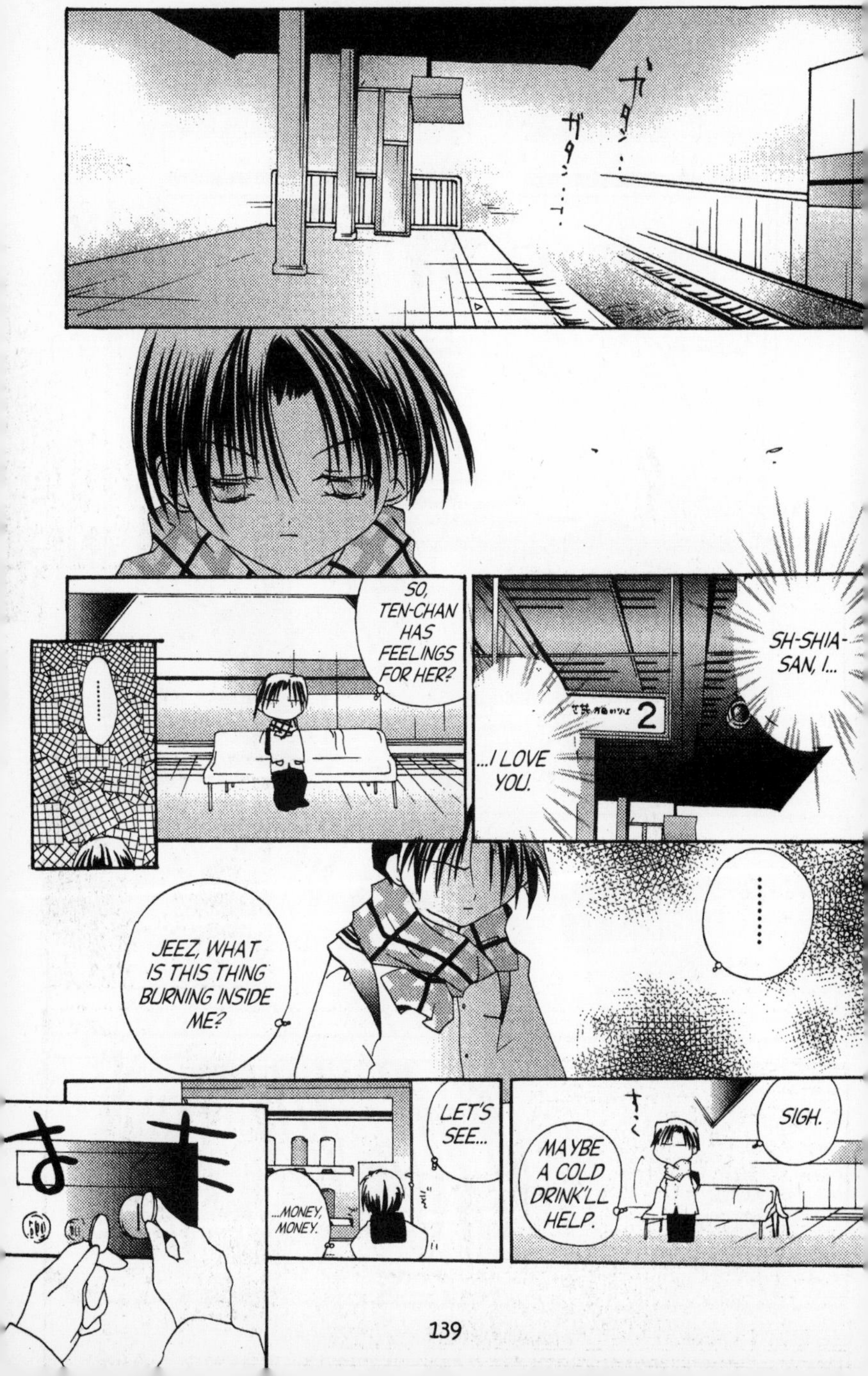
SH-SHIA-SAN, I...
...I LOVE YOU.
SO, TEN-CHAN HAS FEELINGS FOR HER?
......
......
JEEZ, WHAT IS THIS THING BURNING INSIDE ME?
SIGH.
MAYBE A COLD DRINK'LL HELP.
LET'S SEE...
...MONEY, MONEY.

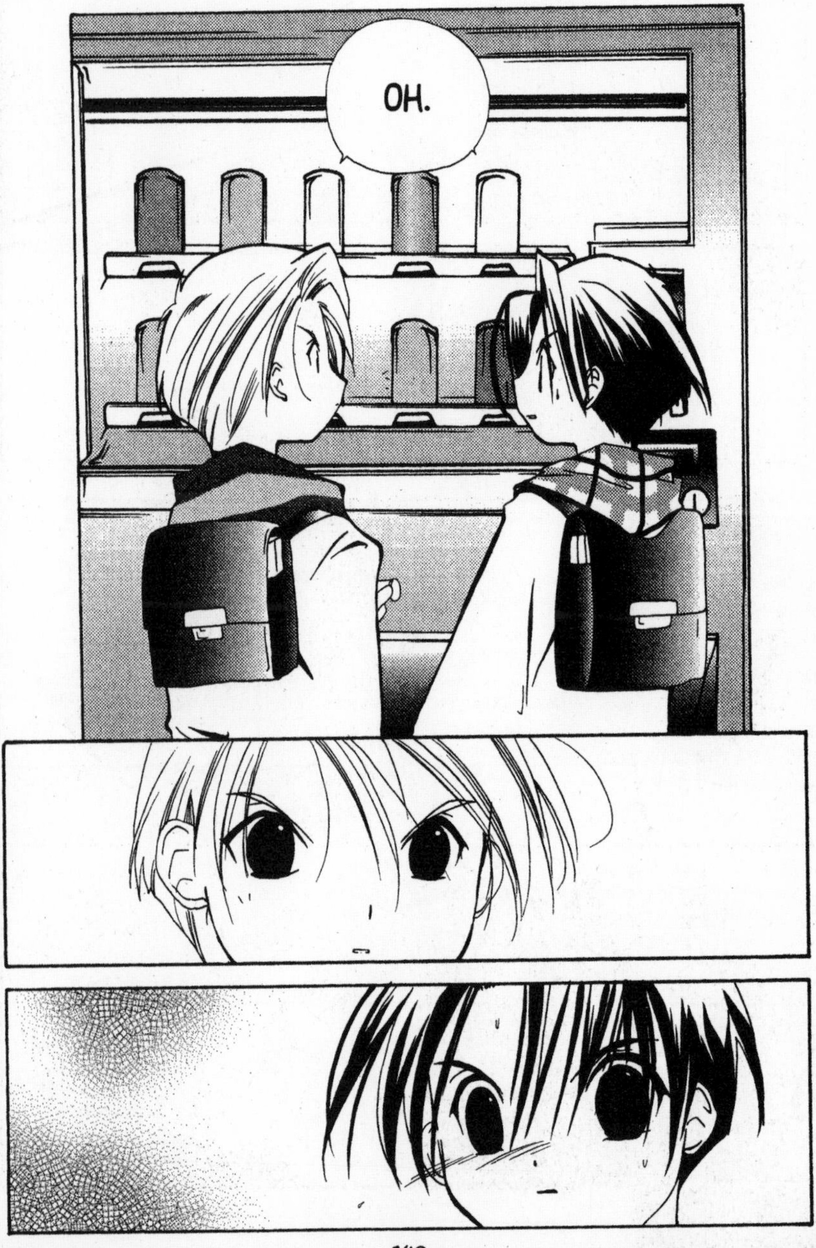
OH.

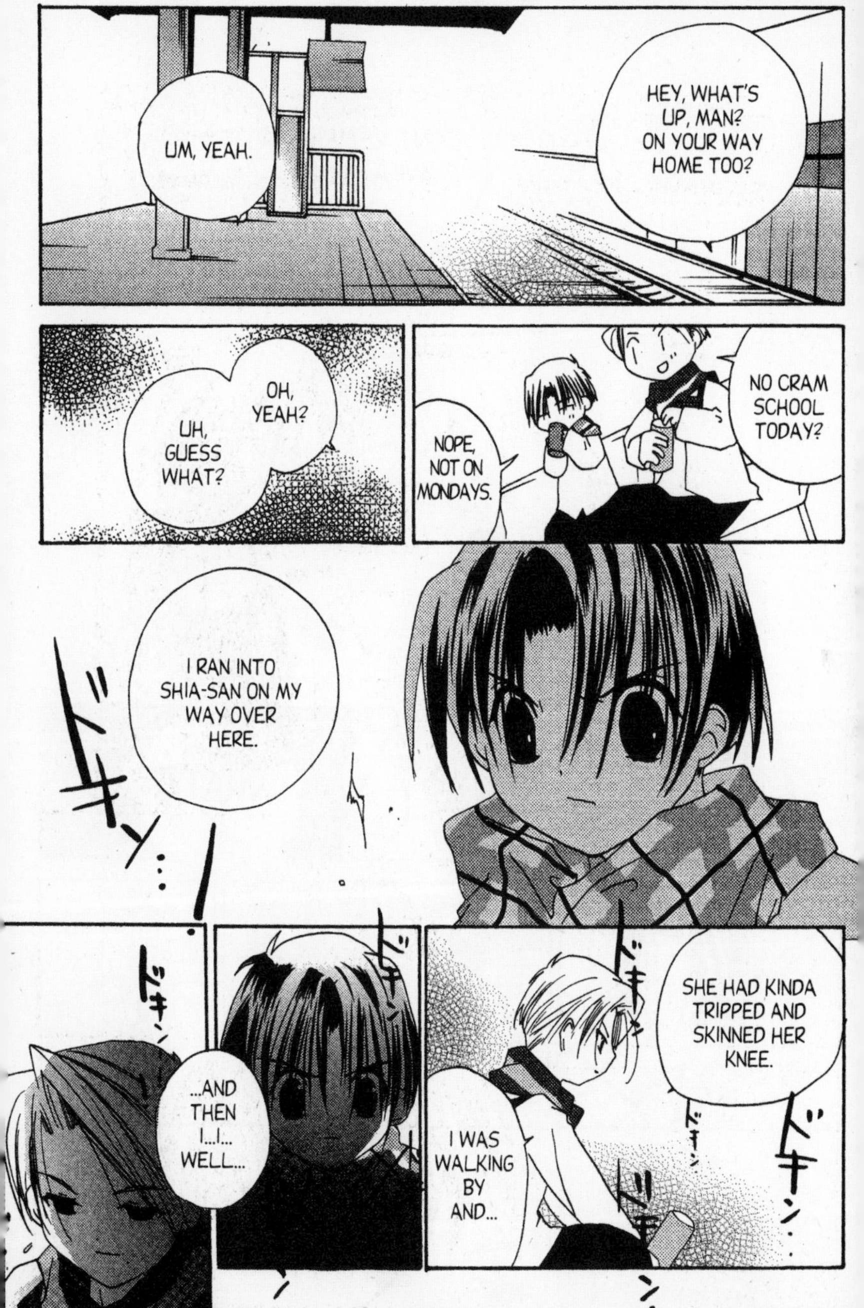
HEY, WHAT'S UP, MAN? ON YOUR WAY HOME TOO?
UM, YEAH.
NO CRAM SCHOOL TODAY?
NOPE, NOT ON MONDAYS.
OH, YEAH?
UH, GUESS WHAT?
I RAN INTO SHIA-SAN ON MY WAY OVER HERE.
ドキン…!
SHE HAD KINDA TRIPPED AND SKINNED HER KNEE.
ドキン…
I WAS WALKING BY AND...
...AND THEN I...I... WELL...

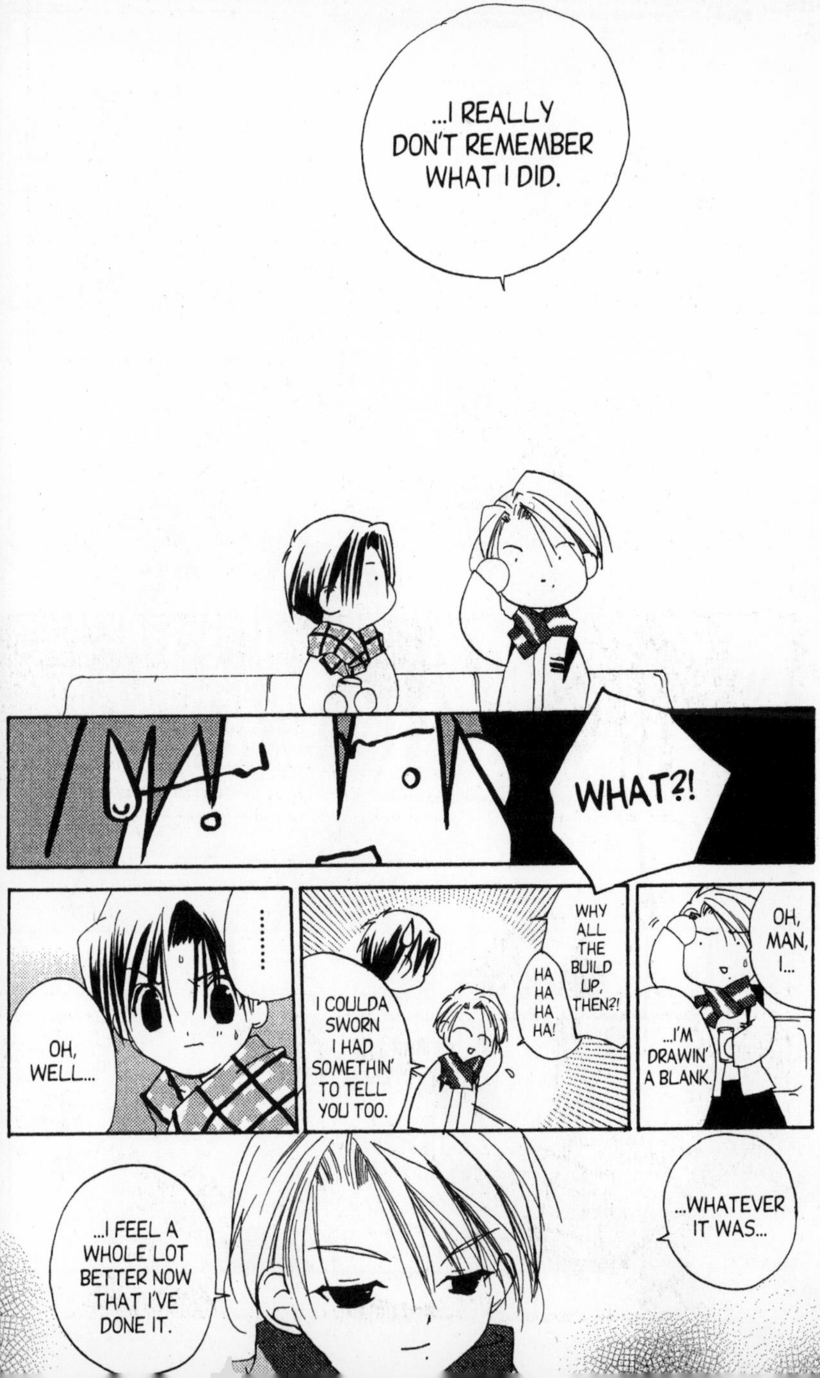
...I REALLY DON'T REMEMBER WHAT I DID.
WHAT?!
OH, MAN, I...
...I'M DRAWIN' A BLANK.
WHY ALL THE BUILD UP, THEN?!
HA HA HA HA!
I COULDA SWORN I HAD SOMETHIN' TO TELL YOU TOO.
......
OH, WELL...
...WHATEVER IT WAS...
...I FEEL A WHOLE LOT BETTER NOW THAT I'VE DONE IT.

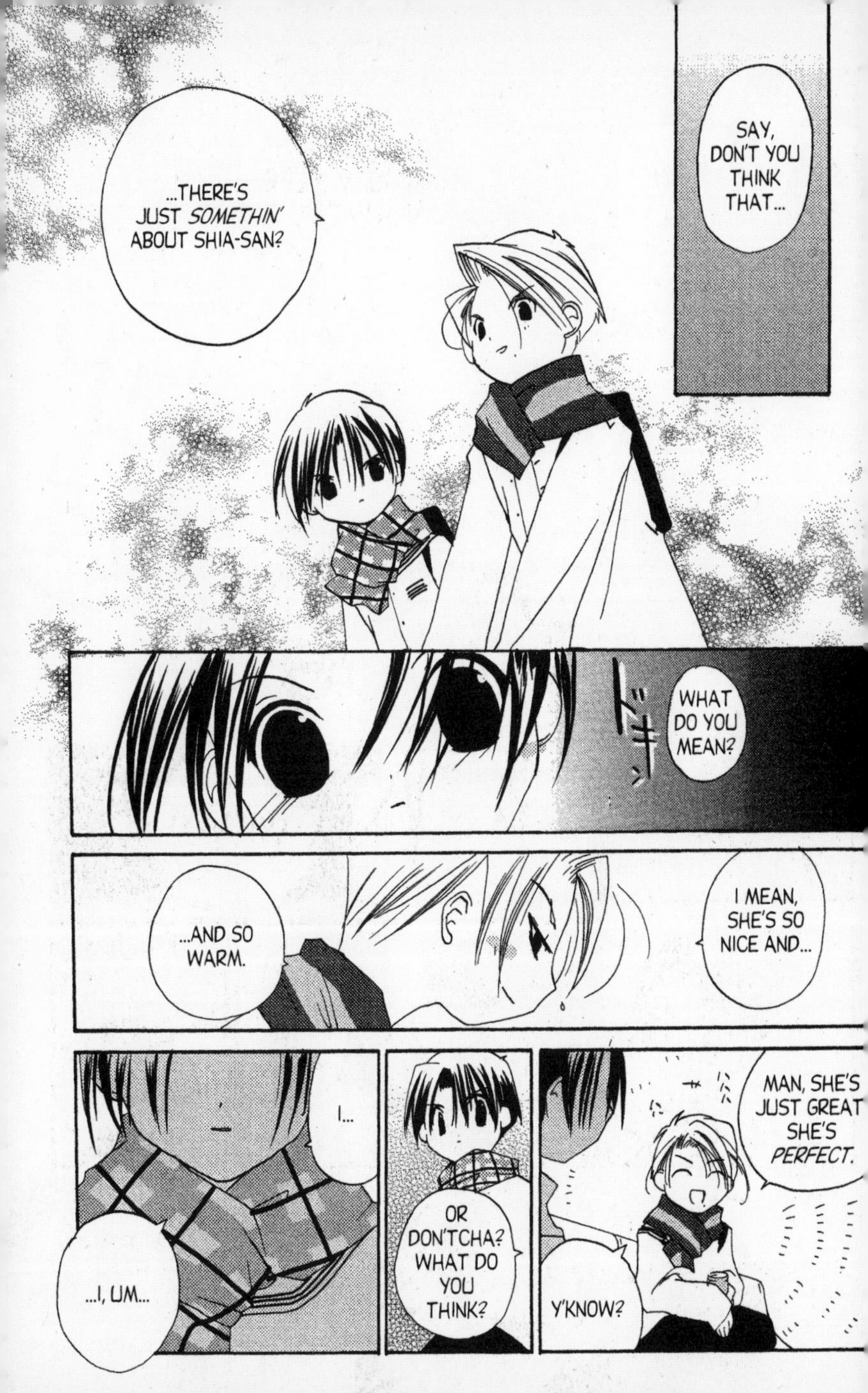
SAY, DON'T YOU THINK THAT...
...THERE'S JUST *SOMETHIN'* ABOUT SHIA-SAN?
WHAT DO YOU MEAN?
I MEAN, SHE'S SO NICE AND...
...AND SO WARM.
MAN, SHE'S JUST GREAT SHE'S *PERFECT.*
Y'KNOW?
OR DON'TCHA? WHAT DO YOU THINK?
I...
...I, UM...

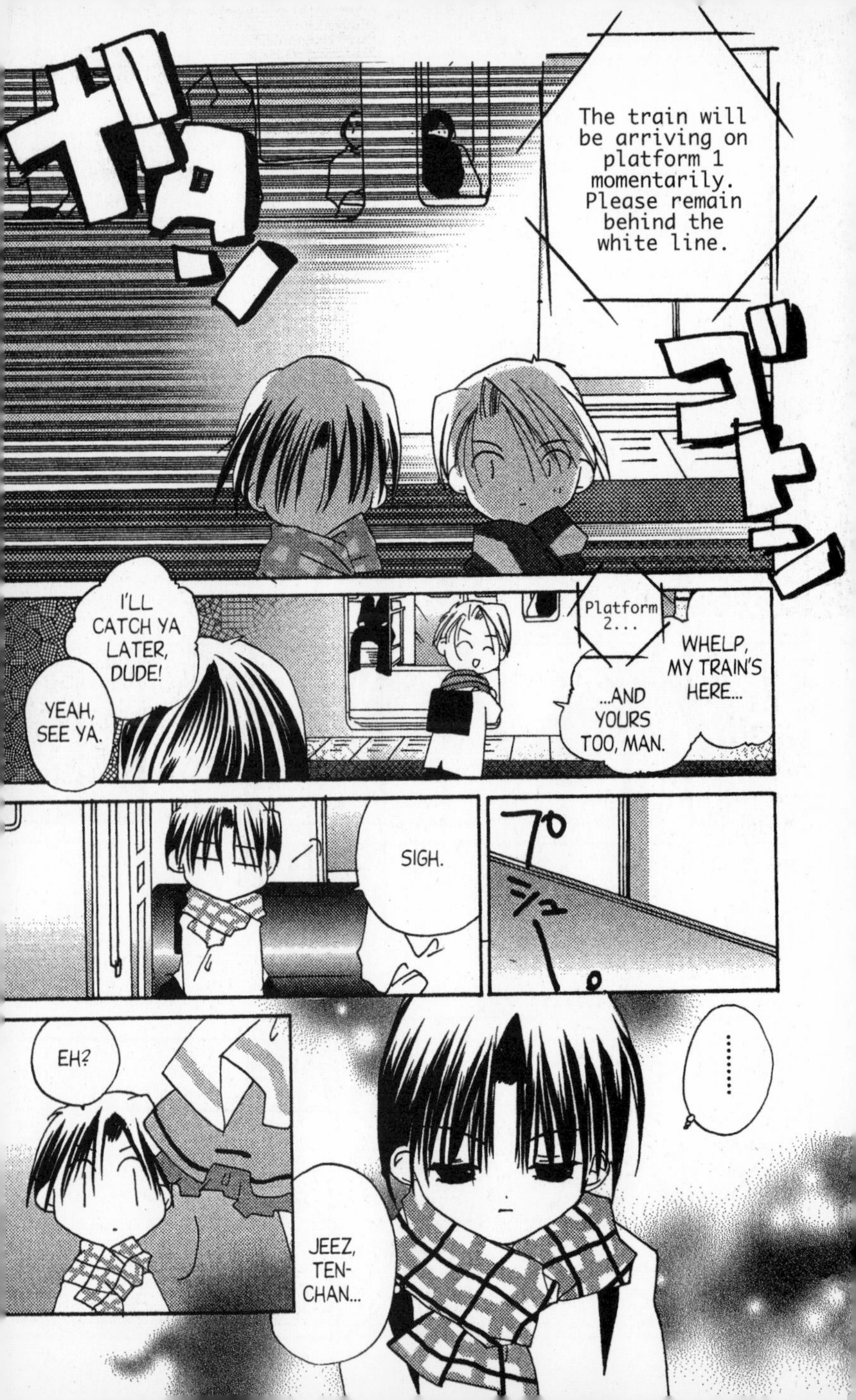
The train will be arriving on platform 1 momentarily. Please remain behind the white line.
Platform 2...
WHELP, MY TRAIN'S HERE...
...AND YOURS TOO, MAN.
I'LL CATCH YA LATER, DUDE!
YEAH, SEE YA.
SIGH.
......
EH?
JEEZ, TEN-CHAN...

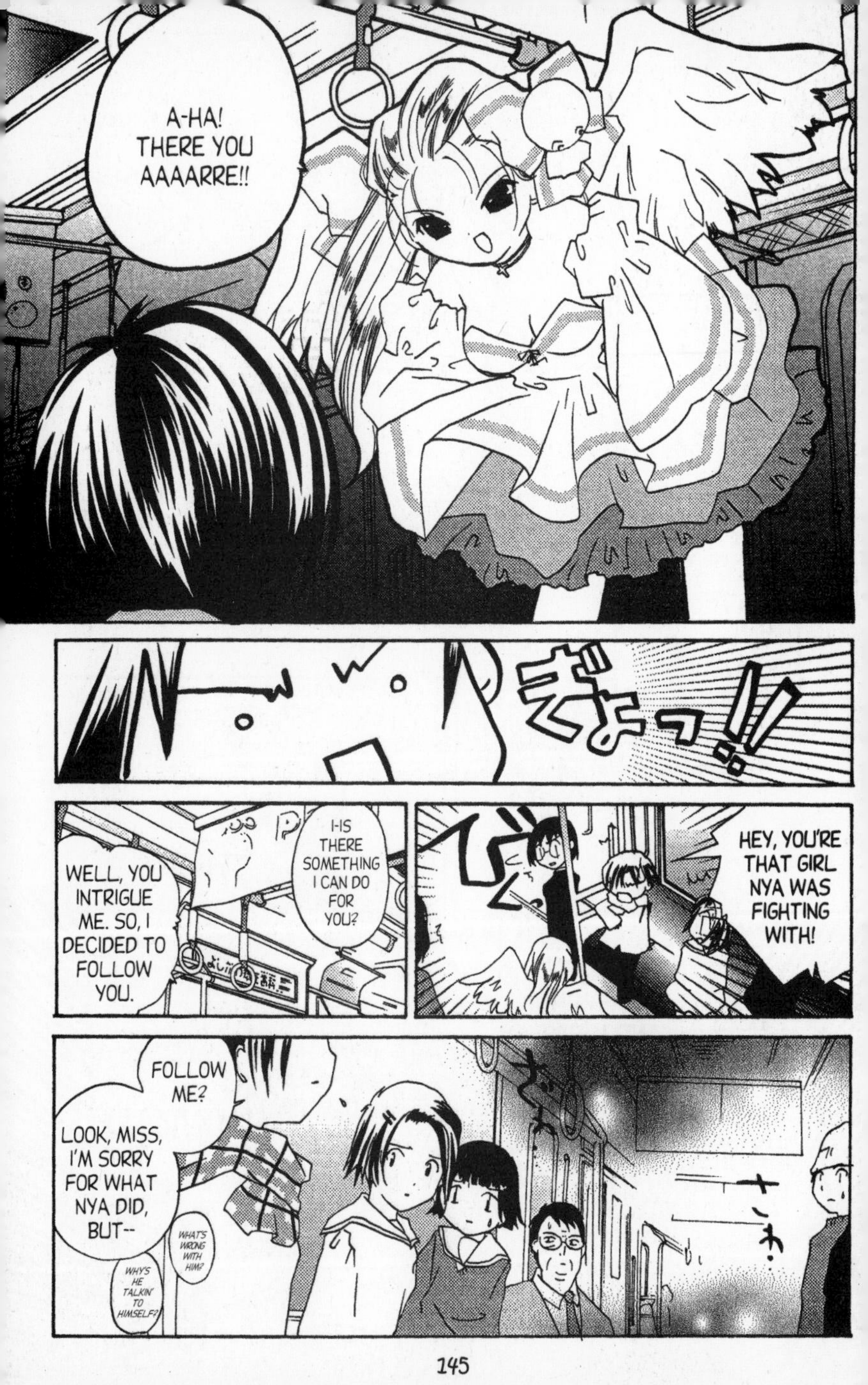
A-HA! THERE YOU AAAARRE!!
ぎょっ!!
HEY, YOU'RE THAT GIRL NYA WAS FIGHTING WITH!
I-IS THERE SOMETHING I CAN DO FOR YOU?
WELL, YOU INTRIGUE ME. SO, I DECIDED TO FOLLOW YOU.
FOLLOW ME?
LOOK, MISS, I'M SORRY FOR WHAT NYA DID, BUT--
WHAT'S WRONG WITH HIM?
WHY'S HE TALKIN' TO HIMSELF?

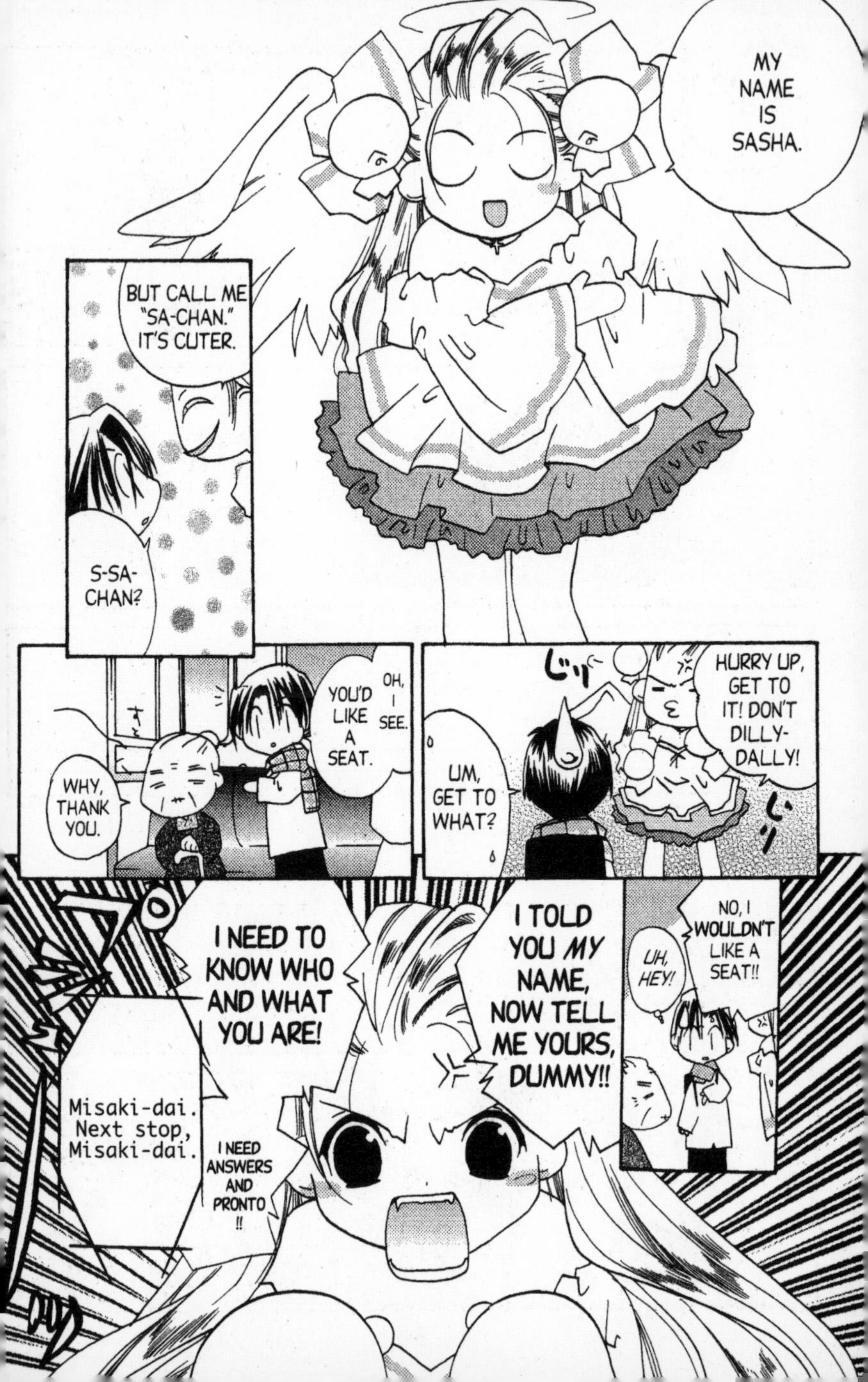
MY NAME IS SASHA.
BUT CALL ME "SA-CHAN." IT'S CUTER.
S-SA-CHAN?
HURRY UP, GET TO IT! DON'T DILLY-DALLY!
UM, GET TO WHAT?
OH, I SEE.
YOU'D LIKE A SEAT.
WHY, THANK YOU.
NO, I WOULDN'T LIKE A SEAT!!
UH, HEY!
I TOLD YOU *MY* NAME, NOW TELL ME YOURS, DUMMY!!
I NEED TO KNOW WHO AND WHAT YOU ARE!
I NEED ANSWERS AND PRONTO!!
Misaki-dai. Next stop, Misaki-dai.

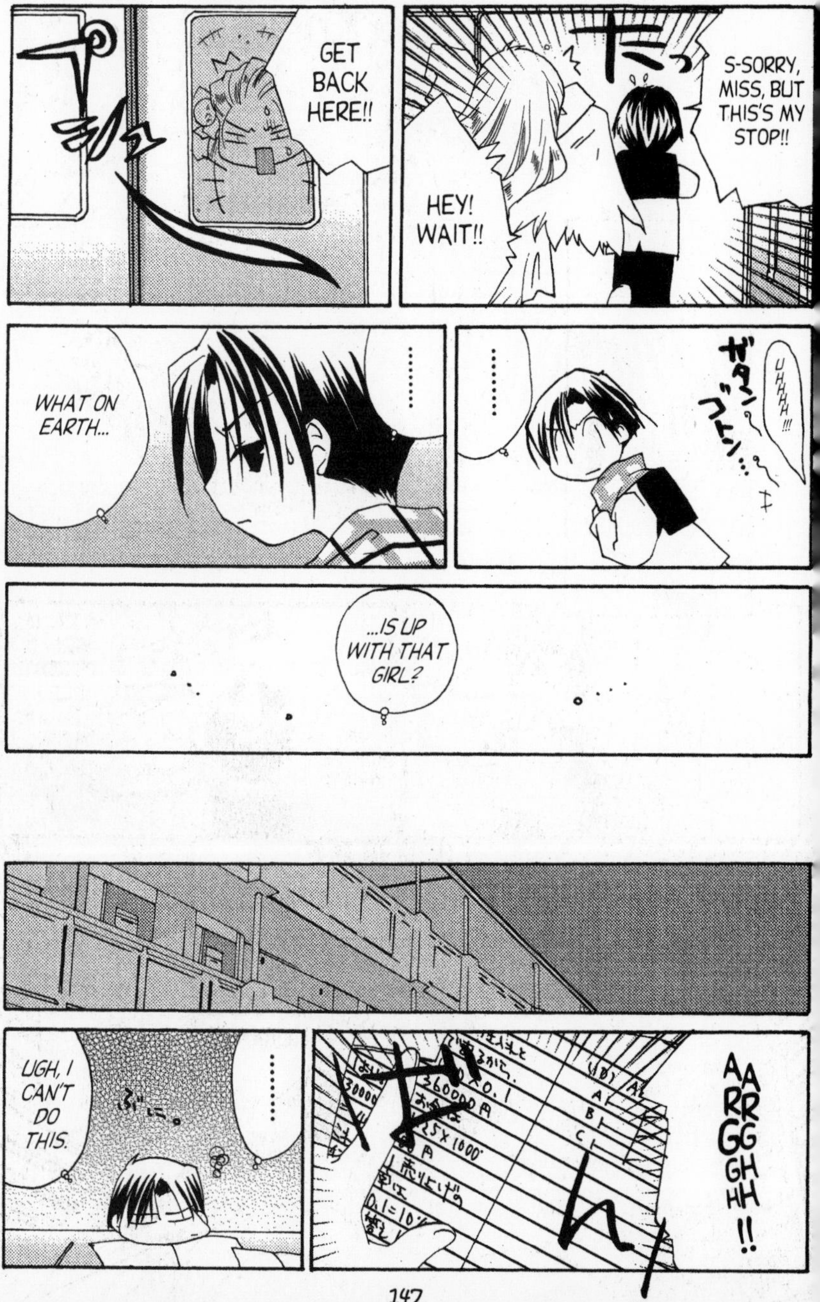
S-SORRY, MISS, BUT THIS'S MY STOP!!
HEY! WAIT!!
GET BACK HERE!!
UHHHH!!!
....
....
WHAT ON EARTH...
...IS UP WITH THAT GIRL?
AARRGGGHHH!!
....
UGH, I CAN'T DO THIS.

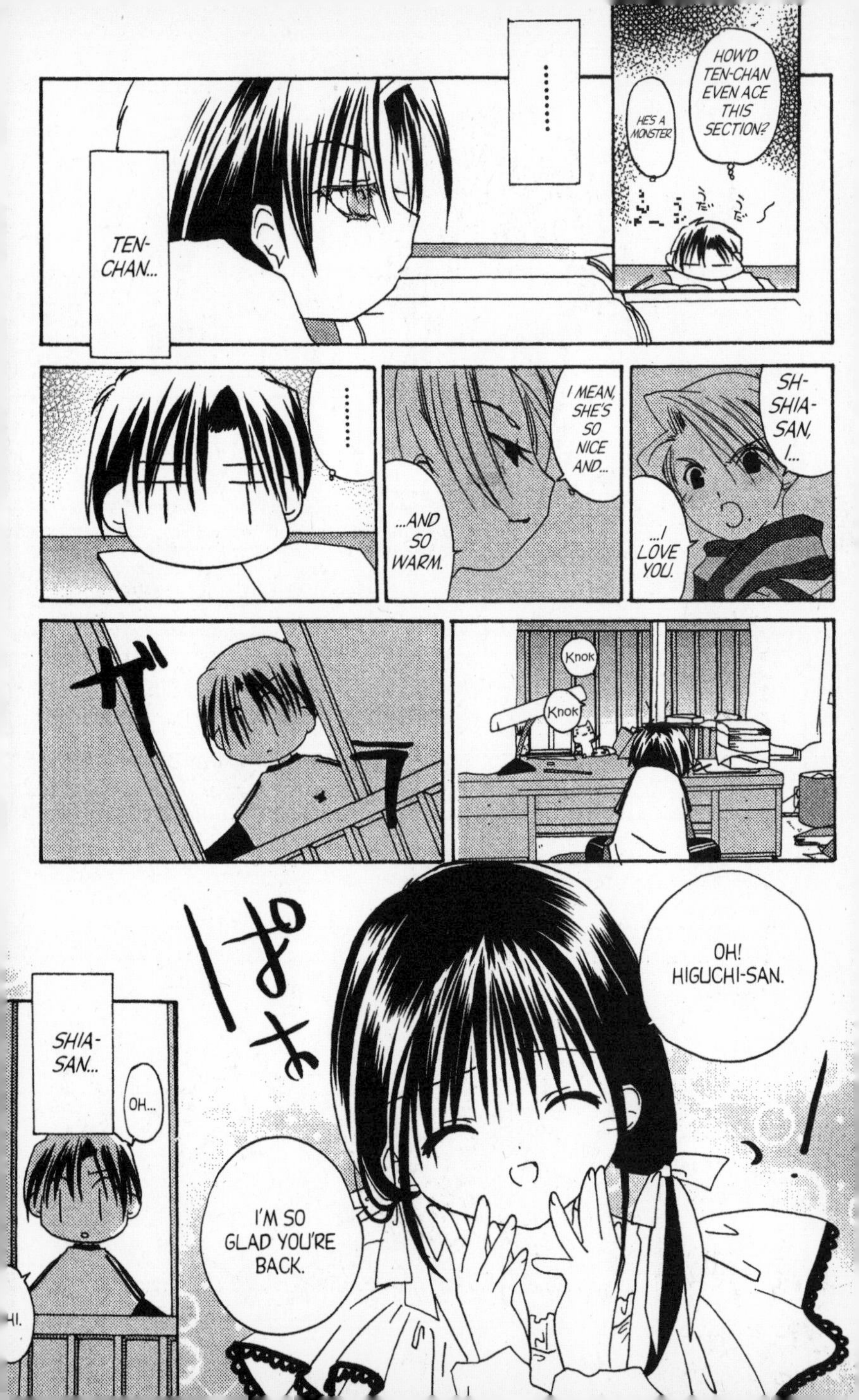
HOW'D TEN-CHAN EVEN ACE THIS SECTION?
HE'S A MONSTER
......
TEN-CHAN...
SH-SHIA-SAN, I...
...I LOVE YOU.
I MEAN, SHE'S SO NICE AND...
...AND SO WARM.
......
Knok
Knok
OH! HIGUCHI-SAN.
I'M SO GLAD YOU'RE BACK.
SHIA-SAN...
OH...
HI.

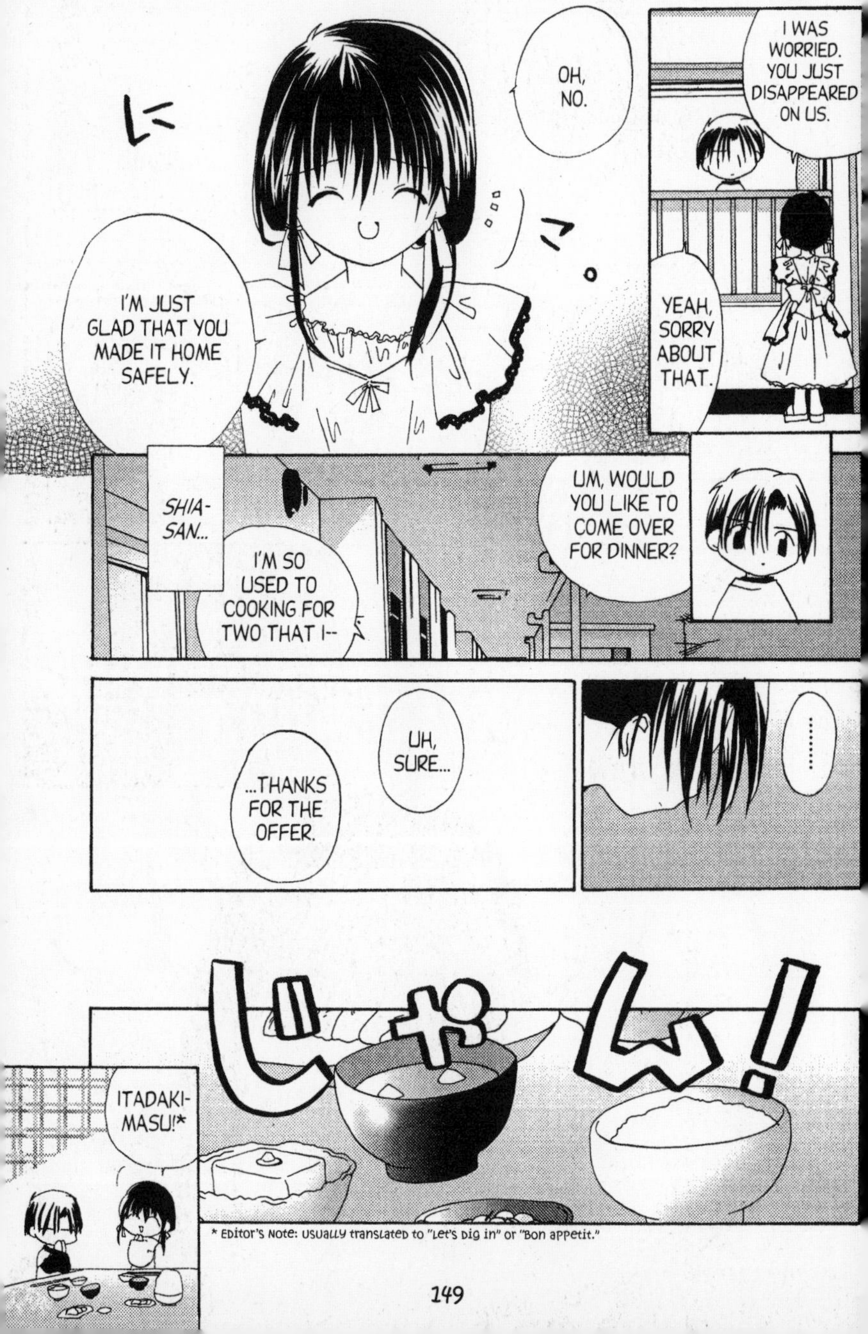
I WAS WORRIED. YOU JUST DISAPPEARED ON US.
YEAH, SORRY ABOUT THAT.
OH, NO.
にこ。
I'M JUST GLAD THAT YOU MADE IT HOME SAFELY.
UM, WOULD YOU LIKE TO COME OVER FOR DINNER?
SHIA-SAN...
I'M SO USED TO COOKING FOR TWO THAT I--
....
UH, SURE...
...THANKS FOR THE OFFER.
じゃん!
ITADAKI-MASU!*

* Editor's Note: Usually translated to "Let's dig in" or "Bon appetit."

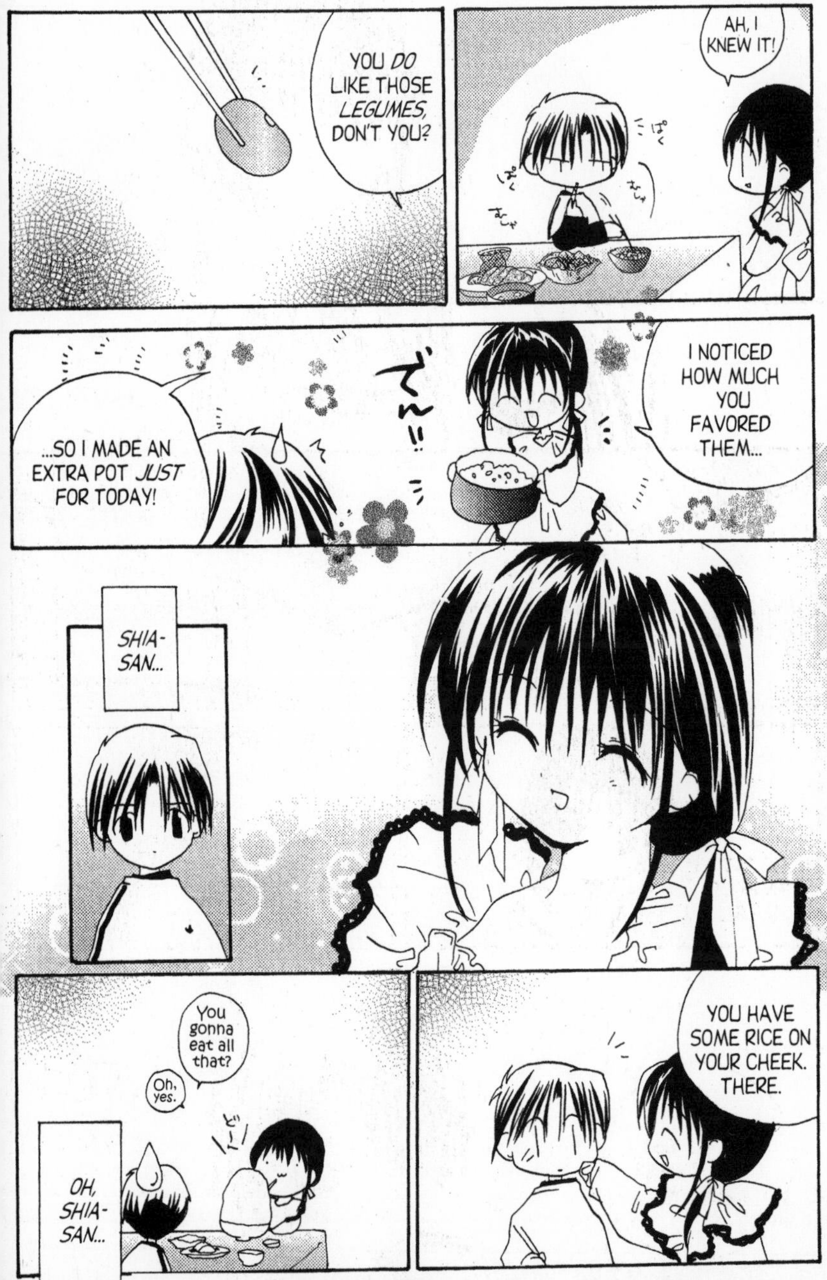

AH, I KNEW IT!
YOU *DO* LIKE THOSE *LEGUMES,* DON'T YOU?
I NOTICED HOW MUCH YOU FAVORED THEM...
でん!!
...SO I MADE AN EXTRA POT *JUST* FOR TODAY!
SHIA-SAN...
YOU HAVE SOME RICE ON YOUR CHEEK. THERE.
You gonna eat all that?
Oh, yes.
OH, SHIA-SAN...

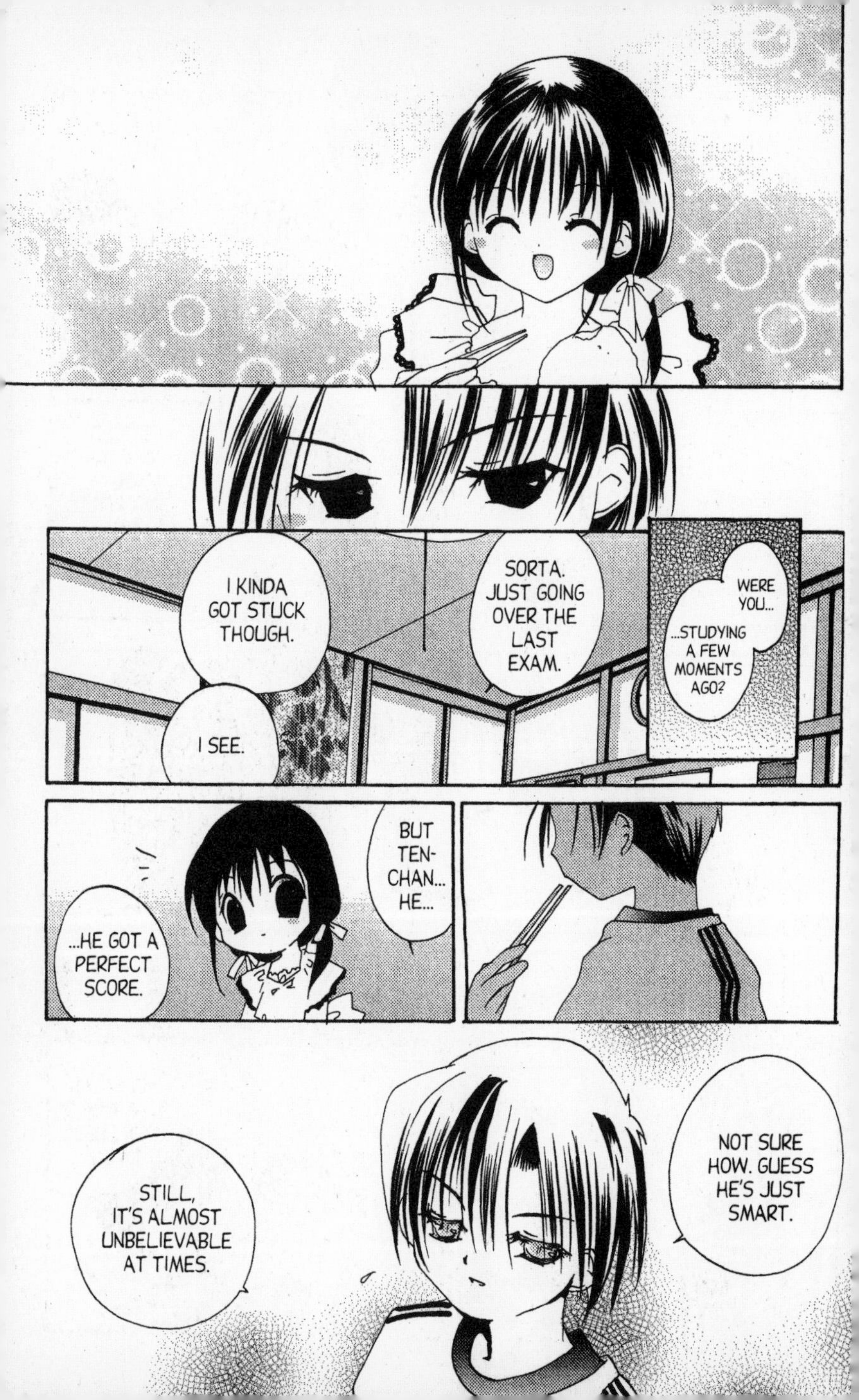
WERE YOU...
...STUDYING A FEW MOMENTS AGO?
SORTA. JUST GOING OVER THE LAST EXAM.
I KINDA GOT STUCK THOUGH.
I SEE.
BUT TEN-CHAN... HE...
...HE GOT A PERFECT SCORE.
NOT SURE HOW. GUESS HE'S JUST SMART.
STILL, IT'S ALMOST UNBELIEVABLE AT TIMES.

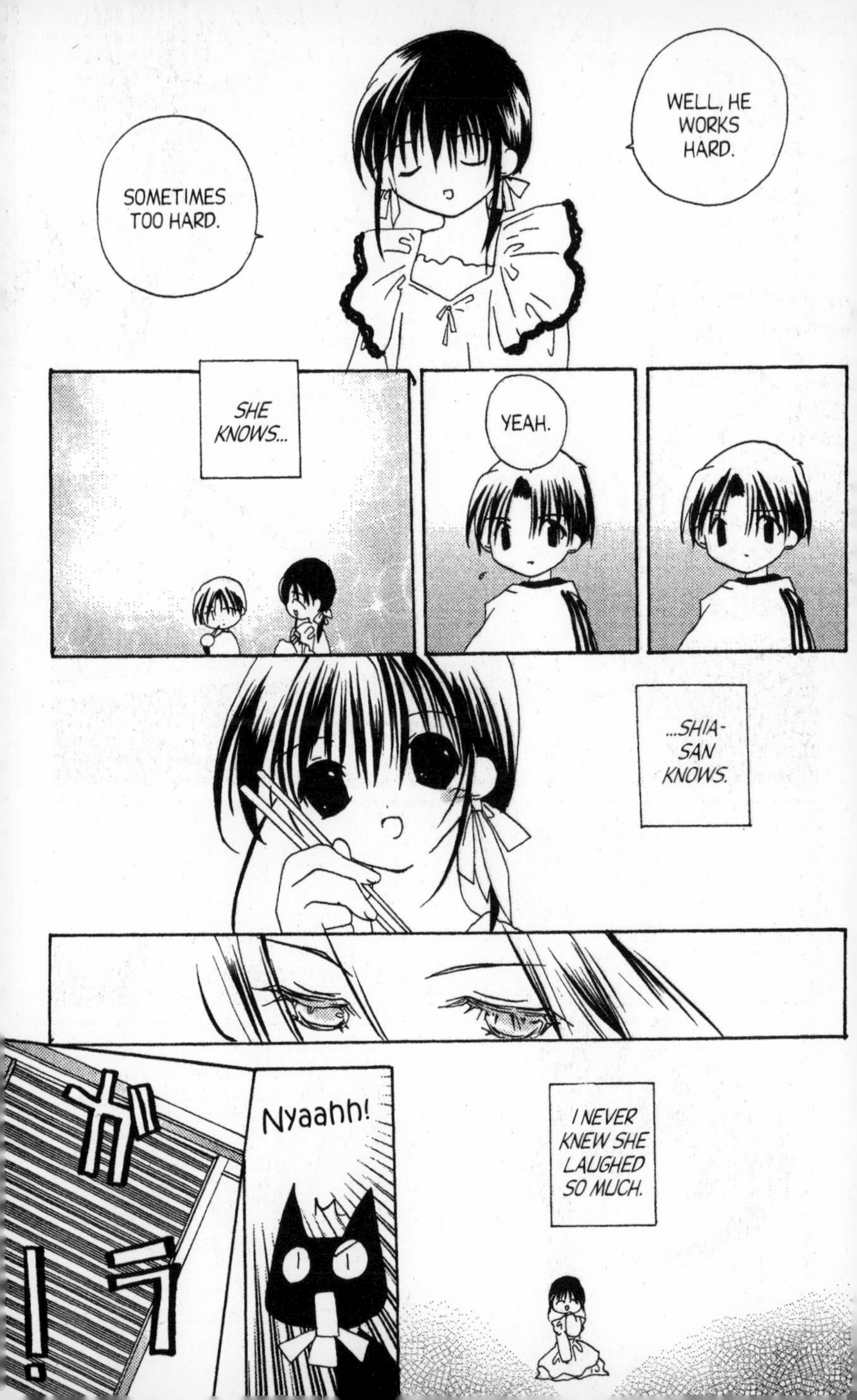
WELL, HE WORKS HARD.
SOMETIMES TOO HARD.
YEAH.
SHE KNOWS...
...SHIA-SAN KNOWS.
I NEVER KNEW SHE LAUGHED SO MUCH.
Nyaahh!
ガラ!

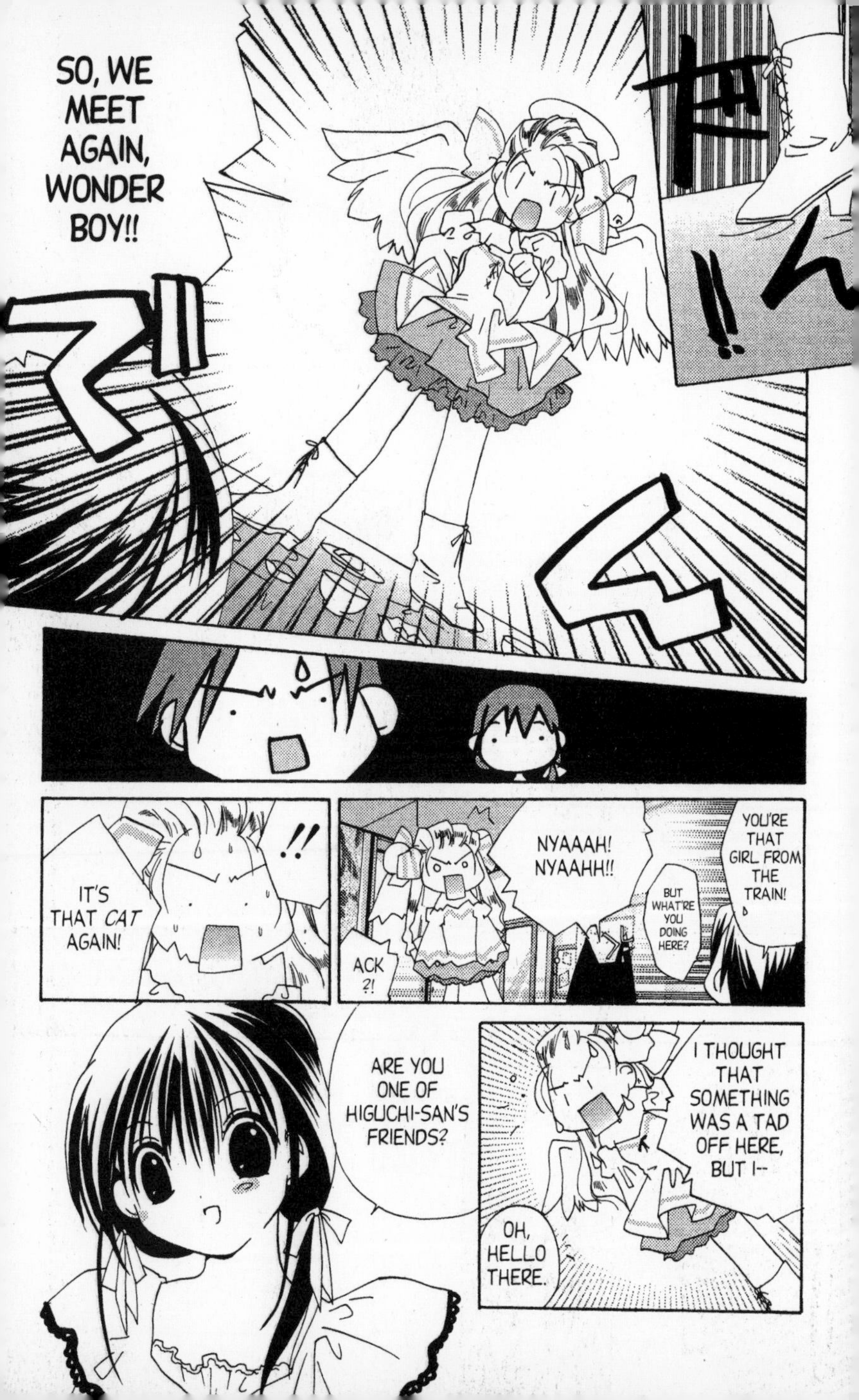
SO, WE MEET AGAIN, WONDER BOY!!
YOU'RE THAT GIRL FROM THE TRAIN!
BUT WHAT'RE YOU DOING HERE?
NYAAAH! NYAAHH!!
ACK ?!
!!
IT'S THAT *CAT* AGAIN!
I THOUGHT THAT SOMETHING WAS A TAD OFF HERE, BUT I--
OH, HELLO THERE.
ARE YOU ONE OF HIGUCHI-SAN'S FRIENDS?

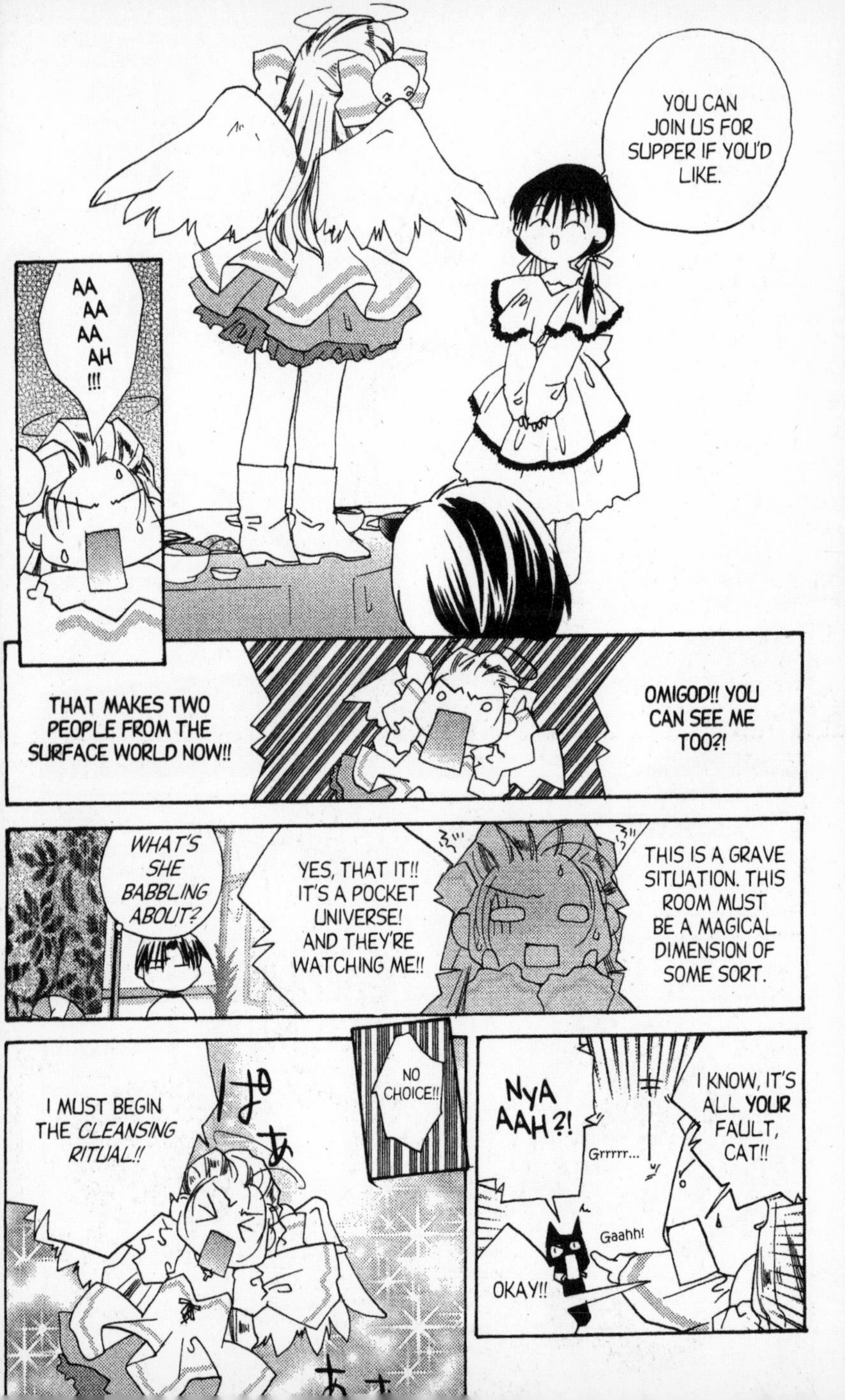
YOU CAN JOIN US FOR SUPPER IF YOU'D LIKE.
AA AA AA AH !!!
OMIGOD!! YOU CAN SEE ME TOO?!
THAT MAKES TWO PEOPLE FROM THE SURFACE WORLD NOW!!
THIS IS A GRAVE SITUATION. THIS ROOM MUST BE A MAGICAL DIMENSION OF SOME SORT.
YES, THAT IT!! IT'S A POCKET UNIVERSE! AND THEY'RE WATCHING ME!!
WHAT'S SHE BABBLING ABOUT?
I KNOW, IT'S ALL YOUR FAULT, CAT!!
NyA AAH?!
Grrrrr...
Gaahh!
OKAY!!
NO CHOICE!!
I MUST BEGIN THE CLEANSING RITUAL!!

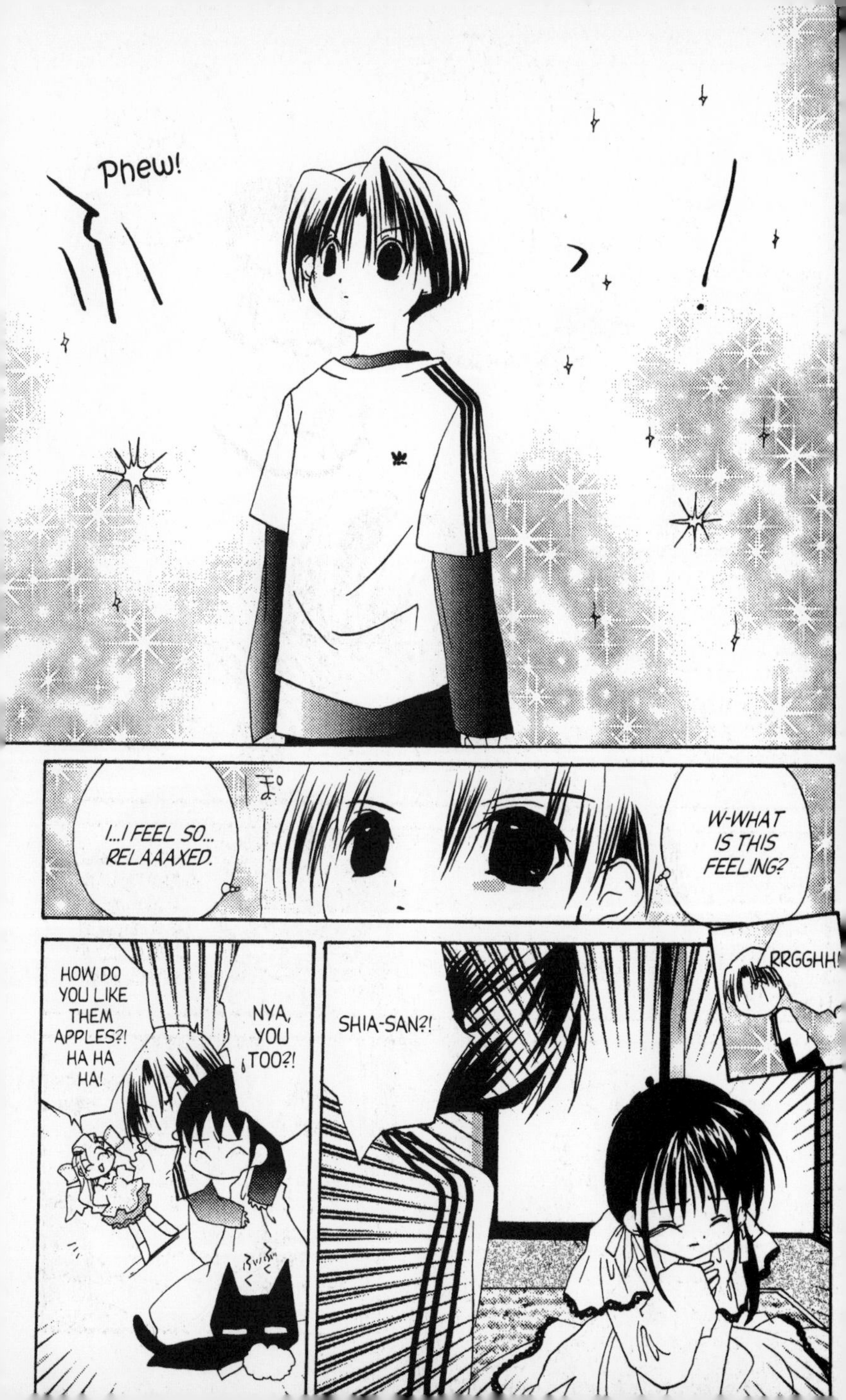
Phew!
W-WHAT IS THIS FEELING?
I...I FEEL SO... RELAAAXED.
RRGGHH!
SHIA-SAN?!
NYA, YOU TOO?!
HOW DO YOU LIKE THEM APPLES?! HA HA HA!

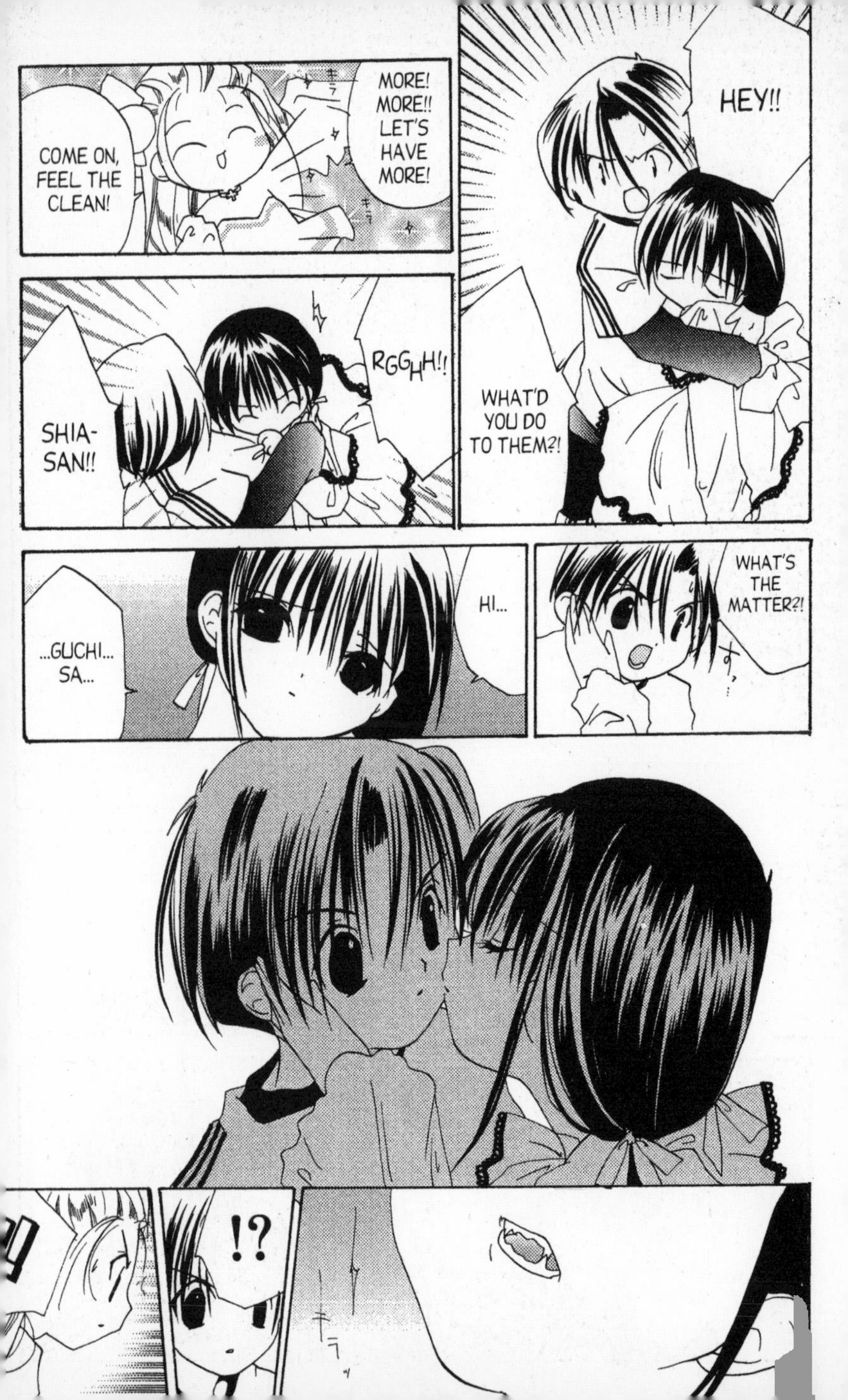
HEY!!
WHAT'D YOU DO TO THEM?!
MORE! MORE!! LET'S HAVE MORE!
COME ON, FEEL THE CLEAN!
RGGHH!!
SHIA-SAN!!
WHAT'S THE MATTER?!
HI...
...GUCHI... SA...
!?

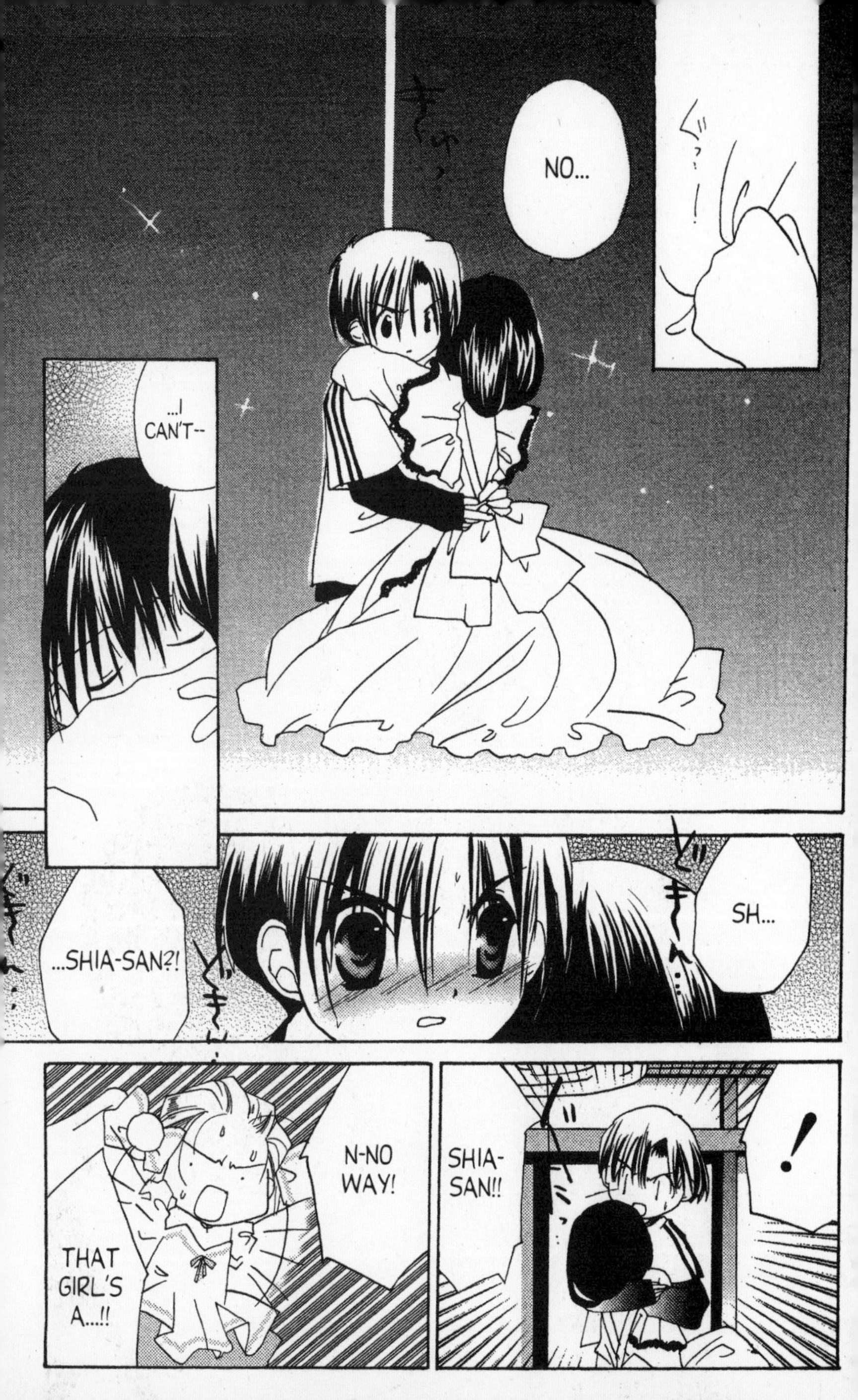
NO...
...I CAN'T--
SH...
...SHIA-SAN?!
SHIA-SAN!!
N-NO WAY!
THAT GIRL'S A...!!

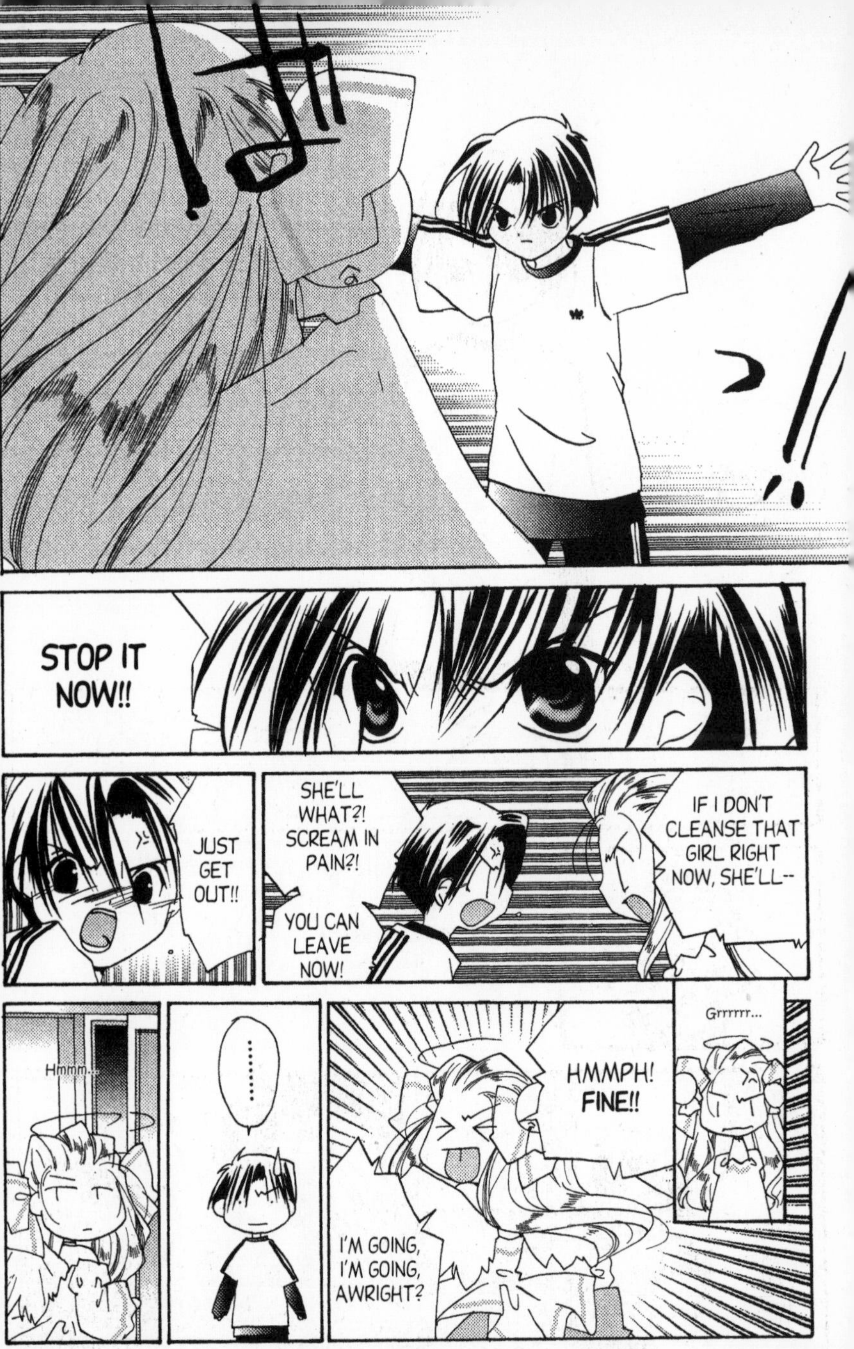
!!
STOP IT NOW!!
IF I DON'T CLEANSE THAT GIRL RIGHT NOW, SHE'LL--
SHE'LL WHAT?! SCREAM IN PAIN?!
YOU CAN LEAVE NOW!
JUST GET OUT!!
Grrrrrr...
HMMPH! FINE!!
I'M GOING, I'M GOING, AWRIGHT?
......
Hmmm...

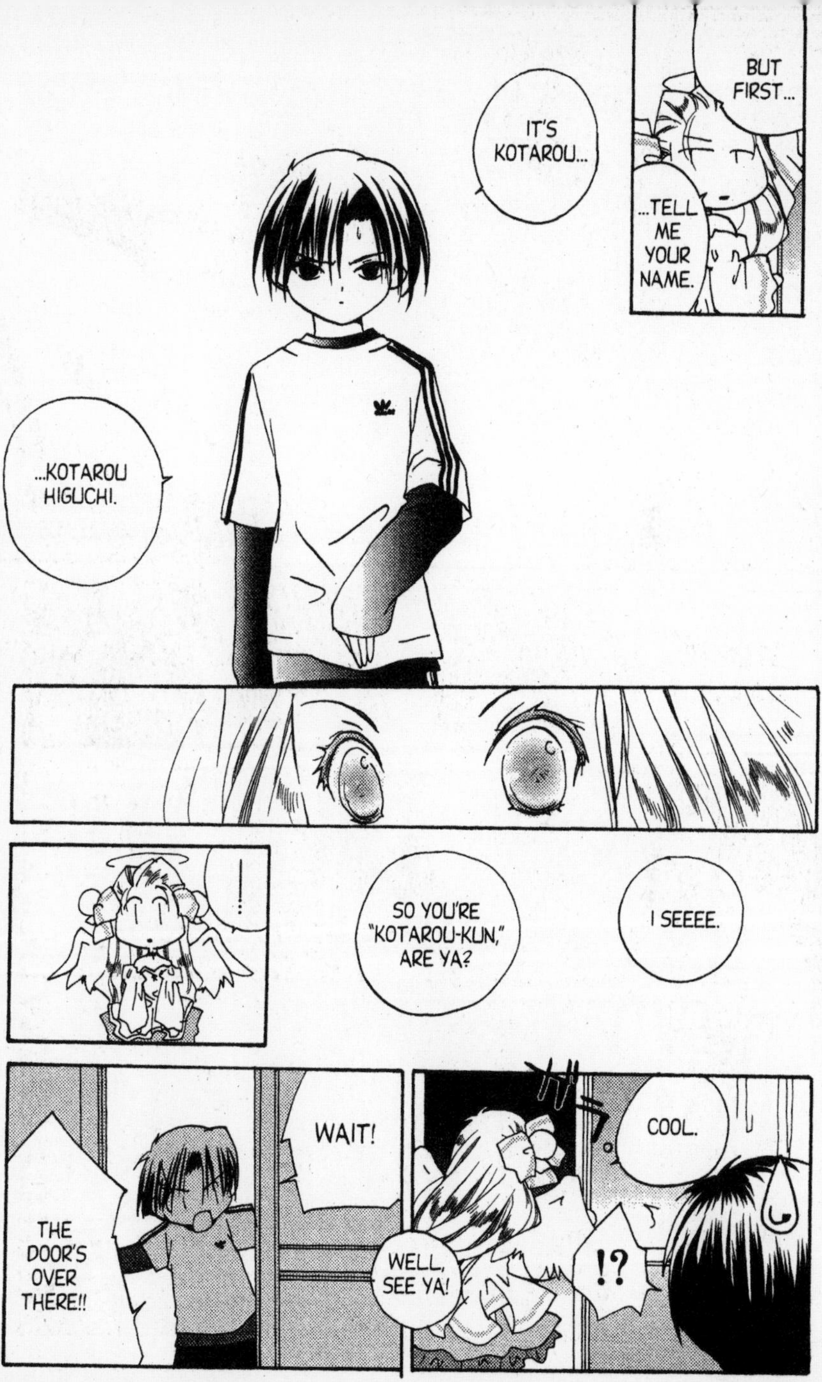
BUT FIRST...
...TELL ME YOUR NAME.
IT'S KOTAROU...
...KOTAROU HIGUCHI.
!
I SEEEE.
SO YOU'RE "KOTAROU-KUN," ARE YA?
!
COOL.
WELL, SEE YA!
!?
WAIT!
THE DOOR'S OVER THERE!!

RRRGHH!!

....

SHIA-SAN, WHAT'S WRONG?!

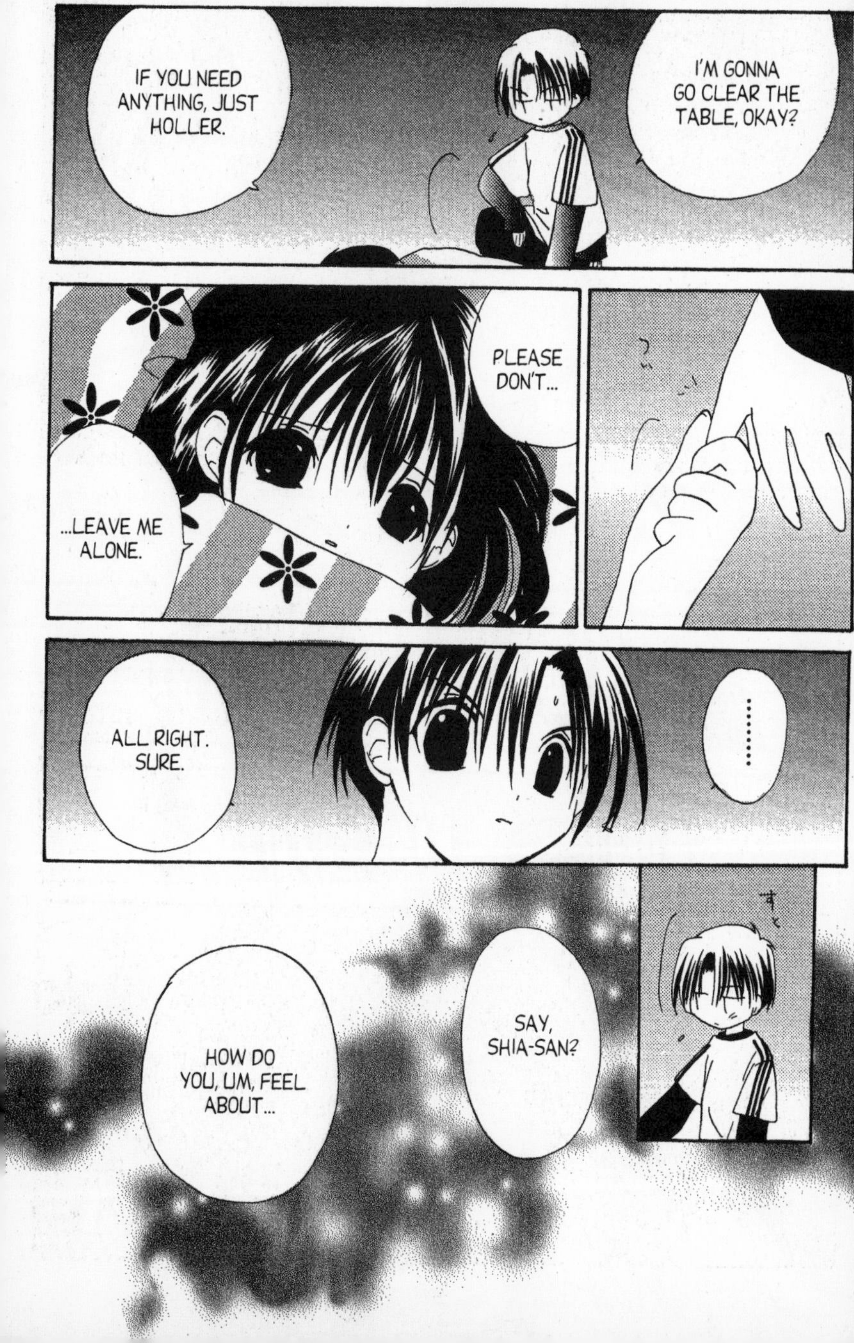
I'M GONNA GO CLEAR THE TABLE, OKAY?
IF YOU NEED ANYTHING, JUST HOLLER.
PLEASE DON'T...
...LEAVE ME ALONE.
......
ALL RIGHT. SURE.
SAY, SHIA-SAN?
HOW DO YOU, UM, FEEL ABOUT...

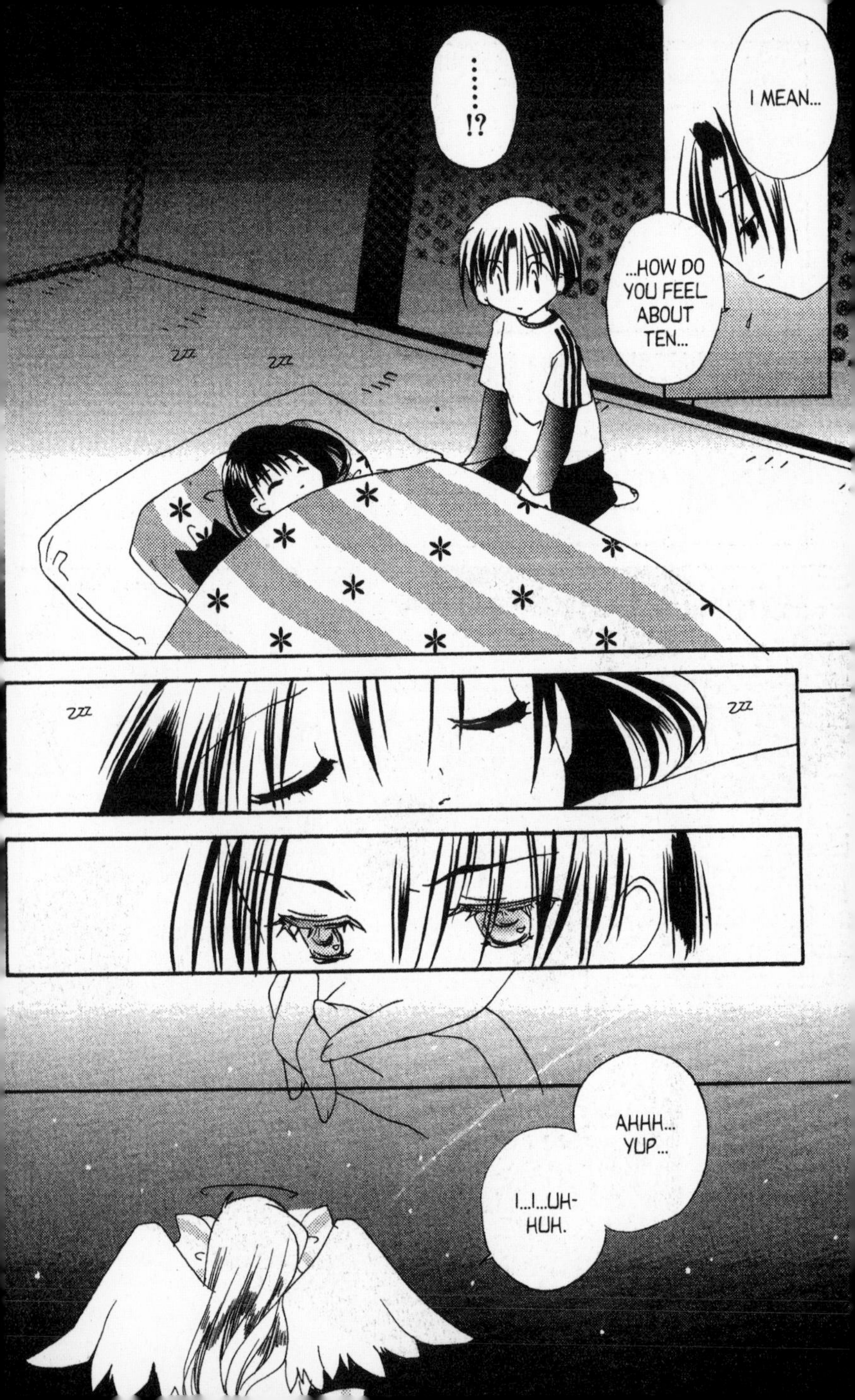
I MEAN...
...HOW DO YOU FEEL ABOUT TEN...
......!?
ZZZ
ZZZ
ZZZ
ZZZ
AHHH... YUP...
I...I...UH-HUH.

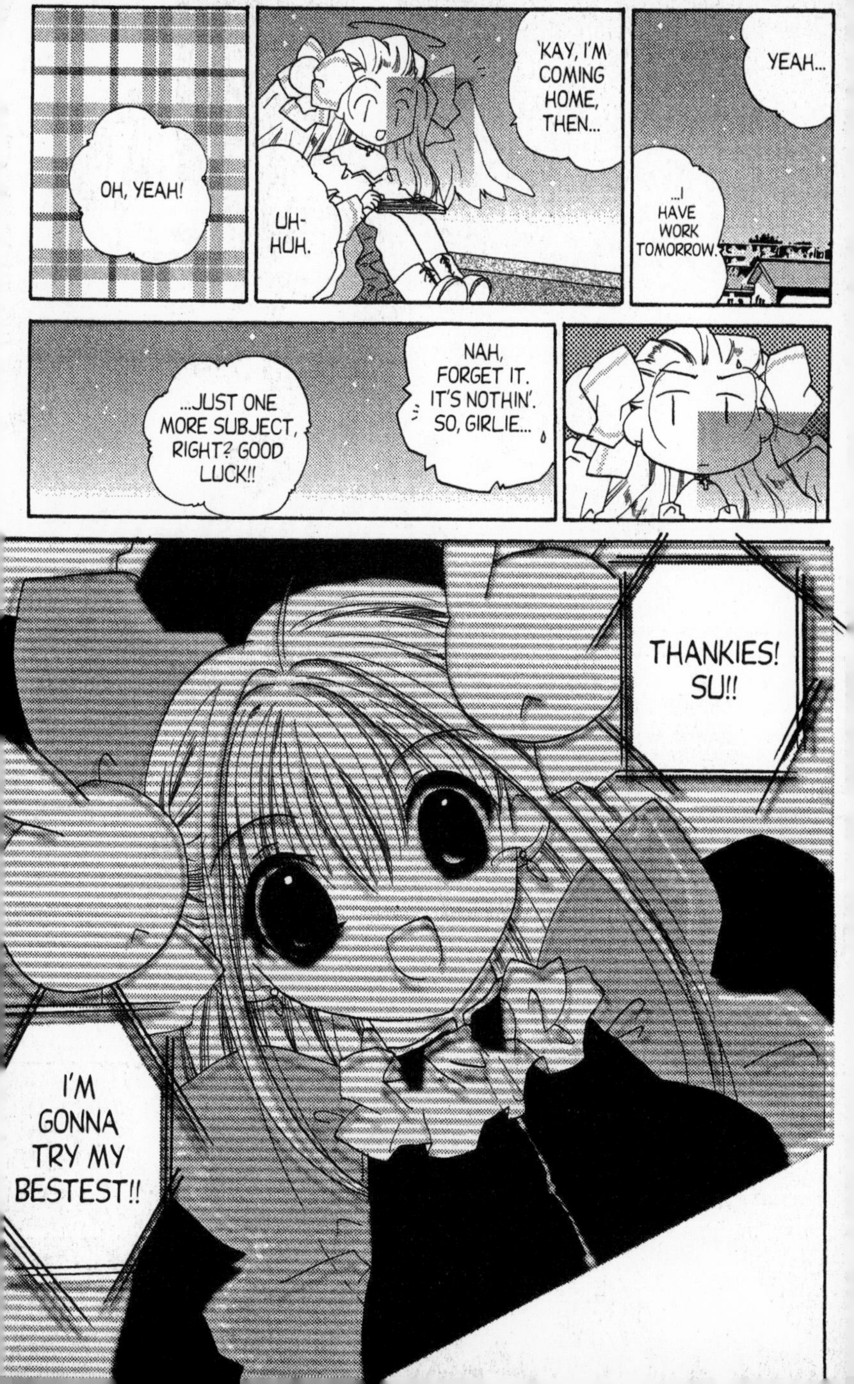
YEAH...
...I HAVE WORK TOMORROW.
'KAY, I'M COMING HOME, THEN...
UH-HUH.
OH, YEAH!
NAH, FORGET IT. IT'S NOTHIN'. SO, GIRLIE...
...JUST ONE MORE SUBJECT, RIGHT? GOOD LUCK!!
THANKIES! SU!!
I'M GONNA TRY MY BESTEST!!

☆ Why, hello! Koge-Donbo here. Yay, Volume 3's out without a hitch! A big thanks goes out to everyone who helped and guided me through this one.

☆ As you've probably noticed, this story has a lot of 6th graders in it. And yes, I do get quite a few comments from all over saying stuff like, "I've never met any 6th graders as grown up as your characters."

But they're absolutely right and I agree too! (I know, I shouldn't.)

☆ But there's an interesting theory I heard that proves that 6th graders are indeed more mature than middle schoolers. See, they're not only the older kids in elementary school, but they're also new students at the same time... and somehow, these two things just kinda mesh and influence their behavior.

(Of course, this is just something I heard. Sounds good, though.) Heh, heh, heh, heh...

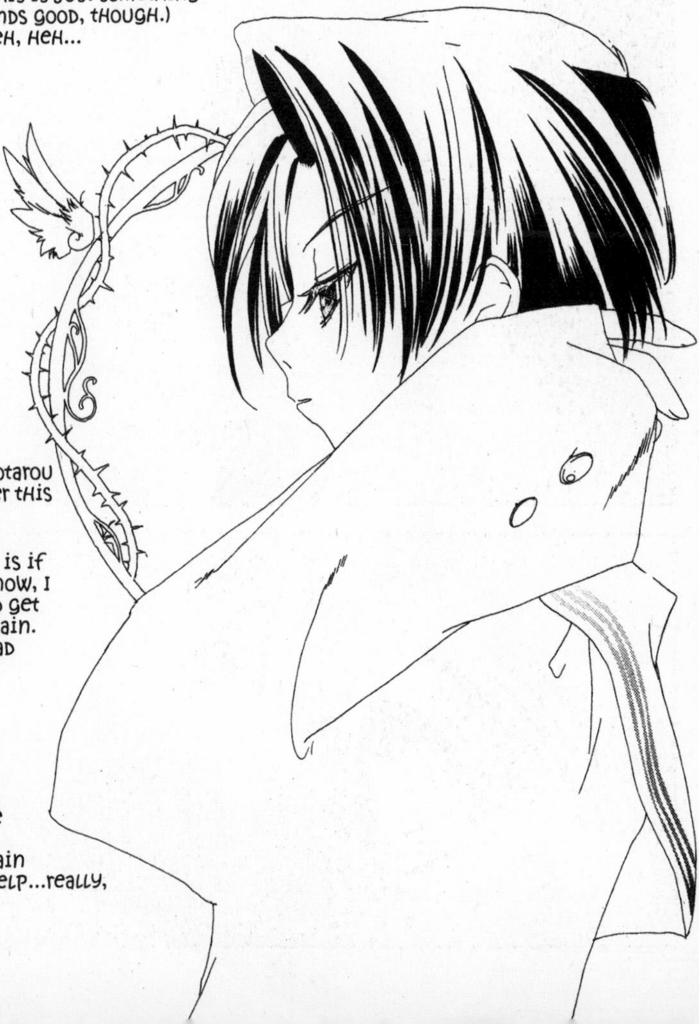

By the way, Kotarou stole the cover this time. →

Reason being is if I didn't do it now, I don't think I'd get the chance again. Doh! What a sad reason.

And special thanks to Kaie Midorino-san. Thank you again for all your help...really, I mean it!

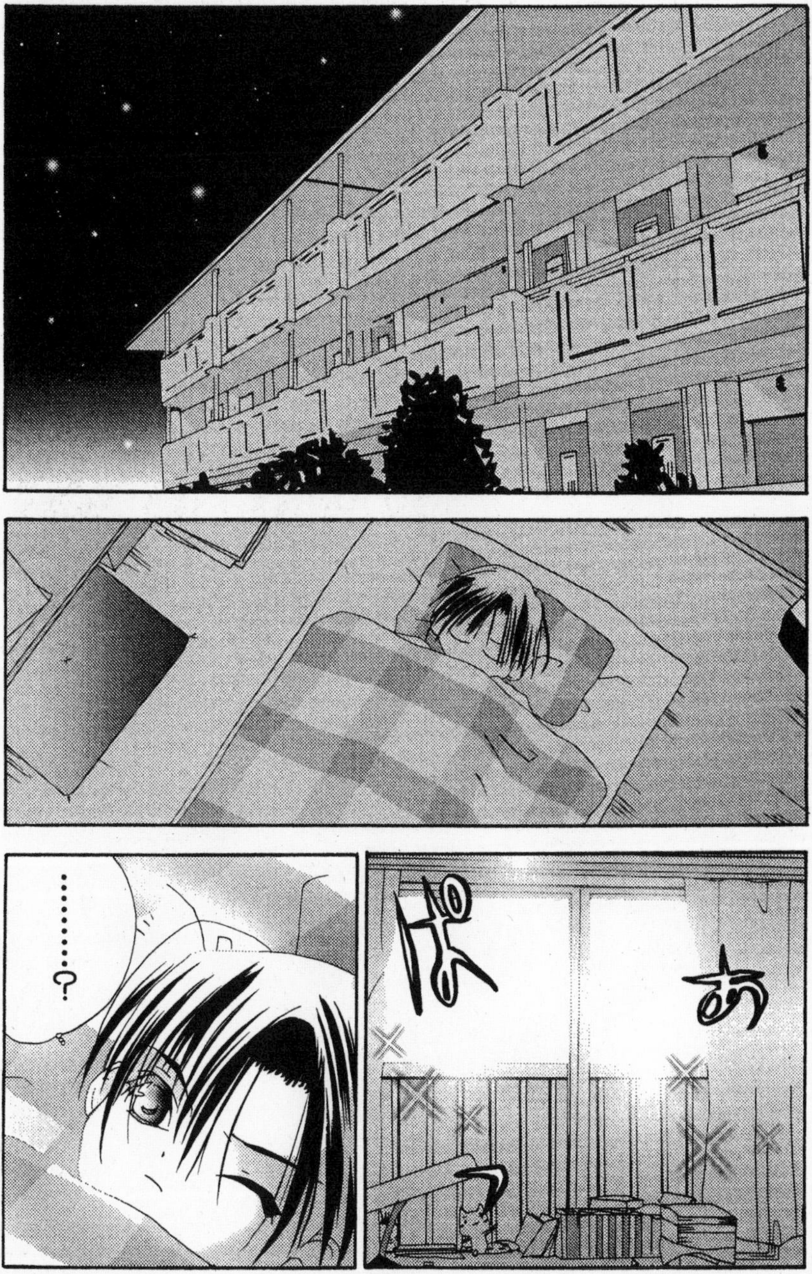
あ
パッ
……?

Lesson 19

How to Help with Chores

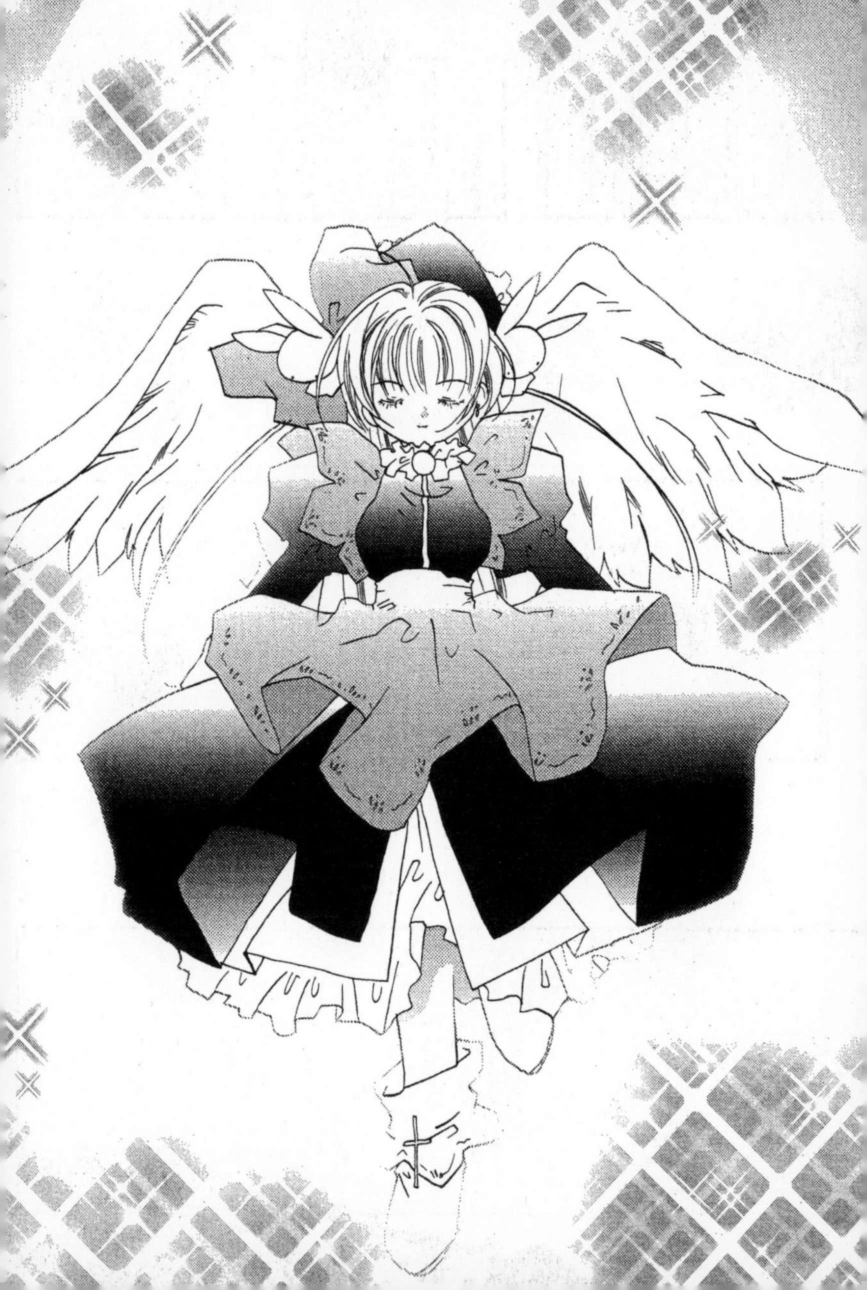

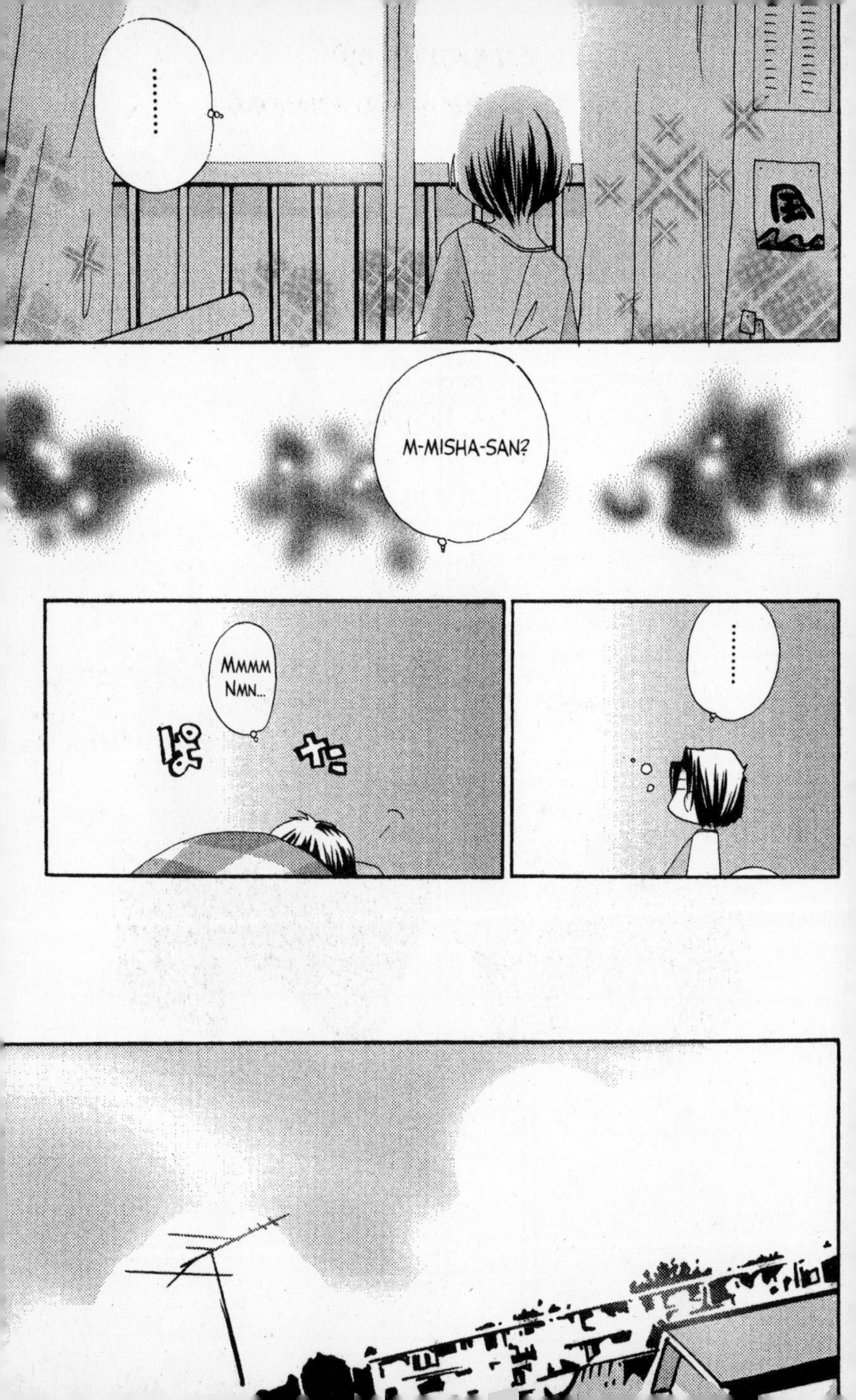
......
M-MISHA-SAN?
....
MMMM NMN...

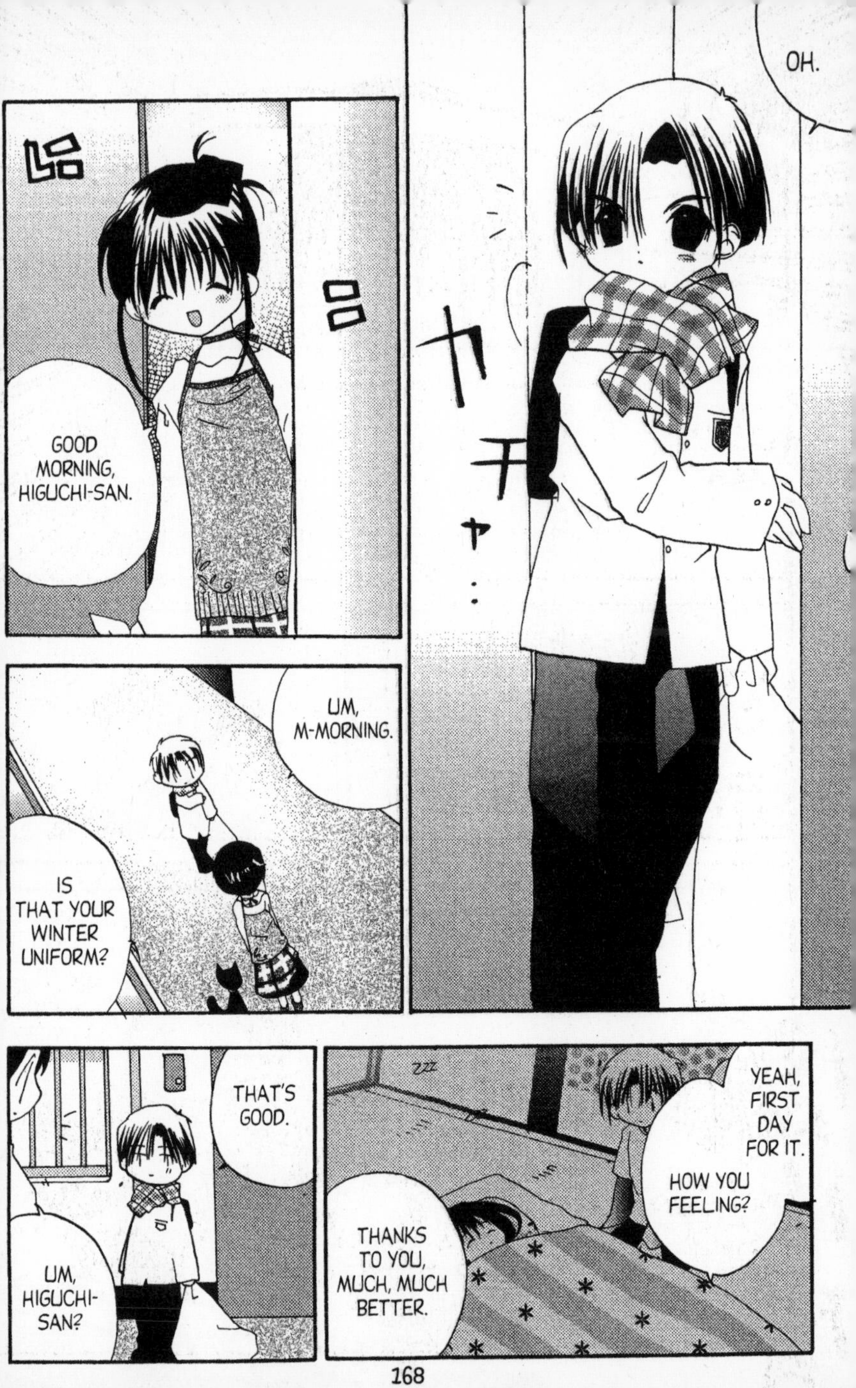
OH.
カチャ‥
GOOD MORNING, HIGUCHI-SAN.
UM, M-MORNING.
IS THAT YOUR WINTER UNIFORM?
YEAH, FIRST DAY FOR IT.
HOW YOU FEELING?
THANKS TO YOU, MUCH, MUCH BETTER.
THAT'S GOOD.
UM, HIGUCHI-SAN?

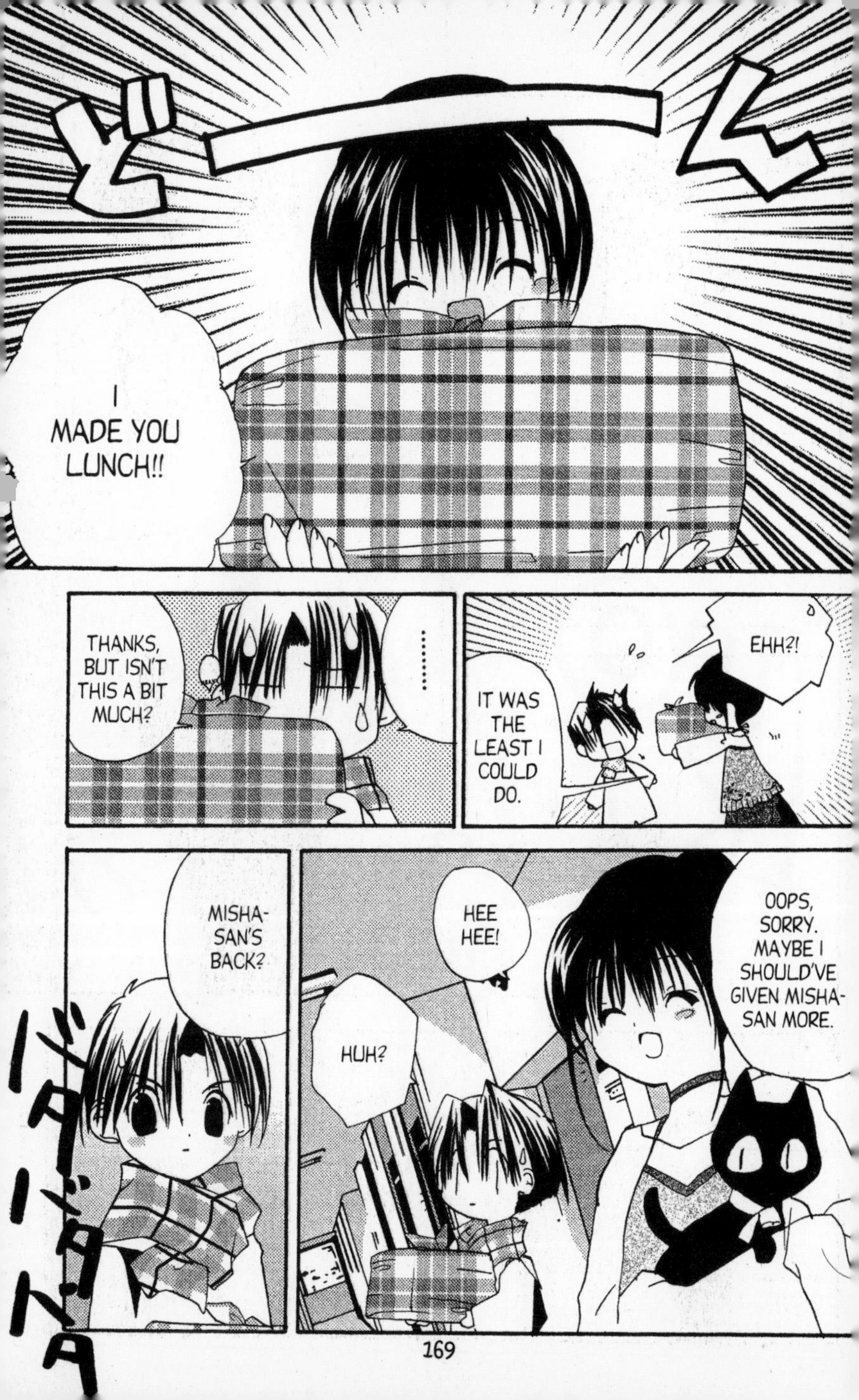
I MADE YOU LUNCH!!
EHH?!
IT WAS THE LEAST I COULD DO.
....
THANKS, BUT ISN'T THIS A BIT MUCH?
OOPS, SORRY. MAYBE I SHOULD'VE GIVEN MISHA-SAN MORE.
HEE HEE!
HUH?
MISHA-SAN'S BACK?

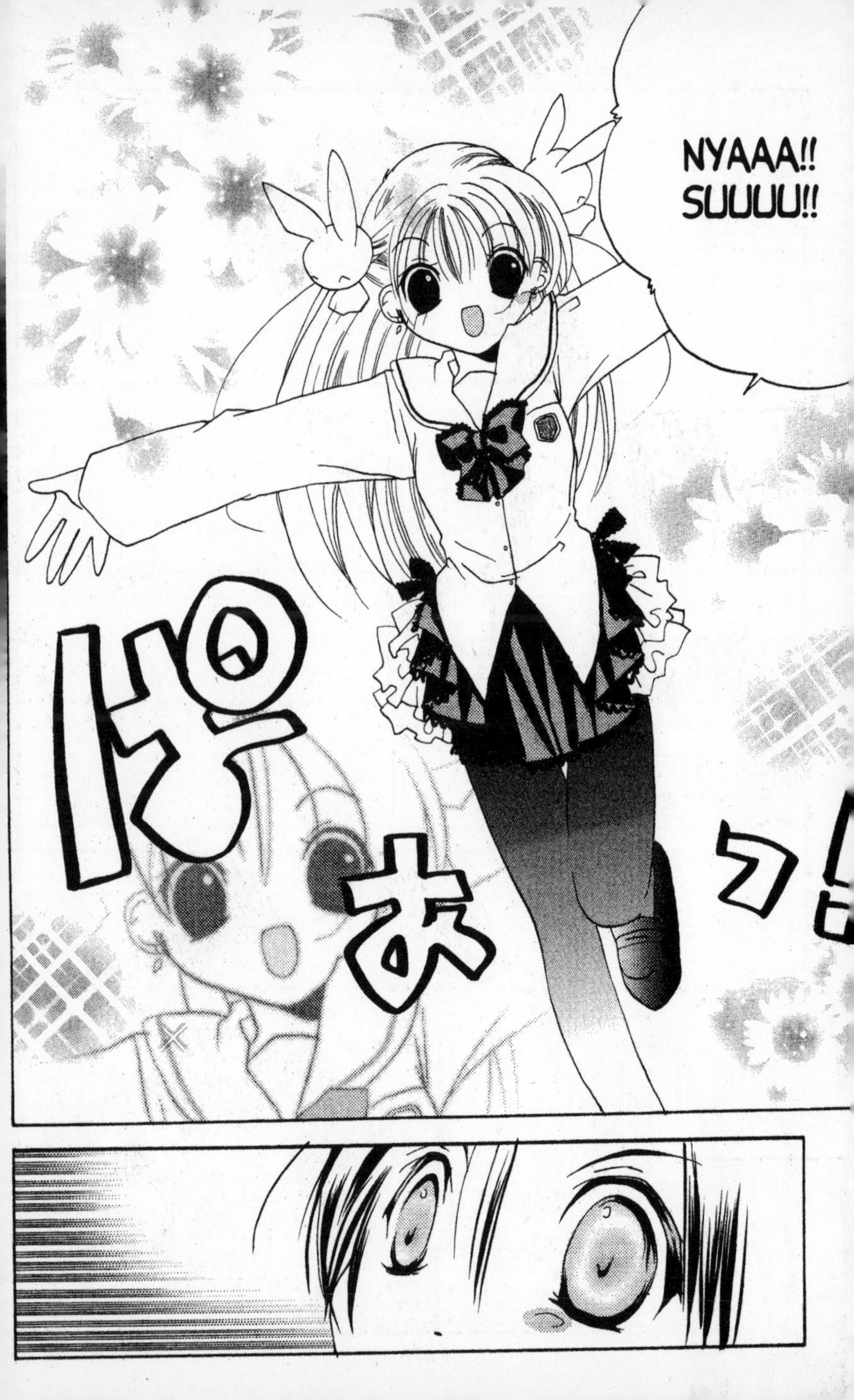
NYAAA!!
SUUUU!!
ぱあっ!

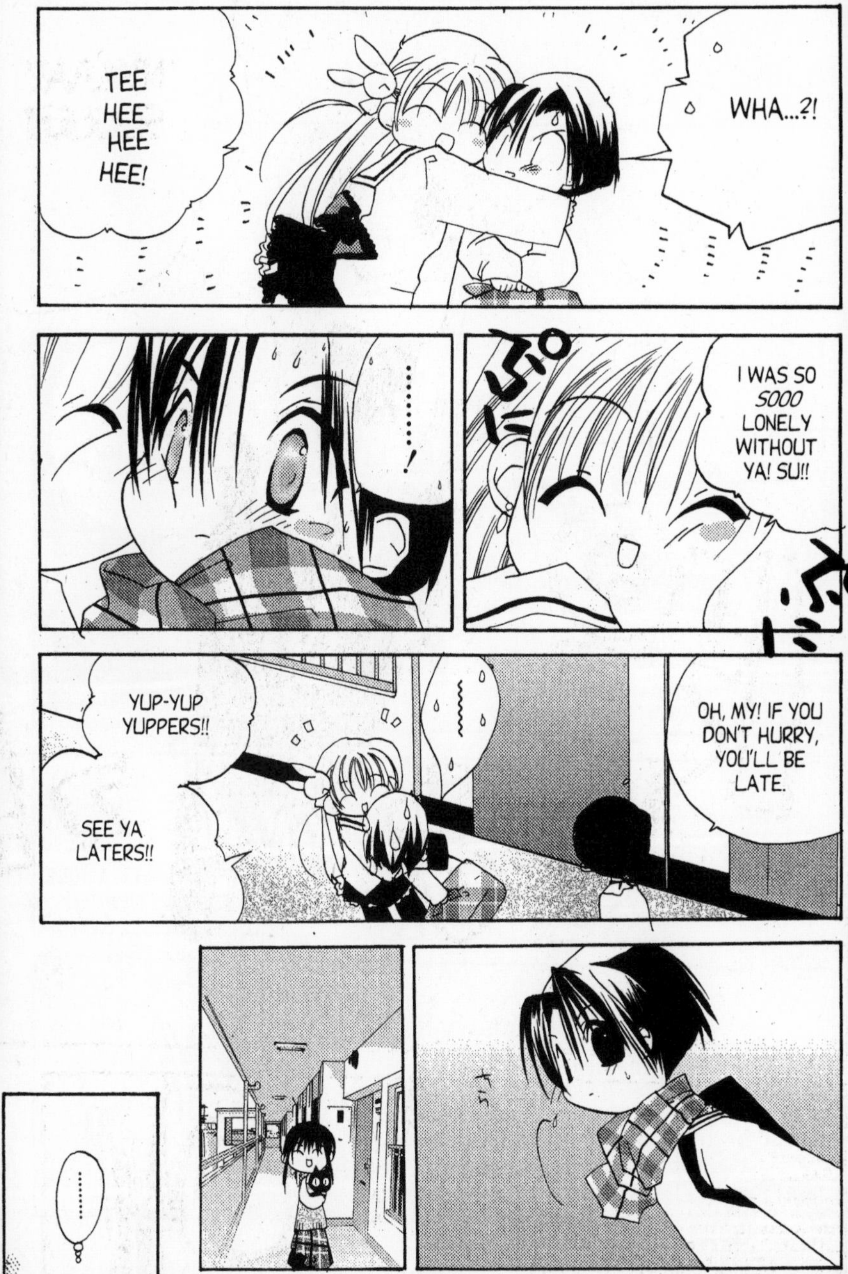
WHA...?!
TEE HEE HEE HEE!
ぷに
I WAS SO SOOO LONELY WITHOUT YA! SU!!
......!
OH, MY! IF YOU DON'T HURRY, YOU'LL BE LATE.
YUP-YUP YUPPERS!!
SEE YA LATERS!!
....

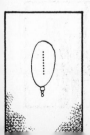

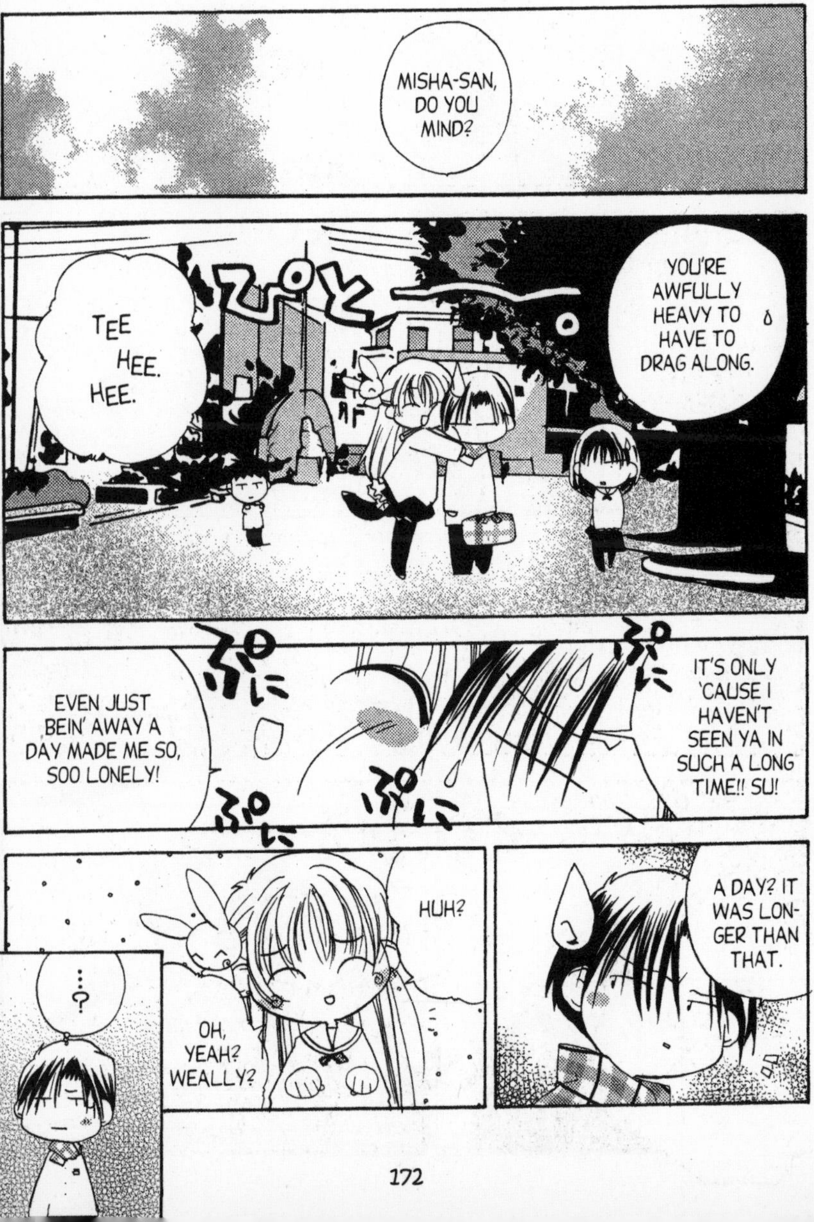
MISHA-SAN, DO YOU MIND?
YOU'RE AWFULLY HEAVY TO HAVE TO DRAG ALONG.
TEE HEE. HEE.
IT'S ONLY 'CAUSE I HAVEN'T SEEN YA IN SUCH A LONG TIME!! SU!
ぷに
ぷに
ぷに
ぷに
EVEN JUST BEIN' AWAY A DAY MADE ME SO, SOO LONELY!
A DAY? IT WAS LONGER THAN THAT.
HUH?
OH, YEAH? WEALLY?
...?

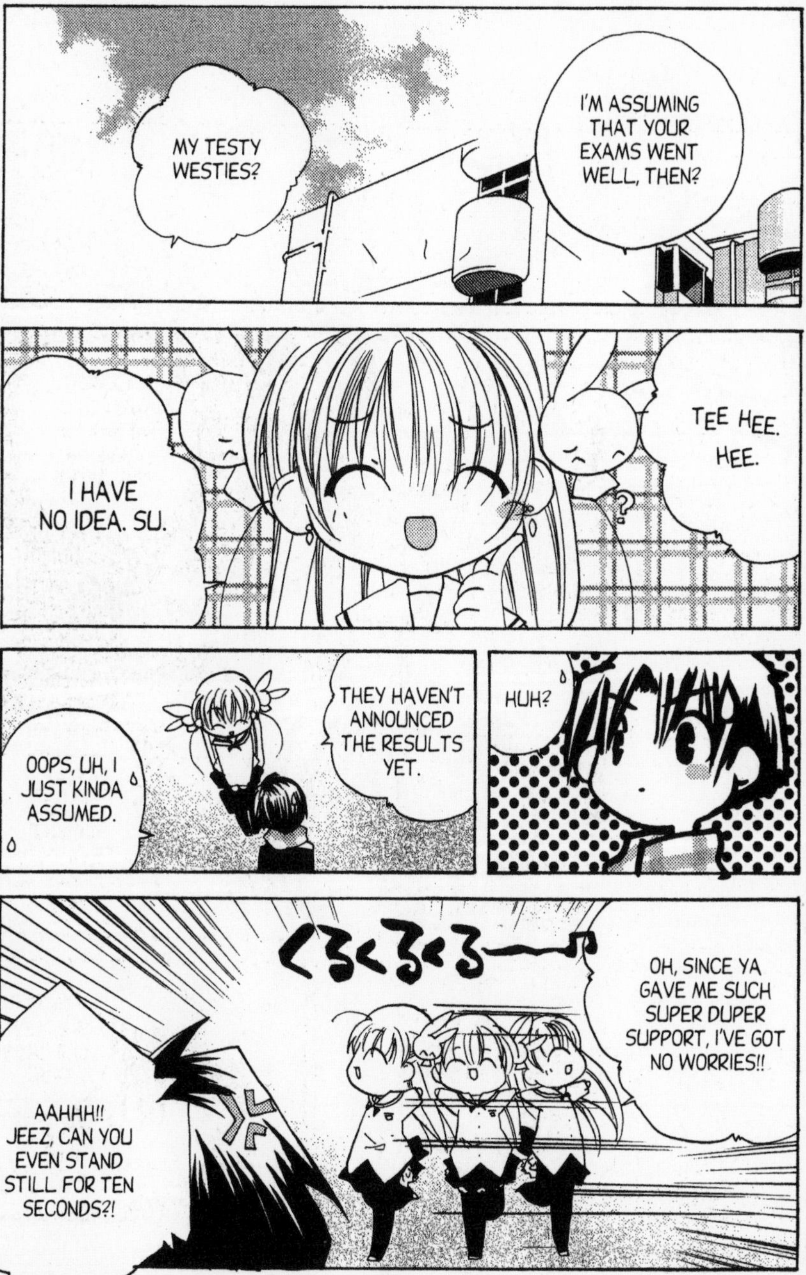

I'M ASSUMING THAT YOUR EXAMS WENT WELL, THEN?
MY TESTY WESTIES?
TEE HEE. HEE.
I HAVE NO IDEA. SU.
HUH?
THEY HAVEN'T ANNOUNCED THE RESULTS YET.
OOPS, UH, I JUST KINDA ASSUMED.
OH, SINCE YA GAVE ME SUCH SUPER DUPER SUPPORT, I'VE GOT NO WORRIES!!
くるくるくる ー♪
AAHHH!! JEEZ, CAN YOU EVEN STAND STILL FOR TEN SECONDS?!

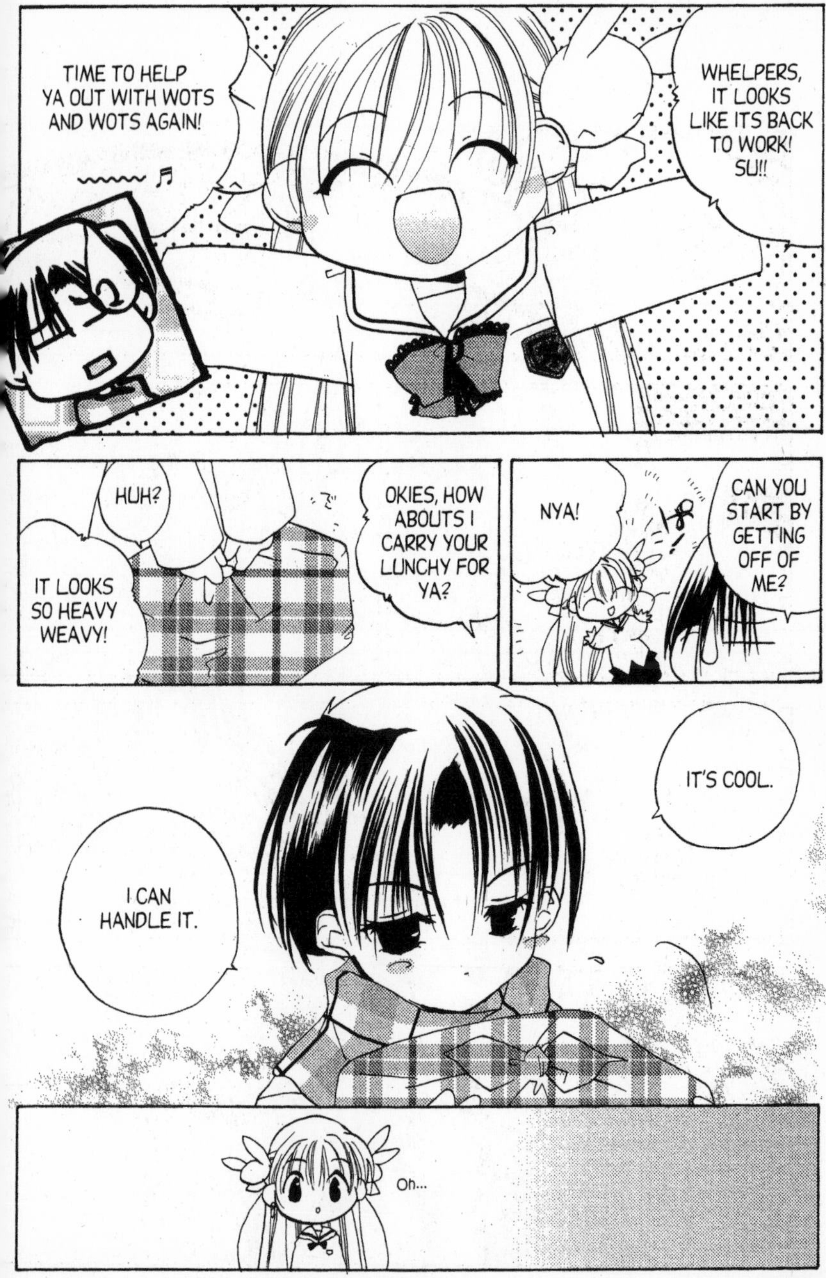
WHELPERS, IT LOOKS LIKE ITS BACK TO WORK! SU!!
TIME TO HELP YA OUT WITH WOTS AND WOTS AGAIN!
CAN YOU START BY GETTING OFF OF ME?
NYA!
OKIES, HOW ABOUTS I CARRY YOUR LUNCHY FOR YA?
HUH?
IT LOOKS SO HEAVY WEAVY!
IT'S COOL.
I CAN HANDLE IT.
Oh...

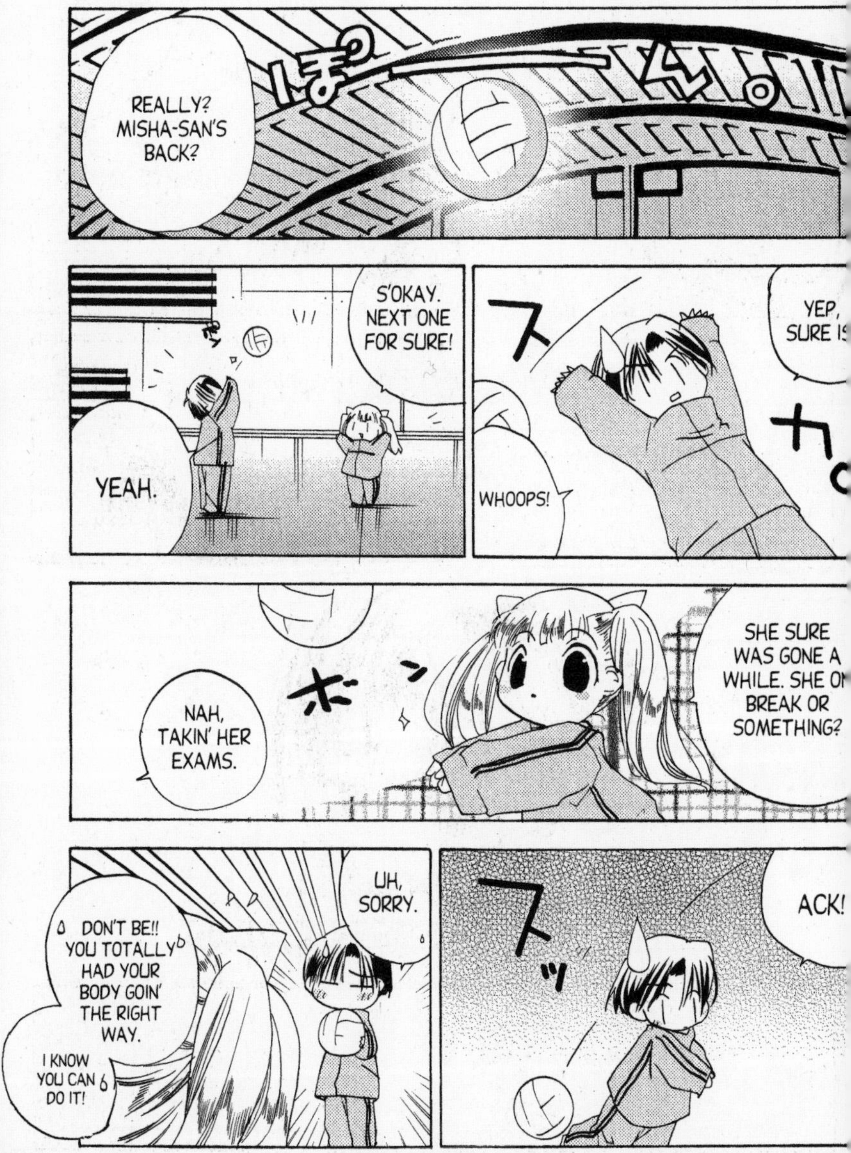
REALLY? MISHA-SAN'S BACK?
YEP, SURE IS
ス
カ
WHOOPS!
S'OKAY. NEXT ONE FOR SURE!
YEAH.
SHE SURE WAS GONE A WHILE. SHE ON BREAK OR SOMETHING?
ボン
NAH, TAKIN' HER EXAMS.
ACK!
スッ
UH, SORRY.
DON'T BE!! YOU TOTALLY HAD YOUR BODY GOIN' THE RIGHT WAY.
I KNOW YOU CAN DO IT!

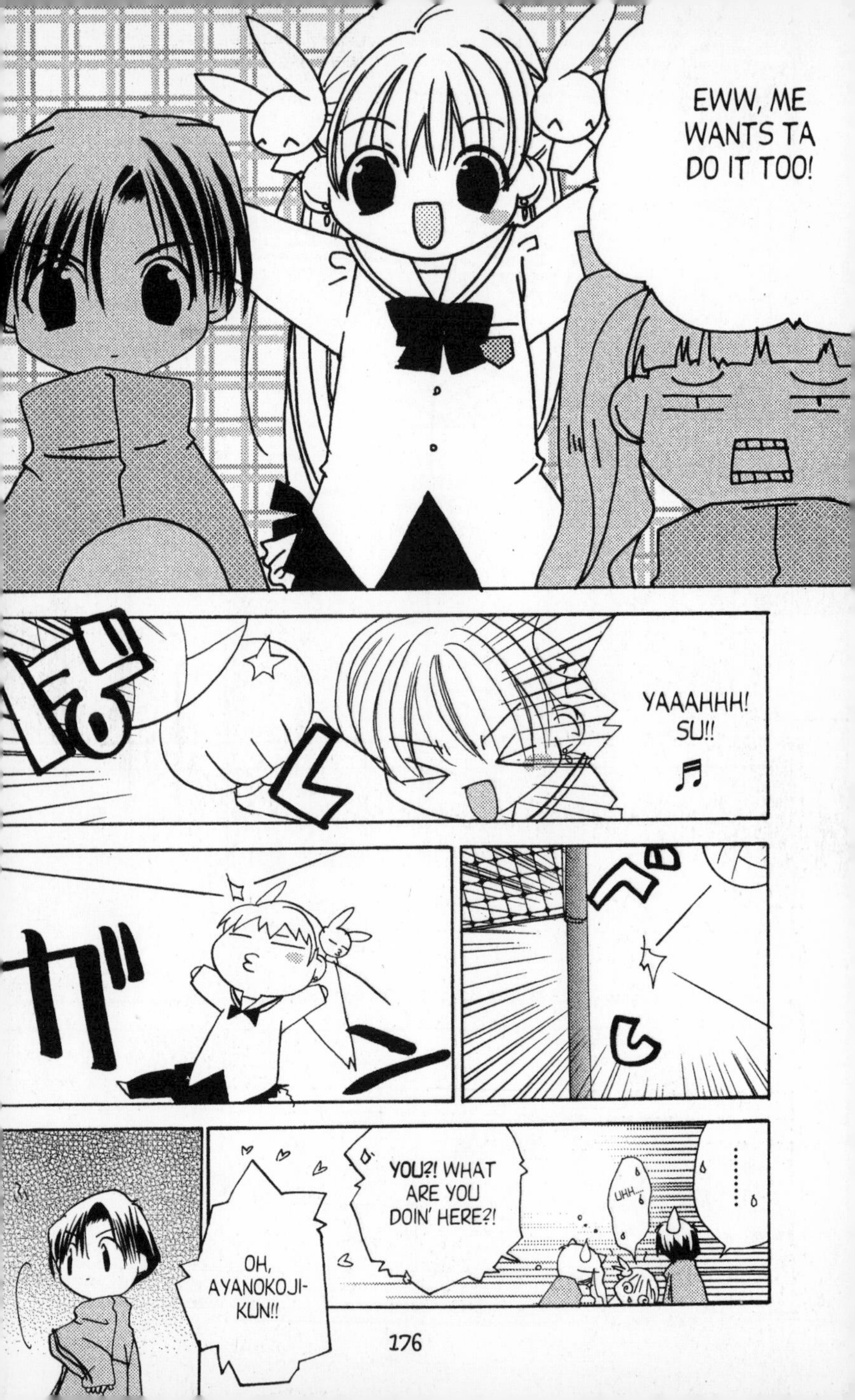
EWW, ME WANTS TA DO IT TOO!
YAAAHHH! SU!! ♪
....
UHH...
YOU?! WHAT ARE YOU DOIN' HERE?!
OH, AYANOKOJI-KUN!!

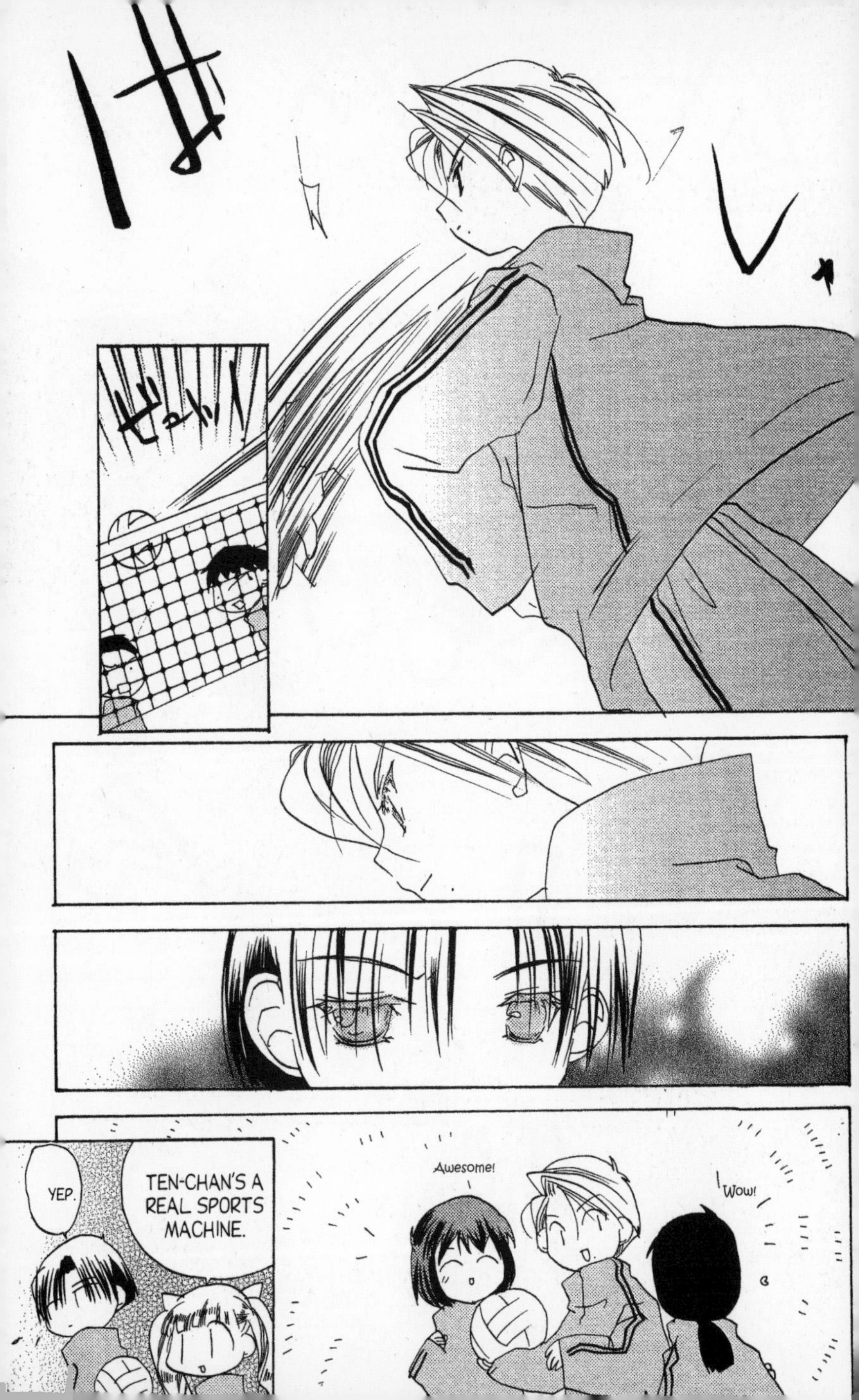
Wow!
Awesome!
TEN-CHAN'S A REAL SPORTS MACHINE.
YEP.

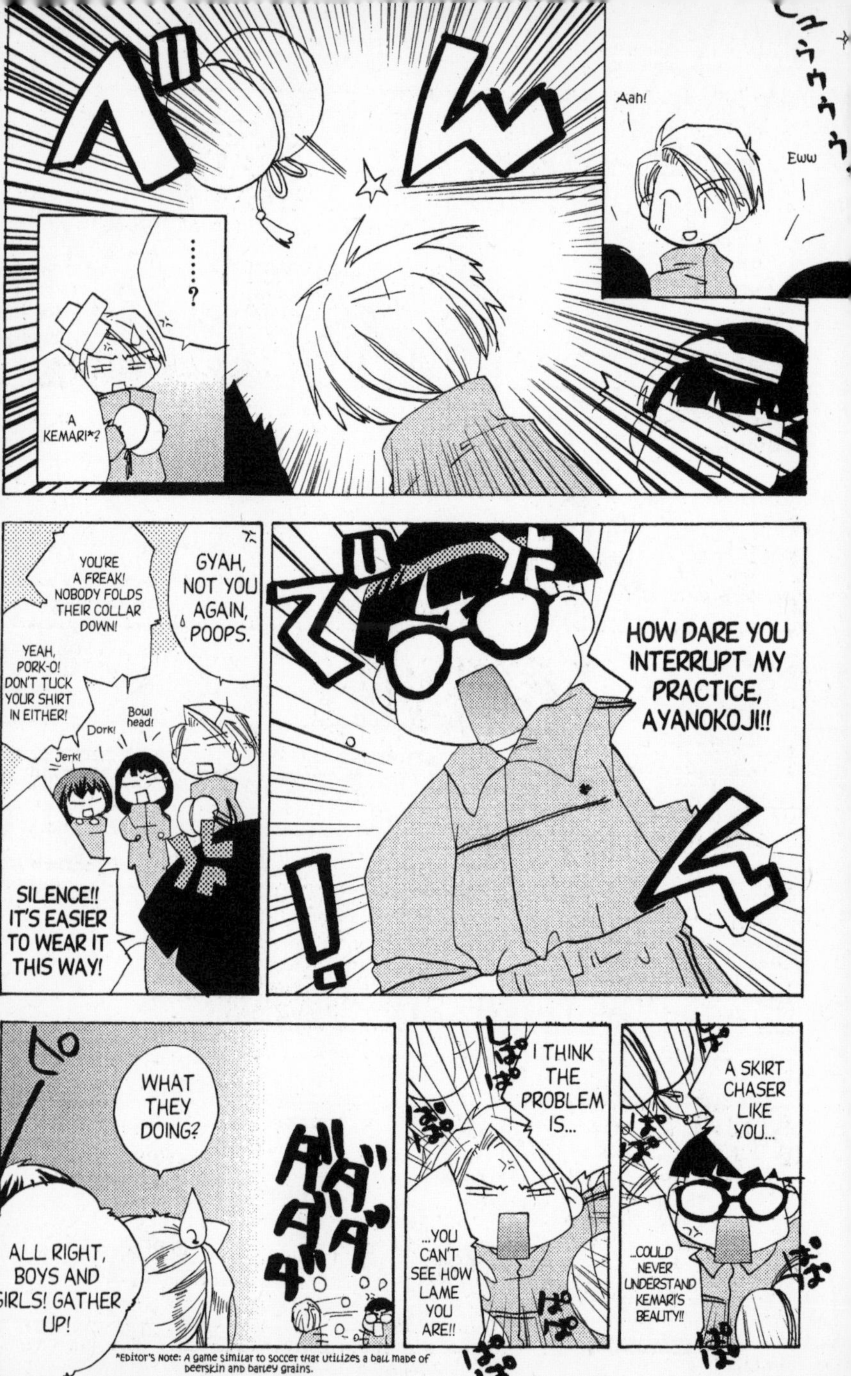
Aah!
Eww
......?
A KEMARI*?
HOW DARE YOU INTERRUPT MY PRACTICE, AYANOKOJI!!
GYAH, NOT YOU AGAIN, POOPS.
YOU'RE A FREAK! NOBODY FOLDS THEIR COLLAR DOWN!
YEAH, PORK-O! DON'T TUCK YOUR SHIRT IN EITHER!
Bowl head!
Dork!
Jerk!
SILENCE!! IT'S EASIER TO WEAR IT THIS WAY!
A SKIRT CHASER LIKE YOU...
...COULD NEVER UNDERSTAND KEMARI'S BEAUTY!!
I THINK THE PROBLEM IS...
...YOU CAN'T SEE HOW LAME YOU ARE!!
WHAT THEY DOING?
ALL RIGHT, BOYS AND GIRLS! GATHER UP!

*Editor's Note: A game similar to soccer that utilizes a ball made of deerskin and barley grains.

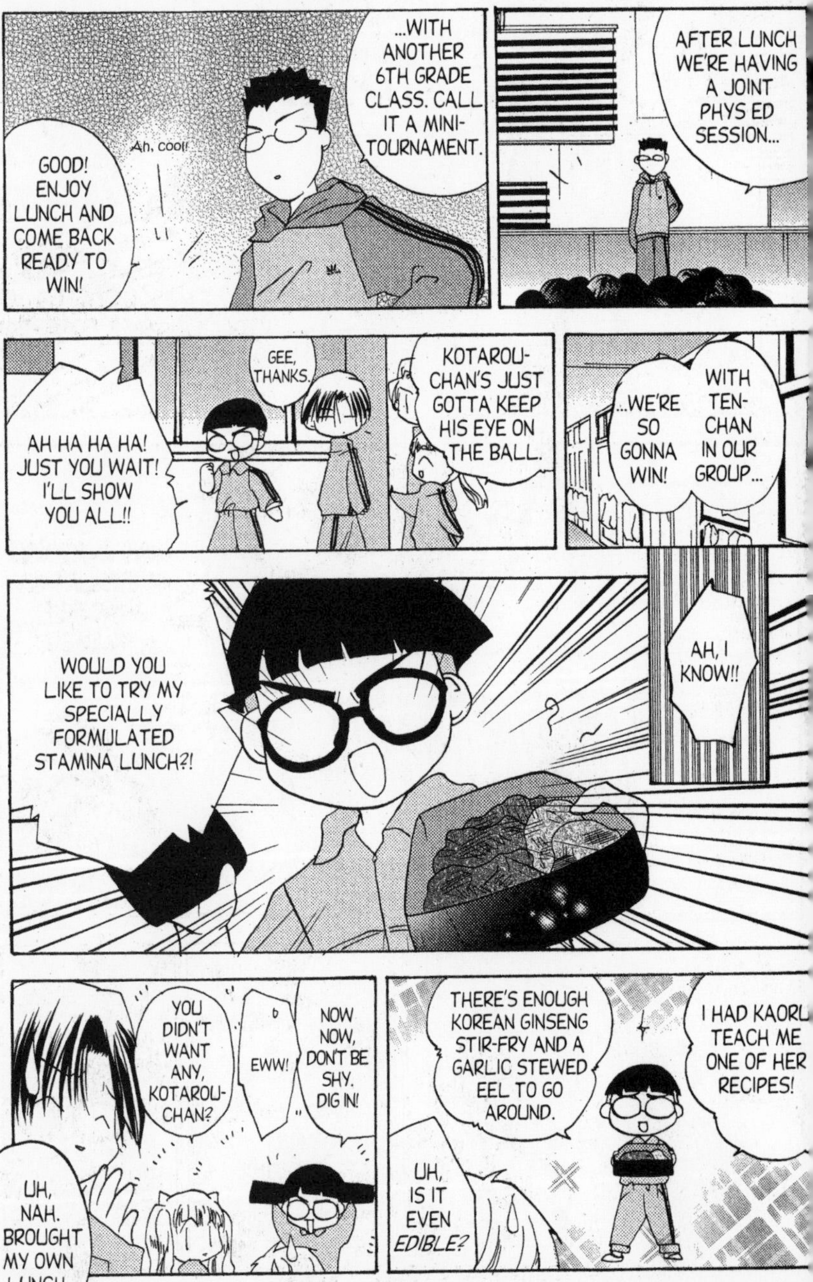
AFTER LUNCH WE'RE HAVING A JOINT PHYS ED SESSION...
...WITH ANOTHER 6TH GRADE CLASS. CALL IT A MINI-TOURNAMENT.
Ah, cool!
GOOD! ENJOY LUNCH AND COME BACK READY TO WIN!
WITH TEN-CHAN IN OUR GROUP...
...WE'RE SO GONNA WIN!
KOTAROU-CHAN'S JUST GOTTA KEEP HIS EYE ON THE BALL.
GEE, THANKS.
AH HA HA HA! JUST YOU WAIT! I'LL SHOW YOU ALL!!
AH, I KNOW!!
WOULD YOU LIKE TO TRY MY SPECIALLY FORMULATED STAMINA LUNCH?!
I HAD KAORU TEACH ME ONE OF HER RECIPES!
THERE'S ENOUGH KOREAN GINSENG STIR-FRY AND A GARLIC STEWED EEL TO GO AROUND.
UH, IS IT EVEN *EDIBLE?*
NOW NOW, DON'T BE SHY. DIG IN!
EWW!
YOU DIDN'T WANT ANY, KOTAROU-CHAN?
UH, NAH. I BROUGHT MY OWN LUNCH.

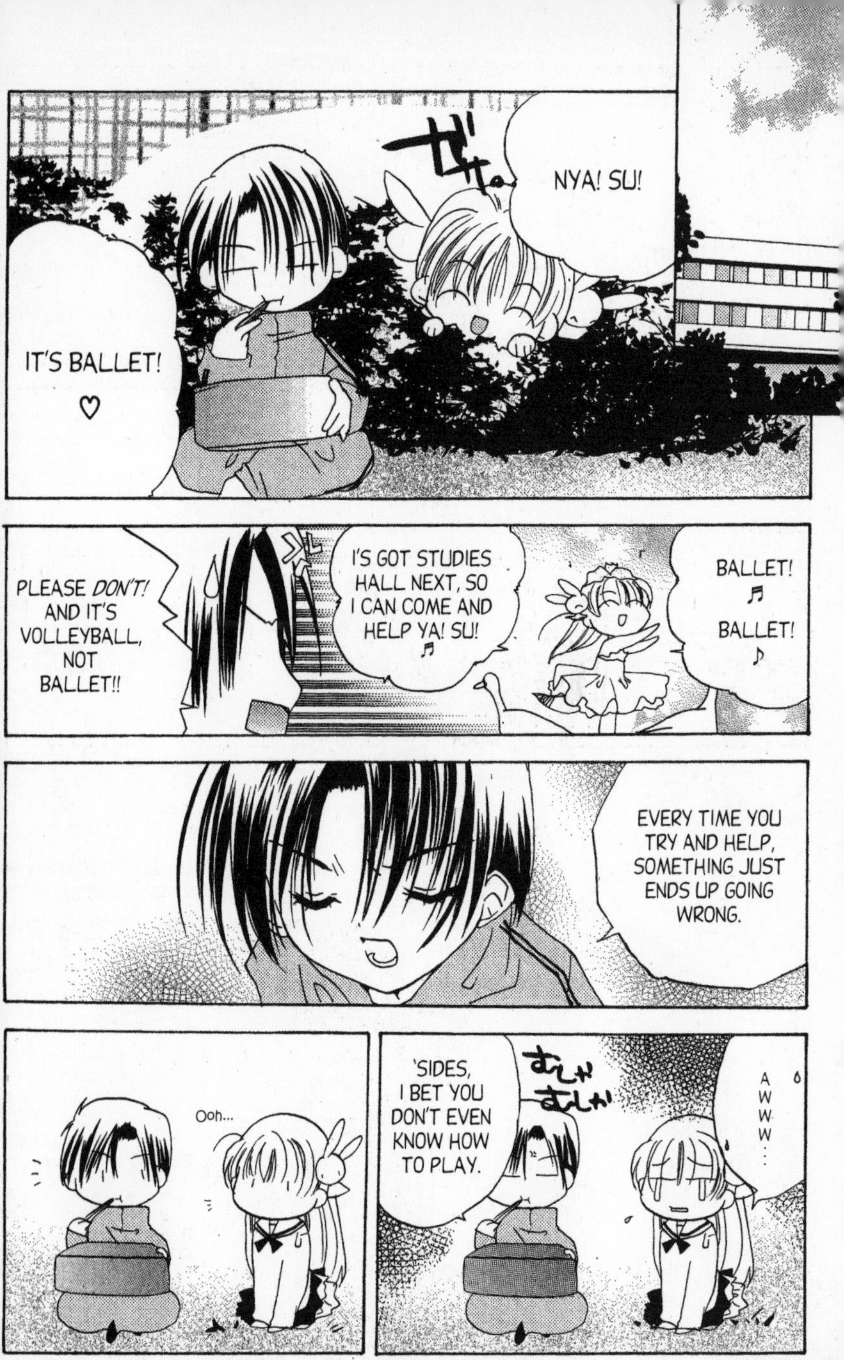
NYA! SU!
IT'S BALLET! ♡
BALLET! ♬ BALLET! ♪
I'S GOT STUDIES HALL NEXT, SO I CAN COME AND HELP YA! SU! ♬
PLEASE *DON'T!* AND IT'S VOLLEYBALL, NOT BALLET!!
EVERY TIME YOU TRY AND HELP, SOMETHING JUST ENDS UP GOING WRONG.
AWWW...
'SIDES, I BET YOU DON'T EVEN KNOW HOW TO PLAY.
むしゃむしゃ
Ooh...

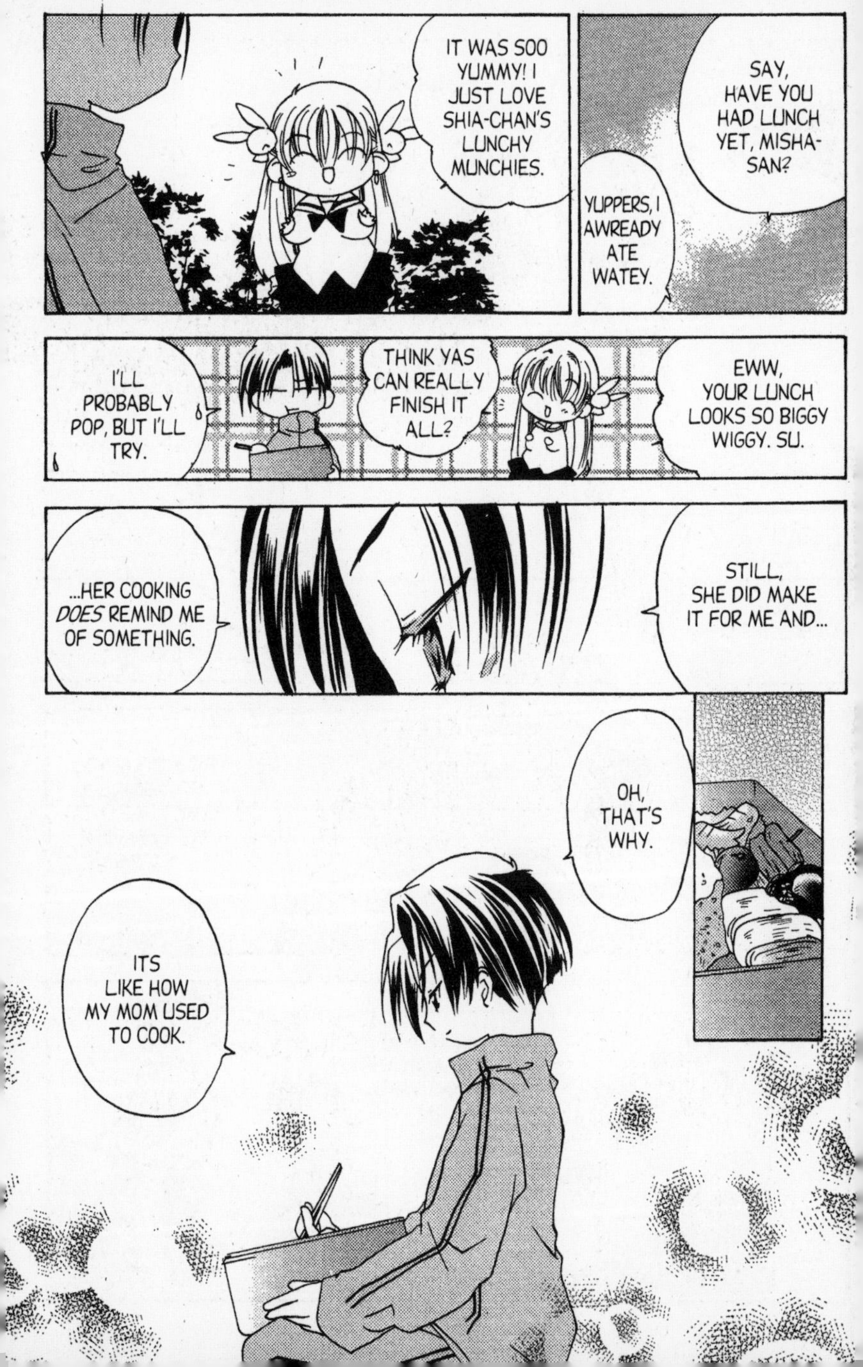
SAY, HAVE YOU HAD LUNCH YET, MISHA-SAN?
YUPPERS, I AWREADY ATE WATEY.
IT WAS SOO YUMMY! I JUST LOVE SHIA-CHAN'S LUNCHY MUNCHIES.
EWW, YOUR LUNCH LOOKS SO BIGGY WIGGY. SU.
THINK YAS CAN REALLY FINISH IT ALL?
I'LL PROBABLY POP, BUT I'LL TRY.
STILL, SHE DID MAKE IT FOR ME AND...
...HER COOKING *DOES* REMIND ME OF SOMETHING.
OH, THAT'S WHY.
ITS LIKE HOW MY MOM USED TO COOK.

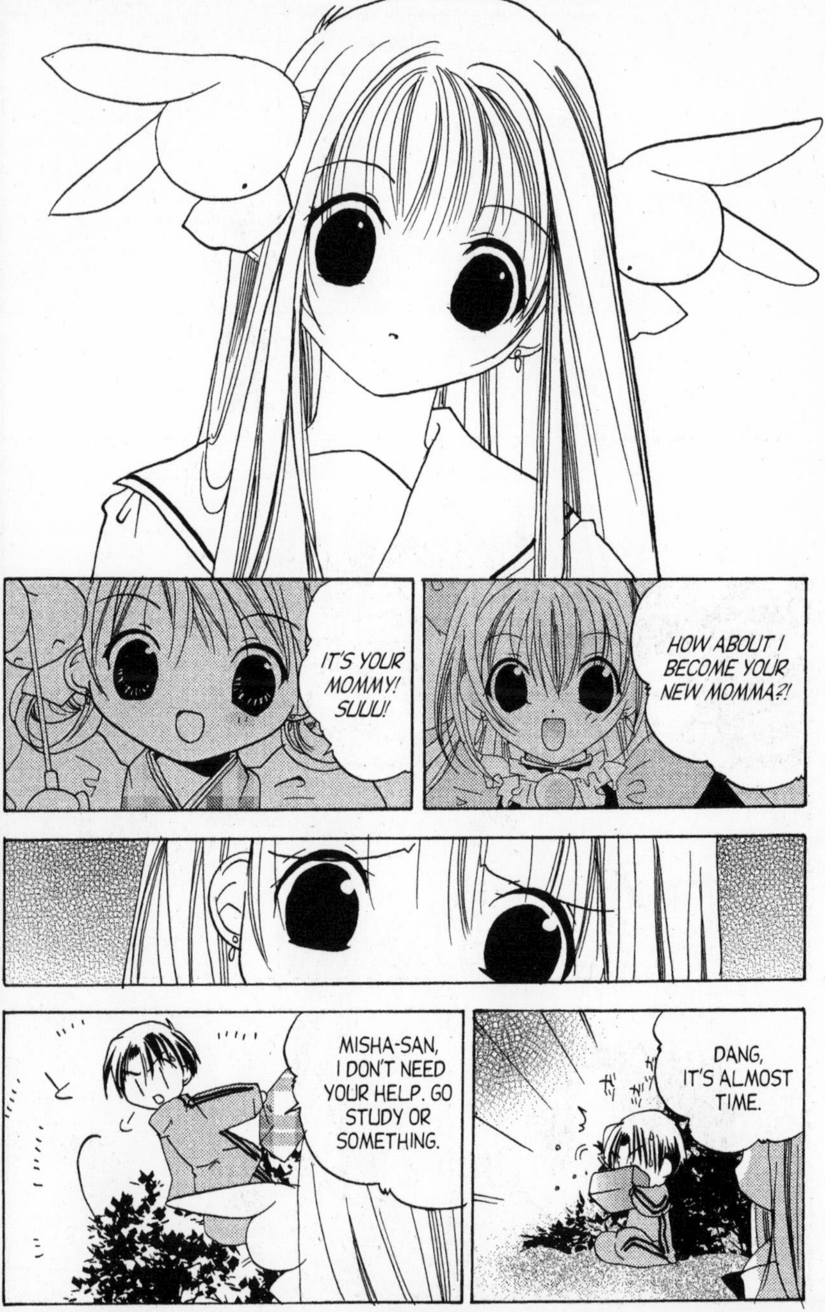
HOW ABOUT I BECOME YOUR NEW MOMMA?!
IT'S YOUR MOMMY! SUUU!
DANG, IT'S ALMOST TIME.
MISHA-SAN, I DON'T NEED YOUR HELP. GO STUDY OR SOMETHING.

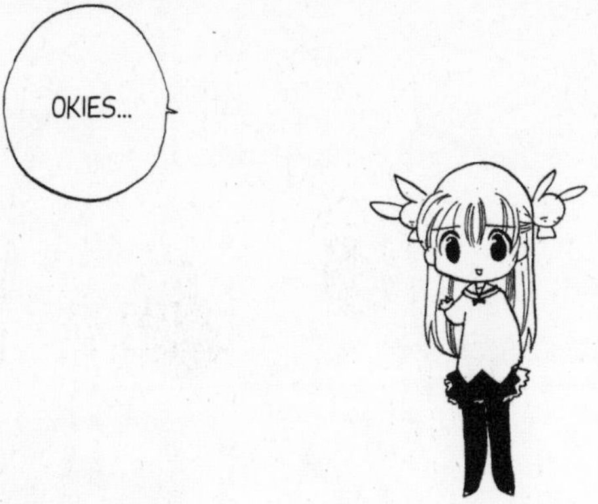
OKIES...

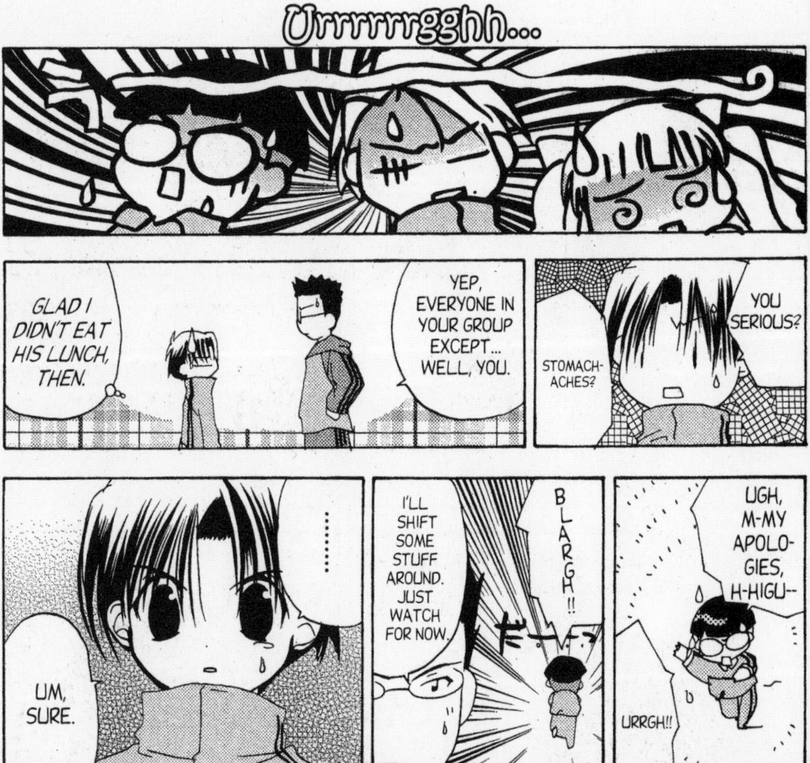
Urrrrrrgghh...
YOU SERIOUS?
STOMACH-ACHES?
YEP, EVERYONE IN YOUR GROUP EXCEPT... WELL, YOU.
GLAD I DIDN'T EAT HIS LUNCH, THEN.
UGH, M-MY APOLOGIES, H-HIGU--
URRGH!!
BLARGH!!
I'LL SHIFT SOME STUFF AROUND. JUST WATCH FOR NOW.
......
UM, SURE.

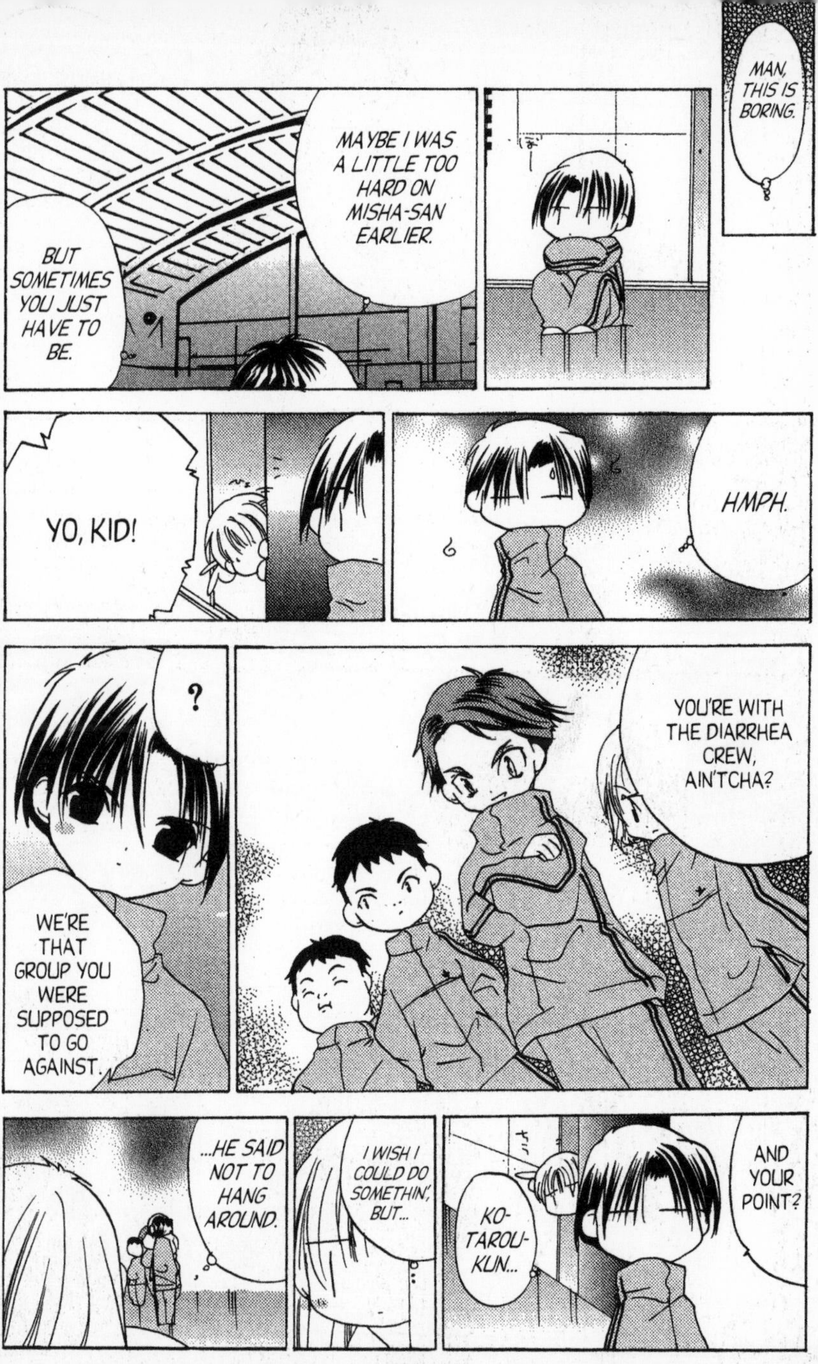
MAN, THIS IS BORING.
MAYBE I WAS A LITTLE TOO HARD ON MISHA-SAN EARLIER.
BUT SOMETIMES YOU JUST HAVE TO BE.
HMPH.
YO, KID!
YOU'RE WITH THE DIARRHEA CREW, AIN'TCHA?
?
WE'RE THAT GROUP YOU WERE SUPPOSED TO GO AGAINST.
AND YOUR POINT?
KO-TAROU-KUN...
I WISH I COULD DO SOMETHIN', BUT...
...HE SAID NOT TO HANG AROUND.

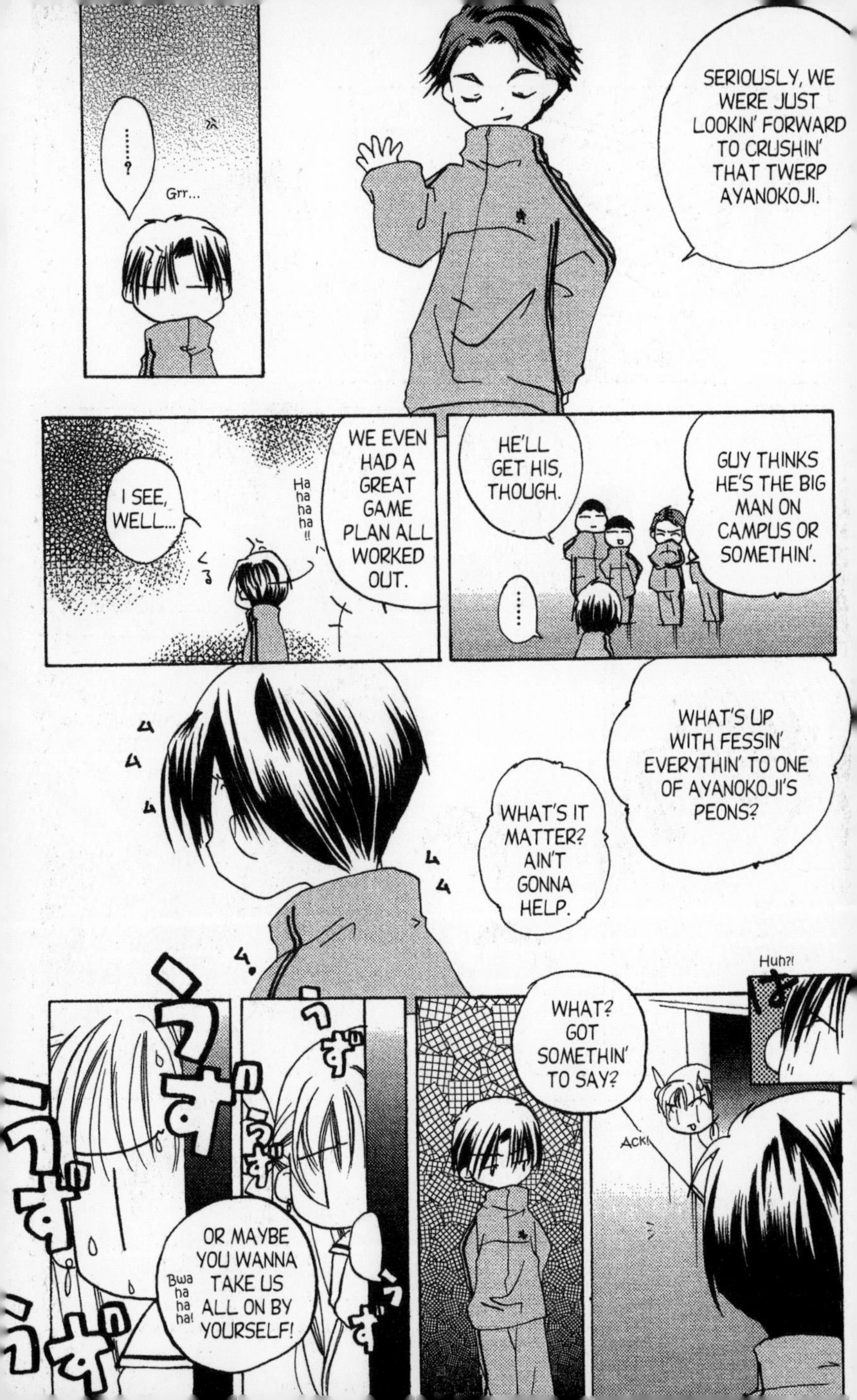
SERIOUSLY, WE WERE JUST LOOKIN' FORWARD TO CRUSHIN' THAT TWERP AYANOKOJI.
......?
Grr...
GUY THINKS HE'S THE BIG MAN ON CAMPUS OR SOMETHIN'.
HE'LL GET HIS, THOUGH.
......
WE EVEN HAD A GREAT GAME PLAN ALL WORKED OUT.
Ha ha ha ha!!
I SEE, WELL...
WHAT'S UP WITH FESSIN' EVERYTHIN' TO ONE OF AYANOKOJI'S PEONS?
WHAT'S IT MATTER? AIN'T GONNA HELP.
Huh?!
Ack!
WHAT? GOT SOMETHIN' TO SAY?
OR MAYBE YOU WANNA TAKE US ALL ON BY YOURSELF!
Bwa ha ha ha!

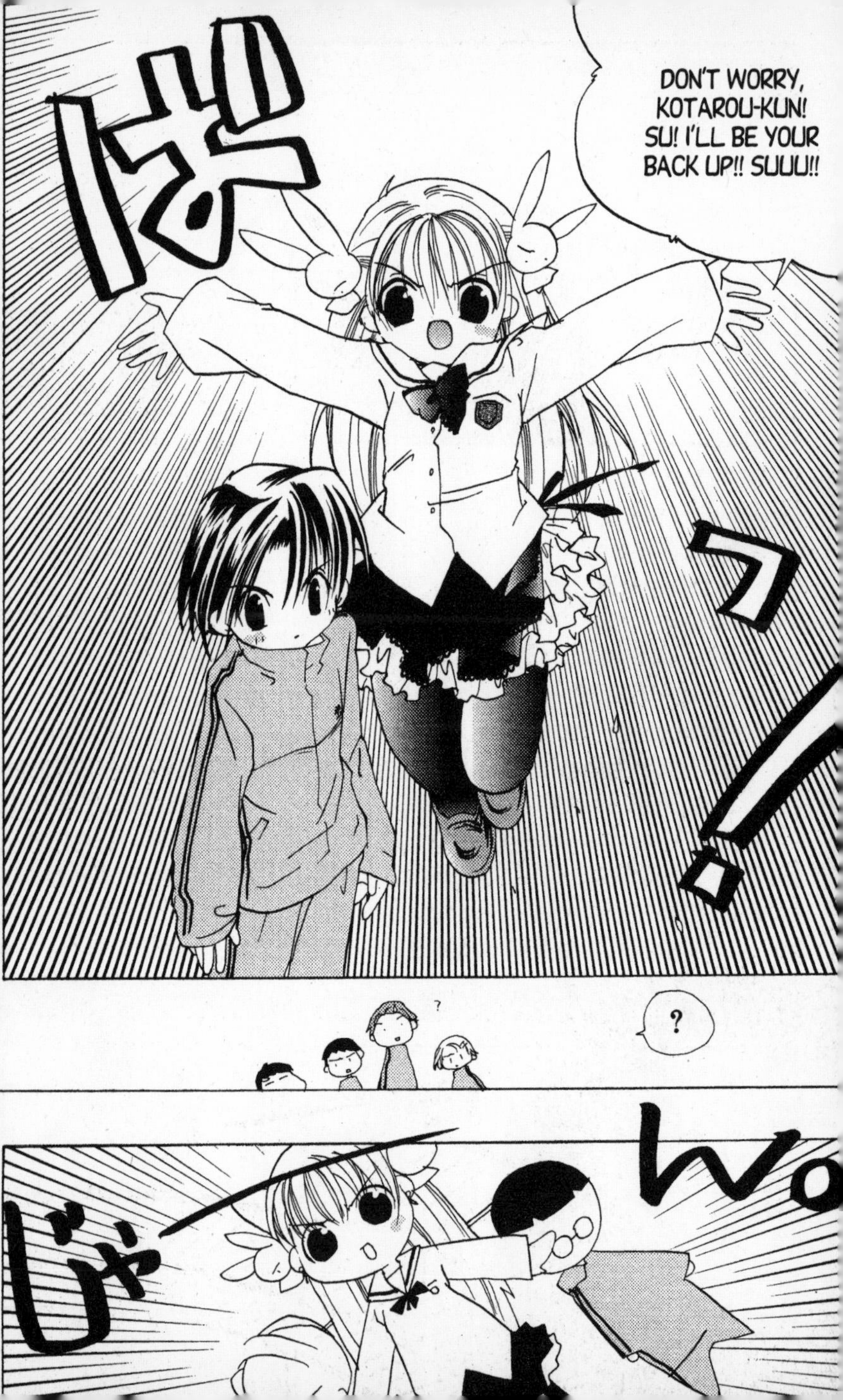
DON'T WORRY, KOTAROU-KUN! SU! I'LL BE YOUR BACK UP!! SUUU!!
?
?

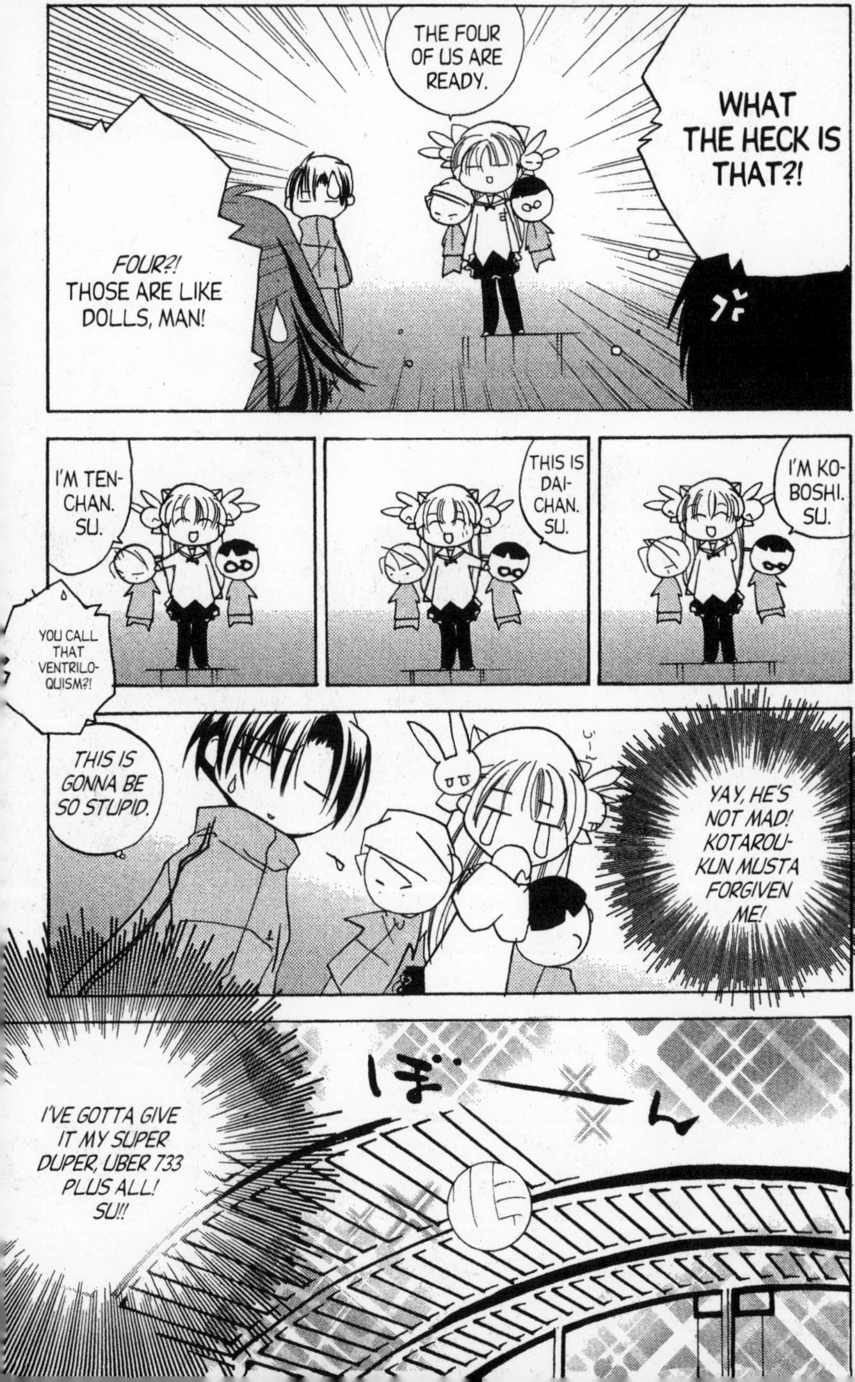
THE FOUR OF US ARE READY.
WHAT THE HECK IS THAT?!
FOUR?! THOSE ARE LIKE DOLLS, MAN!
I'M KO-BOSHI. SU.
THIS IS DAI-CHAN. SU.
I'M TEN-CHAN. SU.
YOU CALL THAT VENTRILO-QUISM?!
YAY, HE'S NOT MAD! KOTAROU-KUN MUSTA FORGIVEN ME!
THIS IS GONNA BE SO STUPID.
ぼーーん
I'VE GOTTA GIVE IT MY SUPER DUPER, UBER 733 PLUS ALL! SU!!

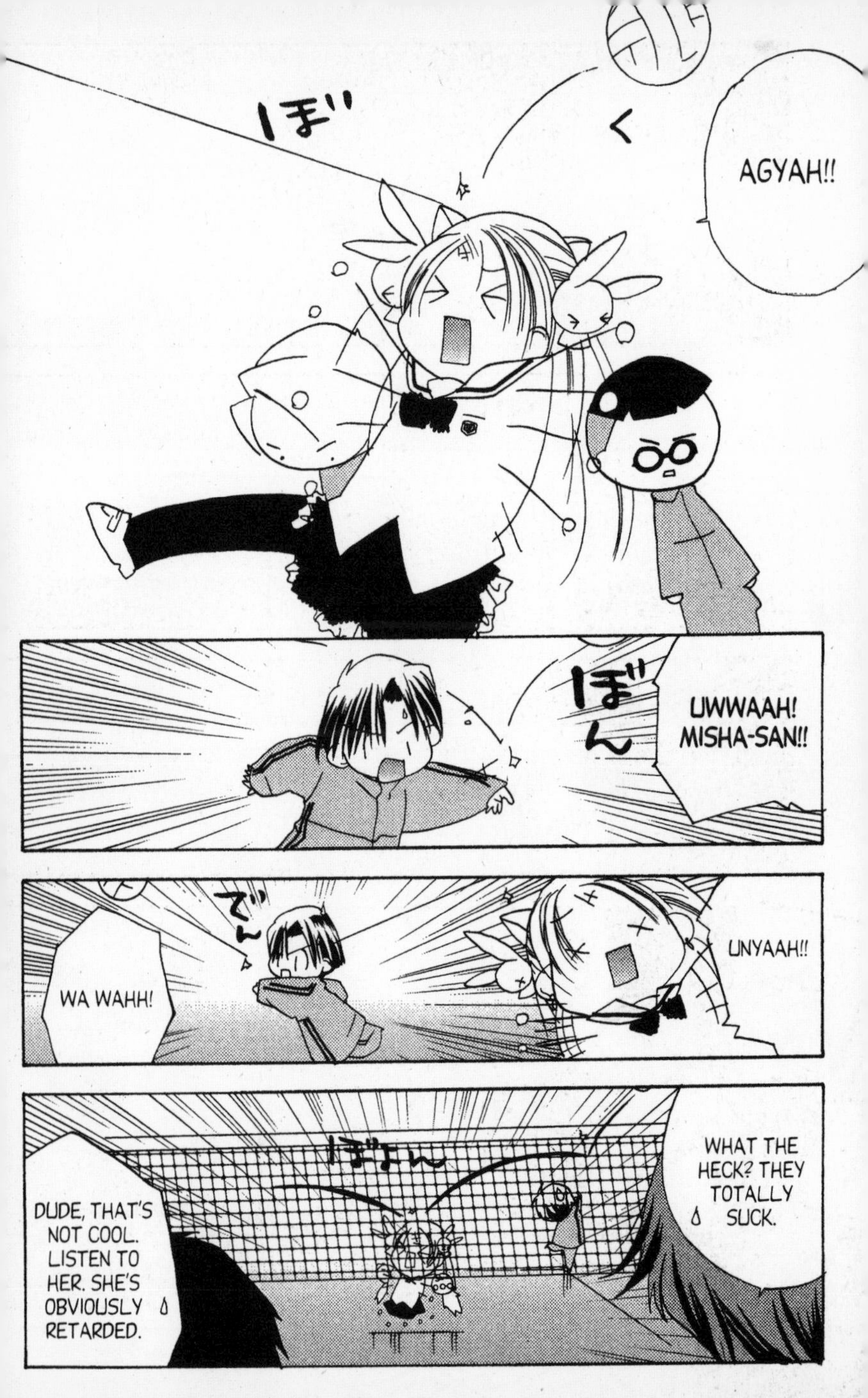
AGYAH!!
く
ぼ
UWWAAH! MISHA-SAN!!
ぼん
UNYAAH!!
でん
WA WAHH!
WHAT THE HECK? THEY TOTALLY SUCK.
ぼよん
DUDE, THAT'S NOT COOL. LISTEN TO HER. SHE'S OBVIOUSLY RETARDED.

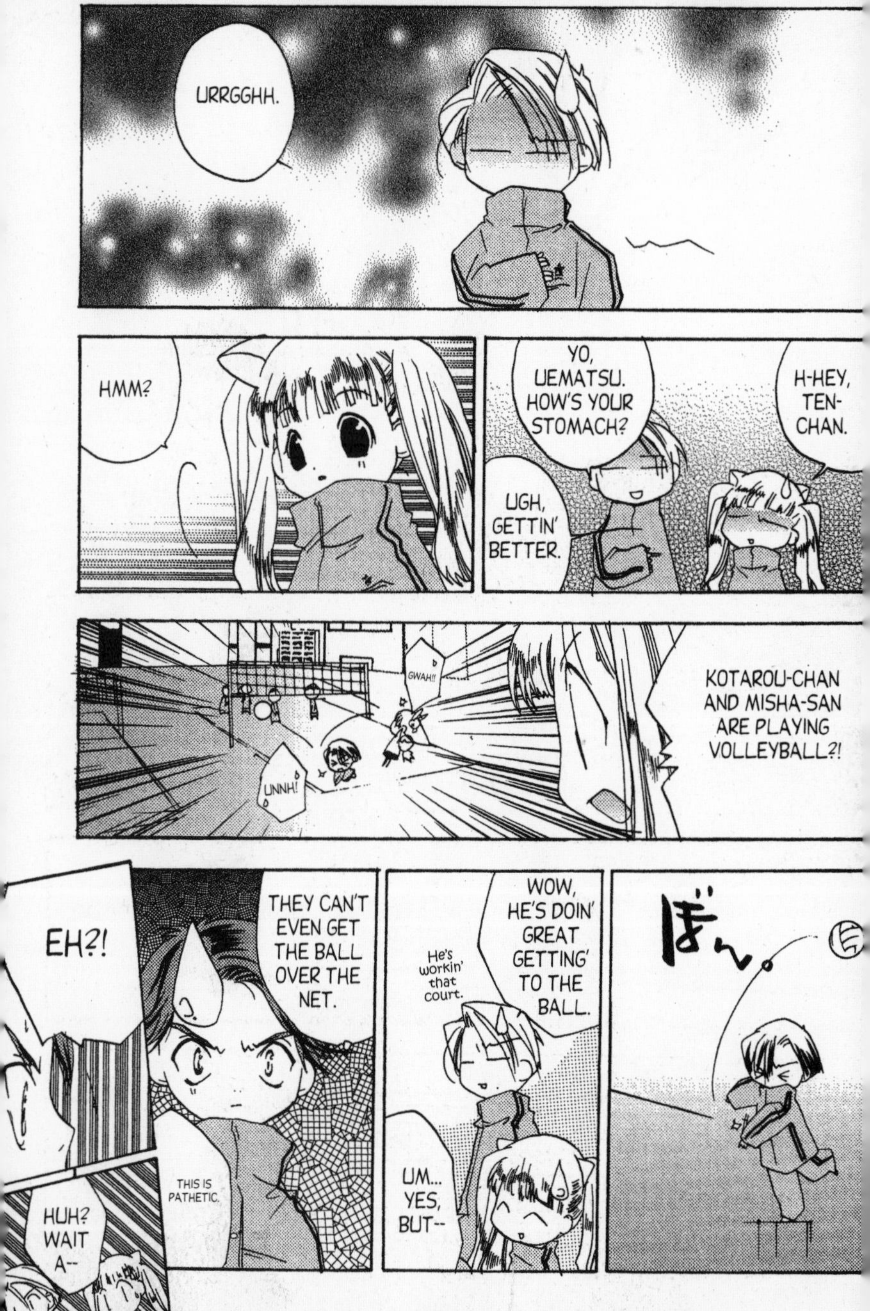
URRGGHH.
H-HEY, TEN-CHAN.
YO, UEMATSU. HOW'S YOUR STOMACH?
UGH, GETTIN' BETTER.
HMM?
KOTAROU-CHAN AND MISHA-SAN ARE PLAYING VOLLEYBALL?!
GWAH!!
UNNH!
ぼん。
WOW, HE'S DOIN' GREAT GETTING' TO THE BALL.
He's workin' that court.
UM... YES, BUT--
THEY CAN'T EVEN GET THE BALL OVER THE NET.
THIS IS PATHETIC.
EH?!
HUH? WAIT A--

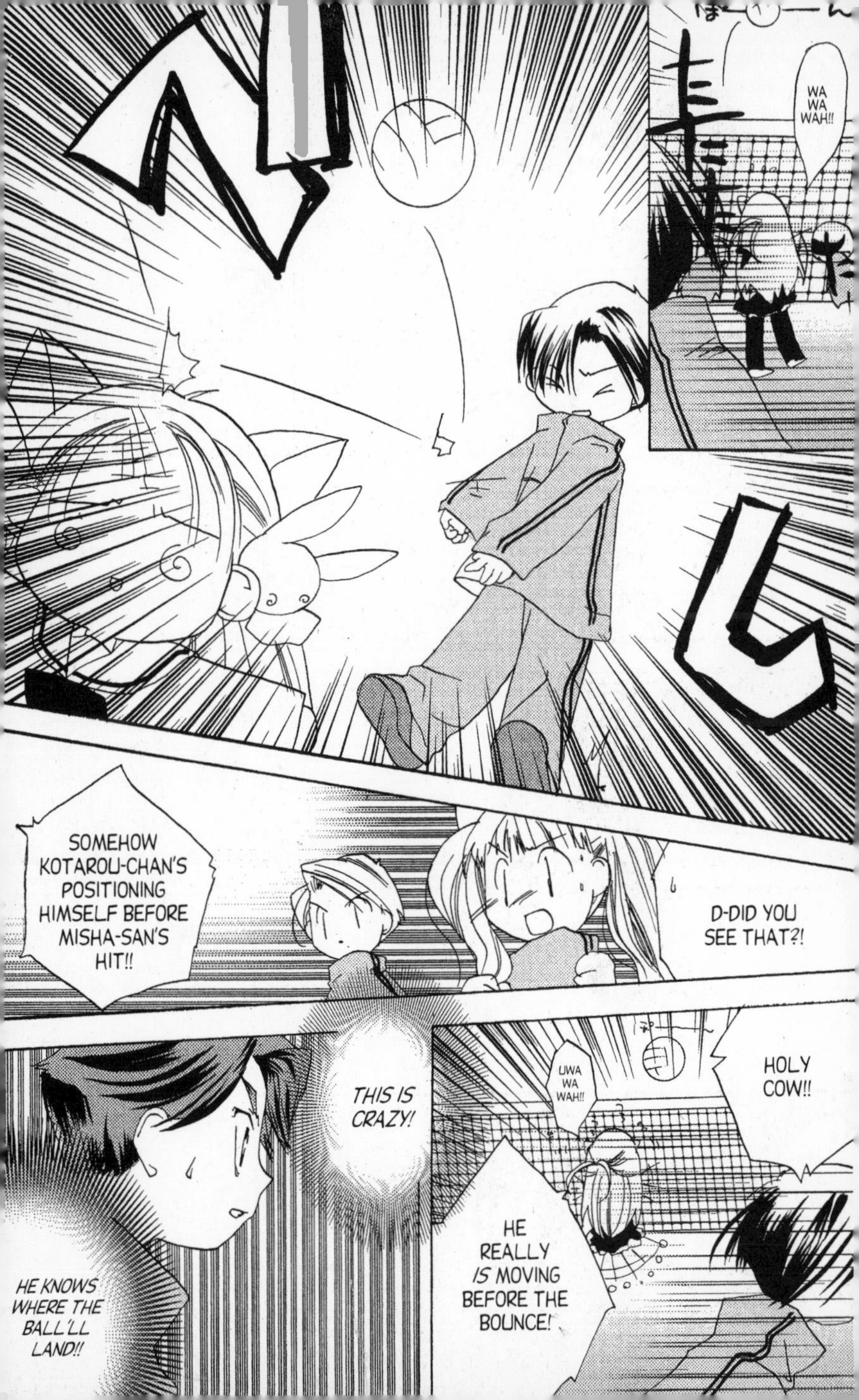
WA WA WAH!!
D-DID YOU SEE THAT?!
SOMEHOW KOTAROU-CHAN'S POSITIONING HIMSELF BEFORE MISHA-SAN'S HIT!!
HOLY COW!!
UWA WA WAH!!
HE REALLY *IS* MOVING BEFORE THE BOUNCE!
THIS IS CRAZY!
HE KNOWS WHERE THE BALL'LL LAND!!

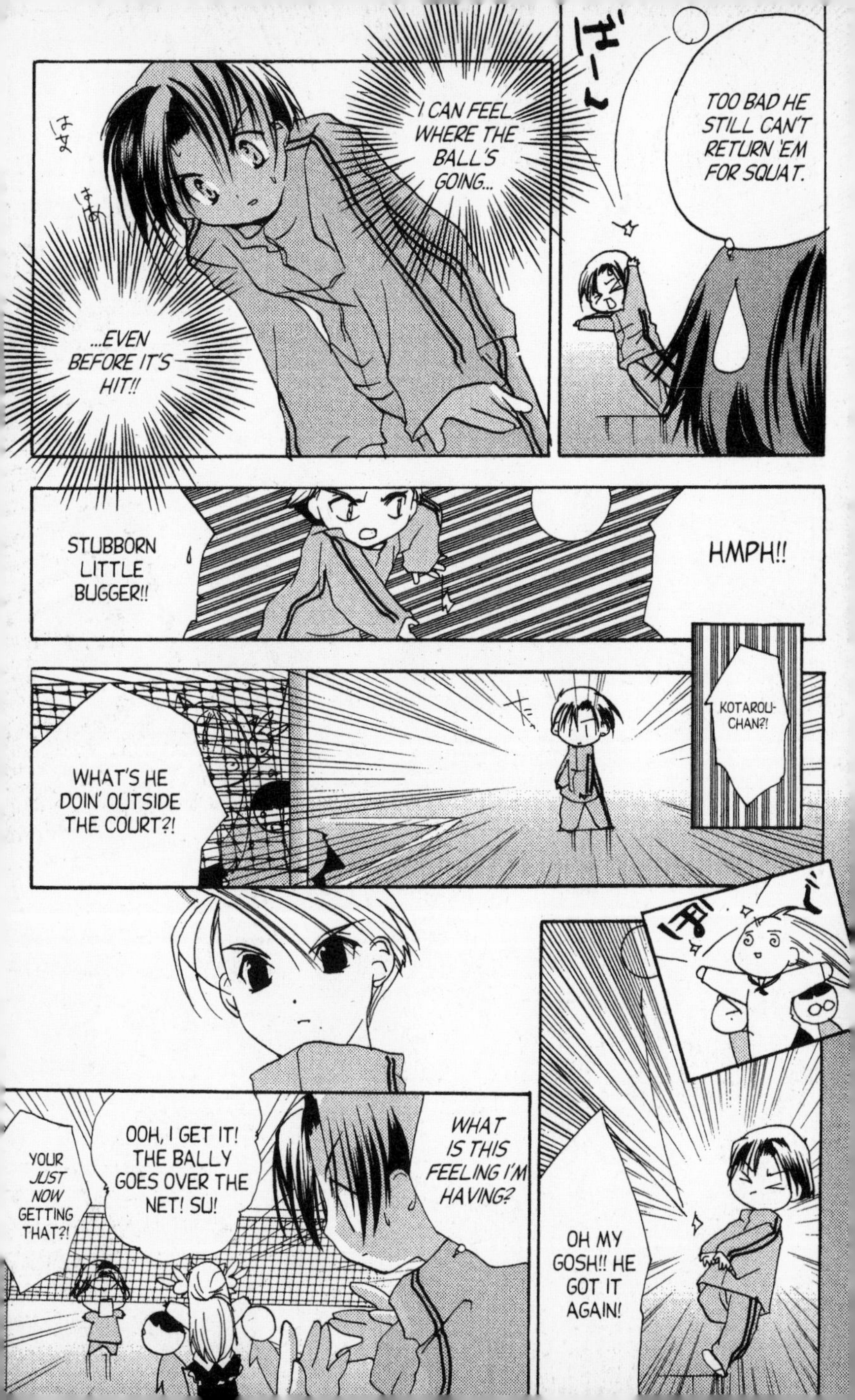
ばーん
TOO BAD HE STILL CAN'T RETURN 'EM FOR SQUAT.
I CAN FEEL WHERE THE BALL'S GOING...
...EVEN BEFORE IT'S HIT!!
HMPH!!
STUBBORN LITTLE BUGGER!!
KOTAROU-CHAN?!
WHAT'S HE DOIN' OUTSIDE THE COURT?!
OH MY GOSH!! HE GOT IT AGAIN!
WHAT IS THIS FEELING I'M HAVING?
OOH, I GET IT! THE BALLY GOES OVER THE NET! SU!
YOUR JUST NOW GETTING THAT?!

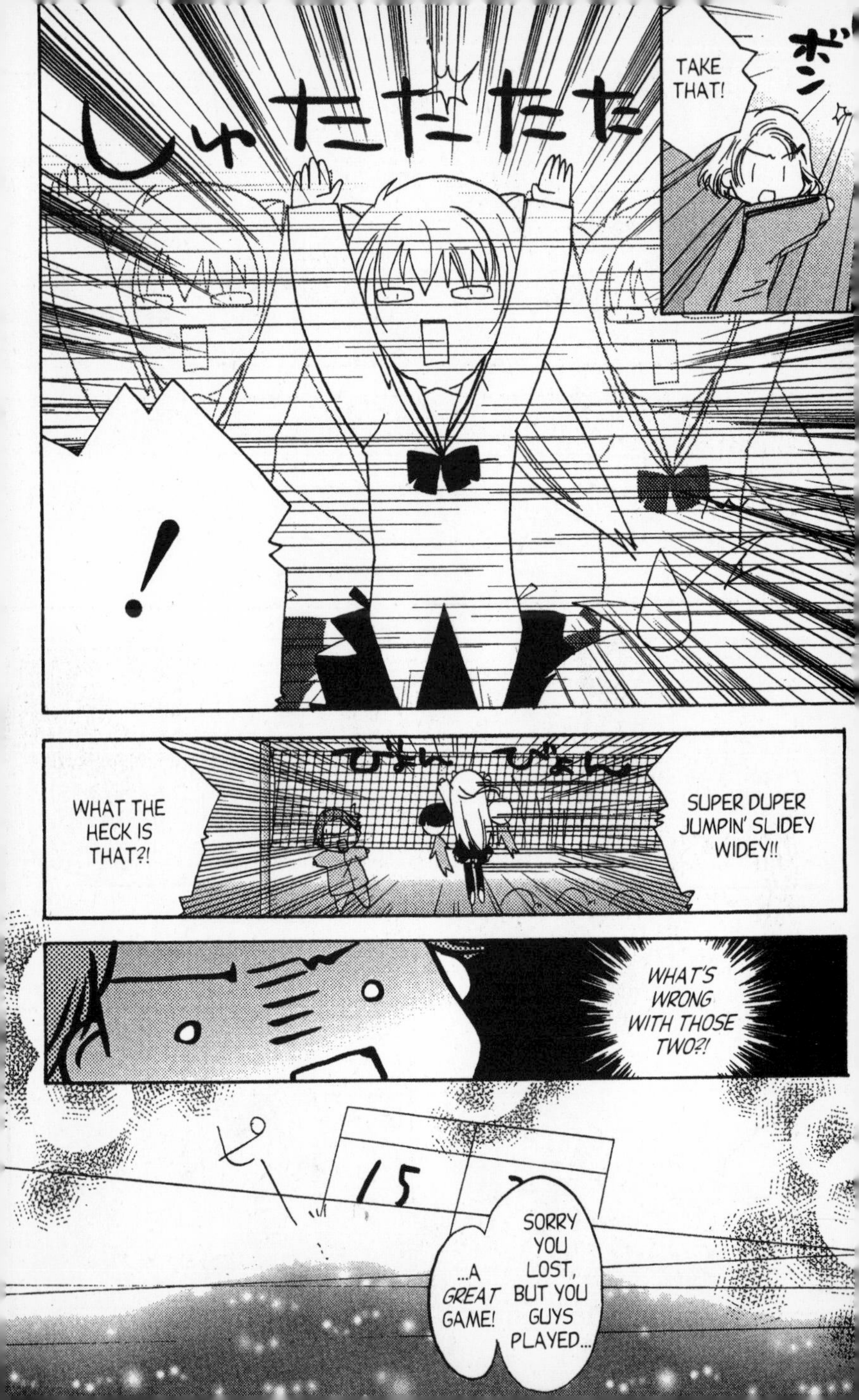
ボン
TAKE THAT!
しゅたたたた
!
SUPER DUPER JUMPIN' SLIDEY WIDEY!!
ぴょん ぴょん
WHAT THE HECK IS THAT?!
WHAT'S WRONG WITH THOSE TWO?!
15
SORRY YOU LOST, BUT YOU GUYS PLAYED...
...A GREAT GAME!

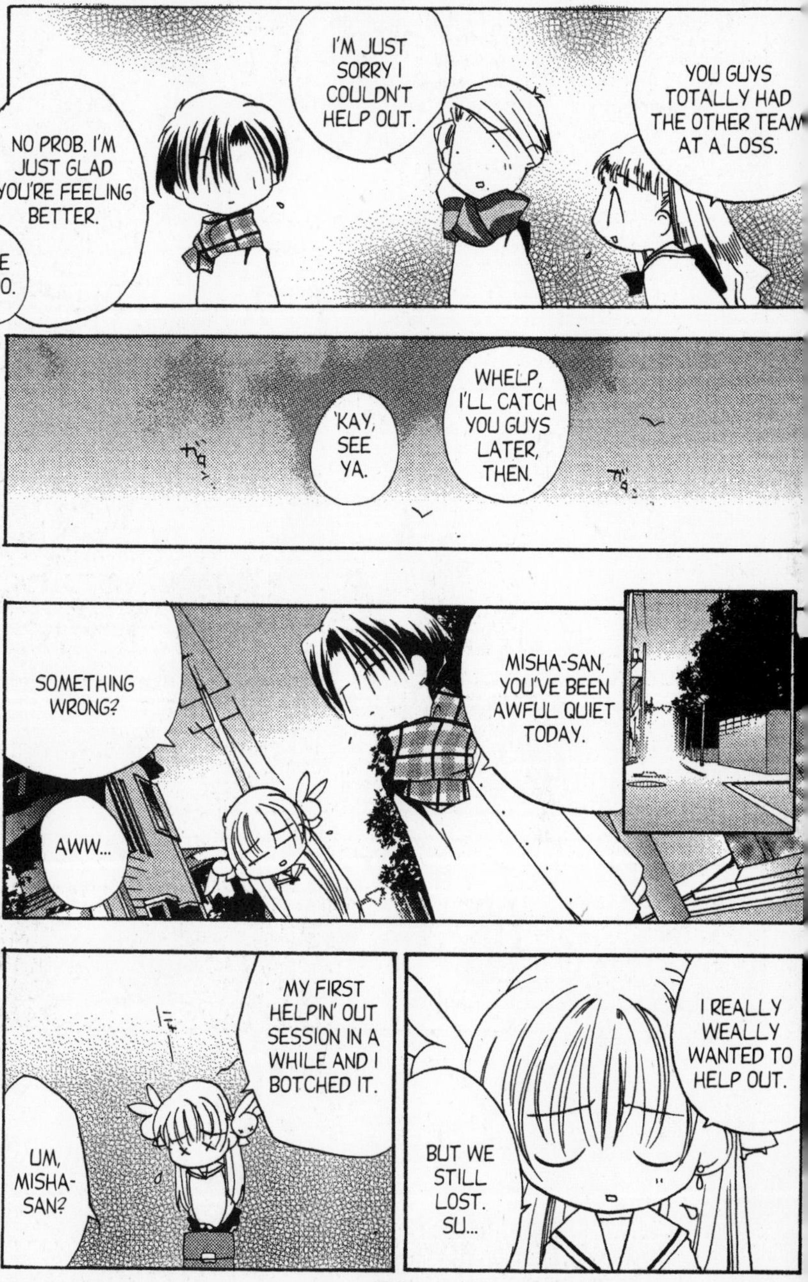
YOU GUYS TOTALLY HAD THE OTHER TEAM AT A LOSS.
I'M JUST SORRY I COULDN'T HELP OUT.
NO PROB. I'M JUST GLAD YOU'RE FEELING BETTER.
ME TOO.
WHELP, I'LL CATCH YOU GUYS LATER, THEN.
'KAY, SEE YA.
MISHA-SAN, YOU'VE BEEN AWFUL QUIET TODAY.
SOMETHING WRONG?
AWW...
I REALLY WEALLY WANTED TO HELP OUT.
BUT WE STILL LOST. SU...
MY FIRST HELPIN' OUT SESSION IN A WHILE AND I BOTCHED IT.
UM, MISHA-SAN?

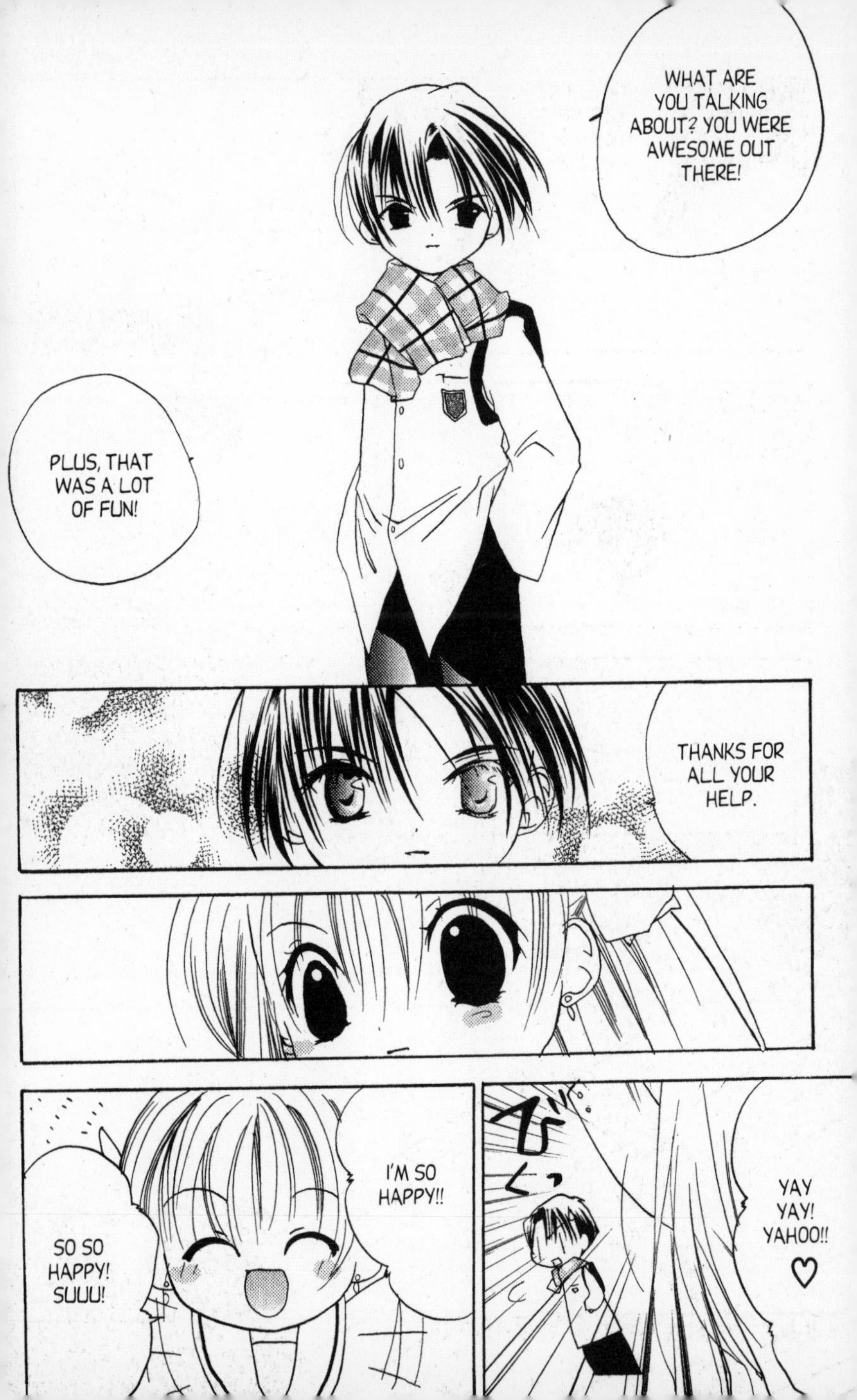
WHAT ARE YOU TALKING ABOUT? YOU WERE AWESOME OUT THERE!
PLUS, THAT WAS A LOT OF FUN!
THANKS FOR ALL YOUR HELP.
YAY YAY! YAHOO!! ♡
I'M SO HAPPY!!
SO SO HAPPY! SUUU!

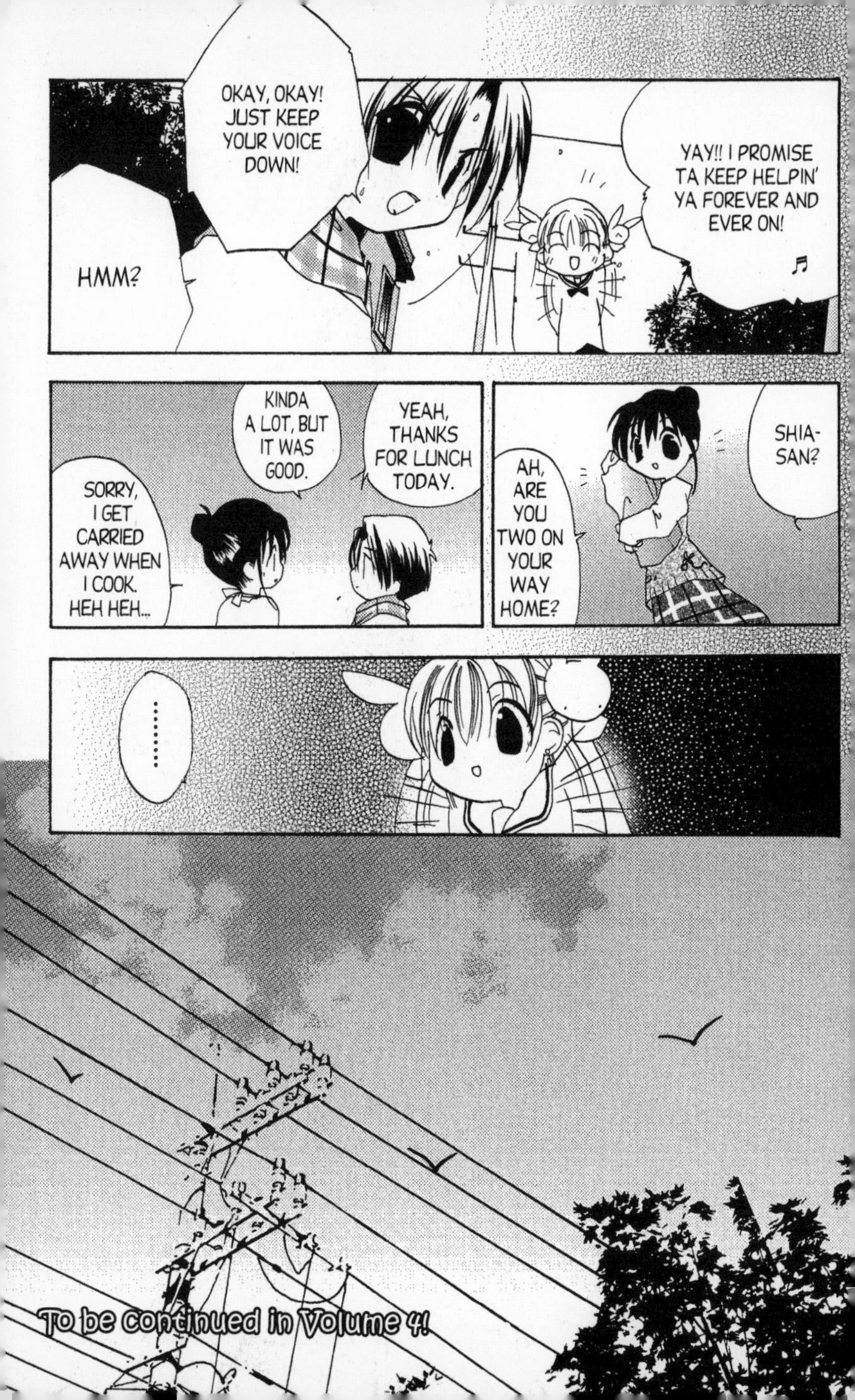
YAY!! I PROMISE TA KEEP HELPIN' YA FOREVER AND EVER ON!
OKAY, OKAY! JUST KEEP YOUR VOICE DOWN!
HMM?
SHIA-SAN?
AH, ARE YOU TWO ON YOUR WAY HOME?
YEAH, THANKS FOR LUNCH TODAY.
KINDA A LOT, BUT IT WAS GOOD.
SORRY, I GET CARRIED AWAY WHEN I COOK. HEH HEH...
......
To be continued in Volume 4!

In the Next Volume of....

PITA-TEN

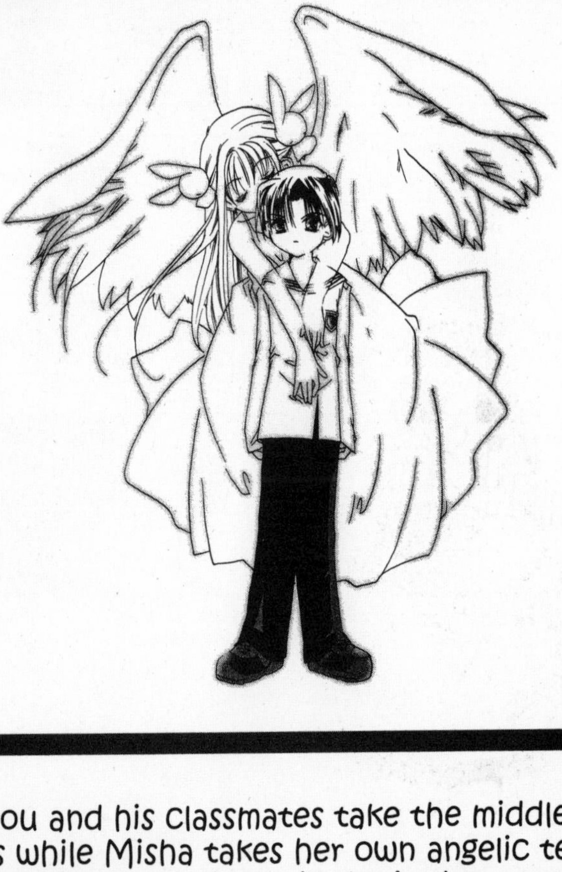

Kotarou and his classmates take the middle-school exams while Misha takes her own angelic test in order to earn her wings—if she is able to pass the test, she will finally be able to prove to Kotarou that she is indeed an angel. Meanwhile, as Ten-chan makes a play for Shia's affections, he discovers that Kotarou also has the hots for her!

ALSO AVAILABLE FROM  TOKYOPOP®

For more information visit www.TOKYOPOP.com

03.03.04T

ALSO AVAILABLE FROM TOKYOPOP

MANGA

.HACK//LEGEND OF THE TWILIGHT
@LARGE
ABENOBASHI: MAGICAL SHOPPING ARCADE
A.I. LOVE YOU
AI YORI AOSHI
ANGELIC LAYER
ARM OF KANNON
BABY BIRTH
BATTLE ROYALE
BATTLE VIXENS
BRAIN POWERED
BRIGADOON
B'TX
CANDIDATE FOR GODDESS, THE
CARDCAPTOR SAKURA
CARDCAPTOR SAKURA - MASTER OF THE CLOW
CHOBITS
CHRONICLES OF THE CURSED SWORD
CLAMP SCHOOL DETECTIVES
CLOVER
COMIC PARTY
CONFIDENTIAL CONFESSIONS
CORRECTOR YUI
COWBOY BEBOP
COWBOY BEBOP: SHOOTING STAR
CRAZY LOVE STORY
CRESCENT MOON
CULDCEPT
CYBORG 009
D•N•ANGEL
DEMON DIARY
DEMON ORORON, THE
DEUS VITAE
DIGIMON
DIGIMON TAMERS
DIGIMON ZERO TWO
DOLL
DRAGON HUNTER
DRAGON KNIGHTS
DRAGON VOICE
DREAM SAGA
DUKLYON: CLAMP SCHOOL DEFENDERS
EERIE QUEERIE!
END, THE
ERICA SAKURAZAWA: COLLECTED WORKS
ET CETERA
ETERNITY
EVIL'S RETURN
FAERIES' LANDING
FAKE
FLCL
FORBIDDEN DANCE
FRUITS BASKET
G GUNDAM
GATEKEEPERS

GETBACKERS
GIRL GOT GAME
GRAVITATION
GTO
GUNDAM BLUE DESTINY
GUNDAM SEED ASTRAY
GUNDAM WING
GUNDAM WING: BATTLEFIELD OF PACIFISTS
GUNDAM WING: ENDLESS WALTZ
GUNDAM WING: THE LAST OUTPOST (G-UNIT)
GUYS' GUIDE TO GIRLS
HANDS OFF!
HAPPY MANIA
HARLEM BEAT
I.N.V.U.
IMMORTAL RAIN
INITIAL D
INSTANT TEEN: JUST ADD NUTS
ISLAND
JING: KING OF BANDITS
JING: KING OF BANDITS - TWILIGHT TALES
JULINE
KARE KANO
KILL ME, KISS ME
KINDAICHI CASE FILES, THE
KING OF HELL
KODOCHA: SANA'S STAGE
LAMENT OF THE LAMB
LEGAL DRUG
LEGEND OF CHUN HYANG, THE
LES BIJOUX
LOVE HINA
LUPIN III
LUPIN III: WORLD'S MOST WANTED
MAGIC KNIGHT RAYEARTH I
MAGIC KNIGHT RAYEARTH II
MAHOROMATIC: AUTOMATIC MAIDEN
MAN OF MANY FACES
MARMALADE BOY
MARS
MARS: HORSE WITH NO NAME
METROID
MINK
MIRACLE GIRLS
MIYUKI-CHAN IN WONDERLAND
MODEL
ONE
ONE I LOVE, THE
PARADISE KISS
PARASYTE
PASSION FRUIT
PEACH GIRL
PEACH GIRL: CHANGE OF HEART
PET SHOP OF HORRORS
PITA-TEN
PLANET LADDER

03.03.04T

When darkness is in your genes,
only love can steal it away.

TOKYOPOP®

D•N•ANGEL

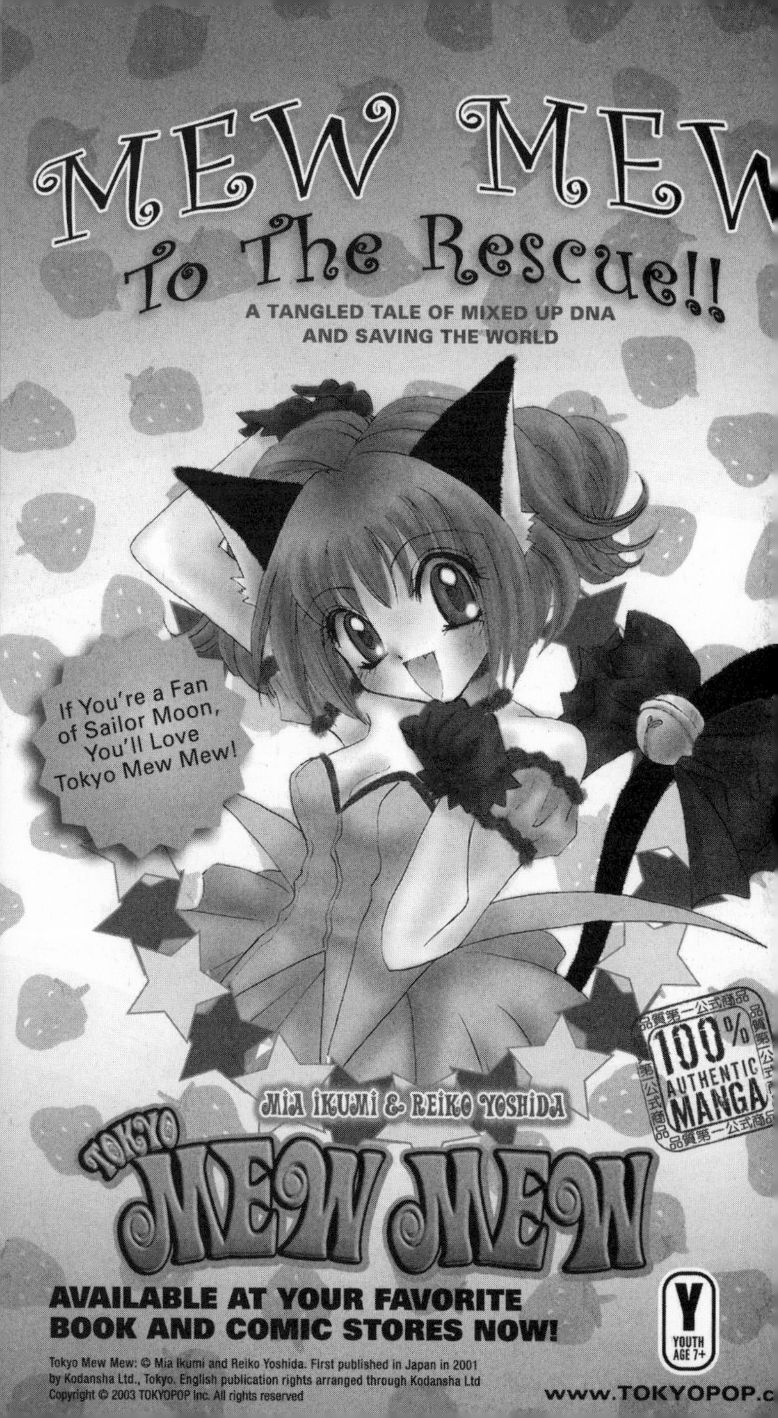
MEW MEW
To The Rescue!!
A TANGLED TALE OF MIXED UP DNA
AND SAVING THE WORLD
If You're a Fan of Sailor Moon, You'll Love Tokyo Mew Mew!
100% AUTHENTIC MANGA
品質第一公式商品
MIA IKUMI & REIKO YOSHIDA
TOKYO MEW MEW
AVAILABLE AT YOUR FAVORITE
BOOK AND COMIC STORES NOW!
Y
YOUTH AGE 7+
Tokyo Mew Mew: © Mia Ikumi and Reiko Yoshida. First published in Japan in 2001 by Kodansha Ltd., Tokyo. English publication rights arranged through Kodansha Ltd
Copyright © 2003 TOKYOPOP Inc. All rights reserved
www.TOKYOPOP.c

PEACH

Miwa Ueda Illustrations

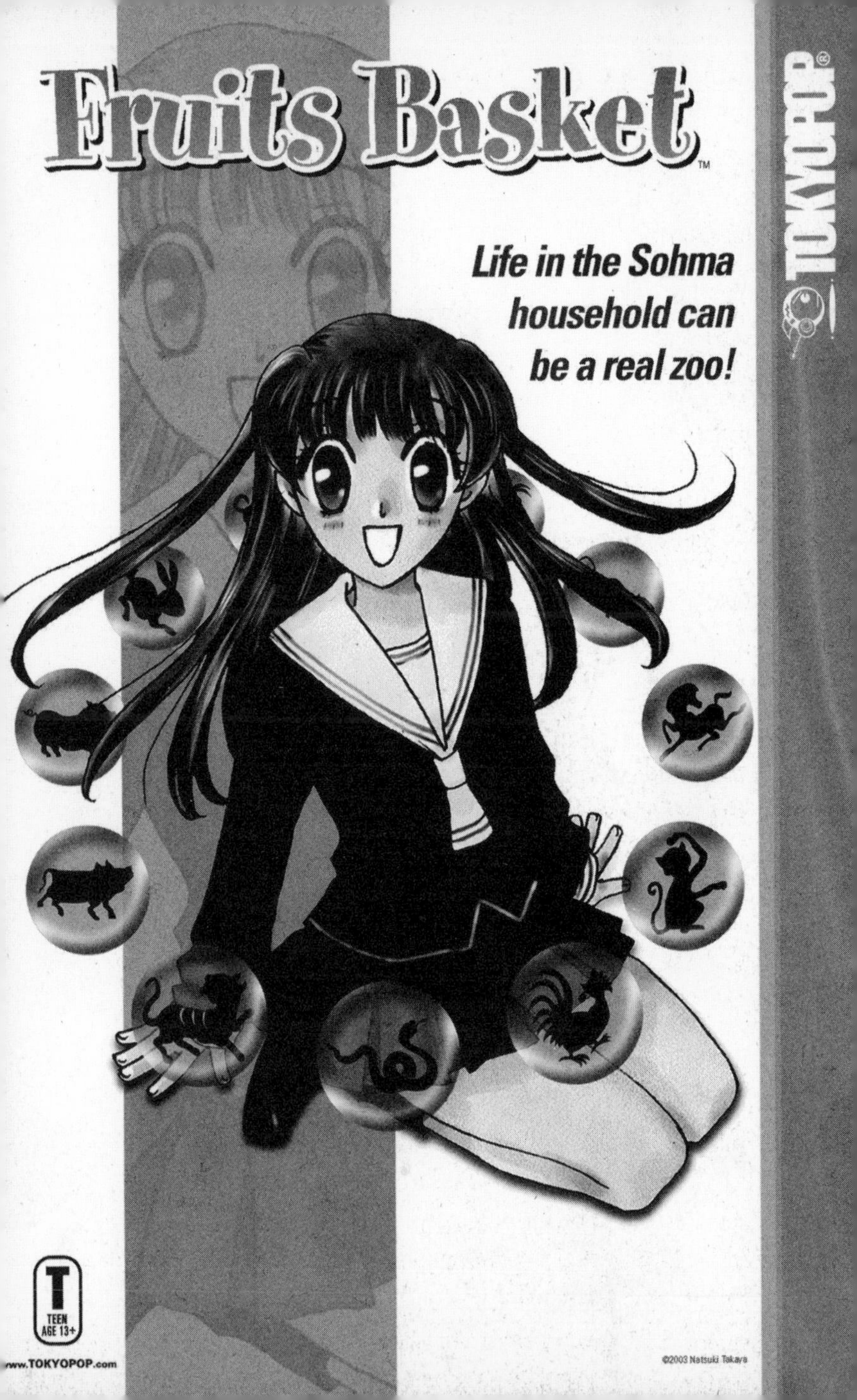

Fruits Basket™
TOKYOPOP®
Life in the Sohma household can be a real zoo!
T TEEN AGE 13+
www.TOKYOPOP.com
©2003 Natsuki Takaya

Heaven help you...
Faerie tales *do* come true!

FAERIES' LANDING ™

Available Now

forbidden Dance

by Hinako Ashihara

Dancing was her life...

Her dance partner
might be her future...

Available Now

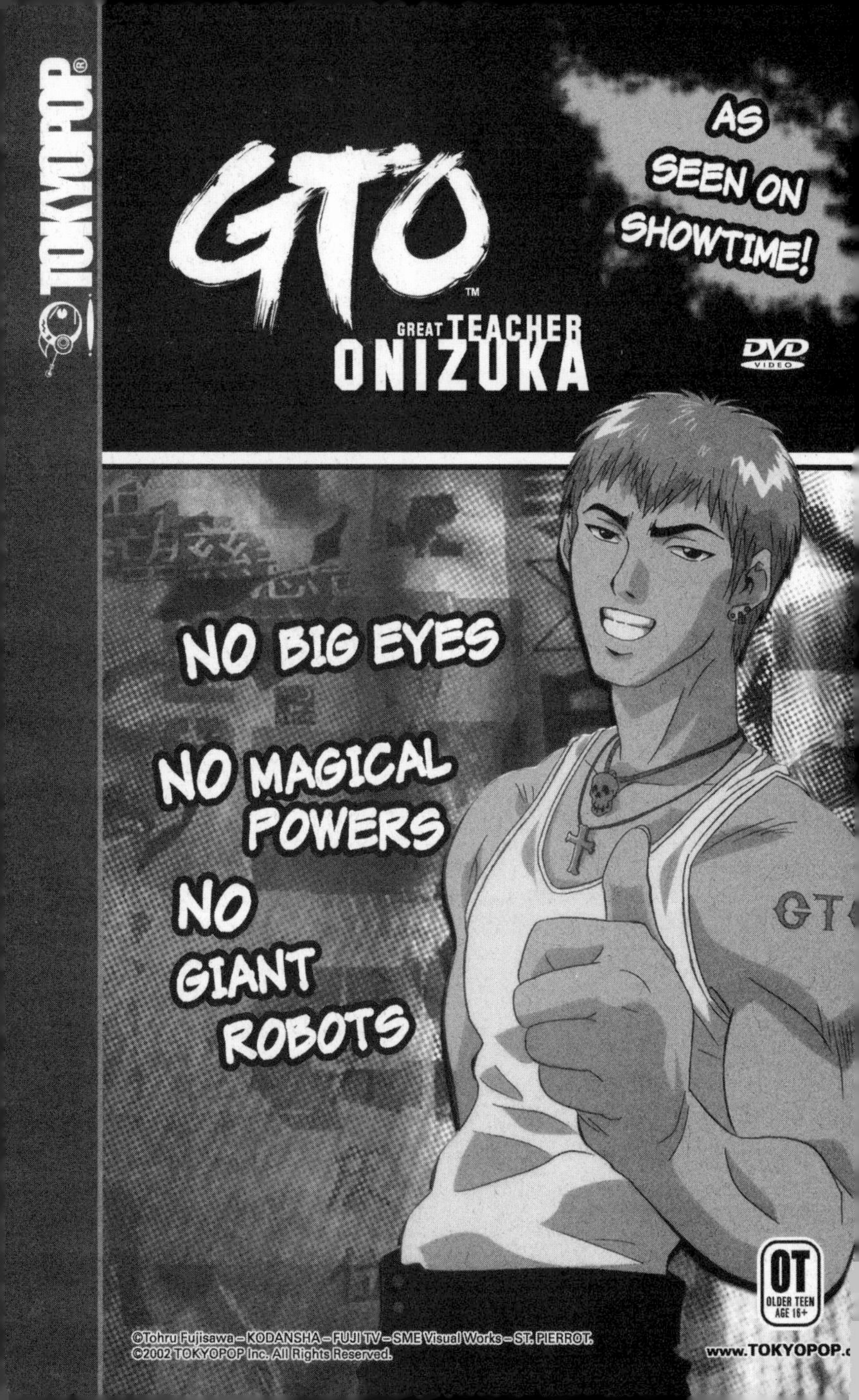

TOKYOPOP®

GTO™
GREAT TEACHER ONIZUKA

AS SEEN ON SHOWTIME!

DVD VIDEO

NO BIG EYES

NO MAGICAL POWERS

NO GIANT ROBOTS

OT OLDER TEEN AGE 16+

www.TOKYOPOP.c

STOP!

This is the back of the book.
You wouldn't want to spoil a great ending!

This book is printed "manga-style," in the authentic Japanese right-to-left format. Since none of the artwork has been flipped or altered, readers get to experience the story just as the creator intended. You've been asking for it, so TOKYOPOP® delivered: authentic, hot-off-the-press, and far more fun!

DIRECTIONS

If this is your first time reading manga-style, here's a quick guide to help you understand how it works.

It's easy... just start in the top right panel and follow the numbers. Have fun, and look for more 100% authentic manga from TOKYOPOP®!